The Development of
Creole Society
in Jamaica
1770-1820

The Development of
Creole Society in Jamaica
1770-1820

Kamau Brathwaite

Introduction by B.W. Higman

Ian Randle Publishers
Kingston • Miami

Published in Jamaica, 2005 by
Ian Randle Publishers
11 Cunningham Avenue
Box 686, Kingston 6
www.ianrandlepublishers.com

Originally published in Great Britain 1971, 1978 by
Oxford University Press

Brathwaite, Kamau
The development of creole society in Jamaica, 1770 - 1820 / Kamau
Brathwaite. - Rev. ed.

p. ; cm.

Includes index

ISBN 977-637-219-5 (pbk)

1. Slavery - Jamaica 2. Jamaica - History 3. Jamaica - Social conditions
I. Title
305.567 - dc 21

Cover design by Shelly-Gail Folkes

Cover image: Baptist Chapel, Spanish Town, c. 1826.
(Baptist Missionary Society, courtesy of BMS World Mission)

TO

MEX

MY MOTHER

AND

THE CARIBBEAN ARTISTS MOVEMENT

. . . in history, time supplies the continuum but not the principle of change. To discover that principle, it is . . . necessary . . . to seek, beyond the narrative of events, a wider understanding of the thoughts, habits, and institutions of a whole society. In the society itself, in its purpose and in its adaptive processes, will be found the true genesis of its history.

Elsa Goveia, *Historiography*

CONTENTS

PART ONE
THE ESTABLISHMENT

PART TWO
JAMAICA AND THE AMERICAN REVOLUTION

PART THREE
THE SOCIETY

PART FOUR
SOCIAL CHANGE

PART FIVE
DOCUMENTATION

INTRODUCTION

B.W. Higman
History Programme, Research School of Social Sciences,
Australian National University

The Development of Creole Society in Jamaica, 1770–1820 holds a central place in the historiography of the Caribbean.[1] It is crucial also to a much larger literature on the essence of what it means to live in the modern world. Being-in-the-world has become a much more intensely understood experience and in order to understand that encounter it is necessary to deploy models of the type advanced by Kamau Brathwaite, linking the local to the global, the colonial to the imperial, the past to the present.[2] Creolization and globalization stand side by side, as social, cultural and economic forces, and it is the roots of the creole element of this dyad that Brathwaite explores on a series of stages, stretching from Jamaica to the Caribbean and the world.

The Development of Creole Society is a 'classic', a 'seminal work', a 'model of interdisciplinary scholarship'.[3] Its importance to the construction of the idea of creolization, argues J. Michael Dash, is that Brathwaite supplies 'a critique of dependency theory and a celebration of resistance in Caribbean folk culture' and 'argues for process and transformation over structures and stasis.'[4] *The Development of Creole Society* is equally central, I believe, to Kamau Brathwaite's extensive and amazingly interconnected oeuvre.[5] The life and career of Brathwaite is evidence of the larger processes of internationalization/localization. The chaos of the individual lived life may be given structure and direction in hindsight and successfully understood in terms of multilayered contexts but that unity of direction and purposefulness is rarely apparent to the eye in the I of the spiritual maelstrom and there can be no doubting that Brathwaite's intense experience of life has been characterized by a willingness to be moved in different, creative directions by the counter-currents of personal and public trauma and tragedy. The intensity with which he has lived his life spills out into his poetry, his history, his drama, the voice and the performance. Ideas and representations change in tandem with change for the person, his very name moving along with the persona.

I first met Kamau in 1968 at the Jamaica Archives in Spanish Town. He had already submitted his Sussex PhD, in August, the thesis having exactly the same title as the book that was to be published by Oxford in 1971. The thesis gave his name as L. Edward Brathwaite but the book called him Edward Brathwaite and that is how he signed the copy he gave me in December of that year. I was given this copy, inscribed 'thanks and power to the people', because I had offered some comments on the thesis — though I can no longer recall what those comments might have been other than that they probably had to do with the demography of slavery which I was in the process of researching. That book is one of the most cherished volumes on my shelves. By December 1971 I had joined the Department of History at the University of the West Indies, Mona, and we became colleagues. We remained together in that Department until 1991 when Kamau moved on to New York and Barbados, his birthplace. I returned to my native Australia in 1996.

The Jamaica of 1968 was a turbulent time and place. There had been just six years of Independence, six years since the collapse of the Federation. Preferred pathways to true economic and cultural self-determination remained contested. In October, days after Brathwaite's return to the island, the government denied entry to Walter Rodney, Lecturer in African History. Rodney, who was Guyanese, had himself returned to Jamaica early in 1968. He spoke on Black Power on the Mona campus and grounded with the brethren on African history in the yards of Kingston. Martin Luther King was assassinated in April. Economic imperialism (American) competed with socialism (Cuban), and the cultures of the black (African, Rasta) and white (European, American) worlds clashed. Reggae replaced rock steady. Brathwaite was a leader in establishing a branch of the Caribbean Artists Movement (to which, along with his wife and mother, he dedicated *The Development of Creole Society*). He read poetry in draft and was in the midst of publishing his trilogy, *The Arrivants*, linking the worlds of Africa and the Caribbean: *Rights of Passage* (1967), *Masks* (1968) and *Islands* (1969). It was a story that marked a personal, private journey as well as a public affirmation of the place of the Caribbean in a larger Atlantic world.[6]

The events of 1968 were important but Brathwaite had already completed the formulation of his concept of the creole society. The origins of the concept must be sought in a deeper history but at the same time located in the contemporary context, a context which later commentators have justly termed a period of intense cultural nationalism.[7] In the Preface to *The Development of Creole Society*, Brathwaite declared that his work 'grew out of a conviction that a study of the forms, institutions, and attitudes of West Indian society during the period of slavery is essential to an understanding of a present which is becoming increasingly concerned with racial and cultural identity and with the West Indian's place in the world'.[8] In this he shared much with contemporary historians, notably his colleague in the Department of History at Mona, Elsa Goveia, who had been installed as the first Professor of West Indian History in 1961. Brathwaite joined the Department in 1963, following a year in Saint Lucia and an extended stay in Ghana. While at Mona, he produced the first drafts of *Rights of Passage*. According to Anne Walmsley, Goveia was in this period Brathwaite's 'inspiration and mentor, the only one in the history department to show sympathy and support for his joint history/literature interests, and for his research into Caribbean creole society'.[9] In 1965, the year Brathwaite commenced his PhD work at the University of Sussex, Goveia published a revised version of her own thesis, *Slave Society in the British Leeward Islands at the End of the Eighteenth Century*, and a potential model for the work of Brathwaite on Jamaica. She concluded with reflections on the contemporary relevance of 'the form of society which slavery had created', and the hope that radical change might enable 'the fragmented territories of the West Indies ... to develop at last a new sense of community, transcending the geographical and political divisions and the alienations of caste and race that have so far marked their common history'.[10]

Goveia's model was not, however, the understanding of history adopted by Brathwaite. Whereas Goveia's focus was found in slavery and 'slave society', Brathwaite looked to creolization and 'creole society'. As Brathwaite put it in his Preface, the 'condition and cultural orientation' of the West Indies circa 1970 were 'as much a result of the process of creolization as the slavery which provided the framework for it'.[11] In this way, he shifted the argument away from slavery as an institution, in the way that it had been dealt with in the traditional historiography of the Americas, and equally away from the slave society concept as developed by Goveia, towards a more holistic, processual understanding of the whole community. Thus, Brathwaite could claim that 'an understanding of the nature and development of interculturation [creolization] in West Indian slave society must *precede*, since it determines, questions of social and national identity.'[12]

The Development of Creole Society might seem to be about a small place and a short period of time. In fact it is Brathwaite's aim to use the example of Jamaica to develop a model of much wider significance, pointing towards the large forces of creolization and globalization. Why did he choose to study Jamaica rather than his native Barbados? The choice is interesting, because it might be argued that a case for creolization and the existence of a creole society during the period of slavery would have been harder to build for Barbados than for Jamaica, at least in the context of scholarly historiography and broad understandings of cultural creativity as they were in the middle of the 1960s.[13] Of course, a more practical explanation might be that Brathwaite found himself living in Jamaica at the time and that the archives were near at hand. A good deal of the documentary evidence deployed in *The Development of Creole Society* did indeed come from the newly organized Jamaica Archives in Spanish Town and this thorough utilization of local resources was at the time unusual. Most West Indian historians still depended exclusively on metropolitan British resources for their doctoral research, as did Goveia and Douglas Hall, for example.[14] Brathwaite did follow their trail to the Public Record Office, the British Museum and other London repositories but he balanced that research by his work in Jamaica. Another factor guiding his choice may have been the advantage to be gained by studying a place other than one's own, a means of establishing a distance and a measuring stick less confused by the personal, individual experience. Goveia similarly studied a different place, the Leeward Islands rather than her native Guyana, though Hall had chosen his own island, Jamaica. In any case, it is fair to say that Brathwaite was already by the middle of the 1960s, well on the way to knowing himself as Caribbean man, belonging to Africa and the Atlantic, the diaspora and the heartland, citizen of the world.[15]

It is equally important to appreciate that Brathwaite's choice of Jamaica did not in itself foreordain the understanding he achieved of Jamaica as a creole society. The obvious point here is that the Jamaican scholar Orlando Patterson, who took a PhD in Sociology at London at the same time as Brathwaite was at Sussex, chose a very similar topic but produced a quite different interpretation. Patterson's thesis appeared as a book in 1967 and Brathwaite wrote an extended review of it in *Race* the following year.[16] Patterson attempted a much longer period than that tackled by Brathwaite, comprehending the entire history of slavery under the British, from 1655 to 1838. As a sociologist, Patterson's principal objective was a precise analysis of social structure, family structure and personality, though building this analysis on introductory chapters that offered a long-term chronological narrative and periodization. Foreshadowing the universal, comparative studies of slavery and freedom he was to produce in years to come, the main title of his book was *The Sociology of Slavery*. But the subtitle — *An Analysis of the Origins, Development and Structure of Negro Slave Society in Jamaica* — pointed to a model closer to that of Goveia than Brathwaite's emerging formulation. By isolating 'Negro slave society' Patterson narrowed the vision of 'slave society' advanced by Goveia, who used the concept to cover the entire community — slave and free; black, white and coloured — rather than merely the people who were enslaved. Patterson's more limited definition was, however, one commonly used by other scholars at the time and since.[17]

Brathwaite's 1968 review of *The Sociology of Slavery* offered an early version of the thesis he was soon to put before the world. He took issue on several points, but the crucial question was the most appropriate way of conceptualizing the society under study. Although Brathwaite accepted that the focus of Patterson's work was on 'an examination of the *slaves*, not the creole society as a whole', he believed that 'this kind of isolation can affect the interpretation of the period and the situation being studied.'[18] Patterson saw Jamaican slave society as 'loosely integrated' and barely warranting the label 'society'. For him, Jamaica was best characterized as merely 'a collection of autonomous plantations, each a self-contained community with its internal mechanisms of power, than as a total social system.'[19] Brathwaite found this vision unacceptable and contrasted it unfavourably with Goveia's more comprehensive understanding of slave society in the Leeward Islands, a vision which Brathwaite believed took into account 'a far greater range of subtlety and groups, and finds, paradoxically, because of this greater complexity, a firmer sense of living wholeness'.[20]

Brathwaite's critique of *The Sociology of Slavery* had also to do with issues of methodology, and the differences he then saw between the disciplines of history and sociology. Drawing on a slightly larger sample of recent writers on slavery — Goveia, M.G. Smith and Douglas Hall — Brathwaite observed that all of these had necessarily combined 'the disciplines of history and sociology in order to arrive at a coherent picture of a type of society whose outlines can only be traced out from inadequate source-material.' In spite of this necessity, Brathwaite believed the study of the past held particular challenges for the sociologist — challenges which Patterson had failed to surmount — because of the problems of dealing with periods 'within which the factors of historical change operate'.[21] This belief in the importance of change and history was emphasized by the epigram placed by Brathwaite at the beginning of *The Development of Creole Society* and drawn from Goveia's influential *Historiography of the British West Indies* (1956). There, Goveia argued that 'in history, time supplies the continuum but not the principle of change. To discover that principle, it is … necessary … to seek, beyond the narrative of events, a wider understanding of the thoughts, habits, and institutions of a whole society. In the society itself, in its purpose and in its adaptive processes, will be found the true genesis of its history.'[22] In this way, Goveia (and Brathwaite) linked the question of historical change with the definition of the unit of study, the 'whole society'.

What was shared by Goveia, Patterson and Brathwaite was a concern with the nature of 'society' and indeed this was the only word shared by the titles of their books. Brathwaite and Patterson did share the word 'development' but Brathwaite believed Patterson both misunderstood the proper unit of analysis (by limiting it to 'Negro slave society') and failed to account for change (by simplifying the history and giving too static a quality to the topics he did subject to detailed sociological analysis). Again, both Goveia and Patterson used the term 'slave society' in their titles, whereas Brathwaite excluded the word 'slave' and indicated the substantial shift he had made by introducing 'creole'. In the Preface to *The Development of Creole Society* he talked explicitly about the meaning of the title, saying he had chosen not to call his book 'The Development of *Jamaican* Society' because 'within the terms of this study, "Jamaica" was little more than a geographical description — an extension of Europe's colonial/mercantilist complex'. The logic behind choosing 'creole' over 'slave' and/or 'Jamaica' was that 'The entire structure of European and European-derived institutional life in the Caribbean was determined by its "creole" development.'[23] Only in the Conclusion to *The Development of Creole Society* did Brathwaite make an explicit break with the slave society concept, in the context of understanding creolization as a creative process affecting the whole of the social body: 'To see Jamaica (or the West Indies generally) as a "slave" society is as much a falsification of reality, as the seeing of the islands as a naval station or an enormous sugar factory.'[24]

Brathwaite's review article of 1968 used the term 'creole society' occasionally, though never quite offering a precise definition or explaining exactly how it differed from the concept of 'slave society' as understood by Goveia. He came closest when offering an alternative periodization of Jamaican development, one that he believed was 'more meaningful' in its application to 'the society as a whole'. In this schema, the years 1655 to 1774 'saw the establishment, growth and first prosperity of Jamaican creole society' and the period 1774-1807 'saw the action on this creole society of external pressures and events'.[25] In *The Development of Creole Society* the issue of definition is tackled at the beginning, in the Introduction. After rehearsing varied meanings of 'creole', Brathwaite indicates that the sense in which the word is used in the book matches that employed in Jamaica during the period of his study, namely 'its original Spanish sense of *criollo*: born in, native to, committed to the area of living', taking both blacks and whites, and with the overtone of 'authentic' or 'culturally autonomous'. The definition is however refined in dealing with 'creole society' in order to exclude indigenous (Taino) and isolated (Maroon) groups whose patterns of social interaction separated them from the process of 'creolization'. This was an exclusion that created problems for the extension of the creole society to the wider Caribbean, especially in terms of mestizo and 'East Indian' involvement, a difficulty Brathwaite was to grapple with in later reflections and revisionings of the concept.[26]

Brathwaite was not the first to use the term 'creole society' but, as far as I can discover, *The Development of Creole Society* is the first work of history to use it in a book title. Probably the history of the term can be traced to earlier sources but the most likely trigger appears to be the proceedings of an inaugural seminar on plantation systems held in Puerto Rico in 1957. The papers and discussions were published in 1959 as *Plantation Systems of the New World*. Brathwaite was not present at the seminar, but the Introduction to *The Development of Creole Society* contained a series of references to the papers of Richard N. Adams, Rémy Bastien and G.A. Béltran. Adams spoke 'On the Relation Between Plantation and "Creole Cultures"' and identified an association between large landed estates dependent on imported forced labour and 'so-called "Creole" societies'. Bastien, commenting on Adams, argued that 'Creole society is characterized primarily by its multiracial composition and secondarily by the predominantly largescale agriculture in which two racial elements are deeply involved for the benefit of a minority of European origin.' Goveia attended the seminar and emphasized the importance of slavery as an influence and concluded that it was 'necessary to ask how much in the evolution of the Creole society in the West Indies in its formative period, was due to European political sovereignty, how much to the plantation, and, perhaps above all, how much was due to slavery'.[27]

Most speakers at the 1957 seminar talked rather of 'creole cultures' and directed their attention to the question how far the regional spread of creole cultures coincided with the limits of 'plantation America'. The scattered references to 'creole society' did not all exactly match the meaning later applied by Brathwaite but they did come close and the way in which they rolled up creolization with the specificity of the plantation and European colonialism did foreshadow the content of Brathwaite's interpretation. The centrality or necessity of the plantation was something that faded away only gradually, in later readings, paralleling the unexpectedly rapid fading of sugar and the literal plantation that took place in the last decades of the twentieth century.

Before anthropologists and historians began talking about creole cultures and creolization the concept had been largely the province of linguistics. The study of creole and pidgin languages, and the processes of pidginization and creolization provided the foundation for the broader social conceptualization of the idea. This was a development firmly rooted in the Caribbean, though it was from the beginning potentially global in its implications. Brathwaite noted the significance of the linguistic roots of the concept, equally the history or etymology of the word 'creole' and the role of disciplinary analysis in the study of creolization as process. In the Introduction to *The Development of Creole Society* he referred to a number of studies published in the 1960s and commented: 'For linguists, the word is used to mean a pidgin or "reduced language" that has "nativised itself"; that is, has become the native language of a speech-community.' In 1971, the year of Brathwaite's book, the anthropologist Sidney W. Mintz published an essay on 'The Socio-Historical Background to Pidginization and Creolization' in a collection edited by the linguist Dell Hymes on *Pidginization and Creolization of Languages*.[28] Thus Brathwaite's extension of the meaning of creole drew on a variety of developments in disciplines, from linguistics to anthropology, yet supplied its own creative originality within the field of history.

The first chapters of *The Development of Creole Society*, especially those purportedly offering a straightforward description of the political and social institutions of Jamaica, appear to have been forged in a traditional — British imperial — school of history-writing and to bear little relation to the apparently much more original chapters that follow. The argument almost catches the reader unawares when it emerges. The notion of a creole society is submerged in the early chapters. It is of course introduced in the Introduction but otherwise the index provides no references to 'creole' or 'creolization' in the first 100 pages of the book. Chapter 7 (pages 80–95) is titled 'A Creole Economy' but the idea is not argued explicitly and indeed falls within the context of Part Two, 'Jamaica and the American Revolution'. Similarly Chapter 8, 'Jamaica: Colonial or Creole' (pages 96–101), introduces the notion of creole political ideas through analysis of the constitutional arguments arising from the debate over the American Revolution. But it is this chapter that provides a bridge to the later sections of *The Development of Creole Society* and the core arguments of the book. In terms of the economy and the political system, the (white) creoles of Jamaica failed to take bold, revolutionary steps, Brathwaite argues, because they were more certainly colonials than creoles, stymied by ambivalence rather than enhanced by the 'creative friction' that could be found in Jamaica's infrastructure and society.

The notion of 'creole economy' has been influential in a subterranean fashion. Although Brathwaite's work has not been seen as central to new varieties of Caribbean economic history, or at least it has been rarely cited in this context, the idea is fundamental to research on the working of the economy outside the plantation system and the traditional emphasis on sugar. Here again it is possible to identify the ambivalence of the colonial and the problem of defining and delimiting the creole.[29] The case of Jamaica is particularly interesting though hardly typical of the smaller and more homogeneous island economies of most of the British colonial Caribbean. Within the period covered by *The Development of Creole Society* the economy of Jamaica did indeed contain elements of diversity and internal linkage that contributed to a truly creole economy but the raison d'être of the system remained rooted in the production of commodities for export. Those export commodities were almost entirely products of plantation agriculture and industry and without them the web of internal connections would have been quite different. At the same time, the internal economy of Jamaica was quite different to that of those islands which depended heavily on the importation of inputs of food and supplies. The significance of Jamaica was that it supported both a strongly integrated internal economy of estates, plantations and pens and a vibrant internal marketing system based on the produce of the enslaved people's provision grounds (and about which Brathwaite had surprisingly little to say). These two connected though separate levels of production and consumption contained a strong variety of creolization, in terms of the organization of cultivation, harvesting and marketing.

One of the more insightful recent reconsiderations of the creole-society concept is that offered by Richard D.E. Burton in his *Afro-Creole* of 1997. Burton distinguishes three 'principal approaches to the study of Afro-Caribbean culture(s)' labeling them 'the Eurogenetic, Afrogenetic, and creativity or creolization hypotheses'. By the end of the twentieth century it was the last of these that held sway, most scholars emphasizing the 'syncretistic or mosaic character' of the cultures though with variations in the weight given different elements.[30] Burton however argues that in the specific case of Jamaica continuity and creativity were both powerful forces in creolization and that the process occurred within the slave community as much as between the enslaved and free sectors of the population. In the end, he rejects 'the idea that anything like a unified creole culture was created, or could have been created, under the conditions of slavery' and follows Orlando Patterson in arguing that 'what took place was a "segmentary" rather than "synthetic" creolization'. Maintaining the linguistic basis of the concept of creolization, Burton identifies 'a continuum of overlapping and competing cultural forms, all of them creole or creolized', stretching from Euro-Creole to Afro-Creole, with an intermediate Meso-Creole ('the "middle culture", corresponding to the mesolect of "middle language", of the free colored classes and certain sections of the slave elite'). Burton puts the emphasis on 'tension and conflict' within this continuum, avoiding the notions of blending, hybridization and homogenization.[31] In doing so, he accepts the critical approach to creolization developed by O. Nigel Bolland.[32]

The ruminations of Burton and Bolland mesh neatly with recent debates in the linguistic analysis of creole genesis. These debates are important for cultural history in the way they provide clues to the chronology and initiation of creolization. Whereas some see relatively 'modern' forms of creole speech firmly in place by about 1700, others argue for a localized version of metropolitan speech continuing into the present, at least for some island variants. Overall, it is becoming clear that creole language emerged along with the 'sugar revolution' which transformed so much else in Caribbean society and economy.[33] If proven, this offers the possibility of a tidy association of language with other aspects of creolization.

Ideas should always be in motion. The possibility that *The Development of Creole Society* might be thought of as a definitive work, a final statement on creole societies and creolization, would be the last thing to enter Brathwaite's mind. I remember that during the production of the book he sought changes at proof stage, much to the perplexity of publisher and printer, and after the volume appeared his thinking about the concepts remained in constant development. Early evidences of the process of rethinking appeared within five years of the publication of *The Development of Creole Society* and were indeed in draft much earlier.[34] There was the expansion of the idea into periods of history and regions of the Caribbean previously unexplored, there was the reconsideration of the place of Africa and, further, the integration of other immigrant groups into the process. Others have encouraged a further expansion into periods outside the 'colonial situation' and an inclusion of the interaction of indigenous and immigrant peoples, variables particularly important for the Hispanic Caribbean.[35] On the other hand, the application of the creole-society concept to North America has been slow and unsteady.[36] This relative neglect no doubt reflects Brathwaite's personal and public search for Caribbean authenticity and locality, and it matches his relatively meagre presence in the North American literary scene compared to other Caribbean writers.[37]

The spread of the concept of creolization through linguistics, globalization and cultural studies has been a dramatic event of the last quarter-century. In linguistics, the *Journal of Creole Studies* began publication in 1977 and the *Journal of Pidgin and Creole Languages* in 1986. The Society for Pidgin and Creole Linguistics held its first meetings in 1989. This Society was the first to remove geographical and lexical source restrictions from the languages it sought to study, the first to unite students of Atlantic creoles and Pacific pidgins, and inclusive of all those interested in 'restructured languages from Central Africa to Siberia'. This expansion of the field of study went together with debates about the place of 'nativization' and the special status of 'true creoles', the latter comprehending the plantation creoles resulting from the uprooting in the Atlantic slave trade.[38]

In the broader fields of anthropology and globalization studies, creolization has sometimes been given a much greater significance. Thus Ulf Hannerz, for example, has written of 'the world in creolisation', moving anthropology and ethnography beyond notions of modernization and cultural nationalism towards 'a general view that there are now no distinct cultures, only intersystemically connected, creolising Culture'. Although it is the Third World that seems to be the true site of creolization, Hannerz contends that 'an understanding of the world system in cultural terms can be enlightening not only in Third

World studies but also as we try to make of anthropology a truly general and comparative study of culture. Creole cultures are not necessarily only colonial and post-colonial cultures. ... In the end, it seems, we are all being creolised.' In this way Hannerz points towards an analysis that overtakes 'regionally restricted conceptions of creolism', such as that offered by Brathwaite's *The Development of Creole Society*.[39]

At the same time Hannerz invokes a future that carries with it all the contradictions of unity and diversity, locality and globality, homogeneity and difference, assimilation and multiculturalism, justice and equality. These are contradictions that perplex and puzzle the world at large. When placed with the Caribbean context they introduce elements that force a fresh consideration of creolization, a fresh analysis of its genesis and development, a fresh struggle between inner plantation and outer plantation. Pride in the outflowing global spread of reggae and Rasta is clouded by the incoming stamp of McDonalds and KFC, the latter now installed on the Mona campus confronting the library. But it is a process with deep roots. CocaColaization has been absorbed by Creolization and regional identity depends, in any case, on the existence of the Other. The diasporic spread of Jamaican language — Creole — is in itself the visible and verbal proof.[40] Then again, the most easily identified outflowing elements of greater Caribbean culture — reggae, Rasta and Jamaican language — are all Jamaican, limiting the regional sharing of pride and introducing a hierarchy of dependencies, perhaps harking back to the alleged temporal and spatial specificity of Brathwaite's *The Development of Creole Society in Jamaica 1770–1820*.

Kamau Brathwaite has a vital yet sometimes ambiguous place in the history of modern Caribbean thought and historiography. Often his central ideas have been taken by others without explicit acknowledgement. This may be viewed in a negative light, in the sense that due respect has not been paid to their author. On the other hand, it is a truism that the most central ideas quickly lose contact with their individual creators and become part of the common pool of thought, accepted as fundamental and common property. This seems a good outcome for something as grounded as the 'miracle' of creolization and Brathwaite's particular contribution the refined concept of creole society.[41]

Notes

1. Edward Brathwaite, *The Development of Creole Society in Jamaica, 1770–1820*. (Oxford: Clarendon Press, 1971). Hereafter, *DCS*.
2. Edward Kamau Brathwaite, 'Caribbean Man in Space and Time,' *Savacou* 11/12 (1975): 11.
3. Verene A. Shepherd, 'Diversity in Caribbean Economy and Society from the Seventeenth to the Nineteenth Centuries,' *Plantation Society in the Americas* 5 (1998): 182, n. 16; Verene A. Shepherd and Kathleen E. A. Monteith, 'Non-Sugar Proprietors in a Sugar-Plantation Society,' *Plantation Society in the Americas* 5 (1998): 216; Howard Johnson, 'Historiography of Jamaica,' in B. W. Higman (ed.), *Methodology and Historiography of the Caribbean*, Volume VI of the *General History of the Caribbean* (London: Macmillan/UNESCO Publishing, 1999): 507–508; David Scott, 'Preface,' *Small Axe* 8 (2000) v.
4. J. Michael Dash, 'Psychology, Creolization, and Hybridization,' in Bruce King (ed.), *New National and Post-Colonial Literatures* (Oxford: Clarendon Press, 1996), 48. See also Michel-Rolph Trouillot, 'Culture on the Edges: Creolization in the Plantation Context,' *Plantation Society in the Americas* 5 (1998): 28; Grey Gundaker, *Signs of Diaspora/Diaspora of Signs: Literacies, Creolization, and Vernacular Practice in African America* (New York: Oxford University Press, 1998), 10–11.
5. See Silvio Torres-Saillant, *Caribbean Poetics: Toward an Aesthetic of West Indian Literature* (Cambridge: Cambridge University Press, 1997), 93–155.
6. Maureen Warner-Lewis, *Edward Kamau Brathwaite's Masks: Essays and Annotations* (Mona: Institute of Caribbean Studies, 1992 [first published 1977]); Gordon Rohlehr, *Pathfinder: Black Awakening in The Arrivants of Edward Kamau Brathwaite* (Tunapuna: the author, 1981); Gordon Rohlehr, 'Dream Journeys,' in Kamau Brathwaite, *DreamStories* (London: Longman, 1994), iii–xv.
7. Johnson, 'Historiography of Jamaica,' 508–509; O. Nigel Bolland, 'Creolization and Creole Societies: A Cultural Nationalist View of Caribbean Social History,' in Alistair Hennessy (ed.), *Intellectuals in the Twentieth-Century Caribbean* (London: Macmillan, 1992), 57–63; David Scott, *Refashioning Futures: Criticism after Postcoloniality* (Princeton: Princeton University Press, 1999), 106–118.
8. *DCS*, p. vii. Cf. David Lowenthal, West Indian Societies (London: Oxford University Press, 1972), 275; Rex M. Nettleford, *Caribbean Cultural Identity: The Case of Jamaica* (Kingston: Institute of Jamaica, 1978), 59.
9. Anne Walmsley, *The Caribbean Artisits Movement, 1966-1972: A Literary and Cultural History* (London and Port of Spain: New Beacon Books, 1992), 39–43, 97, 190–94.
10. Elsa V. Goveia, *Slave Society in the British Leeward Islands at the End of the Eighteenth Century* (New Haven: Yale University Press, 1965), 337–51.
11. *DCS*, p. vii.
12. *DCS*, p. vii (emphasis in original).

13. Cf. Jerome S. Handler and Frederick W. Lange, *Plantation Slavery in Barbados: An Archaeological and Historical Investigation* (Cambridge, Mass: Harvard University Press, 1978), 215.

14. B.W. Higman, *Writing West Indian Histories* (London: Macmillan, 1999), 103–106; Goveia, *Slave Society*; Douglas Hall, *Free Jamaica, 1838-1865: An Economic History* (New Haven: Yale University Press, 1959).

15. Edward Kamau Brathwaite, 'Caribbean Man in Space and Time,' *Savacou* 11/12 (1975): 1–11.

16. Orlando Patterson, *The Sociology of Slavery: An Analysis of the Origins, Development and Structure of Negro Slave Society in Jamaica* (London: McGibbon and Kee, 1967); Edward Brathwaite, 'Jamaican Slave Society, A Review' *Race* 9 (1968): 331-42. For the essential absence of the idea of a creole society in the early period of colonization, in a contemporary history, see Richard S. Dunn, *Sugar and Slaves: The Rise of the Planter Class in the English West Indies, 1624-1713* (Chapel Hill: University of North Carolina Press, 1972), 332-40.

17. B.W. Higman, *The Invention of Slave Society* (Mona: Department of History, University of the West Indies, 1998), 3.

18. Brathwaite, 'Jamaican Slave Society,' 333 (emphasis in original).

19. Patterson, *Sociology of Slavery*, 70.

20. Brathwaite, 'Jamaican Slave Society,' 333.

21. Brathwaite, 'Jamaican Slave Society,' 331.

22. *DCS*, p. vi; Elsa V. Goveia, *A Study on the Historiography of the British West Indies to the End of the Nineteenth Century* (Mexico: Instituto Panamericano de Geografia e Historia, 1956), 177.

23. *DCS*, p. vii (emphasis in original).

24. *DCS*, p. 307. Cf. Woodville K. Marshall, 'A Review of Historical Writing on the Commonwealth Caribbean since c.1940,' *Social and Economic Studies* 24 (1975): 279-80.

25. Brathwaite, 'Jamaican Slave Society,' 332.

26. *DCS*, pp. xv, 310. Cf. Brian L. Moore, *Race, Power and Social Segmentation in Colonial Society: Guyana After Slavery, 1838-1891* (New York: Gordon and Breach Science Publishers, 1987), 202; Brian L. Moore, *Cultural Power, Resistance and Pluralism: Colonial Guyana 1838-1900* (Barbados: The Press University of the West Indies, 1995), 167, 305.

27. [Vera Rubin (ed.)], *Plantation Systems of the New World* (Washington, DC: Pan American Union, 1959), 61, 74, 80.

28. *DCS*, p. xv; Sidney W. Mintz, 'The Socio-Historical Background to Pidginization and Creolization', in Dell Hymes (ed.), *Pidginization and Creolization of Languages* (Cambridge: Cambridge University Press, 1971), 481–96. Cf. R.B. Le Page, *Jamaican Creole: An Historical Introduction to Jamaican Creole* (London: Macmillan, 1960).

29. Shepherd, 'Diversity in Caribbean Economy and Society,' 182–83; Shepherd and Monteith, 'Non-Sugar Proprietors in a Sugar-Plantation Society,' 205–222.

30. Richard D.E. Burton, *Afro-Creole: Power, Opposition, and Play in the Caribbean* (Ithaca: Cornell University Press, 1997), 2–3.

31. Burton, *Afro-Creole*, 5–6, 42–46. See also Chris Smaje, *Natural Hierarchies:*

The Historical Sociology of Race and Caste (Oxford: Blackwell Publishers, 2000), 208–210; Cf. Mechal Sobel, *The World They Made Together: Black and White Values in Eighteenth-Century Virginia* (Princeton: Princeton University Press, 1987), 6.

32. Bolland, 'Creolization and Creole Societies,' 63.

33. John R. Rickford and Jerome S. Handler, 'Textual Evidence on the Nature of Early Barbadian Speech, 1676-1835,' *Journal of Pidgin and Creole Languages* 9 (1994): 221, 243–44; John Victor Singler, 'Theories of Creole Genesis, Sociohistorical Considerations, and the Evaluation of Evidence: The Case of Haitian Creole and the Relexification Hypothesis,' *Journal of Pidgin and Creole Languages* 11 (1996): 226; Jean Aitchison, *Language Change: Progress or Decay?* (Cambridge: Cambridge University Press, 2001, third edition), 228–34.

34. See particularly Edward Brathwaite, *Contradictory Omens: Cultural Diversity and Integration in the Caribbean* (Mona: Savacou Publications, 1974); Brathwaite, 'Caribbean Man in Space and Time' (1975); Edward Kamau Brathwaite, 'Caliban, Ariel, and Unprospero in the Conflict of Creolization: A Study of the Slave Revolts in Jamaica 1831–32,' *Annals of the New York Academy of Sciences* 292 (1977): 41.

35. Franklin W. Knight, 'Pluralism, Creolization and Culture,' in Franklin W. Knight (ed.), *The Slave Societies of the Caribbean*, Volume III of the *General History of the Caribbean* (London: Macmillan/Unesco Publishing, 1997), 271–86.

36. See, for example, Gwendolyn Midlo Hall, *Africans in Colonial Louisiana: The Development of Afro-Creole Culture in the Eighteenth Century* (Baton Rouge: Louisiana State University Press, 1992), 158–59; Sobel, *The World They Made Together*, 3–11; Robin Blackburn, *The Making of New World Slavery: From the Baroque to the Modern 1492–1800* (London: Verso, 1997), 449–51; David Turley, *Slavery* (Oxford: Blackwell Publishers, 2000), 79–88.

37. Torres-Saillant, *Caribbean Poetics*, 141.

38. Francis Byrne and John Holm, 'Introduction: Perspectives on the Atlantic and Pacific ... and Beyond,' in Francis Byrne and John Holm (eds), *Atlantic Meets Pacific: A Global View of Pidginization and Creolization* (Amsterdam: John Benjamins Publishing Company, 1993), 1–7.

39. Ulf Hannerz, 'The World in Creolisation,' *Africa* 57 (1987): 551, 557 and 557 n.5. Cf. Wilson Harris, 'Creoleness: The Crossroads of a Civilization?' in A.J.M. Bundy (ed.), *Selected Essays of Wilson Harris: The Unfinished Genesis of the Imagination* (London: Rouledge, 1999), 237–47.

40. Cf. Neil J. Savishinsky, 'Transnational Popular Culture and the Global Spread of the Jamaican Rastafarian Movement,' *New West Indian Guide* 68 (1994): 259–81; Bill Maurer, 'Creolization Redux: The Plural Society Thesis and Offshore Financial Services in the British Caribbean,' *New West Indian Guide* 71 (1997): 259–61.

41. Trouillot, 'Culture on the Edges,' 8; See also Verene A. Shepherd and Glen L. Richards (eds), *Questioning Creole: Creolisation Discourses in Caribbean Culture* (Kingston: Ian Randle Publishers, 2002), a book of essays 'in honour of Kamau Brathwaite.'

PREFACE

THIS book is in substance a doctoral thesis of the same title accepted by the University of Sussex in 1968. It grew out of a conviction that a study of the forms, institutions, and attitudes of West Indian society during the period of slavery is essential to an understanding of a present which is becoming increasingly concerned with racial and cultural identity and with the West Indian's place in the world. Our present condition and cultural orientation, it seems to me, are as much a result of the process of creolization as the slavery which provided the framework for it. One of the arguments of this book, in fact, is that an understanding of the nature and development of interculturation in West Indian slave society must *precede,* since it determines, questions of social and national identity. The entire structure of European and European-derived institutional life in the Caribbean was determined by its 'creole' development. I have therefore called the book, 'The Development of *Creole* Society' rather than 'The Development of *Jamaican* Society', since, within the terms of this study, 'Jamaica' was little more than a geographical description — an extension of Europe's colonial/mercantilist complex.

For encouragement and the practical step of making time and money available to undertake my research, I am indebted to Sir Philip Sherlock, then Vice-Chancellor of the University of the West Indies, Professor Douglas Hall, Head of the Department of History of the University of the West Indies, Professor Asa Briggs and Dr. Donald Wood who also supervised my work while I was attached to the University of Sussex. The Government of Barbados' nomination of a Commonwealth Scholarship made it possible for me to complete the study.

I should also like to thank the Directors and Librarians of the University Library, Mona, Jamaica; the Jamaica Archives, Spanish Town; the West Indian Reference Library, Institute of Jamaica; the University Library, Sussex; the British Museum; the Public Record Office, London; the Library of the Royal Commonwealth Society; the Library of the West India Committee; the University of London Library; the Institute of Historical Research, the School of Oriental and African Studies Library, the Institute of Commonwealth Studies, all of the University of London; the Library and Archives of the Baptist Missionary Society, London;

The Church of England Archives, Fulham Palace, London; the Moravian Church, Mt. Tabor, Barbados; the Moravian Church, Malvern, Jamaica; the Moravian Church Archives, London; the Wesleyan Methodist Missionary Society, London, and Worthy Park Estate, Jamaica, for their assistance in making material available and for permission to use extracts from their manuscripts and holdings, as cited.

I am also grateful to the authors of the unpublished theses and papers, listed in the bibliography, for permission to cite and quote from the results of their research.

Finally, I should like to thank Professor D.A.G. Waddell of the University of Stirling, Scotland, Professor Goveia and Dr. Woodville Marshall of the University of the West Indies, Mrs. Linda Wolf of the University of Chicago, Mr. Barry Higman of the University of Sydney (both of them engaged in research at the University of the West Indies) for reading the manuscript and helping with revision; Donald Wood and H.P. Jacobs for not only reading and correcting the manuscript, but for supplying information and suggesting additional source material; Wilma Williams of the Institute of Social and Economic Research, University of the West Indies, for drawing the maps and helping with the geographical background to the study, and Doris Monica for preparing the manuscript for publication.

LIST OF MAPS

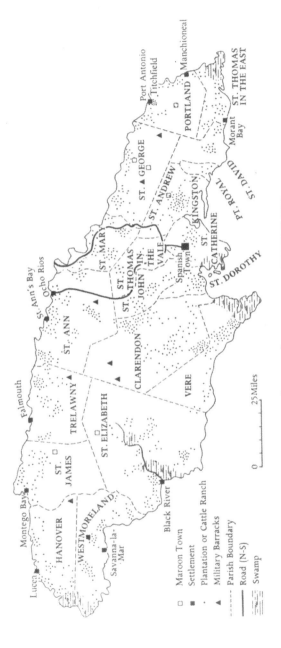

MAP I. JAMAICA: LAND USE AND SETTLEMENTS 1790

□ Maroon Town
■ Settlement
· Plantation or Cattle Ranch
▲ Military Barracks
--- Parish Boundary
═ Road (N-S)
Swamp

0   25 Miles

Lucea
Montego Bay
Falmouth
St. Ann's Bay
Ocho Rios
Port Antonio
Titchfield
Manchioneal

HANOVER
ST. JAMES
TRELAWNY
ST. ANN
ST. MARY
ST. GEORGE
PORTLAND
ST. THOMAS IN THE EAST

WESTMORELAND
Savanna-la-Mar
ST. ELIZABETH
Black River
CLARENDON
VERE
ST. JOHN
ST. THOMAS IN THE VALE
ST. ANDREW
ST. CATHERINE
ST. DOROTHY
Spanish Town
KINGSTON
PT. ROYAL
ST. DAVID
Morant Bay

INTRODUCTION

This study of Jamaica during the fifty years, 1770–1820, is an attempt to examine the nature of a society, based on slavery, from the point of view of its institutions, its social groupings, and the attitudes of individuals and groups to each other and to the institutions of their society. The term 'institutions' is not being used in this context in its abstract sociological sense to refer to kinship, marriage, law, property, religion, education, etc.;[1] it is used here to refer to those legally established and constitutionally recognized bodies such as the Church, the vestries, the militia and above all the House of Assembly, which served the society as a whole and through which the society regulated itself. The Press, though not legally 'established', was recognized as a constituent element of the society, and is therefore included under the term.

The material being presented here argues that the people, mainly from Britain and West Africa, who settled, lived, worked and were born in Jamaica, contributed to the formation of a society which developed, or was developing, its own distinctive character or culture which, in so far as it was neither purely British nor West African, is called 'creole'; that this 'creole culture' was part of a wider New World or American culture complex,[2] itself the result of European settlement and exploitation of a new environment; and that Jamaican development (like that of the Caribbean generally), was significantly affected by realignments within this complex caused by the two major upheavals in the area during the period of this study: the American and what may be described as the 'Humanitarian' Revolutions.

The American Revolution, a specific political event in British imperial history, isolated Jamaica, in certain important respects, from the wider English-speaking New World area of which it was part, thus causing the island, on the one hand, to rely more and more on the essentially 'absentee' cultural and material influence of the Mother Country, and on the other, to turn in upon itself to look for solutions to its problems. An understanding of Jamaica during this period, in other words, depends as much on an appreciation of its external colonial relationship with

Britain, as on an examination of its internal social structure and problems, which centred around the black/white dichotomy created by slavery. The 'Humanitarian Revolution' (by which is meant those movements of and for slave emancipation which had their first significant effects in the Caribbean with the response to the French Revolution in St. Domingue, and among elements of the slave populations of the islands generally,[3] along with Abolitionist and missionary activity in the area), exploited and tested this social dichotomy. But paradoxically, as will be discussed in the body of this work, these Revolutions also contributed to a certain integrating of the society as a cultural unit (even though its 'plural' nature remained), by bringing about a measure of 'creolization' of both black and white *vis-à-vis* each other and the society as a whole. The American Revolution in this sense, raised a question which the 'Humanitarian Revolution' (which did not end with Emancipation and is still in progress) 'answered'.

This, then, in outline, is the structural *rationale* of this monograph. It is an historical study with a socio-cultural emphasis, seeking to understand the workings of a 'creole' society during the central period of British West Indian slavery. Before proceeding into the details of this work, however, the word 'creole' as used within this text must be defined, since it is often used in different ways by different people and has been used to refer to a variety of societies and cultures. The word itself appears to have originated from a combination of the two Spanish words [4] *criar* (to create, to imagine, to establish, to found, to settle) and *colono* (a colonist, a founder, a settler) into *criollo*: a committed settler, one identified with the area of settlement, one native to the settlement though not ancestrally indigenous to it. In Peru, for example, the word was used in this sense to refer to people of Spanish descent who were born in the New World, who 'were of the upper social reaches but distinctly below their peninsular born relatives'.[5] In Brazil, the term was applied to Negro slaves born locally.[6] In Louisiana, the term was applied to the white francophone population, while in New Orleans it applied to mulattoes. In Sierre Leone, 'creole' refers to descendants of former New World slaves, Maroons and 'Black Poor' from Britain who were resettled along the coast and in Freetown especially and who form a social élite distinct from the African population. [7] For linguists, the word is used to mean a pidgin or 'reduced language' [8] that has 'nativised itself'; [9] that is, has become the native language of a speech-community.[10] In Jamaica, during the period of this study, the word was used in its original Spanish sense of *criollo*: born in, native to, committed to the area of living, and it was used in relation to both whites and slaves. It is in this sense that the word is applied in this book, with the overtone as may be heard, say, in present-day Puerto Rico, of 'authentic', 'culturally autonomous'.

The use of the term 'creole society' has also to be defined since the designation 'born in the New World' would have to include groups such as Caribs, Black Caribs, Central American *ladinos,* Brazilian *caboclos,* Maroons and others, whose development, according to one authority,[11] did not involve them significantly, during this period, in social interaction with others outside their group; did not involve them, to put it another way, in the process of 'creolization'. 'Creole', in the context of this study, presupposes a situation where the society concerned is caught up 'in some kind of colonial arrangement'[12] with a metropolitan European power, on the one hand, and a plantation arrangement on the other;[13] and where the society is multi-racial but organized for the benefit of a minority of European origin.[14] 'Creole society' therefore is the result of a complex situation where a colonial polity reacts, as a whole, to external metropolitan pressures, and at the same time to internal adjustments made necessary by the juxtaposition of master and slave, élite and labourer, in a culturally heterogeneous relationship.[15]

Notes

1   R.H. Lowie, *Social Organisation* (London, 1949), pp. 3-4.
2. See for example, R.C. West and J.P. Augelli, *Middle America: Its Lands and Peoples* (New Jersey, 1966), p. 11.
3   J. H. Parry and P. M. Sherlock, *A Short History of the West Indies* (London, 1956, 2nd reprint 1960), pp. 161-6; Betty Russell, 'The Influence of the French Revolution upon Grenada, St. Vincent and Jamaica' (unpublished paper, Dept. of History: Postgraduate Seminars, U.W.I., Mona, 1967). It has never been clearly established that there was direct intervention in Jamaica from Haiti, but the whites interpreted slave unrest and revolt during this period in this light. See, for example, C.O. 137/110: Nugent to Hobart, 19 Nov. 1803, 11 Mar. 1804; C.O. 137/118: Coote to Windham, 9 Jan. 1807 and M.C. Campbell, 'Edward Jordan and the Free Coloureds: Jamaica, 1800-1865'. Unpublished Ph.D. Thesis, University of London, n.d. [1968], pp. 19-24, 145-8.
4. M. Sidney Daney, Histoire de la Martinique, 3 vols. (Fort Royal, 1846, reprint 1963), Vol. 1, p. 415.
5. Richard N. Adams, 'On the Relation Between Plantation and "Creole Cultures"' in *Plantation Systems of the New World*, Social Science Monographs, VII, Pan American Union (Washington, D.C., 1959), p. 73.

6. Gilberto Freyre, *The Masters and the Slaves* (trans. New York, 1946), pp. 66, 67, 301.
7. A. T. Porter, *Creoledom* (London, 1963), pp. 5-6. 19-47; *Proceedings of the Conference on Creole Language Studies*, ed. R.B. Le Page (London, 1961), p. 1.
8. Robert Hall, *Pidgin and Creole Languages* (New York, 1966), p. xi.
9. M.C. Alleyne, 'The Cultural Matrix of Caribbean Dialects'. Unpublished paper, University of the West Indies, Mona, Jamaica, n.d., p. 1.
10. R. Hall, op. cit., p. xii.
11. Adams, op. cit., p. 73.
12. ibid., p. 74.
13. ibid.
14. Rémy Bastien, *Plantation Systems*, p. 80.
15. A distinction might also be drawn between *mestizo* creole societies and *mulatto* creole societies (see G.A. Beltrán, *Plantation Systems*, p. 67). *Mestizo* creole cultures involve *one* group (the Amerindians) native to the New World, while in *mulatto* societies, both groups, European and African, are cultural strangers. Jamaica is an example of this latter type of society, where the problems of cultural rehabilitation are of a radically different order from those in *mestizo* societies.

PART ONE

THE ESTABLISHMENT

JAMAICA: BACKGROUND

JAMAICA, approximately 140 miles from east to west and fifty miles at its widest, with an area of some 4,207 square miles, lies ninety miles south of Cuba and about the same distance west of the long and narrow peninsula of Haiti in that northern section of the Caribbean archipelago known as the Greater Antilles. It was inhabited by Amerindian Arawaks when discovered by Columbus in 1494. It was occupied by the Spaniards in 1509. In the course of the first century of its settlement the Arawaks were destroyed and West African Negro slave labour was imported into the colony, first by the Spaniards and then by the English who captured the island in 1655. The Jamaican novelist, John Hearne, has described it as

a long jagged backbone of mountains set in a ring of gently sloping plain which varies in depth, from a ribbon under sheer, forested walls on the north-east to wide, dry savannahs on the south-west. The Blue Mountains of the east are high, peaks of five to six thousand feet jumbled around the seven thousand four hundred foot of the Peak. . . . It is a terrain of steep misty valleys funnelling up to the peaks, long ridges, narrow as a mule's spine, with cool, tart air blowing up the flanks under the rain clouds.[1]

It is within this 'ring of gently sloping plain', especially (see Map I) around Savanna-la-Mar in Westmoreland, Black River in St. Elizabeth, the Clarendon–St. Catherine area (on the south coast), the eastern Westmoreland–Hanover plain, the northern coastal strip from Lucea to Ocho Rios, the St. Mary lowlands running, because of a geological fault in the mountain chain (see Map II), into the appropriately named St. Thomas-in-the-Vale, that the Spaniards, then the English, settled, first as herdsmen and small farmers, afterwards mainly as sugar planters and cattle ('pen') keepers, with cotton, cocoa, ginger, pimento, and logwood as subsidiaries and some coffee in the mountains.[2] The central mountains acted as a barrier between

[1] In *Ian Fleming Introduces Jamaica*, ed. Morris Cargill (London, 1965), p. 47.
[2] *Journals of the Assembly of Jamaica*, 14 vols. (Jamaica, 1803–26) (hereafter cited as *JAJ*); Vol. I. Appendix, p. 50.

the settled coasts and were inhabited by Maroons[1] and runaway slaves who posed a continual security problem for the settlers. Because of this, contact between south and north was mainly by coastal shipping: from Kingston in the south to Montego Bay, Falmouth and St. Ann's Bay in the north, via Savanna-la-Mar on the south-west and Port Antonio in the north-east. The main north–south road connection, called the River Road,[2] was from Spanish Town (St. Iago de la Vega), the capital, along the Rio Cobre via Bog Walk and Linstead and from there west over Mount Diablo into St. Ann; and east, following the Rio d'Oro into St. Mary.

This central mountain barrier preventing easy communication between the settled coasts was one factor militating against full settlement of the island. But the nature of the island's soil was another. Apart from the ancient Blue Mountain ridges, the great mass of the central highland is in essence a pitted (karsted) white limestone plateau occupying four-fifths of the total area of the island.[3] This is difficult soil and terrain to cultivate and the heavy seasonal rainfall (annual average 30–100 inches with possibilities in the mountains of up to 200 inches),[4] followed by long periods of drought, causes erosion. Irrigation and conservation of water, especially given the skills available in the eighteenth century, were also difficult because of the porous quality of the limestone, and the sharp descent of the plateau on to the narrow coastal strip created flooding and overflowing of the island's rivers, many of which, again because of the nature of the terrain, shrank to trickles or became 'dry river' gullies during the dry season (normally December to April). Soil exhaustion was a condition of these factors. Hurricanes, earthquakes, drought, fire and famine were also constantly recurring hazards to life, property and crops. Within the period of this study alone, there were at least seventeen earthquakes,[5] ten hurricanes,[6]

[1] See p. 7, n. 4, below.

[2] *JAJ*, Vol. VII, 605 of 18 Nov. 1783. See also G. E. Cumper, 'Labour Demand and Supply in the Jamaican Sugar Industry, 1830–1950', *Social and Economic Studies*, Vol. ii (1954), no. 4, pp. 53–4 and Map 1.

[3] Charles Schuchert, *Historical Geology of the Antillean-Caribbean Region* (New York, 1935), p. 412.

[4] Schuchert, p. 411; Maxwell Hall, *The Meteorology of Jamaica* (Kingston, 1904), p. 21.

[5] 1771, June 1780, Oct. 1780, 1781, 1784, 1796, 1798, 1799, 1801, 1802, 1806, June 1812, July 1812, Nov. 1812, Aug. 1813, Oct. 1813, 1818. See Maxwell Hall, *Notes of Hurricanes, Earthquakes, and other Physical Occurrences in Jamaica up to . . . 1880* (Kingston, 1916), pp. 3–6.

[6] 1780, 1781, 1784, 1785, 1786, 1812, 1 Aug. 1813, 28 Aug. 1813, 1815, 1818. See Hall, *Notes*, pp. 3–6.

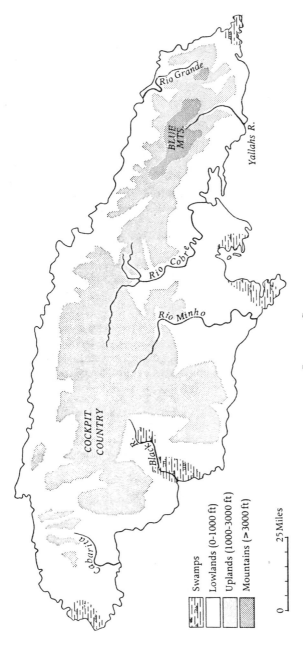

MAP II. JAMAICA: SURFACE FEATURES

Swamps
Lowlands (0-1000 ft)
Uplands (1000-3000 ft)
Mountains (>3000 ft)

0   25 Miles

Rio Grande

BLUE MTS.

Yallahs R.

Rio Cobre

Rio Minho

COCKPIT COUNTRY

Black

Cabarita

four droughts and famines[1] and nine great fires.[2] In addition, health was, and remained, a major problem for both the white and black elements of the population,[3] especially for newcomers. Sanitary arrangements, particularly in the towns, were deplorable; soldiers lived in hot, overcrowded barracks usually on low ground; slaves in the towns were relegated to hot, overcrowded quarters; those on the estates were overworked and undernourished, many were yaws-bitten; and though the creole whites had on the whole successfully adapted their way of living to tropical conditions, they remained vulnerable to malaria and yellow fever since the source of these evils —the *anopheles* and *Aedes aegypti*—whined on at large and un-regarded. These physical and environmental factors, and the kind of incalculability they introduced,[4] were to play an important part in the (slow) development of the society.

From 1655 to 1664, however, English-occupied Jamaica was run as a conquered territory by the Army—an administration of major-generals and colonels. The 2,000 or so soldiers[5] were expected to turn their swords to cultivation. These military farmers were supple-mented by more conventional settlers from other West Indian islands, Bermuda, New England and Surinam, and by convicts and inden-tured servants from England, Scotland, and Ireland.[6] It was not a prosperous time for the colony,[7] except for the wealth of plunder brought in by buccaneers and privateers.[8] The island's stock of wild cattle, hogs, and horses did not long survive indiscriminate sport and slaughter,[9] and small-scale diversified planting, although officially

[1] 1772, 1780, 1786, 1815. See Hall, *Notes*, pp. 3–6.

[2] 1779 at Savanna-la-Mar, 1780 in Kingston, 1782 in Kingston, 1795 in Montego Bay, 1798 in Montego Bay, 1808 in Falmouth, 1808 in Montego Bay, 1811 in Montego Bay, 1815 in Port Royal. See Hall, *Notes*, pp. 3–6; *JAJ*, VII, 499 of 14 Nov. 1782 and XII, 372 of 12 Nov. 1811; Frank Cundall, *Historic Jamaica* (London, 1915), p. 321.

[3] See Chapter 18.

[4] See Douglas Hall, 'Incalculability as a Feature of Sugar Production during the Eighteenth Century', *Social and Economic Studies*, Vol. x (1961), no. 3.

[5] A. P. Thornton, *West-India Policy under the Restoration* (Oxford, 1956), p. 39.

[6] Add. MS. 11410 f. 16–17, 'The Relation of Collonell Doyley upon his returne from Jamaica'; Add. MS. 12408 f. 6; *Calendar of State Papers (Colonial), America and West Indies*, hereafter cited as *C.S.P.*, 1574–1660, pp. 431, 491–2; 1661–8, nos. 292, 350; 1675–6, nos. 239, 260, 504, 610, 675, 740, 800 (p. 344).

[7] *C.S.P.*, 1661–8, no.68; John Thurloe, *A Collection of the State Papers of John Thurloe, Esq.*, Vol. IV (London, 1742), p.153.

[8] Bryan Edwards, *The History, Civil and Commercial, of the British Colonies in the West Indies* (London, 1793) ed., 1801, 3 vols. Vol. I, pp. 211–12.

[9] See, for example, Add. MS. 11410 f. 17–18; Bryan Edwards, op. cit., p. 204. Also Thurloe, op. cit., p. 635: Copy of Instructions to Fortescue, Goodsonn, Sedgwick and Serle:

'you are hereby authorized and required, to give such rules and directions from time to time concerning the killing of cattle, as that the stock and breed of cattle be not

encouraged,[1] was by the 1690s failing as a result of natural disasters (a cocoa blight, the hurricane of 1689, the earthquake of 1692, for instance),[2] the losses and uncertainties as to the future brought about by a French 'commando' raid among small settlements in 1694,[3] continuing Maroon depredations,[4] and the increasing competition from privileged settlers who had been acquiring large land-grants[5] and were turning these lands over to sugar production.[6] As sugar was an increasingly lucrative commodity in overseas markets,[7] these producers were soon able to attract the kind of capital[8] necessary to establish full-scale sugar estates and the West African slave labour that went with them. By the third decade of the eighteenth century, large-scale sugar production was the chief and most characteristic economic activity within the colony, and the interest in 'small' white settlement had declined.

Politically, the first major change in the island's constitution came when Army rule was exchanged for a form of representative government by Governor, Council, and Assembly. A Council of twelve was elected early in 1660 though there is no record of the election or of how representation was arranged.[9] Thereafter, Councils were

destroyed thereby; which we are informed will be done in a very short time by the great numbers, which are yearly killed for their hides. . . .'

[1] See, for example, *C.S.P.*, 1669–74, pp. 145–7; Anon., *Colonization of the Island of Jamaica* (no imprint, 1792), p. 7.

[2] *The Universal Magazine* for Apr. 1773, pp. 169–70; Edwards, op. cit., Vol. I, pp. 230–2; W. J. Gardner, *A History of Jamaica* (London, 1873), 2nd ed. 1909, pp. 73, 75–8, 83.   [3] Gardner, op. cit., pp. 101–4.

[4] ibid., pp. 53–4. These Maroons were Spanish slaves who had seized the opportunity of the English take-over of the island to revolt in 1655. They inhabited the central highlands, remaining generally separate from the English slaves but receiving steady accretions of runaways from them from time to time. See R. C. Dallas, *The History of the Maroons*, 2 vols. (London, 1803), Vol. I, pp. 25–31. The Jamaica government reached a settlement with them after the first Maroon War, 1730–9.

[5] Gardner, op. cit., p. 52. By 1670, there were forty-five holdings of 1,000 acres or more in the island (C.O. 138/1).

[6] 'The sugar cane was early cultivated here by the Spaniards; they probably obtained their plants from the Brazils; their plantations served only to furnish them with sugar for their own consumption; for it does not appear that they exported any. The Nevis planters, who came hither with General Brayne, entered more largely upon this article; and after their example, Colonel Barrington and other officers of the army formed some few sugar plantations; but so unskilful were they in the manufacture of it, that what they made was of very bad quality, black, and of no grain; upon Sir Thomas Modiford's appointment to the government, in 1664, he instructed the inhabitants in the art of management, as then practised at Barbadoes; and from this period their produce grew into esteem at the British market.' Edward Long, *The History of Jamaica*, 3 vols. (London, 1774), Vol. I, p. 435.

[7] Richard Pares, *Merchants and Planters* (Cambridge, 1960), *Economic History Review Supplement*, no. 4, pp. 22–4.

[8] See ibid. pp. 38–50, which discusses this for the West Indies generally.

[9] *C.S.P.*, 1661–8, no. 108; A. M. Whitson, *The Constitutional Development of Jamaica*, 1660–1729 (Manchester University Press, 1929), p. 20, n.2.

appointed by the Governor acting on behalf of the Crown. The first Assembly was convened in January 1664. From the outset, it asserted its right to speak and act on behalf of the colony, to control local taxation, and supervise its expenditure within the colony.[1] By an Act of 1674 (confirmed in 1683), the Assembly established its institutional integrity by setting out the number of representatives eligible to sit for the various constituencies of the island.[2] It also insisted on its right to choose its own Speaker,[3] to control its members, order its business[4] and decide for itself the merits of disputed elections.[5] An act of 1711 declared 'what persons shall be qualified to sit in Assemblies'[6] and an Act of 1716 sought to regulate the conduct of elections.[7] In 1741 the first attempts were made by the House to limit the life of Assemblies, though legislation under this head was not accepted by the British Government until 1779.[8] Between 1677 and 1680, it was the Assembly's action that prevented the establishment of a system of direct Crown rule in the colony, modelled on Poyning's Law for Ireland.[9] This was perhaps the single most important constitutional 'victory' for the island during this period. By 1728, most of the Assembly's claims to institutional integrity—to being a kind of overseas House of Commons—had been tacitly admitted by the British Government in exchange for the granting, by the Assembly, of a fixed permanent revenue to the Crown, for use within the island, of £8,000 per annum.[10]

It is from this kind of background that the Jamaica Assembly had emerged within the creole Establishment by the beginning of our period.

[1] Whitson, *Constitutional Development*, pp. 25, 160; F. G. Spurdle, *Early West Indian Government* (Palmerston North, New Zealand [1962], pp. 25–6. At the time, these claims were ahead of House of Commons practice.

[2] Spurdle, op. cit., p. 70.   [3] Whitson, *Constitutional Development*, pp. 42–3.
[4] Ibid, p. 40.   [5] Spurdle, op. cit., p 71.

[6] 10 Annae, c. 5. Laws identified with this kind of numbering in this text are from *Laws of Jamaica*, 6 vols. (St. Iago de la Vega, 1792, 1802, 1793–1817) and volumes for 1817, 1818, 1819, and 1820–1 (St. Iago de la Vega, 1818, 1819, 1820, 1821).

[7] Spurdle, op. cit., p. 71. The 1716 Act was disallowed on a legal technicality. In 1733, the Assembly passed another Act to secure the freedom of elections. This was neither approved nor disapproved in Britain and thus remained in force in Jamaica until 1780, when a more comprehensive Act (21 Geo. III, c. 15) was introduced and passed.

[8] Spurdle, op. cit., p. 72.

[9] Whitson, *Constitutional Development*, pp. 78–110; Sir Alan Burns, *History of the British West Indies* (London, 1954), pp. 331–2. It was proposed that two rules should be adopted from Poyning's Act: (1) that no assembly should in future be called without the King's express direction; (2) that no law should be consented to by the Governor until it had been approved by the Crown.

[10] Whitson, *Constitutional Development*, pp. 152–7.

2

POLITICAL AND SOCIAL INSTITUTIONS (1)

The Legislature

The Governor, a Council of twelve appointed members, and the Assembly constituted the legislature of Jamaica. Within the period of this study, all legislation originated in the Assembly. After three readings, including a committee stage, the passed bills were sent to the Council where a similar procedure was followed. The Council had power to amend all bills, though from about 1710 it had tacitly given up the right to amend money bills.[1] From time to time, however, it disputed with the Assembly its right to amend clauses in bills to do with expenditure.[2] Bills passed by both Houses were sent to the Governor by the Assembly, usually near the end of the session (in December), for his approval and assent. They then came into force locally unless specifically stated otherwise, though technically they still had to receive the royal consent. Acts that contravened British policy or principles were disallowed by the Crown, though this power was not generally exercised, since it was the Governor's responsibility, in the first place, not to assent to bills that contravened his Instructions. Faced with recalcitrance, a Governor could, as a last resort, prorogue or dissolve an Assembly, though here he ran the risk of not being voted the money necessary for running his government.[3] To avoid local disputes, Governors sometimes allowed

[1] See Spurdle, op. cit., pp. 31, 223 n.11. Spurdle's work was of great value in the preparation of this and the sections on Administration and Executive below, especially where it relates to the years before the beginning of this study.

[2] See, for example, *JAJ*, VIII, 558 of 21 Dec., 559 of 22 Dec. 1789; IX, 89 of 8, 9 March 1792. For a full account of these conflicts see A. L. Murray, 'Constitutional Developments in Jamaica 1774–1815' (unpublished M.A. Thesis, University of London, 1956), pp. 226–67.

[3] The Governor derived his permanent revenue from the Revenue Acts of 1728 and 1794 (1 Geo. II, c. 1 and 35 Geo. III, c. 9). This amounted to £10,000 per annum in 1794. Over this the Assembly had no control whatever, though the Governor could not spend this money without consulting the Council. But government could not be run on £10,000. To meet this problem, the Assembly had to provide funds from annual taxation. Estimates for 1788 were £163,500; the Ways and Means figure for 1796 was £656,223 15s. 10d. for 1805, £578,578 15s. 1d.; Estimates for 1805 amounted to

certain bills to pass but confidentially recommended their disallowance to the Crown. Sometimes the Crown's legal officers disallowed
bills that Governors had approved. In practice, the local Assembly
got around the stumbling block of royal disallowances by passing
bills on an annual basis (it usually took more than a year for bills
from the colonies to be considered by the Board of Trade), unless, as
already mentioned, such bills contained specific clauses suspending
their operation until they had received the royal consent.[1] When
constitutional conflicts *did* arise—after 1799, for instance, over
various matters to do with slavery in Jamaica—the royal disallowance
was used, notably in the Privy Council's rejection of the Slave Preaching Bills of 1802, 1807, and the Consolidated Slave Bill of 1808.[2]

Administration

This was carried out by certain Boards—the Committee of Correspondence, the Commission of Public Accounts, the Commission
of Forts, Fortifications, Barracks and Public Buildings, the Board
of Works, the Council of War, and the Ecclesiastical Commission—
two of which—the Board of Works and the Ecclesiastical Commission— were established within the period of this study. These Boards,
mainly composed of representatives of all three branches of the
legislature, were statutorily recognized and in effect may be seen as a
form of collaboration between Crown and colonists in the work of
running the island. Crown officers were available to advise these
Commissions as the need arose.[3] Boards for other specific purposes
were established from time to time as necessary.

The Committee of Correspondence, first established in 1693,[4]

£444,990 11s. 9d.; normal statutory expenditure alone (Governor's additional salary,
the Speaker's salary, the clergy's salary, the free schools, subsistence of troops, road
grants, etc.) in 1816 totalled over £137,377. (See *JAJ*, VIII, 483–5 of 19 Dec. 1788; IX,
521 of 30 April 1796; X, 462 of 11 Feb. 1800; XI, 828 of 21 Dec. 1815.)

[1] What Crown officers usually did, in fact, was neither to approve nor disapprove
of the generality of colonial laws before them. Unless the bills were such that they
required specific or immediate action, they were simply allowed to 'lie by'. For a full
account of the Assembly's disputes with the Crown over suspending clauses, see A. L.
Murray, op. cit., pp. 4–38, and *JAJ*, XII, 166–72 of 16 Nov.; 240–1 of 13 Dec. 1809.

[2] For these, see C.O. 139/51, no. 1221 (1802); *JAJ*, XII, 166–72 of 16 Nov. 1809;
A. L. Murray, op. cit., pp. 36–7; C.O. 137/125, no. 65, Manchester to Castlereagh,
29 Oct. 1809.

[3] Crown officers, for instance, attended the Commission for Forts and Fortifications.
See William Beckford, *A Descriptive Account of the Island of Jamaica* . . . 2 vols.
(London, 1790), Vol. I, p. xxxv.

[4] Spurdle, op. cit., p. 205, citing *Laws of Jamaica*, 1684–1698, 2 vols. (London,
1684–98), Vol. II, p. 52. This Committee, however, is referred to by title for the first
time in the Act 6 Geo. II, c. 18 of 1733.

was responsible for appointing, and conducting correspondence with, the Island Agent in London. Petitions to the British Government, and attempts to influence the course of colonial legislation in the Commons,[1] were normally conducted through this channel. From 1767 to 1794 this Committee consisted of seven Councillors and twenty-three Assemblymen, with a quorum of five, of which one at least had to be a Councillor.[2] After 1794, the entire Council and Assembly constituted this Committee.[3]

The Commission of Public Accounts,[4] which was really two committees—one for inspecting the Public Accounts and the other for settling them, consisted (from 1774) of the entire House of Assembly[5] —appropriately enough, since the House alone was responsible for local finance.

The Commission for Forts, Fortifications, Barracks and Public Buildings (established in 1742),[6] was responsible for inspecting and managing the items mentioned in its title, though the Crown also retained a Supervisor of Forts and Fortifications.[7] Between 1769 and 1778, this Commission consisted of the Governor, seven Councillors and an increasing[8] number of Assemblymen. After 1778, the entire House sat on the Board with the Governor and seven Councillors.[9] In 1792, a separate Board of Works, specially concerned with public buildings (including hospitals, gaols and barracks, was set up, on which sat the Governor, the President of the Council, the Attorney General, the Chief Justice, the Speaker of the House,

---

[1] On 27 January 1795, for instance, the Committee of Correspondence wrote to the then Agent, Robert Sewell, that he ought to endeavour to obtain a seat in the House of Commons so that he could more accurately report what went on there and be in a better position to represent the interests of the West Indies, 'It being deemed of essential importance to this Island that you should have not only the most accurate information of all the proceedings in the House of Commons, but also the earliest opportunity of interposing on our behalf in any measure there proposed which may be likely to affect our Interests . . .' (The Hon. Committee of Correspondence, 1794–1833, Minute Book. Minute no. 6 of 27 Feb. 1795.) Sewell complied and gained a seat (see Minute no. 1 of 15 Aug. 1796).

[2] Spurdle, op. cit., p. 207.   [3] 35 Geo. III, c. 4 of 1794; Laws, Vol. III, p. 90.

[4] Established by 4 Geo. II, c. 9 of 1732; but a Committee of the Assembly to inspect the Public Accounts was in operation from as early as 1679 (Spurdle, op. cit., p. 120).

[5] 15 Geo. III, c. 4 of 19 Nov. 1774; Laws, Vol. II, pp. 148–9.

[6] JAJ, III, 609 of 28 May; 613 of 3 June, 1742. The Assembly and Council, however, had a joint committee of inspection from as early as 1679. (Spurdle, op. cit., pp. 129 and 246, n.7.)

[7] See p. 15 below, n. 4.   [8] Spurdle, op. cit., p. 140.

[9] C.O. 139/35, no. 396 of 1778. This Commission had a quorum of five, of whom one had to be a Councillor and at least three, Assemblymen. By 1799, the whole Council also sat on this Commission, still with the same quorum. (See 40 Geo. III, c. 10 of 1799; Laws, Vol. IV, p. 33; JAJ, VII, 176 of 12 Nov. 1779.)

and nineteen Assembly members. All members of this Board were specified by name in the Act and its various renewals.[1]

The Council of War,[2] called only during emergencies, consisted until 1779 of the Governor as Commander-in-Chief and Chairman, members of the Council, and senior military and naval officers.[3] After 1779, it was made up 'of the Governor or Commander in Chief for the time being, the several members of the Privy Council of [the] Island, the Speaker and the Members of the Assembly for the time being, General Officers of the Militia, Field Officers Actually Commanding Regiments and the Field Officers of such . . . Regiments of the Militia in Actual Commission for the time being, and no other person Whatsoever. . . .'[4]

The Ecclesiastical Commission, consisting of five local rectors, was set up by the Act 39 Geo. III, c. 23 of 1799.[5] It replaced the Bishop of London's ordinary jurisdiction over the clergy of the island. The Commission had power 'to give institution to benefices, and to grant licences to curates, and to visit all rectors, curates, ministers, and incumbents, of all the churches and chapels [in the] island . . . and all other priests and deacons in holy orders of the church of England, resident in [Jamaica], with all and all manner of ecclesiastical jurisdiction, power, and coercion, that may be requisite in the premises'.[6] Any three of this Commission could suspend any of the island clergy for a period not exceeding one year. In cases of dismissal, or of suspension for more than one year, the Governor's confirmation had to be obtained, and the clergyman or clergymen involved had the right of appeal to the Crown.[7]

Executive

During the period of this study, as will be noted from the section above, the Assembly and/or locally resident bodies had encroached on, and had gained an increasing measure of participation in and control of, the colony's administration at the expense of the Crown. The execution of legislative decisions and of British Govern-

[1] C.O. 139/47, Acts of Jamaica (1790–2, nos. 755–860), no. 851.
[2] This Council probably existed from the time of the establishment of English government in Jamaica. The first reference to it occurs in the 'Act for settling the Militia' of 1681.   [3] Spurdle, op. cit., p. 230 n.31.
[4] C.O. 139/37A, no. 437 of 23 Dec. 1779: 'An Act for Ascertaining who shall Compose future Councils of War'.
[5] 'An act for annulling so much of an act of this island [21 Geo. II, c. 6 of 1748] as gives power to the bishop of London to exercise ordinary jurisdiction in this island, as far as the same appertains to the ecclesiastical regimen of the clergy only. . . .'
[6] *JAJ*, X, 485 of 11 Dec. 1800.   [7] ibid.

ment policy was still, however, in the hands of officials appointed by the Governor, British government departments or patent office-holders in Britain holding their grant direct from the king. All, of course, were in theory at least, subject to the authority of the Governor while in Jamaica, if not effectively controlled by him.

Some of the oldest, most important, and most lucrative posts were the patent-held offices, executed by means of deputies while the substantive holder resided in Britain and shared the profits with his surrogate. Some of these patent holders held the same office in several islands.[1] In Jamaica, the most important of these posts were those of Island Secretary, the deputy Provost-Marshal-General, the Surveyor-General, the Clerk of the Supreme Court, the Registrar of the Court of Chancery, the Clerk of the Patents, the Clerk of the Court of Common Pleas, the Clerk of the Crown and the Peace, the Receiver-General, the Attorney-General, the Auditor-General, the Solicitor-General, the Naval Officer,[2] the Agent-General,[3] and the Clerk of the Markets. All these, within the period of this study, were deputies, except the Attorney-General and the Clerk of the Crown and the Peace.[4]

Executively, the most important of these posts was perhaps that of Island Secretary, who was also automatically Clerk of the Council and ex-officio Secretary to the Governor,[5] though by about 1747 the Governor had obtained for himself a Private Secretary,[6] recognized

[1] The Hon. Chas. Wm. Wyndham, for example. See C.O. 325/12, and C.O. 325/19, Returns of Appointments, 1809 and 1817 respectively.

[2] The Naval Officer's duty was 'to enter and clear all Merchant Vessels of every description trading to the Island. To examine their Dockets, bill of Stores, certificates of bonds, and to record same; To take account of Cargo, regulate their tonnage, and all dutyable articles, granting certificates thereof, with marks, Numbers and packages to the Receiver General and collector of the Customs, taking affidavits of Stores being part of such dutyable articles, regulating the same and to examine all vessels for those uncertified. . . . To take affidavits of the due measurement of all lumber imported, to take cognizance of all vessels coming into Port from stress of weather or in distress, reporting them to the Governor. . . .' (C.O. 137/125.) The Naval Officer relied entirely on fees. His average income here was over £3,600 sterling, of which £1,500 went to his principal.

[3] It was the (Deputy) Agent-General's 'right to require that all Stores and Provisions shall be consigned to him or his Deputy or Deputies, and that he . . . do everything with respect to such Stores and Provisions that appertains to his Trust as Commissary and Steward General . . .' (C.O. 137/125, Miscellaneous. Copy of Treasury Minute dated 5 April 1809).

[4] See C.O. 137/125, no. 64: Manchester to Castlereagh, 29 Oct., 1809: and Returns of Appointments, C.O. 325/12 and 325/17.

[5] C.O. 137/125, as cited above. The potentially powerful Receiver-General was under the effective control of the Assembly's Commission of Public Accounts.

[6] Spurdle, op. cit., p. 260 n.7.

by statute in 1783.[1] The Island Secretary's duty was to register all deeds, keep and transcribe all the island's laws and transmit them in original and duplicate to London annually. As Clerk to the Council, his responsibility was to keep the record of its proceedings and transmit them, also in original and duplicate, annually to London. In his capacity of Clerk to the Governor, he acted as Ordinary and as such prepared papers for proving and administering wills. He also acted as Notary Public and, in addition, as Clerk of the Court of Error, kept all its records. The office was worth about £3,000 sterling per annum in 1809, mostly from fees.[2] At least two offices in this category, however, were worth even more. The Clerk of the Supreme Court (also prothonotary of the King's Bench and Common Pleas), received £3,882 sterling after deductions, £2,500 being retained by the patentee.[3] The Clerk of the Patents (this post was usually combined with that of Registrar in Chancery), received £4,694 in salary and fees.[4] (The salary came out of the British Treasury. The fees came out of Jamaica.) The Provost-Marshal-General[5] reported that, between June 1808 and June 1809, he had derived some £11,000 from fees though his net receipts were only £3,644 sterling, £2,100 of which went to Lord Braybrooke, the patentee.[6]

In the second category of public offices in Jamaica were those appointed from and financed by British Government departments: the Comptroller of Customs, the Collector of Customs, the Commissioner of Stamp Duties (by the British Treasury and/or Customs) the Deputy Postmaster-General (by commission for the joint Postmasters-General), the Judge, the Registrar, the Marshal of the Court of Vice-Admiralty and the Advocate-General (from the High Court of Admiralty). All these, except, in 1809, the Registrar and the Marshal of the Court of Vice-Admiralty, executed their offices in person, the Customs Officers having deputies in the various ports of the island.[7]

In a third category were lesser offices, directly under the Governor's

[1] 23 Geo. III, c. 22 of 1 March 1783; *Acts of Assembly Passed in the Island of Jamaica: from 1770, to 1783, inclusive* (Kingston, 1786), No. 106: '. . . to regulate the fees of the Governor's private secretary'.

[2] C.O. 137/125.   [3] ibid.   [4] ibid.

[5] His duties were the keeping of the peace, the execution of writs, sentences, etc., and the conduct of elections. He was also in charge of the gaols of the island. See 'Commission of Inquiry into the Administration of Civil and Criminal Justice in the West Indies', First Report, 2nd Series, Jamaica, 1826–7; *Parliamentary Papers*, hereafter cited as *P.P.*, Vol. XXIV (559), p. 90.

[6] C.O. 137/125. In other words, the Provost-Marshal depended on fees for running his office as well as for providing himself with a living.

[7] ibid.

appointment and control.[1] These included the *custodes rotulorum* or Chief Magistrates of the various parishes,[2] and the Justices of the Peace, the five Superintendents of the Maroon Towns (Trelawny, Accompong, Moore Town, Charles Town and Scott's Hall),[3] the Harbour Masters of Kingston, Black River, and Falmouth, the Superintendent of Forts and Fortifications (the Island Engineer)[4] and the Island Barrack-Master-General. In 1809, the Marshal of the Court of Vice-Admiralty also held his appointment from the Governor.[5]

Individually, there is no evidence to gainsay the competence of these officials. They apparently executed their duties as efficiently as prevailing conditions permitted. The fees system, however, made for abuses, and as early as 1664, when the first Jamaican Assembly met, efforts were being made to regulate this. Between 1664 and 1750, in fact, Acts were passed regulating the fees of most of the senior public officers as well as of coroners and various legal officers in the law courts of the island.[6] These legal restrictions, however, were regarded as a violation of property rights by patentees, supported by the Board of Trade and the Privy Council.[7] Within the period of this study, nevertheless, the fees of certain public officers continued to be regulated by Jamaican statute: the land surveyors (assistants and deputies of the Surveyor-General), by 11 Geo. III, c. 21 of 1770 and various renewals, the Governor's (Private) Secretary by 23 Geo. III, c. 22 of 1783, the Collector of Customs and the Naval Officer by 24 Geo. III, c. 12 of 1783 and thereafter by renewal. In 1801, the Receiver-General was granted 'an annual allowance, or

[1] See Spurdle, op. cit., pp. 209 and 263, n. 35.

[2] See H. P. Jacobs's useful brief description in 'Roger Hope Elletson's Letter Book', *Jamaica Historical Review*, hereafter cited as *JHR*, Vol. ii, no. 1 (Dec. 1949), pp. 67–73.

[3] See Map I.

[4] The Governor had been trying to have an official of this description appointed in 1777. A Lt. Nepean, 'one of his majesty's engineers' (*JAJ*, VII, 558 of 20 Feb. 1783) arrived sometime in 1782 and was warmly recommended by the Governor. The Assembly, surprisingly, agreed to his appointment. (See *JAJ*, VII, 559 of 20 Feb. 1783.)

[5] C.O. 325/12.

[6] See *Acts of Assembly, Passed in the Island of Jamaica; From the Year 1681, to the Year 1754, inclusive* (St. Iago de la Vega, 1769), no. 150 of 1747 (Assay-Master); no. 56 of 1711 (Attorney-General, Collector, Clerk of the Supreme Court, Clerk of the Crown, Clerk of the Warrants, Surveyor-General, Clerk of the Markets and coroners); nos. 9 (1681), 38 (1696), 56 (Clerk of the Peace); nos. 25 (1683), 37 (1696), 56 (Clerk of the Patents); nos. 46 (1703), 56 (Naval Officer); nos. 56, 105 (1735), 147 of 1747 (Provost-Marshal); nos. 56, 70 (1721), 86 of 1728 (Receiver-General); nos. 20 (1681), 26 (1683), 37 and 38 of 1696, 56, 70, 86 (Island Secretary): see also *The Laws of Jamaica, Passed by the Assembly, And confirmed by His Majesty in Council April 17, 1684* (London, 1684), 'An Act for Regulating Fees', pp. 91–103.

[7] Spurdle, op. cit., p. 67.

salary, in lieu of commissions'[1] and by 55 Geo. III, c. 26 and c. 27 of 1814, the fees of the Clerk of the Supreme Court and of the Island Secretary were further regulated.

The Assembly was able also within this period to control to some extent the discharge of duties with respect to some of these offices. In 1774, for instance, the Island Secretary, the Provost-Marshal, the Clerk of the Supreme Court and the Clerk of the Patents, were forced by law to make deposits as sureties 'for the faithful discharge of their respective offices'.[2] In 1780, an Act compelled the Provost-Marshal 'to enter satisfaction, in his books, upon all executions now returned into his office . . . and to oblige the persons hereafter executing that office, to enter satisfaction . . . upon all executions that shall be hereafter lodged. . . .'[3] By 51 Geo. III, c. 17 of 1810, 55 Geo. III, c. 27 of 1814 and 60 Geo. III, c. 23 of 1819, the office of the Island Secretary was further regulated. 43 Geo. III, c. 1 of 1802 disqualified collecting constables (agents of the Receiver-General), from sitting in the House of Assembly. By 1816, despite the failure of legislation under this head, most of the public officers, like the Receiver-General, the Provost-Marshal, the Chief Justice and the Attorney-General, who had previously sat in the House, no longer did so.[4]

But these, taken all in all, were limited controls only. The efficiency of these offices, as a civil service, was vitiated by the fact that the most important posts continued to be held by non-residents. The lack of a single person or body to whom all public servants might have been, in effective terms, responsible, meant that there could be little overall control of their functions and very little, if any, long-term planning.

Courts of Law

These were of two kinds: the 'royal' courts—the Court of Sessions, Chancery, the Court of Error, the Court of Vice-Admiralty and the Court of Ordinary[5]—representing British policy and presence in Jamaica, and the civil courts—the Supreme Court, the courts of Assize for the counties of Surrey and Cornwall, and the Courts of Common Pleas and Quarter Sessions. For the county of Middlesex,

---

[1] 41 Geo. III, c. 10.   [2] 15 Geo. III, c. 7.   [3] 21 Geo. III, c. 23.
[4] See pp. 56–9, below, for a fuller discussion of this.
[5] John H. Howard, ed. *The Laws of the British Colonies in the West Indies and other parts of America concerning real and personal property, and manumission of slaves, with a view of the constitution of each colony*, 2 vols. (London, 1827), Vol. I, pp. 27–33.

the functions of the Assize Court were performed (from 1758)[1] by the judges of the Supreme Court. The Surrey Assizes were held three times a year in three-week sessions in Kingston; the Cornwall Assizes for the same period at Savanna-la-Mar and, after 1815, at Montego Bay.[2]

The jurisdiction of the Supreme Court, both civil and criminal, was co-extensive with that of the King's Bench, Common Pleas, Insolvent Debtors and Exchequer in England.[3] It was also a court of appeal from the inferior courts of Common Pleas.[4] It sat at the official seat of government, St. Iago de la Vega, three times in the year for three weeks per session. Actions in this court were tried before the Chief Justice and four assistant judges (unpaid until 1810),[5] any three of whom were sufficient to make a court, and a common jury of twelve qualified Middlesex persons, although upon special application by either the plaintiff or defendant, a special jury could be struck for trial of the cause.[6]

The two Assize courts consisted of an unlimited number of justices and a common jury of twelve, with provisions, as within Middlesex, for appeal against the jury's composition. Three justices had to be present to constitute a court. 15 Geo. III, c. 6 of 1774 allowed a single justice to open and adjourn these courts; and the same law permitted a judge of the Supreme Court to do the same in the Supreme Court. Like the Chief Justice and the assistant judges of the Supreme Court, the justices of Assize were appointed by the Governor by a commission under the broad seal of the island.[7]

The Courts of Common Pleas were held in the same precincts as the quarter sessions. These courts sat once in every three months, though some had the privilege of sitting more often. Their jurisdiction extended to all cases, excepting freehold or slaves, where the value of the suit did not exceed £20 with costs, though the Governor, as Chancellor, could allow them to hold pleas to any amount. Judges of these courts were appointed by the Governor and appeals from them were heard in the Supreme Court.[8]

The Courts of Quarter Sessions dealt with all matters, except land titles, that did not exceed 40s. in value. Cases here were heard

[1] Spurdle, op. cit., p. 52.
[2] Montego Bay was made county capital of Cornwall by 56 Geo. III, c. 20 (1815).
[3] See Car. II, c. 25 (1681), preamble of 17 Geo. III, c. 27 (1776), and John H. Howard, op. cit., Vol. I, p. 27.
[4] John H. Howard, op. cit., p. 27.   [5] See 51 Geo. III, c. 27 and p. 20, below.
[6] John H. Howard, op. cit., Vol. I, p. 27.
[7] ibid., pp. 28–9.   [8] ibid., p. 30.

and determined by any Justice of the Peace for the area, without appeal.[1] Justices of the Peace were appointed by the Governor and removable at pleasure.

The Courts of Chancery, Error, Vice-Admiralty and Ordinary were mainly concerned with the Crown's interests in Jamaica and took their form directly from the English courts to which they corresponded. In all these courts the Governor had direct control. He sat as Chancellor of the Court of Chancery and presided over the Court of Ordinary which determined ecclesiastical matters.

The Court of Vice-Admiralty had two distinct jurisdictions: it was an Instance court for deciding maritime causes; and also a Prize Court. Its presiding judge was appointed in England and held office during the Royal pleasure.[2] The Court of Error, consisting of the Governor and five members of Council who had to be entirely un-connected with other courts of law,[3] was the local court of appeal—under certain restrictions—in matters arising from the Supreme and Assize courts.[4] There was also appeal from this court and the Court of Chancery to the King in Council, under certain restrictions.[5]

There was, for the period of this study, an average of about thirty judges in the island.[6] According to Moreton, there were about seventy attorneys-at-law and twenty barristers in the island in 1790,[7] many of them trained at the various London Inns of Court,[8] in addition to the Attorney-General, the Solicitor-General, the Advo-cate-General, and the Provost-Marshal who was the executive officer of the courts, responsible for summoning juries and executing writs and orders.[9] The Provost-Marshal also acted as Returning Officer

[1] John H. Howard, op. cit., Vol. I, p. 30.   [2] ibid., p. 52.
[3] See C.O. 137/131, Morrison to Liverpool, 18 May 1811.
[4] John H. Howard, op. cit., Vol. I, p. 31.   [5] ibid., p. 31.
[6] A. L. Murray, op. cit., p. 205.
[7] J. B. Moreton, *Manners and Customs of the West India Islands* (London, 1790), pp. 63–4.
[8] The Middle Temple was one of the most popular with Jamaicans. Between 1770 and 1820, the following are recorded in the Register there: Willoughby Knowles (1771), Barnabas Riley (1772), Robert Irvin (1773), John Lyon, John Wall (1779), Edward Pinnock (1780), George Scott (1782), Edmund Pusey Lyon (1783), Gilbert Mathison (1790), George Lyon (1791), James Lewis (1793), R. J. Dunn (1794), T. B. V. Symes (1802), Walter Minto (1804), Hugh James (1807), Richard Cargill (1810), Henry Burke, T. J. Hall (1811), J. E. W. Panton (1817), H. A. S. Symes, W. B. Dean (1819). (*Middle Temple Register*, 1501–1902, ed. H. F. Macglagh and H. A. C. Sturgess, 2 vols. (London, 1949). See also *Register of Admissions to Gray's Inn*, 1521–1889, com-piled by J. Foster (London, 1889); *Records of the Honourable Society of Lincoln's Inn*, 1420–1893, 2 vols. (London, 1896).
[9] D. J. Murray, *The West Indies and the Development of Colonial Government 1801–1834* (Oxford, 1965), p. 19.

in Assembly elections.[1] It was felt, though, that there were not enough barristers and law officers in the country, and that professional standards of conduct and training were unsatisfactory.[2] A committee of the Assembly reported in November 1782, for instance, that the Supreme Court had not met for five days during sessions because of 'non-attendance of judges'.[3] The Chief Justice answering this criticism said that he had 'applied to most of the gentlemen of distinction in the country, to permit their names to be inserted in the commission and to qualify for justices of assize; but that they had all, without exception, declined'.[4] The only really dependable law officer in the island appeared to be the Attorney-General,[5] who was appointed by letters-patent from the King[6] and was removable by him alone,[7] though even this officer was not above criticism: 'Attorney-Generals, in some of the British Islands, are originally only Attorney's clerks who with a smattering of Latin, by some little interest procure those births [*sic*]; and they are as grasping as the Bow-street magistrates. . . .'[8]

In 1781 a law was passed,[9] making the appointment of judges and justices *quamdiu se bene gesserint* instead of at pleasure, though their suspension remained in the power of the Governor and five councillors. In 1785 the Assembly attempted, doubtless under pressure from the judiciary, to provide salaries for judges. Whatever the arguments against this,[10] there is no doubt that since the judges were unpaid, their judicial duties often suffered since they could not devote all their time to them. This point was made by Chief Justice

[1] See n. 5, p. 14, above.   [2] *JAJ*, VIII, 223 of 19 Dec. 1786.

[3] ibid., VII, 514 of 23 Nov. 1782.

[4] ibid. See also the Assembly's Inquiry into the Administration of Justice: *JAJ*, XII, 234 of 8 Dec. 1812, and the Assembly Committee Inquiry into the Conduct of Chief Justice Lewis; *JAJ*, XII, 745–72 of 14 Dec. 1812.

[5] Writing in 1816, Governor Manchester said '[a] constant and confidential Intercourse with the Governor and the Ease and indeed Success of his Administration materially depends upon the prudence and good Judgement of the Attorney-General'. (C.O. 137/142, Manchester to Bathurst, December 1816 (undated.) See also Frank Cundall, ed. *Lady Nugent's Journal* (hereafter cited as *LNJ* (Cundall)) (London, 1907), p. 60.

[6] In 1809, however, he held his commission from the Governor. See C.O. 325/12, no. 64 as cited.

[7] The Governor, of course, could suspend the Attorney-General, and all officers, in Jamaica, though this action had to be confirmed. (See for example C.O. 137/28/28, Knowles to Council of Trade and Plantations, 25 June 1754.) In the nineteenth century, these officers were usually selected from the local Bar. (See C.O. 137/114, Nugent to Castlereagh, 17 Nov. 1805.)

[8] Moreton, op. cit., p. 184.   [9] 21 Geo. III, c. 25.

[10] Judges, previous to this, had been paid in Jamaica until 1683. See *JAJ*, I, 74 of 5 Oct. 1683. No reason is given in the *Journals* for the decision to stop payment at that time.

Lewis during his examination before an Assembly committee in 1810. Lewis was asked if he thought justice would be affected if the judges remained unpaid. Lewis replied that he 'rather thinks the difficulty will increase in the supreme court, and his reason for thinking so is, that Mr. Vidal, one of the judges of that court, from whom he has hitherto received great assistance, will not sit again, as it interferes with his private concerns.'[1] But the Assembly's attempt to introduce salaries in 1785 and again in 1788, was defeated by the weight of public opinion;[2] and Lewis' suggestion in 1810 that the House might consider 'a certain annual sum to the gentlemen of the country' (i.e. those who lived outside Spanish Town) to help with travel expenses[3] was apparently not taken up. It was, however, agreed[4] that the two senior assistant judges of the Supreme Court and the two senior assistant judges of the Surrey and Cornwall Assize courts were to receive £700 and £500 per annum, respectively, on condition of regular attendance. Absence from more than one court was deemed 'irregular'. Clause x of this Act also stipulated that in future, Chief Justices[5] should be appointed from the ranks of the assistant judges of the Supreme Court only, or from barristers of more than five years' professional practice in the island—clearly a creole attempt to exclude expatriates from some of the juicier jobs in the island.

Vestries

The island was divided into parishes by one of its earliest Acts[6] and the powers and duties of vestries were set out in 29 Car. II, c. 1 of 1677.[7] Each vestry consisted of twelve elected men, two of whom were churchwardens, a varying number of local magistrates,[8] the parochial rector, and the *custos rotulorum*, as chairman. Churchwardens and vestrymen were elected by freeholders qualified to vote

[1] *JAJ*, XII, 291 of 21 Nov. 1810.

[2] See, ibid., VIII, 109 of 22 Nov.–135 of 8 Dec. 1785.

[3] ibid, XII, 291 of 21 Nov. 1810.   [4] 51 Geo. III, c. 27 of 15 Dec. 1810.

[5] In 1804 (see 45 Geo. III, c. 17), the Chief Justice had been transferred from fees to salary (£4,000 currency per annum) and by 58 Geo. III, c. 18 of 1817, this was raised to £5,600. Until then he had received a salary of £120 currency (plus fees), dating from 1683.

[6] 'An act for dividing this his majesty's island of Jamaica into several parishes and precincts.' See *JAJ*, I, 1, undated [1664].

[7] For 29 Car. II, c. 1, see C.O. 139/5/20–2.

[8] An attempt in 1789 to limit the number of magistrates sitting on vestries failed. (See *JAJ*, VIII, 538 of 12 Dec., 547 of 17 Dec., 557 of 21 Dec., 1789.) According to Stewart, however (J. Stewart, *A View of the past and present state of the island of Jamaica; with remarks on the moral and physical condition of the slaves and on the abolition of slavery in the colonies* (Edinburgh, 1823, p. 148) the number of magistrates sitting on vestries had been limited to two by 1823.

for members of the Assembly. The votes of at least six freeholders were necessary to make an election valid. Election days for the several parishes were fixed by 22 Geo. II, c. 16 of 2 December 1749. Each vestry held its election on a different day—St. Catherine on the second Tuesday in January, Port Royal on the second Wednesday in January, Kingston on the second Thursday in January, and so on. Elections were held annually. Vestries apparently met whenever there was business to be transacted or discussed. The quorum was fixed at two justices and six vestrymen. In Kingston (the busiest vestry), there were between twenty-one and twenty-five meetings a year.[1] In the smaller parishes there were sometimes not more than five meetings a year.[2] Where there were no vestry buildings, meetings were held in the Court house (if and when convenient) or in private houses or taverns.[3]

The vestries' function was to carry out local administration: the running of local workhouses, gaols (where these were separate from workhouses), the tracking down of runaway slaves, the protection of slaves (after 1801, through the Council of Protection set up by the Act 41 Geo. III, c. 26 of 15 March 1801), preparing jury lists for the courts of Assize, providing for the education of poor children and other local charities, keeping the roads in repair,[4] providing for the accommodation and feeding of troops during martial law, supervising the settling in of new settlers and, in the case of Kingston, particularly, looking after, first, the American loyalist refugees,[5] and later the French from St. Domingue; investigating the manumission claims of freed slaves, providing for and inspecting the parish churches where these existed (St. John, St. David, St. George, St. Mary, and Westmoreland did not have parish churches during the period of this study),[6] granting licences to Non-conformist preachers

---

[1] This is an average obtained from the seven Kingston Vestry and Common Council Minute Books (cited hereafter as *K.C.C.* Minutes), consulted at the Jamaica Archives, Spanish Town (1744–9, 1760–92 (Accounts), 1769–70, 1781–8, 1795–1805, 1805–15, 1815–20).

[2] See, for example, St. David Vestry Minutes, 1785–93, 1793–1800, 1806–13; St. George Vestry Minutes, 1801–16.

[3] See, for example, St. Ann Vestry Proceedings, 1791–1800, p. 161. Minute dated 28 May 1796. Also Minute dated 26 Jan. 1799. The Vestry purchased a house for its own use in March 1799 (Minute dated 28 March 1799).

[4] Every slave-owner, on pain of fine, had to contribute a certain number of slaves for work on the roads in each parish every year. The St. Ann Vestry was particularly efficient in organizing this work. See St. Ann Vestry Orders, 1767–90; St. Ann Vestry Proceedings, 1791–1800, 1800–9, 1817–23.

[5] See pp. 88–92, below.

[6] See 30 Geo. III, c. 13, section 3 of 1789; *JAJ*, X, 63 of 15 Dec. 1797; G. W. Bridges, *The Annals of Jamaica*, 2 vols. (London 1827); 2nd ed., Vol. I, pp. 561–7.

(after 1802),[1] providing relief after hurricanes, fires, etc.; being responsible for local police, fire, and security arrangements, the shipping of sick poor-whites out of the island on compassionate grounds, the regulation of markets, the licensing of hawkers and tavern keepers, and the levying and collecting of parish taxes and rents.

The vestries, naturally, pressed the legislature for measures that interested them—for example the St. James/Westmoreland dispute over the location of the county court which lasted from 1770 to 1815, when the court was moved from Savanna-la-Mar to Montego Bay;[2] and St. Ann's suit to have St. Ann's Bay made a Port of Entry.[3] On a few occasions, the vestries showed a will of their own. In 1785 and 1790, for instance, they disagreed with Assembly proposals to put all judges on salary.[4] In 1791, St. Ann and St. David objected to giving a salary to the Speaker of the Assembly.[5] In 1806, the Kingston Common Council, as it had become in 1801,[6] supported the city's printers in a dispute with the House,[7] and in 1818 all the vestries objected to the Assembly investigation into the office of the Chief Justice.[8] But on the whole, they were useful and obedient instruments of Assembly policy. After the 1802 Bill against Non-conformist ministers preaching to slaves was disallowed by the Privy Council, for instance, responsibility for carrying out the policy was imposed, without their objection, on them. In any case, there was a close personal relationship between the two bodies. The Custos was usually a member of the Assembly (or Council), and most vestries had at least one of their number in the legislature. The St. Catherine Vestry of 1813 had four of its members on the Assembly, and another was Clerk of the House. There were also two Councillors on this Board at the time. In general, the vestries were efficient, hardworking journeymen of local policy and administration. Through them, white control and domination of the society was assured. Consequently, as agents of social change, they were hardly effective. As may be inferred from their objections to the payment of judges

[1] See pp. 249–50, below.   [2] 56 Geo. III, c. 20 of 1815.
[3] St. Ann Vestry Minutes 1767–90, Minute dated 28 June 1790.
[4] See *JAJ*, VIII, 109 of 22 Nov. 1785; *Daily Advertiser* (Kingston), 5 Nov., and 13 Nov. 1790. The Assembly proposals were discussed on p. 20, above.
[5] St. Ann Vestry Minutes 1785–93, Minute dated 22 Oct. 1791.
[6] By 41 Geo. III, c. 29.
[7] See Kingston Common Council Proceedings 1803–15, Minutes dated 1 and 8 Dec. 1806; 14 Sept. 1807. The dispute is discussed under 'The Press' on pp. 38–9, below.
[8] See *Royal Gazette* (Kingston, Jamaica), hereafter cited as *R.G.*, XL (1818), 52, pp. 25, 28.

and the Speaker of the House, they represented the 'old guard' Establishment of middle-range creole planters, attorneys and traders who were making a reasonable living locally. They were more conservative, as such bodies usually are, than the legislature.

The Church

The Church of England was the 'established' church in Jamaica, but until 1799 when a local Ecclesiastical Commission was set up, it was not an organized corporate body. In fact, it may be argued that it did not become an organized corporate body until 1825, when the first Bishop of Jamaica was appointed.[1] Until then there was no local head, no synods, no local ecclesiastical Conferences where collective policy could be discussed, though until 1799 the Bishop of London had a commissary in the island who heard complaints and reported back to London.[2] But during the period of this study, the Church of England in Jamaica was no more than a collection of qualified individuals,[3] representative of a British institution. From 1748 to 1799 the Bishop of London was vested with the exercise of ordinary jurisdiction in the island as far the ecclesiastical regimen of the clergy was concerned,[4] though the Crown, through the Governor as Ordinary, retained the authority to present and induct ministers to the several parishes of the island, and on petition from parishioners, to suspend and/or dismiss them from the temporal and spiritual exercise of their functions.[5] Before appointment, clergymen had to be licensed as qualified by the Bishop of London.[6] By 39 Geo. III, c. 32 of 1799, the ordinary jurisdiction of the Bishop of London was transferred to a local Ecclesiastical Commission.[7] The authority to license clergy was retained, however, by the Bishop of London acting on behalf of the Crown.

[1] *Acts of Parliament: Great Britain: Public General Acts* (London, 1825); 6 Geo. IV, c. 88.

[2] See Church of England Archives, Fulham Palace: General Correspondence, West Indies; Vol. XVIII, Jamaica 1740—undated; ff. 53–4 (William May to Bishop Sherlock, 21 June 1751); 65–70 (William Stanford to Bishop Porteus, 22 July 1788); 102–5 (William Scott to Porteus, 22 and 26 May 1798); 171–2 (R. Tabor to Bishop Robinson, undated).

[3] A. Caldecott, *The Church in the West Indies* (London, 1898), p. 52. It must be pointed out, however, that in law, the 'clergy' and not individual clergymen were recognized as being pastorally present in the island.

[4] 'Ecclesiastical Establishment: Church and Clergy', p. 1 in *The Political Constitution of Jamaica* (London, 1844); Fulham Palace Papers, cited in n. 2, above, ff. 100–1.

[5] Caldecott, op. cit., pp. 51–2.

[6] John B. Ellis. *The Diocese of Jamaica* (London, 1913), p. 33.

[7] See p. 12, above.

Each parish in the island had, or should have had, a rector[1] who sat *ex-officio* on the vestry of his parish and was maintained out of parish taxes until 38 Geo. III, c. 24 of 1797 when the Assembly assumed responsibility for the salaries of the various rectors. Payment of this salary was made dependent upon regular attendance to duty, and each vestry had to issue a 'work certificate' on behalf of its rector for this.[2]

The clergy who came to Jamaica 'passed as educated men'[3] and by their position took rank in the upper reaches of the society, with entrée to King's House.[4] The rector of St. Ann (1804–5) and of Hanover (1806–24), the Rev. Daniel Warner Rose, of Antigua, had been educated at Charterhouse and Jesus College, Cambridge. The rector of St. Catherine (1792–1809), a regular diner at Government House when the Nugents were there, was a Winchester and New College, Oxford, man and had taught at Winchester and at Wolmer's (in Kingston) before becoming rector. The rector of St. John (1798–1805) and of St. Dorothy[5] were also Oxbridge men.[6] These, however, appear to have been exceptions. On the whole, the Church of England clergy in Jamaica were boorish and poorly educated and, like their counterparts in England, were usually, like the rector of St. Mary (1802–21), the Rev. Colin Donaldson, who came to Jamaica in 1800 as a clerk to a Kingston merchant house,[7] products of primogeniture—younger sons without a chance of inheriting property and with little prospect, besides, of promotion in their vocation in Britain.[8] They were therefore exceedingly dependent upon Jamaica for their livelihood and consequently very prone to support the Establishment and the established way of life in the island. Their function was to preach to mainly white (and free coloured) inhabitants and baptize their children into the Church and (the local interpretation of) the Christian religion.

With growing fears after 1807 that Non-conformist missionary

[1] 33 Car. II, c. 18 of 1681.

[2] See, for instance, the Kingston Common Council Minutes, 14 April 1817: 'That Certificates in the usual form be granted to the Rev. Isaac Mann Rector of this City and Parish of residence and performance of the duties required by law between the 31st day of December and 31st day of March last.'

[3] Caldecott, op. cit., p. 58.

[4] See *Lady Nugent's Journal*, ed. Philip Wright (Kingston, 1966), hereafter cited as *LNJ* (Wright); entries for 23, 29 Aug.; 27 Sept. 1801; 12, 23 May; 6, 20, 23 June 1802, among many others.

[5] The Rev. Edward Ward. He was a non-resident incumbent.

[6] The information on these rectors is derived from *LNJ* (Wright) Index—a most thoughtful and useful compilation.

[7] Wright (*LNJ*) Index.　　　　[8] Caldecott, op. cit., p. 58.

activity was designed to undermine the very structure of society (see pp. 260–1 below), an attempt was apparently made to institutionalize into the local Church of England, the religious instruction of the slaves. In February 1808, a Committee of the Kingston Common Council reported that 'it is extremely proper and desirable the plan stated in the Rectors letter of affording religious instruction to people of every description according to the principles of the Church of England be . . . adopted'.[1] By 57 Geo. III, c. 24 of 1816 an arrangement was set up whereby curates were to be paid to provide religious instruction to slaves deemed suitable to receive it. In March 1820, a Moravian missionary was complaining that some overseers 'had resorted again to the practice of having their negroes baptized by the clergymen of the parish'.[2] The Church of England in Jamaica, however, never had enough clergy to contribute effectively to white (or black) religious welfare, even if it had consistently wished to. There was, for the period of this study, something like one Church of England clergyman per 1,500 white inhabitants—one clergyman per 15,000–18,000 of the total population.[3] The main religious activity in Jamaica centred around the missionaries and the Black Baptists, as will be discussed later.[4]

---

[1] K.C.C. Proceedings, 1803–15, 8 Feb. 1808.
[2] (Moravian) *Periodical Accounts*, Vol. VIII (1820), p. 72.
[3] Dallas, op. cit., Vol. II, p.442; *Wesleyan Methodist Missionary Society Report*, hereafter cited as *WMMS Report*, Vol. I (1819), p. 42.
[4] See pp. 161–4 and 252–64, below.

3

POLITICAL AND SOCIAL
INSTITUTIONS (2)

The Militia

An efficient militia, as many concerned with Jamaica realized,[1] was essential if the island was to be able to defend itself and to enjoy internal security from slave rebellion. This body, set up in 1681 by the 'Act for Settling the Militia',[2] consisted of local free men—white, coloured, black and Jew[3]—between the ages of sixteen and sixty,[4] with three regiments of horse, twenty regiments of infantry (in 1820)[5] and detachments of artillery operating with the infantry. Militia men were responsible for the supply of their own uniforms and small-arms, and were mustered once a month for drill and once a quarter for field inspection,[6] according to company or regiment, at the 'most convenient places'[7] in the several parishes.[8] Militia duty was compulsory on all persons qualified for it,[9] and it could not be

[1] Long, *History*, Vol. I, pp.123–7, 136–55; Alexander Dirom, *Thoughts on the State of the Militia of Jamaica, November, 1783* (Jamaica, 1783); King's Manuscripts, 214: 'A Memoir Relative to the Island of Jamaica, 1782 . . . by Major General Archibald Campbell'; Edwards, op. cit., Vol. I, pp. 279–81. Campbell was Lt. Governor of Jamaica, 1781–4, and wrote his 'Memoir' as a plan for the island's defence.

[2] 33 Car. II, c. 21.

[3] In 1778, 800 to 900 Jews, mostly from Kingston, were reported in the militia. See *The Present State of the West Indies, containing an accurate description of what parts are possessed by the several powers in Europe* (London, 1778), pp. 58–9; also Wright, *LNJ*, pp. 55, 235. [4] 50 Geo. III, c. 17, section 1 of 1809.

[5] See *The Jamaica Almanack for the Year 1821* (Kingston, n.d.), pp.64–82. There was one regiment of Horse per county. In 1793, there were fourteen regiments of Foot militia (Edwards, op. cit., Vol. I, p. 280). In 1805 there were eighteen Foot regiments contributed as follows: Middlesex 7, Surrey 6, Cornwall 5. (See *JAJ*, XI, 310–12 of 4 July 1805.) Two more regiments were being contributed from Middlesex by 1820, one from the parish of Manchester, formed in 1815.

[6] Stewart, *View*, p. 160. [7] 33 Car. II, c. 21; *Laws*, I, p. 28.

[8] The Rio Nova Company of the St. Mary Regiment, for instance, met 'at the Tamarind Tree, on the road leading to White River near the house now occupied by Mr. William Matthews' (*RG*, XVI (1794) 15, 17). Places of muster were revised in the Act 43 Geo. III, c. 18 of 1802; but to the very end of the period of this study the complaint was still being heard that 'a great part of the militia . . . are compelled to travel very long distances to the general musters, and the fatigue, deprivations and sufferings sustained . . . are in many cases excessive . . .' (*JAJ*, XIII, 497 of 6 Dec. 1820).

[9] Members of the Council, the Speaker of the Assembly, the Chief Justice and retired officers were exempted. (See 43 Geo. III, c. 18 of 1802.)

avoided, as in England, by providing a substitute,[1] no doubt due to the overall shortage of white men, though it was the practice for some of the more influential citizens to avoid the rigours of duty and the boredom of muster by having themselves registered as gunners, quarter-gunners, etc., to the several forts of the island, whether these emplacements were operative or not.[2] During martial law the militia came under the control of the Governor (as Commander-in-Chief) and the Council of War and had to remain on permanent duty—a source of considerable irritation and expense to the small white population—while it remained in force.[3] For the period of this study, the average muster of the Jamaican militia was about 8,000 men.[4] These, augmented by the 2,000 regular British troops quartered in the island, comprised its main internal defence.

The Jamaica militia, however, was not only a para-military organization. It was a social institution as well. It reflected, *par excellence*, the hierarchical nature of the society. Militia officers (whites only) were commissioned by the Governor, usually on the recommendation of the various militia colonels.[5] Commissions cost (in fees to the Governor's Secretary), £30 for generals, £21 for colonels, £12 10s. for majors and £3 5s. for the ranks of ensign, adjutant and quartermaster.[6] The qualification for militia commissions was two years' service in the ranks and a respectable income,[7] but since high militia rank was an indication of status,[8] this service in the ranks was often overlooked if the aspirant had influence in the right places.[9] This meant that the militia could become an army of officers.

[1] Stewart, *View*, p. 160.   [2] *JAJ*, IX, 63–4 of 12 Dec. 1791.

[3] While on permanent militia duty, privates and N.C.O.s received 5s. a day and rations (officers' service was an uncompensated privilege), but this could hardly make up for the enforced absence from work, etc. During martial law, the Government could also (and did) 'command the Persons of any of His Majesty's Liege People, as also their Negroes, Horses and Cattle . . . and . . . pull down Houses, Cut down Timber' etc. (33 Car. II, c. 21 of 1681). For an instance of a landholder suffering under this ordinance, see pp. 148–9, below.

[4] This figure is derived from Militia Returns in *JAJ*. Sample returns for the period of this study are as follows:

1764	5,398	(*JAJ*, I, Appendix, p. 50).
1783	6,126	(*JAJ*, VII, 662 of 23 Dec. 1783).
1796	7,796	(*JAJ*, IX, 649–50 of 1 Aug. 1797).
1802	8,172	(Edwards, op. cit., Vol. I, p. 280).
1805	9,672	(*JAJ*, XI, 309 of 4 July 1805).
1817	8,909	(*JAJ*, XIII, 161 of 28 Nov. 1817).

[5] Stewart, *View*, p. 158.   [6] ibid., p. 159.

[7] ibid., pp. 158–9. Stewart does not indicate the actual income qualification.

[8] L. J. Ragatz, *The Fall of the Planter Class in the British Caribbean, 1763–1833* (New York, 1928), reprint 1963, p. 31. Many Assemblymen and Councillors were high-ranking militia officers. See Appendix I.

[9] See Stewart, *View*, p. 159.

Stewart was not exaggerating when he wrote in 1823 that it was not unusual to see 'a battalion of about three hundred men have about fifty commissioned officers attached to it, besides nearly an equal number of non-commissioned officers'.[1] The 1783 Returns bear this out: 507 officers, 286 sergeants and 5,207 rank and file[2]—quite close to Stewart's claim of 'one commissioned and one [N.C.O.] to every seven men'.[3]

But although, as Long had said, 'It is not a red coat that imparts valour to ... soldiers',[4] the socially conscious white Jamaicans became very sensitive whenever there was an indication, imagined or otherwise, that their seniority of militia rank was being encroached upon by professionals.[5] In 1779 (to provide only one example), the House of Assembly, which boasted an impressive number of major-generals among its ranks[6] complained to the Governor with a hint of restrained asperity, that

The house have . . . to observe, that though, in order to strengthen the hands of your excellency, they did, in their address in answer to your excellency's speech at the opening of this session, request that your excellency would exert your judgment in calling forth such persons, whether from amongst the regulars or the militia, as you should deem capable of taking the command of the grand divisions of the militia, and to give them proper commissions, to enable them to take such command, during the continuance of martial law; and, though full approbation is due to the gentlemen appointed to those high commands, yet, the house were little aware, that the intimation so given, would have been extended to the nominating of young officers of the regulars to the command of sub-divisions, *to the exclusion of almost all the field officers of the militia; some of whom may be presumed to have more experience, and equal military abilities.*[7]

What the Assembly/militia officers were really objecting to, of course, was not only their redundancy in the presence of the Army; they were reacting to the loss of social 'face'. The greatest prestige, needless to say, attached itself to the Horse Militia, with its blue

[1] See Stewart, *View*, p. 158.   [2] *JAJ*, VII, 662 of 23 Dec. 1783.
[3] Stewart, *View*, p. 158.   [4] Long, *History*, Vol. I, p. 136.
[5] For reasons of efficiency (the militia, for example, did not make a very good showing in the early stages of the 1795–6 war with the Maroons), it was necessary for regular Army officers to take command of some, at least, of the militia units during emergencies. See the Whitehall circular dated 18 Dec. 1793, for instance, printed in *R.G.*, XVI, 34, 25.
[6] See Appendix I.
[7] *JAJ*, VII, 162 of 11 Sept. 1779, my italics. See also *R.G.*, XVI, 51, 20 for a similar reaction in 1794.

officers' coatees with red facings, cuffs, cape, yellow buttons, and narrow gold vellum lace on the button holes of the facings, cuffs and cape; white waistcoats, blue pantaloons, horsemen's boots with spurs, round black hats, sashes, yellow mounted sabres with buff shoulder belts, and above all—most exclusive symbol—the horse worth at least £50, even for privates.[1] Small wonder that no free coloureds, not to mention blacks—no matter how wealthy—could possibly be admitted into this body, although the numbers of these (especially free coloureds) were steadily growing throughout our period.[2] In fact, even in the 'ordinary' (foot) militia to which this class of citizen was confined, he could not ever rise above the rank of sergeant.[3] But as was said earlier, this merely reflected the hierarchical structure and divisive nature of the whole society. As in the society,

[1] *Laws*, Vol. IV, pp. 391–2.

[2] The following figures indicate the growth of the free coloured/free black participation in the militia:

	white	col.	
1764	4,068	830	(*JAJ*, I, Appendix, p.50.)
1796	4,584	2,301	(*JAJ*, IX, 650 of 1 Aug. 1797.)
1804	5,630	2,399	(*JAJ*, XI, 256 of 5 Dec. 1804.)
1817	5,644	3,265	(*JAJ*, XIII, 161 of 28 Nov. 1817.)

If the white Horse Militia figure (on average 750 men) is excluded, the free coloured/ black contribution to these forces will be appreciated more fully. In 1817, in fact, free coloured/black foot militiamen outnumbered the whites in Surrey 1085/1158 and got pretty close to it in Middlesex (1087/1036). In 1819, free coloured/black infantry outnumbered white Foot Militia troops in the following parishes (figures for white troops are placed first):

Middlesex

	rank and file	sergeants
St. Catherine	121/315	10/25
St. Thos.-in-the-Vale	89/104	4/4
St. John & St. Dorothy	85/113	3/5

Surrey

	rank and file	sergeants
Kingston	549/583	35/34
St. Andrew	107/171	9/10
Port Royal	54/110	7/8

Cornwall

	rank and file	sergeants
St. Elizabeth	172/301	14/26

(*JAJ*, XIII, 161 of 28 Nov. 1817; 355–6 of 23 Nov. 1819).

[3] Sheila Duncker, 'The Free Coloured and their fight for Civil Rights in Jamaica 1800–1830', unpublished M.A. Thesis, University of London, 1960, pp. 224–5. Mrs. Duncker, however, does not cite her authority for this statement and nothing relevant to it appears in the statute books. Section 15 of 43 Geo. III, c. 18, setting out the 'Qualifications requisite in such as shall be recommended for commissions', stipulates that candidates should be over 21 years old and, except for overseers, not 'in the service or employ of another, upon salary or hire'. No mention is made of colour. It is clear from the Militia Returns, however, that black and free coloureds never reached commissioned rank within the period of this study. The prohibition was probably customary. When, for instance, in 1797 a British general officer raised a regiment of free coloureds 'on a footing of equality' with the rest of the militia, he was censured by the Assembly for introducing a system 'contrary to . . . practice' (*JAJ*, IX, 648 of 28 July 1797).

there was a clear division observed in the militia between officers and men, between cavalry and infantry,[1] between privileged whites and lesser privileged whites, between white and non-white. Yet they were all expected to serve, and they all served, with varying rectitude and efficiency, in this body set up for the defence of the country.

In this sense, then, the militia was a creole institution. But it was also a colonial force, under the command of a British Governor and/or Commander-in-Chief. It was the Governor, therefore, who introduced, first under Nugent (the regulations contained in the 1802 Militia Act[2] were the results of his planning), then under Eyre Coote, the first real reforms of this body during the period of this study. In two messages to the Assembly on 12 November 1806, Coote informed the House that he had found, on inspecting the militia, 'several corps in the country parishes in a state so imperfect that their best exertions could be of very little utility',[3] and that not only were there irregularities in the issue of arms to the militia (in the country districts the proprietors of plantations supplied part, the public arsenal the rest),[4] but that 'the arms of many regiments [were] very bad and of unequal calibre'.[5] Coote suggested a new Code of rules and regulations. Arms should be uniform, and militiamen should be kept under regular rather than spasmodic training. 'Interior' regiments should be established in Hanover, Westmoreland, and St. James to make it possible for settlers in the interior of these parishes to forgo the long journey to muster at the coastal towns of Savanna-la-Mar, Montego Bay, and Lucea.[6] Most importantly, the militia was to be subject to military discipline and training by professional officers, and the local men manning forts were to be replaced and/or reinforced by a core of soldiers and artillerymen.[7] By 53 Geo. III, c. 23 of December 1812, a southern interior regiment was set up for Vere, Clarendon, and St. Elizabeth, to match the northern interior force already established. In 1816, the island was divided into six militia districts under Major-Generals of the Militia, whose duty was to inspect the local units at least once a year and report back to the Governor.[8] There is no evidence, however, that the militia ever reached anything like reasonable efficiency or preparedness during

---

[1] There was even a restriction on moving from Infantry to Horse—'Sufficient Cause before a Court-Marshal' had to be shown. (Act 177 of 1751, *Acts of Assembly*, 1681–1754.)

[2] 43 Geo. III, c. 18.   [3] *JAJ*, XI, 456 of 12 Nov. 1806.   [4] ibid.

[5] ibid.   [6] ibid., 467 of 13 Nov. 1806.

[7] ibid., 435 of 21 Oct. 1806; 488 of 21 Nov. 1806.

[8] ibid., XIII, 58 of 26 Nov. 1816; *R.G.*, XXXVIII, 50, 17.

this period. The preamble to the Militia Act of 1816[1] setting up the district officers confessed that

Whereas the safety of this island depends, and must always in a great measure depend, upon the actual strength, constant readiness for service, and good discipline, of the militia, and also upon the fit state and condition of the arms and accoutrements, appointments, and ammunition, and other articles, which have been or shall be issued, out of the island store or otherwise. . . . And whereas periodical inspections, by general officers of districts, . . . greatly contribute to the augmentation of its present number, and to the improvement of its discipline, and to the prevention of further enormous loss to the public, by repeated carelessness, neglect, or waste [the institution was still in an unsatisfactory condition].[2]

The Press

The newpapers of Jamaica were strong supporters of the Establishment and were also, where necessary (as will be discussed below), controlled by it. Within the period of this study, some fifteen different newspapers appeared in Jamaica, though only one of these, *The St. Iago de la Vega Gazette* (1755) was published throughout the entire period. Kingston probably had the highest readership, having by far the largest urban population, and nine of the fifteen newspapers originated there. *The Jamaica Mercury & Kingston Weekly Advertiser* (1779), called *The Royal Gazette* from 1780, became in a sense the Government's semi-official organ and was still going strong in 1820, as was *The Kingston Chronicle & City Advertiser* and the *Jamaica Courant*, both started in 1805. *The Daily Advertiser* was started in 1790 but appears to have disappeared by about 1804. Five of the fifteen newspapers appeared on the North Coast—*The Jamaica Mercury & Trelawny Advertiser* (1791–1813?) and the *Cornwall Gazette & Northside General Advertiser* (1818–23) at Falmouth; *The Cornwall Chronicle & County Gazette* (1773) at Montego Bay; *The Cornwall Mercury & Savanna-la-Mar Weekly Advertiser* (1782) and *The Savanna-la-Mar Gazette* (1788) at Savanna-la-Mar. Most papers appeared weekly except *The Diary and Kingston Daily Advertiser* (1795–1802?), *The Daily Advertiser*, *The Kingston Chronicle* and the *Jamaica Courant*, which were dailies. *The Kingston Mercantile Advertiser* (1801?–2?) appears to have been published on alternate days.[3]

[1] 57 Geo. III, c. 21.   [2] *Laws*, Vol. VI, pp. 488–9.
[3] See Frank Cundall, *The Press and Printers of Jamaica Prior to 1820* (Worcester, Mass., 1916). The examples from newspapers used in this section are mainly from the

These newspapers were what might be called 'independent journals', run by local entrepreneurs. During the 1780s, editors were very much taken up with the war in North America[1] and in the 1790s, until Waterloo, with the war against the French and the progress, decline, fall, escape, and escapades of Bonaparte.[2] For the rest of our period, the central figure in the Jamaican newspapers was the Duke of Wellington. Royal affairs, as always, were high on the list of popular topics. If there were royal scandals (Her Royal Highness Princess Caroline, for instance),[3] so much the better. Royal deaths (Queen Charlotte Sophia's[4] in 1818), State Trials,[5] biographies,[6] poetry (Southey, Scott, and Byron in particular),[7] were clearly in demand. There was also a great deal of occasional verse, some of it fashioned by local craftsmen; like 'On the Proceedings Against America' (March 1775):

> Lost is our old simplicity of Times
> The world abounds with laws and teems with crimes
> ......
> Commerce from frequent Marts no more her own
> Exiled, to foreign coasts compelled, is flown.
> On useless keels, with helm neglected, ride
> Britannia's bulwark and Britannia's pride.[8]

When Governor Williamson's wife died in 1794, her passing was marked with this eulogy:

Royal Gazette. More editions of this paper, for the period of this study, are available than any other, and the *Gazette*'s coverage was wider than that of any other paper within this period. It may be taken as typical.

[1] See for example, the *Jamaica Mercury*, Vol. II (1780), nos. 35, 52, 53, 55, 56, 76, 77, 78, 79, 81, (*Royal Gazette*) 88, 99, 100, 101, 102, 106, 113, etc.

[2] See for example, *R.G.*, XXXVII (1815), 10, 4–6, 10–11, etc.; 22, 1–5; 23, 11–12, etc.

[3] See, for example, *R.G.*, XXXV (1813), 21, 9–12; 22, 7–8; 23, 17–18; 25, 20–1. The Princess Caroline (1768–1821) was the second daughter of Charles William, Duke of Brunswick-Wolfenbuttel and of George III's sister, Augusta. In 1795 she married the future George IV, then Prince of Wales. Domestic incompatibility led to their separation and rumours concerning the lady's misconduct. Although these rumours turned out to be well founded, the Princess, who was turned away from the door of Westminster Abbey at the coronation in 1821, received wide public support and sympathy. *Dictionary of National Biography*, hereafter cited as *DNB* (London, 1893); *Chambers' Biographical Dictionary* (London, 1946 ed.).

[4] The wife of George III.

[5] Warren Hastings' (1788–95), Lt.-General Sir John Murray's, among others.

[6] Most of the great political and warrior figures of England, Europe and North America were treated; but, as in so much in this field, local figures were ignored. 'Monk' Lewis' death for instance, was noticed only by a single correspondent in a letter to the Editor (*R.G.*, XLI, 15, 27, of 10 April 1819).

[7] For Byron, see, for example, *R.G.*, XXXIV (1812), 38, 1–4.

[8] *Royal Gazette*, 10 March 1775.

> If condescension, kindness, sympathy;
> Truth, wisdom, honour, virtue, piety;
> All that could glad and grace the private scene;
> All that could represent ev'n Britain's queen;
> All that cou'd dearest, dignified aver
> The human, female, Christian character—
> Command, to excellence departed, praise . . .[1]

More frequent, however, if not more characteristic, was the 'imported' timely verse, like 'The Lamentation of an Unfortunate Queen' (Marie Antoinette), which began:

> How dark is my Prison how hollow the wind
> Which so suddenly blows o'er the Tower . . .[2]

Headlines (more discreet than they are today) such as: 'Mrs. Siddons' Retirement',[3] 'Mr. Kemble's Farewell',[4] 'The Ionian Islands',[5] 'Recent Fracas at the General Post-Office, London',[6] illustrate the orientation of the Jamaican reading public at this time.[7] In all this, the percentage of local news coverage was low; though the papers were clearly regarded as a sure means of disseminating information about properties, houses for sale, arrivals of supplies and people from Britain, departures, deaths, marriages, dissolutions of business partnerships, runaways, theatre, horse-racing, etc. The following inventory of the lay-out of part of the *Royal Gazette*, Vol. XVI, no. 44, Saturday 25 Oct.–Saturday 1 November 1794, may be taken as typical:

Page 1   Advertisements: ships sailing;
              (British) State Papers: Proclamation of the Prince of Coburg.
Page 2   State Papers (cont.);
              Jamaica Public Advertisements.
Page 3   Advertisements: Imports, For Sale, Ran Away, Midwifery.
Page 4   Botanic Gardens Report (ordered to be printed by the Assembly)
              Imports;
              Private Advertisement.
Page 5   Council Order: Aliens (published in English and French);
              Imports;
              Morant Bay Workhouse: list of runaways taken up;
              St. Catherine Pound: list of stray cattle taken up;

[1] *R.G.*, XVI (1794), 39, 23,   [2] ibid., XV (1793), 1, 2.
[3] ibid., XXXIV (1812), 44, 4.   [4] ibid., XXXIX (1817), 35, 9–11.
[5] ibid., 27, 10.   [6] ibid., 9–10.
[7] Things have not changed much in 160 years, as a perusal of Jamaican and West Indian newspapers will reveal.

'The Conduct of France in Bribing Foreign Powers'.

The newspapers, also, from time to time, published learned discourses on sugar cane manufacture and coffee production either from local correspondents or copied from British journals,[1] items of botanical and horticultural interest,[2] and treatises on the yellow fever and/or other local diseases, sometimes sparking off very personal and bitter debate among members of the medical profession in the island.[3] There was not as much on slavery as might perhaps have been expected. It was as if the white residents were deliberately turning their backs on the most difficult and important subject in the island. Was it perhaps necessary for them to do so? Or was it that (there is not enough evidence to offer answers) they had long ago taken the institution for granted? But anti-slavery books and tracts received long, hostile reviews, often heavy with ridicule, from anonymous or pseudonymous correspondents in the island. Reviewing Gilbert Mathison's *Notices respecting Jamaica, in 1808, 1809, 1810*,[4] one local critic wrote:

[1] See, for example, *R.G.*, XXXV (1813), 33, 13; XXXVIII (1816), 27, 9–10; XXXIX (1817), 9, 4–5; and the 'Essay on the Culture of Coffee' in the *Jamaica Almanack for 1787*, pp. 74–7.

[2] See, for example, *R.G.*, XVI, 11, 9–11; 14, 1–3.

[3] See, for example, *R.G.*, XVI, 18, 1–2; 28, 23; 29, 23; 30, 20; 31, 20; 32, 20; 33, 21; 34, 1–3, 15.

[4] (London, 1811); see n. 1, p. 35, below.

Had Mr. M[athison] entitled his book '*The Lucubrations, Opinions, and Amusements of the idle hours of Gilbert Mathison, Esquire, during a solitary residence of two years in Jamaica*', he would have come nearer to the point. But 'Notices respecting Jamaica' is a title which carries with it a bold, pompous, and authoritative tone; which commands us to read in spite of ourselves—to our great disappointment and mortification; and only serves to remind us of the old Greek proverb—'The hills and the mountains were in great trouble; at length—*forth came a mouse*.'[1]

The ridicule technique, in fact, was reserved for Abolitionists generally:

We are credibly informed, that a gentleman of this parish, not more distinguished for his abilities, person and address, than his opulence, now on a return from London, has publicly and repeatedly declared, that he is a perfect disciple of the humane Mr. Wilberforce; and fully determined to emancipate his Slaves on his return, and hire them. But we are assured, that he must look more ways than one for them, as *all his Slaves*, have taken care to save him the trouble of emancipation, by *taking their own freedom*.[2]

On the other hand, extracts from the 1793 (1st edition) of Bryan Edwards's *History* (following severe criticism of his constitutional position), appeared in instalments in the *Royal Gazette* during 1794.[3]

The newspapers were also great upholders of what was deemed proper conduct between the races. When the Naval Commander-in-Chief at Port Royal entertained a delegation of black Haitian Ambassadors at his table in 1818, he was accused by the *Royal Gazette* of a 'most glaring and flagrant breach of all forms of outward decorum, [here]tofore observed in these Colonies'.[4] However, the paper refrained from making further 'open animadversions on his conduct, trusting that, whenever an opportunity should be afforded', the House of Assembly would record 'their most marked and unqualified disapprobation' of his conduct.[5] But the Assembly made no comment and, to make matters worse, the *St. Iago de la Vega*

[1] *R.G.*, XXXIII (1811), 33, 11. Italics in text. Mathison, a local planter, had served briefly in the Assembly in 1795, had gone to England but returned to Jamaica in 1808 for two years. His *Notices* was published in London in 1811. (See *JAJ*, IX, 401 of 28 Nov. 1795; L. J. Ragatz, *A Guide for the Study of British Caribbean History, 1763–1834, including the Abolition and Emancipation Movements* (Washington, 1932), p. 229.)
[2] *Daily Advertiser*, 16 Jan. 1790, italics in text.
[3] The *Gazette* concentrated especially on Edwards's sections dealing with slavery. Edwards, as far as the white creoles were concerned, was 'reasonable' on this subject. His constitutional position is discussed on pp. 75–9, below.
[4] *R.G.*, XL (1818), 46, 19.   [5] ibid.

Gazette and the *Morning Chronicle* came out in support of the Admiral's action. This brought upon them an attack from the *Cornwall Gazette:*

The Editor of The Morning Chronicle, if we are not misinformed, is a near relative to the Messrs. Lunan of this island. When Sir Home Popham [the Naval C.-in-C.] came to Jamaica, he brought a letter of introduction from Mr. Perry to one of these Gentlemen. The only newspaper in Jamaica, which presumed to defy the public displeasure, and to attempt an excuse for the Rear-Admiral, was the St. Iago Gazette, of which Mr. John Lunan is the Editor . . .[1]

On the other hand, the *Royal Gazette* came out with a surprising tribute to the (Black) 2nd West India Regiment when it was leaving the island in 1819.[2] This was the Regiment, much distrusted in Jamaica, whose 'mutiny'[3] had scared Kingston and the island in 1808.

The departure of the Second West-India Regiment from this island affords a proper occasion for speaking with approbation of the discipline and deportment of that Corps. It is perhaps peculiarly just that this tribute to the good conduct of the Regiment should emanate from the press of this city. No other part of the island has had an equal opportunity with this vicinity of observing the demeanour and regularity of the officers and men. If prejudices have existed towards troops of this description, the conduct of the Second West-India Regiment has deservedly made a most favourable impression in their favour, at least upon those who have had opportunities of observing their habits and manners.[4]

Still, although the *Gazette* was able to make this generous statement —how much of it out of relief cannot be determined—it was not prepared to support the 'un-Jamaican' argument of accepting black troops in principle, though it admitted that in practice, the 2nd

[1] *R.G.*, XL (1818), 46, 19.
[2] The 2nd West India Regiment arrived in Jamaica from Trinidad and the Danish West Indies, despite Jamaican opposition, in 1801. It was sent to St. Domingue in 1809, and after duty in the Bahamas and Georgia (1809–16), returned to Jamaica for another three years. Its H.Q. was transferred to West Africa in 1819. In 1825 it was back in the Bahamas, Jamaica became its Headquarters in 1857, though units had already been re-stationed there in 1839 (Spanish Town) and 1841 (Up-Park Camp). In 1861, the H.Q. was moved to Belize, but the regiment arrived back in Jamaica in 1865 to help put down the Morant Bay 'rebellion'. (See James E. Caulfeild, *One Hundred Years' history of the Second Battalion, West India Regiment, from the date of raising, 1795–1898* (London, 1899), pp. 214–21.)
[3] For a full account of this, see *JAJ*, XII, 98–115 of 16 May 1809. Also Edwards, *History*, 1819 ed., Vol. V, p. 97.
[4] *R.G.*, XLI, 12, 19 of 13–20 March 1819.

West India Regiment had proved the Army's point[1] that this kind of soldier was undoubtedly an asset in the West Indies:

Upon any considerations of public policy, as connected with similar troops, we abstain from speaking; but of their utility in relieving European soldiers, under the severities of tropical service, no doubt can be entertained.[2]

The Jamaican Press therefore was a force to be reckoned with in the formation and expression of public opinion—something the Assembly knew and recognized. If, in the period of this study, it could not be regarded as a critic of the Establishment, it was nevertheless an institution to be watched and controlled. In 1779, for example, two newspapers, the *Kingston Journal* and the *Jamaica Mercury*, printed a document said to be signed 'by all the officers of the troops of horse [militia]' disaffected, they claimed, for want of proper subsistence and accommodation during the Emergency period of Martial Law in 1778/9.[3] The Assembly had, before this item appeared, and in response to the complaint, denied that the Horse Militia was being improperly treated. The House wanted to know, in fact, if the cavalry felt themselves to be better than foot soldiers[4]—a rhetorical question, since they did. But the publication of their grievances, in this manner, was taken by the House as 'a scandalous libel', misrepresenting the proceedings of the House.[5] John Lewis, compositor of the *Kingston Journal* and Messrs. Douglass and William Aikman of the *Mercury*, were called to the Bar of the House, but discharged when no direct blame against them could be established.[6]

It was not always easy, however, to get printers to *appear* before the House. In 1787, George Eberall and John Lewis of the *Kingston Morning Post* and Joseph Preston of the *Jamaica Gazette*, were ordered before the House to answer 'a false, scandalous and malicious libel' published by them, 'grossly reflecting upon the proceedings of the select committee of [the] house' in the matter of a controverted election for the parish of St. Mary.[7] Five days after the order, the Messenger acquainted the House that he had been able to serve notice on two only of the printers involved. 'John Lewis . . .

---

[1] See Portland to Balcarres, dated Whitehall, 9 Aug. 1797; Frederick, F. M. to Portland, dated Horse Guards, 1 Aug. 1797 in *JAJ*, X, 4–5 of 1 Nov. 1797.
[2] *R.G.*, XLI, 12, 19.   [3] *JAJ*, VII, 170 of 19 Sept. 1779
[4] ibid., 149 of 20 Aug. 1779.   [5] ibid., 169 of 18 Sept. 1779.
[6] ibid., 170 of 20 Sept. 1779.   [7] ibid., VIII, 337 of 13 Dec. 1787.

had secreted himself, [and] could not be found'.[1] No further action was taken in this case that session, because the House was prorogued shortly after. But at the start of the new session on 24 December 1787, the order against the printers was reissued.[2] Five days later the Messenger reported that he was informed John Lewis was sick; that George Eberall said he would not attend the house; and that Joseph Preston not only refused to obey the said warrant, but said that the house might do their worst.[3] The cat-and-mouse game dragged on until January 1788 when Lewis was finally caught.[4] But nothing appears to have come of this incident.

In 1806, there was a much more serious encounter between the Assembly and the Press, involving this time an attack, through the Press, on the Assembly's handling of public money. On Friday 5 December 1806, the editors of three Kingston papers: *The Daily Advertiser*, the *Kingston Chronicle & City Advertiser* and the *Royal Gazette*, had apparently inserted in their pages, certain resolutions signed 'Daniel Moore, chairman'.[5] No copy of this edition of these newspapers is extant,[6] but it appears that the newspaper item related to resolutions adopted at a meeting of freeholders of Kingston (both city and parish), at which the Assembly's decision to vote 3,000 guineas for a gift of plate to Admiral Duckworth in recognition of his victory over the French fleet off St. Domingue[7] (this in addition to £1,000 already voted for a ceremonial sword), was regarded by the freeholders as a wanton and improvident expenditure of the public money.[8] The House, it was felt, 'had forfeited every claim to the confidence of the good people of [the] island, by its inconsistent, extravagant, and unconstitutional conduct . . .'.[9] This resolution appeared in the three papers already referred to, and on 8 December, the *Jamaica Courant* joined in with a copy of similar resolutions passed at a meeting of the St. Andrew Vestry.[10] This was clearly a serious matter and was taken seriously by the House:

That any set of individuals presuming to censure the proceedings of this house is a breach of the privileges, and destructive of the freedom, of this house. . . .

That the editors of . . . The Daily Advertiser, The Kingston Chronicle and City Advertiser, and The Courant, for having inserted in their several

[1] *JAJ*, VIII, 340 of 18 Dec. 1787.   [2] ibid., 350 of 24 Dec. 1787.
[3] ibid., 363 of 29 Dec. 1787.   [4] ibid., 368 of 3 Jan. 1788.
[5] ibid., XI, 517 of 6 Dec. 1806.   [6] Cundall, *Press and Printers*, p.51.
[7] *JAJ*, XI, 498 of 25 Nov. 1806.   [8] ibid., 517 of 6 Dec. 1806.
[9] ibid.   [10] Cundall, *Press and Printers*, p. 53.

newspapers of Friday the 5th December, 1806, certain resolutions signed 'Daniel Moore, chairman', are guilty of a breach of the privileges of this house. . . .

That it tends to the subversion of the constitution of this house to call any part of its proceedings a wanton and improvident expenditure of the public money. . . .

That it is a breach of the privileges of this house for any set of individuals to say that this . . . house has forfeited every claim to the confidence of the good people of this island, by its inconsistent, extravagant, and unconstitutional conduct in respect to the disposal of the public money.[1]

What the House was disputing here was the right of any Jamaican body, outside itself, to challenge its actions. It was very narrowly defining the limits of free speech and encroaching upon the freedom of the Press. As George Strupar of the *Courant* told the Assembly, 'if he had not published the resolutions he might as well have shut up his office altogether'.[2] Andrew Lunan of the *Chronicle* said that if he had refused to publish the resolutions of 'such a respectable meeting', he would have been financially ruined.[3] What is interesting here—and it is a damaging observation on the nature of white Jamaican creole society—is that not one of these gentlemen of the Press made a stand on the *rights* of the Press to freedom of expression. Instead, the appeals were to self-interest; their dependence on their readership. They were all released from custody on apologizing to the Assembly.[4]

After this, there is no further evidence of criticism of Assembly action until 1819, when Andrew Lunan of the *Kingston Chronicle* fell foul of the House for 'alluding to the observations of certain Members, made by them in the House'.[5] The Assembly, in other words, was vindicating its claim to be *the* representative institution of the society. Such a position was seen to be essential if the society was to be controlled and maintained in its constituted form. Rivals to authority or opinion could only mean a weakening of the Establishment. In this conviction and the realization of it, the Assembly was to prove itself, functionally, the most important and finely adapted of all Jamaica's institutions—the most perfect expression of (white) creole society. It will be necessary, therefore, to take a closer look at this body.

[1] *JAJ*, XI, 517 of 6 Dec. 1806.   [2] ibid., 519 of 9 Dec. 1806.   [3] ibid.
[4] ibid., 520 of 10 Dec.; 527 of 11 Dec.; 533-4 of 12 Dec.; 536 of 16 Dec. 1806.
[5] *R.G.*, XLI (1819), 49, 20.

THE ASSEMBLY

Members

From the outset, the Assembly of Jamaica gave expression to
Jamaican aspirations and interests.[1] From the beginning it was
a truly creole institution, containing people from all walks of (white)
Jamaican life. Predominant, of course, were the planters. In 1750,[2]
two of the really big landowners (men with over 10,000 acres) were
Assemblymen: Andrew Archdeckne, 12,712 acres, and Sir Charles
Price, 13,651 acres. In 1820, William Shand (St. John) owned 1,294
slaves; Henry Cox (St. Mary) had 942 slaves and 705 head of stock;
Benjamin Crossley (St. George) owned 801 slaves and 662 stock;
John Meek (Kingston) owned 675 slaves and John Crosman, also a
representative for Kingston, owned 647 slaves and 547 head of stock.
Walter Minto (St. James) owned 594 slaves and Charles Grant (St.
Mary) had 537 slaves and 649 stock. Abraham Hodgson (St. Mary)
owned 525 slaves and 425 head of stock. William Rowe (St. Elizabeth)
had 535 slaves and 521 head of stock.[3] It is often said that the
members of the Council were the richest men in the island. This is not
borne out by the returns. In the 1750s, not one Councillor was in the
over 10,000 acres class and only three were in the 5,000 acre group.
On the other hand, there were sixteen Assemblymen with 5,000 acres
or more in that period. In 1820, only one Councillor (Samuel
Jackson)[4] would have rated with the nine Assemblymen listed above.
Perhaps the richest individual proprietor during the period of this
study was Simon Taylor, member of Assembly for Kingston (1763–
81) and St. Thomas-in-the-East (1784–1810).[5] Taylor owned at least
seven large estates, one of which, Holland, cost him £100,000.[6]

---

[1] See Whitson, *Constitutional Development*; A. L. Murray, op. cit.; George Metcalf, *Royal Government and Political Conflict in Jamaica, 1729–1783* (London, 1965).

[2] See Add. MS. 12436: List of Landholders in Jamaica, 1750.

[3] Figures obtained from *The Jamaica Almanack for 1821*. For a list of Assemblymen, see John Roby, *Members of the Assembly of Jamaica from the institution of that branch of the legislature to the present time* (Montego Bay, 1831).

[4] *Jamaica Almanack for 1821*, p. 23.

[5] See *LNJ* (Cundall), p. 41, n.; *LNJ* (Wright), p. 318.   [6] *LNJ* (Cundall), p. 41, n.

John Thorp (or Tharp), one of the members for Trelawny in 1772, was regarded, after Taylor, 'as the richest and most extensive proprietor in Jamaica'.[1] In 1820, the nine Thorp properties in Trelawny still had more than 2,800 slaves between them,[2] and when John Shand[3] died in 1825, he left £127,348 in 3 per cent Government annuities, in addition to estates in Scotland and Jamaica, with legacies of about £5,000 to each of his ten illegitimate coloured children.[4]

But even if the planters predominated, they certainly did not have a monopoly of Assembly seats. There were doctors, merchants, barristers, and attorneys-at-law. Until 1802,[5] the Chief Justice sat in the Assembly. The Receiver-General remained eligible for election until 1809.[6] Besides their Assembly work (and during sessions this was quite arduous—standing committees, parochial and individual petitions to be dealt with, on-the-spot investigations and inspections, reports, the preparation of bills), members served as judges, *custodes*, magistrates, justices of the peace, collecting constables,[7] and officers in the militia.[8] John Jaques, the first mayor of Kingston,[9] was also a member of the Assembly.[10] Of the 229 Jamaicans who went to Oxford[11] or Cambridge[12] during the period under consideration, thirty-three (a high proportion of those who *did* return to Jamaica),[13] sat in the Assembly. Edmund Pusey Lyon (St. Catherine, 1797), who was appointed Island Agent in 1803, was a Middle Temple man (1783), as were Gilbert Mathison (Trelawny, 1772, 1774),[14] Henry Burke (Portland, 1819), and T. J. Hall (St. John, 1818).[15] Walter Minto (Trelawny, 1815) went to the Middle

---

[1] See, Philo Scotus (pseud.), *Reminiscences of a Scottish Gentleman* (London, 1861), p. 186.

[2] *Jamaica Almanack for 1821*, p. 132.

[3] Brother? of William Shand, above, and like him, member for St. John (1801–18).

[4] P. Wright, op. cit., p. 316.   [5] See *JAJ*, XI, 3 of 19 Oct. 1802.

[6] ibid., XII, 145 of 31 Oct. 1809.   [7] Until 1802. See *JAJ*, XI, 10 of 28 Oct. 1802.

[8] See Appendix I.

[9] K.C.C. Minutes, 1795–1805; 15 Nov. 1802. This entry comes after that of 30 Dec. 1802.

[10] 1796–1812. (See *JAJ*, IX, 529 of 28 Oct. 1796; XII, 426 of 27 Oct. 1812.)

[11] See *Alumni Oxonienses: The Members of the University of Oxford, 1715–1886: Their Parentage, Birthplace and Year of Birth, With a record of their Degrees, being the Matriculation Register of the University* . . . arr. Joseph Foster, 4 vols. (London, 1887, 1888).

[12] *Alumni Cantabrigienses: A biographical list of all known Students, Graduates and Holders of Office at the University of Cambridge, from the earliest times to 1900*, comp. J. A. Venn; Part II, 1752–1900, 6 vols. (Cambridge, 1940–54).

[13] Most Jamaicans educated overseas remained abroad, many of them achieving considerable distinction in their careers. (See op. cit., n. 11 and 12, above.)

[14] Probably the father of the Gilbert Mathison referred to on pp. 34–5, above.

[15] See *Middle Temple Register*.

Temple before going on to Cambridge in 1797. There were also eight Etonians, of whom James Lawrence (Hanover, 1806) went to Oxford, Charles Gray (Port Royal, 1818) went to Cambridge, James Trower (St. Catherine, 1775 and 1781) went to Lincoln's Inn, and Sam Whitehorne (St. Catherine, 1796) went to Lincoln's Inn and Cambridge. At least three Assemblymen were Harrovians.[1] During the period of this study, the Assembly could also boast of members like Alexander Aikman, Snr. and John Lunan, printers and publishers; Bryan Edwards, the historian; Hinton East, Receiver-General (1779) and botanist;[2] Chief Justice Fearon and Sir Charles Price, men with stately homes and reputedly fine libraries; Daniel Moore, publisher[3] and agriculturalist; John Nixon and Edward Woollery, local sugar cane experts, and W. D. Quarrell, who was very much involved in the 1795–6 campaign against the Maroons. (He brought the infamous bloodhounds from Cuba. Dallas[4] dedicated his *History of the Maroons* to him.) Yet Quarrell was interested enough in horticulture to send back a collection of plants from Nova Scotia while he was there in 1796/7 supervising the transportation of the said (Trelawny Town) Maroons.[5]

There was also in the Assembly during the period of this study Dr. Quier, 'an eminent and experienced Practitioner', who, according to a colleague, 'carried the practice of Inoculation to a much greater length, than [had] been done by any of the boldest empirics in Europe'.[6] There was Robert Scarlett, surveyor and Cambridge

[1] See J. Foster. *Men at the Bar: a biographical handlist of the members of the various Inns of Court . . .* (London, 1885); *Register of Admissions to Gray's Inn*; the *Eton College Register, 1753–1790*, ed. Richard A. Austen-Leigh (Eton, 1921); *The Eton School Lists, from 1791 to 1850*, comp. H. E. C. Stapylton (London and Eton College, 1864); *The Harrow School Register, 1571–1800*, comp. and ed. W. T. T. Grin (London, 1934); *The Harrow School Register, 1801–1823*, ed. R. C. Welch (London, 1894); *Records of . . . Lincoln's Inn*; *Alumni Oxonienses*; *Alumni Cantabrigienses*.

[2] See Cundall, *Historic Jamaica*, p. 228, East's Gardens in Gordon Town were purchased by the Government in 1793 (34 Geo. III, c. 23). A catalogue of plants, prepared by East and revised and enlarged by Dr. Arthur Broughton, another resident botanist, was published in 1792 under the title *Hortus Eastensis*.   [3] See p. 38, above.

[4] Born Kingston, 1754, of an American/British family. Read law at Inner Temple. Lived for two short periods in Jamaica; left for good some time after 1782, because of wife's health. *History of the Maroons* (1803) based therefore not on personal experience but on 'the relations of participants', chief among whom was probably Quarrell. Died in Normandy in 1824. (See James Dallas, *The History of the Family of Dallas . . .* (Edinburgh, 1921), pp. 495–6, 498; Ragatz, *Guide*, p. 197; *DNB*.)

[5] See *JAJ*, X, 70 of 18 Dec. 1797.

[6] Thomas Dancer, *The Medical Assistant: or Jamaica practice of physic: designed chiefly for the use of families and plantations* (Kingston, 1801), p. 153. There were at least three other M.D.s in the Assembly during our period—William Elphinstone (St. George, 1775, 1781) John Gordon (St. Ann, 1770) and Archibald Sympson (Vere, 1775–97).

graduate; Matthew Wallen, a botanist; Henry Shirley, one of the most articulate members of the Assembly, whose reports on the Sugar Trade and Botanical Gardens were models of their kind;[1] and John Shand, already mentioned,[2] leader of 'the patriotic [i.e. creole] party in the House',[3] who was said to have been responsible for the passing of the ameliorative legislation in favour of the free coloureds in 1813.[4]

Membership

In 1758, Jamaica had been divided into three counties of nineteen parishes,[5] as follows:

County of Middlesex
St. Catherine, St. John, St. Dorothy, St. Thomas-in-the-Vale, Clarendon, Vere, St. Mary, St. Ann.

County of Surrey
Kingston, Port Royal, St. Andrew, St. Thomas-in-the-East, St. David, Portland, St. George.

County of Cornwall
St. Elizabeth, Westmoreland, Hanover, St. James.

In 1773,[6] the parish of Trelawny was created out of part of St. James; and in 1814, the parish of Manchester came out of Vere, Clarendon, and St. Elizabeth.[7]

Each of these parishes was represented by two men in the Assembly, with Port Royal, Kingston and St. Catherine (the parishes containing the three senior towns of Port Royal, Kingston, and Spanish Town/ St. Iago de la Vega), returning three representatives each. (The parish of Kingston was created in 1693 out of St. Andrew, following the

[1] See *JAJ*, IX, 144–59 of 23 Nov. 1792; 247–8 of 27 Nov. 1793; 507 of 23 April 1796; 513–14 of 27 April 1796; X, 69–75 of 18 Dec. 1797.

[2] See pp. 40, 41, above.

[3] Governor Nugent, quoted in P. Wright, op. cit., p. 316.

[4] The attribution occurs in the novel *Marly* (Glasgow, 1828), pp. 188–9. References for other names mentioned in the text are Aikman: Cundall, *Press and Printers*, p. 24; *R.G.*, XL, 47, 20–2; *JAJ*, IX, 270 of 11 Dec. 1793; XIII, 283 of 11 Dec. 1818. Fearon: *Jamaica Mercury*, Vol. I, no. 8, 12–19 June 1779; Gardner, op. cit., p. 166; Richardson Wright, *Revels in Jamaica, 1682–1838* (New York, 1937), p. 131. Price: Gardner, op. cit., p. 166. Lunan: Cundall, *Press*, p. 59; *JAJ*, XII, 600, 725; S. P. Hendrick, *Sketch of the History of the Cathedral Church of St. Iago de la Vega* (Spanish Town, 1911), p. 4. Nixon: W. A. Feurtado, *Official and other personages of Jamaica, from 1655 to 1790 ...* (Kingston, 1896), p. 72; *JAJ*, VI, 476–7, 512. Woollery: *JAJ*, VI, 350, 366–7. Scarlett: *JAJ*, VI, 376. Wallen: Cundall, *Historic Jamaica*, p. 25.

[5] 31 Geo. II, c. 15.   [6] 14 Geo. III, c. 31.   [7] 55 Geo. III, c. 23.

build-up of the town of Kingston after the destruction of Port Royal in the earthquake of 1692.)[1] The Assembly, in other words, contained forty-one members in 1770, forty-three in 1774 and forty-five after 1816.[2] The division figures[3] indicate an average attendance of twenty-nine members per daily session (about 67 per cent of total membership), during the period of this study. Since 1678 (at least), the quorum necessary to constitute a House had been twenty-one.[4]

The Franchise

The qualifications of the electors were that they be white ('pure' or above four removes from a Negro ancestor), 21 years or more of age, and possessed of a freehold of at least £10 per annum in the parish in which they proposed to vote. Persons seeking election had to possess a minimum freehold of £300 per annum (this could be in any part of the island) or a personal estate of at least £3,000.[5] These arrangements were first set out in 10 Annae c. 5 of 1711: 'An act declaring what persons shall be qualified to sit in Assemblies'; and in the Acts of 1716 and 1735, 'To secure the freedom of elections'. In December 1780, legislation under this head was revised and remained operative for the rest of the period under review. There was to be a forty-day period between the issue of writs of election and their return; freeholders were to have five days' notice of the time and place of the election; no two parishes were to be elected for on the same day (a similar regulation applied to Vestry elections);[6] and if writs were not issued on the day appointed, no new writ was to be issued until after the opening of the Assembly.[7]

Elections

The average electoral vote per Assembly member for the years 1810 and 1816, which may be taken as typical, was thirty-six—five *higher* than it was in the 1860s.[8] Only once (in the available figures)

[1] Cundall, *Historic Jamaica*, p. 42.

[2] Although the law making Manchester a parish was passed in 1814, there was no election until 1816. The first members for the parish took their places in the Assembly in November 1816. (See *JAJ*, XIII, 4–5 of 29 Oct.; 36 of 19 Nov. 1816.)

[3] See Appendix II.

[4] See *JAJ*, I, 24 of 3 Sept. 1678.

[5] Edwards, op. cit., Vol. I, p. 273; R. Renny, *A History of Jamaica* (London, 1807), p. 108.

[6] See p. 21, above.   [7] 21 Geo. III, c. 15. of 30 Dec. 1780.

[8] See M. G. Smith, *The Plural Society in the British West Indies* (University of California Press, 1965), p. 153; *Handbook of Jamaica for 1883*, ed. A. C. Sinclair and L. R. Fyfe (Kingston, 1883), p. 65.

did more than 500 people[1] vote in a single election (Kingston in 1809), during the period of this study. At the other end of the scale, only four people turned up to return, and returned, the representatives of the parish of St. George in 1771—though here, according to one of the candidates, this was due to bad weather and because no proper notice of election had been given.[2] The election return figures available between 1790 and 1820 are as follows:[3]

	1790	1803	1810	1816	1820
Kingston				263	293[4]
St. Thos. in the V.				28	82
St. George			80	83	81
Trelawny	138		108	145	
St. John			26	30	
St. Mary			36	45	
St. Elizabeth			42	33	53
St. David	55		55	39	28
St. Ann	195		101	86	
Hanover			40	115[5]	99
Clarendon			103	36	
St. Thos/East			74	44	
Vere			54	19	
St. Dorothy			46	27	
Portland	107	139	42	33[6]	94
Manchester				38	74[7]
St. Andrew	181	192		153	
St. James		260	150	74	
Westmoreland		151	127	104	
Port Royal		221	144	78	
St. Catherine		314	126	99	

With such small voting figures, electoral arrangements had necessarily to be as generous as possible. The clause limiting elections to one parish at a time, for instance, must be understood in this context. Many electors owned property in several parishes and were no doubt expected (and perhaps wished) to vote in the constituencies for which they were qualified.[8] Each qualified freeholder therefore had two votes. Since elections were seldom disputed,[9] most candidates were

[1] 554. See House of Assembly Poll Book, 1803–43; MS. Jamaica Archives, Spanish Town.   [2] *JAJ*, VI, 365 of 29 Nov. 1771.

[3] Assembly Poll Book; except figures for 1790 from *Daily Advertiser*, 12, 26, 30 Jan. 1790.   [4] *R.G.*, XLII (1820), 28, 17 gives this figure as 383.

[5] 121 according to *R.G.*, XXXVIII (1816), 24, 19.

[6] 30 according to *R.G.*, XXXVIII (1816), 25, 20.   [7] *R.G.*, XLII (1820), 28, 17.

[8] For a similar situation in Virginia, see D. J. Boorstin, *The Americans*; Vol. I, *The Colonial Experience* (New York, 1958), London ed. 1965, p.137: 'Virginia law permitted a gentleman freeholder to vote in every county where he possessed the property qualification. If he was qualified in three counties he could vote for three sets of Burgesses.'   [9] But see pp. 47–9, below.

Pol. Inst.

simply returned with an equal number of votes between them.[1]

It is not clear how electors voted, but it was probably by 'voice'. When in December 1788 Bryan Edwards presented to the House a motion for a bill to choose the members of the Assembly by ballot,[2] it was rejected by 17 votes to 14.[3] In the 1750s similar bills had failed to pass the House or had been disallowed in Britain.[4]

It seems, also, that persons could be elected without having even put themselves up for election:

Mr. Speaker laid before the house a letter from Robert Jackson, esquire, who had been returned as a representative for the parish of Port-Royal, in the room of Oliver Hering, esquire, whose seat the house had vacated, intimating his wish to decline the honour intended him by the freeholders of the said parish.[5]

George Richards was elected for Vere in November 1815, although he had 'declined to accept this favour, when proposed to [him] some few months since'.[6] The Hon. James Stewart of Trelawny, speaking at a public farewell dinner for him in Falmouth in 1820, told the electorate that

As one of their representatives he thought it his duty to announce his intention of going off the island soon; perhaps, before the dissolution of the Assembly, when they would be called upon to elect their representative ... that he would therefore recommend to the parish, to elect some other gentleman in his place, of greater abilities, who could give his personal attendance to the duties of the country; but if, from their kindness or partiality, they still thought proper to re-elect him, he pledged himself to give the earliest intimation of his intention of returning, or remaining, in Europe.[7]

Henry Shirley, member for St. George, was returned in the 1803 elections, although he was in England and had in fact left Jamaica in 1801.[8] In 1755, as a matter of fact, the Assembly had actually made an attempt to put a stop to this practice of absentee election. The House resolved 'That it is contrary to the public good and

---

[1] See Assembly Poll Book: St. Thomas-in-the-Vale 1808; and St. George, Trelawny, St. Mary, St. Elizabeth, Vere, St. Dorothy, St. Thomas-in-the-East, Hanover, for 1810. The Poll Book contains a record of votes cast for each voter. By a strange oversight, it seems that the two-vote system applied to Kingston, Port Royal and St. Catherine as well, although these parishes returned three representatives.

[2] *JAJ*, VIII, 459 of 1 Dec. 1788.   [3] ibid., 462 of 4 Dec. 1788.
[4] e.g. 24 Geo. II, c. 5 of 1751.   [5] *JAJ*, X, 321 of 6 Nov. 1799.
[6] *R.G.*, XXXVII (1815), 48, 23.   [7] *R.G.*, XLVI (1820), 17, 16.
[8] *JAJ*, X, 587 of 20 Oct. 1801.

welfare . . ., to elect members to serve in this assembly, who are
absent . . . at the time of election, and not in the country to take
their seat, at the meeting of the house next after such their election.'[1]
This could of course be interpreted—and clearly was—to mean that
election was in order as long as the candidate got back to Jamaica in
time. And as the case of Shirley (above) demonstrates, there was not
much to be done if he did not arrive in time, except to expel him
eventually for non-attendance. Indeed when a candidate for election was abroad, he often had an agent (some worthy well-known
friend and member of the community) to canvass supporters for
him:

Gentlemen,
    The seat of your late worthy Member Thomas Murphy, Esq., being in
his absence vacated by the Honourable House of Assembly, I, as representing him in his private capacity, beg leave to inform you, that I am in
daily expectation of his return to the Island, also on his behalf to solicit
the honour of your suffrages for his re-election . . .[2]

It was also, apparently, the 'done thing' for gentlemen to be
returned unopposed. Thomas Dance in November 1794 informed the
freeholders of St. Thomas-in-the-Vale:

Gentlemen,
    When I offered myself to your notice for the honour of representing you
in the Assembly, I did it under an idea of there being no opposition. The
event has turned out otherwise, and from a quarter little to be expected.
As I have too great a respect for my Brother Freeholders to be the most
distant means of erecting anything like a division in the Parish, I beg leave
to resign for the present, the pretensions which your partiality had induced me to form . . .[3]

This was connected with the fact that there were no parties, in the
modern political sense, and that the white élite, it would seem, knew
themselves to be too small a group and felt themselves too busy
otherwise, to waste time, money, and energy on election campaigns.
One exception to this was William Bolt, the rumbustious, wealthy,
hard-working, long-serving, and influential vestryman for St. Ann,[4]
who put himself up for Assembly election in 1790 against the
'approved' candidates. Late in December 1789, on the eve of election,

---

[1] *JAJ.*, IV, 541 of 23 Oct. 1755.   [2] *R.G.*, XVI, 50, 9. Letter dated 10 Dec. 1794.
[3] ibid., 45, 20.
[4] See St. Ann Vestry Orders 1767–90, 1791–1800; St. Ann Vestry Proceedings,
1800–9, *passim*.

he shot this salvo at the Establishment through the columns of the *Daily Advertiser*:

It having been intimated to me by some of my friends of great respectability among you, at the time Mr. Blagrove signified his intention of vacating his seat in the Assembly, that it was their wish I should offer myself to succeed him as one of your representatives. . . .

Permit me however to say, that notwithstanding I offer myself to be your representative, I do not solicit your votes, for though I may be singular in my opinion, I declare it to be that the electors and not the elected are obliged if fairly represented, and so it was considered at the first institution of Parliament, before its wise and virtuous purposes were shamefully subverted, by affording a sanctuary to swindlers and thereby defrauding the honest and fair trader; *I must furthermore add that, as I shall not consider myself under any obligation to such as may think fit to vote for me, the opposition of such as are indebted to me shall not provoke rigour.* . . .[1]

The reaction to this began with a *Daily Advertiser* editorial of 15 January: 'It is believed the Freeholders of St. Ann are so much disgusted with a certain Gentlemen's address, that the road to senatorial honour will be completely barred and *bolted* against him. . . .'[2]

But Bolt did not only spark off editorial wit. His stand produced some local election verse, ridiculing his position:

An Election Song

Tune—'A Tinker and a Taylor'

Avaunt! ye Rogues and *Swindlers*
Degenerated dwindlers,
Your halcyon days are past,
Jamaica's rouz'd at last:—

Chorus:
Huzza! for Billy B—lt,
Huzza! for Billy B—lt,
Avaunt! ye Rogues and Swindlers,
Make way! for Billy B—lt.[3]

Another verse went:

The House of Assembly I'll quickly reform,
I care not a d—m how they bluster and storm,
Both sides I'll attack, but with neither unite,
For *virtuous* I am, and for *virtue* I'll fight.

[1] *Daily Advertiser*, 2 Jan. 1790, my italics.   [2] ibid., 15 Jan. 1790, italics in text.
[3] ibid., 18 Jan. 1790.

No longer shall Edwards, that brow beating fellow,
Alone on all subjects continue to bellow;
Nor thin sided Redwood, nor outlandish Shirley,
Prevent me from sharing the grand hurly burly.

Not all the dam'd junto, William Mitchell, John Rodon,
And the rest who too long over poor members have trod on,
Will e'er tred on me, they shall know that William Bolt Sirs
Goes always well mounted with pistols in holsters.[1]

It was all very well for Bolt's supporters to counter with:

> Assert your rights, protect them whilst you live,
> Not every age to you a B— will give . . .[2]

Bolt, despite his parochial achievements, had offended the legislative Establishment, and his social status did not help matters either:

> PEDRO MEN remark
> Your QUONDAM PARISH CLERK
> In independent strains
> Your suffrages disdains . . .[3]

But the biggest attack was to come in prose. 'To my astonishment', wrote 'A Landholder' in a letter to the *Advertiser* dated Spanish Town, 5 January 1790:

I learnt he was one of the partners of a store on St. Ann's Bay, *possessing a pittance of land and, perhaps, half a dozen negroes*; that . . . his father had been many years in the *capacity of Clerk* to the Honourable House of Assembly; and . . . the present gentleman had himself held the *same honourable appointment in the Vestry of St. Ann* . . .[4]

'Not even the proud and haughty Child of Wealth', 'A Landholder' went on, 'nurtured from the cradle in the *boast of a Illustrious Pedigree* and highly gratified with splendid abilities, would have presumed, in any other country, to issue forth such a contemptuous Address to the People . . .'[5]

Duration of Assemblies

Since 1741, the House had been pressing for some constitutional limitation on the life of Assemblies.[6] This was finally obtained through 20 Geo. III, c. 3 of 26 November 1779, limiting the duration

[1] *Daily Advertiser*, 2 Feb. 1790.   [2] ibid., 25 Jan. 1790.
[3] ibid., 18 Jan. 1790.   [4] ibid., 19 Jan. 1790.
[5] ibid., my italics. After this, the campaign deteriorated into personal insult and invective. But Bolt was elected. (See *JAJ*, VIII, 560 of 23 March 1790.)
[6] See p. 8, above.

Γ

of any given Assembly to a maximum of seven years. Before this, the Governor could, in effect, keep an Assembly in session (with prorogations) for as long as he liked—the record being the nine-year Assembly (with twenty-three separate sessions) of 9 March 1736 to 13 July 1745.[1]

Meetings of the House

'. . . . the inhabitants of the island began about the year 1756 to erect, at their own expense, an immense pile of spacious apartments, rather than a regular house [of assembly]. These [were] calculated to contain, under one roof, the Assembly room . . . , the speaker's chamber, the court-house, and jury-room, on the upper story; and on the ground floor, suitable offices for the secretary of the island, the provost marshal, the register of the court of chancery, and the clerks of the crown and of the courts of law. Such a vast undertaking necessarily made but a slow progress, the sums requisite to complete the whole being paid in by instalments; so that it was upwards of thirty years before it was entirely occupied'.[2] By 1762,[3] however, the Assembly was occupying and using its section of this building.

The House was usually in session from October to December, except when specially summoned or detained by the Governor to complete work, or because of the declaration of martial law stemming from a threat of invasion or Black insurrection. It sat, beginning at nine in the morning, with a break for lunch, for four days a week: Tuesdays to Fridays, with Saturdays and when necessary Sundays and Mondays added, especially towards the end of a session, in order to expedite business.[4] But usually, the Assembly members reserved the long weekend to attend to their private affairs;[5] and on Wednes-

---

[1] Spurdle, op. cit., p. 72.
[2] Thomas Coke, *A History of the West Indies containing the Natural, Civil, and Ecclesiastical History of each Island: with an account of the Missions instituted in those islands, from the commencement of their civilization; but more especially of the Missions which have been established in that archipelago by the Society late in Connexion with the Rev. John Wesley*, 3 vols. (Vol. I, Liverpool, 1808. Vols. II and III, London 1810 and 1811), Vol. I, p. 339.
[3] Cundall, *Historic Jamaica*, p. 101; Clinton V. Black. *The Story of Jamaica* (London 1965), p. 84. See also *JAJ*, V, 323 of 4 Feb. 1762.
[4] See, for example, *JAJ*, VI, 324 of 16 Dec., 337 of 23 Dec. 1770; 436 of 20 Dec. 1772; VII, 59–60 of 21 Dec. 1777; 460 of 3 March 1782; IX, 386 of 27 Sept. 1795; 525 of 1 May 1796; XI, 430 of 22 Dec. 1805 (all referring to Sunday sessions); and the sessions of Sat. 24 Oct., Sat. 12 Dec. 1801; Sat. 19 June, Mon. 21 June, Sat. 27 Nov., Sat. 11 Dec., Sat. 18 Dec. 1802; Mon. 15 April, Sat. 20 April, Sat. 30 Nov., Sat. 14 Dec., Mon. 16 Dec., Sat. 21 Dec., Sun. 22 Dec., Mon. 23 Dec. 1805. After Dec. 1805 there were no Sunday sessions within our period.   [5] See *LNJ* (Cundall), p. 166.

days (at least when Nugent was Governor), there seems to have been a regular dinner at King's House.[1] Session time, in fact, was the social season for Spanish Town. Lady Nugent's *Journal* is full of references to having members to breakfast, dinner, cards, and/or dances; and other sources within the period also provide evidence of this aspect of social life.[2]

Procedure

When a newly elected House met, its first act was to choose a Speaker and inform the Governor of the choice. The Governor formally acknowledged the House's choice, heard the Speaker's oath of allegiance to the Crown and confirmed him in his traditional privileges. The House then listened to the writs of election and dealt with controverted elections. After this the Rules of the House were read and the House's officers (clerk, messenger, chaplain) appointed or confirmed in their positions, as was necessary. The House was then summoned by the Provost-Marshall to the Council Chamber to hear the Governor's speech outlining British policy and requirements. The Speaker 'to prevent mistakes', obtained a copy of this speech, which after being read by the Clerk of the House was entered in the records. A committee to reply to the Governor's Speech was then appointed, followed by the standing committees of the House. There were eight of these committees: Privileges and Elections, Grievances, the Public Accounts Committee, the Committee dealing with the Courts of Justice, the Public Offices Committee, the Committee responsible for dealing with expired laws, the Committee responsible for the Minutes of the House, and the Committee appointed to inspect the Journals of the Council.[3] These Committees, with the exception of Public Accounts, were separate from the Administrative committees[4] in which the Assembly also participated. These standing committees were small (average five members with a quorum of three). The largest was that of Public Accounts (between eleven and twelve members with a quorum of three); the smallest, those dealing with Minutes (two members with a quorum of one). The Privileges and Grievances Committees varied from seven to eleven members, with a quorum of five demanded for Privileges.

[1] *LNJ* (Cundall), p. 166.

[2] See, for example, *Letters to Jane from Jamaica 1788–1796*, ed. Geraldine Mozley (London, n.d.), *passim*; *RG*, XXXV, 46, 18, announcing the Assembly and 'Colts' Balls to be held during session time on 13 and 25 November 1813.

[3] See, for example, *JAJ*, VI, 444 of 19 Oct. 1779; VII, 73 of 20 Oct. 1778; XII, 688 of 20 Oct. 1815.   [4] See pp. 10–12, above,

The more active members of the House sat on most of these committees.

Privileges

As suggested by the importance accorded the Committee of
Privileges, the House of Assembly was particularly sensitive and
concerned about its status as a 'House of Commons'. Most of its
privileges, in fact, had been claimed and accepted in the early
period of its career—from its establishment to about 1728. In 1679,
it had won the right, from the Governor, to appoint its own Clerk,[1]
had stopped the Governor from coming to the House,[2] had asserted
unilaterally, its right to consent to 'convenient' imperial laws only,[3]
and to inspect the Receiver-General's books.[4] In 1682, it had claimed
the right to meet annually for at least ten days,[5] and in 1686 had
secured for its Messenger the privilege of being free from Court
Summonses while the House was in session.[6] In 1698 it had made it
clear that its members' servants should not be struck,[7] and (in 1702)
that they should not be committed to prison while members were
attending the House.[8] (This led to certain abuses, however, which
were not corrected until Olyphant's Case in 1764.)[9] The House
had also established its right to prevent expelled members being
re-elected unless it wished otherwise.[10] It tried, unresolved, to assert
a right to call any officer of Government before it;[11] it attempted, and
failed, in 1706, to win the privilege of adjourning itself 'for a longer
time than *de die in diem*'.[12] Its right to decide controverted elections—
for its representatives to be 'sole judges of their own members and
elections'[13]—was admitted in 1722. In 1725, the House successfully
resolved that 'no member of the council hath any right to vote in the
election of any member to serve in any assembly'.[14]

These, then, by 1770, were the generally recognized privileges, won
by the House *vis-à-vis* its constitutional rivals and connected with its

---

[1] *JAJ*, I, 47 of 28, 29 Oct. 1679.   [2] ibid., 47 of 30 Oct. 1679.
[3] ibid., 53 of 14 Nov. 1679.   [4] ibid., 55 of 21 Nov. 1679.
[5] ibid., 58 of 21 Sept. 1682.   [6] ibid., 95 of 18 August 1686.
[7] ibid., 187 of 19 Nov. 1698.   [8] ibid., 253 of 15 Aug. 1702.
[9] See *The Privileges of the island of Jamaica vindicated . . .* (Jamaica, 1766).
[10] See *JAJ*, I, 309–13 of 17 Sept.–2 Oct.; 320 of 29 Oct. 1703.
[11] See, for instance, *JAJ*, I, 351 of 6 Oct. 1704: 'That the attorney-general is obliged;
by his office, not only to attend the service of the council, as they are part of the
legislative power, but also on this house, whenever his assistance and attendance is
required. . . .' See also Carmichael's case, p. 107, below.
[12] *JAJ*, II, 40 of 5 June 1711.   [13] ibid., 425 of 24 Oct. 1722.
[14] ibid., 531 of 1 Oct. 1725.

public prestige. But the Assembly was also concerned with its own internal integrity.

Control of Members and Membership

In this connection, the House claimed the right to censure any member who, in its opinion, brought discredit to it.[1] In April 1770, for instance, Nathaniel Grant, a representative for Portland, apparently said in a debate on the Rum Bill, 'that he never expected that a majority of forty-one members . . . would have betrayed the rights of the people'.[2] This was regarded by the House as an imputation of its status as a representative institution, and Grant was ordered, under Standing Order IX—'That the speaker and assembly have power to imprison such of their members as shall misbehave themselves . . .'[3] —to be placed in the Messenger's custody. To make matters worse, Jasper Hall (Kingston), in the very close division over Grant (the decision to place him in custody was carried by 17 votes to 15), was apparently very critical of the House's decision. It was found that 'Jasper Hall, Esquire, a member of this house, has, in debate this day, made use of words reflecting on the honour and dignity of this house. . . .'[4] The case against Hall, however, never developed, and Grant was released from custody after admitting, formally, that he had no intention of offending the House.[5] But there was no doubt where power lay.

The Assembly also began to exert stricter control over members' absence without leave; or rather, it would seem that compared with the period before 1770 when a high proportion of Assemblymen were expelled for being absent over-long without leave, or for being absent beyond the maximum permitted time,[6] the representatives during the period of this study had come to be somewhat more scrupulous about observing the House regulations on this subject. There were in fact three Assembly rules covering members' absence. The first stated that

every member, who shall absent himself without leave of the house or the speaker, be, without further order, taken into custody; and that the speaker

---

[1] See Whitson, *Constitutional Development*, pp. 47–8.
[2] *JAJ*, VI, 271 of 13 April 1770. [3] ibid., 267 of 10 April 1770.
[4] ibid., 271 of 13 April 1770. [5] ibid., 272.
[6] Between 1725 and 1727, the rules of the House stipulated a permitted length of absence of six months (see *JAJ*, II, 522 of 14 Sept. 1725 and 601 of 1 March 1727). After this, no time limit is written into the rules until Rule XXII of 1801 which offered a year's grace. There were twenty-five expulsions under these rules during the period 1710–69.

shall, and . . . is empowered and required to, sign warrants for those purposes.[1]

The second rule warned that

if any member of [the] house shall go off [the] island without leave of the house, if sitting, or without acquainting the speaker with his intention of so doing, in case the house be not sitting, or, having had leave to go off the island, shall not return within the time limited for such leave (unless sufficient cause is shewn to the contrary), he shall be expelled.[2]

These two rules had been in operation from the early eighteenth century.[3] A third rule, introduced in 1801, closed the loophole that until then was still being used as a means of 'escape':

. . . and that no member, departing from the island for Great-Britain, shall have leave of absence from the house, unless such member, on applying for that leave, shall expressly declare his intentions of returning, and resuming his place in the house; and that, after twelve months leave of absence had, the same shall not be renewed, unless under special circumstances, and shall on no account be extended beyond the session in which such further leave shall be applied for.[4]

During the fifty years covered by this study, as a matter of fact, only two Assembly members (Sir Simon Clarke in 1773,[5] and P. P. Livingston in 1774)[6] were actually *expelled* under the House rules for non-attendance. Thirteen others[7] lost their seats because their leave had expired and they had not reapplied, had left the island without permission, or (after 1801) having sought permission had not declared an intention of returning. The majority of absent members simply wrote in to request the vacating of their places.[8]

Having established this point, however, the House attempted to go even further in the matter of controlling its members. In 1798, Philip Redwood was placed in custody for poor attendance.[9] The following year the Assembly threatened Robert Jackson for declining

[1] See Rule XVII of 25 Oct. 1808; first introduced 14 Sept. 1725.
[2] See Rule XXI of 25 Oct. 1808; first introduced 1 March 1727.
[3] See n. 6, p. 53, above.
[4] See Rule XXII of 25 Oct. 1808; first introduced 20 Oct. 1801. (*JAJ*, X, 587.)
[5] See *JAJ*, VI, 450 of 3 Nov. 1773.   [6] ibid., 512 of 25 Oct. 1774.
[7] Edward Clarke, Sam Alpress, John Campbell (1772), Thomas Bourke (1776), Henry Shirley (1783), James Lewis (1786), Sir Thos. Champneys (1791), Edmund Jordan (1792), Thos. Murphy (1794), Hungerford Spooner (1801), R. Lake (1808) Geo. Howell (1814) and Andrew Bogle (1815).
[8] There were ninety-nine such cases. See *JAJ*, VI–XIII, *passim*.
[9] *JAJ*, X, 128 of 6 Nov. 1798. Redwood became Speaker in 1802. (See *JAJ*, XI, 1 of 19 Oct. 1802.)

the honour of being elected. Jackson had sat for St. James from 1776 to 1787.[1] Now he was put up (to him, put upon) by the freeholders of Port Royal. Jackson informed the House that he did not wish to accept the seat. He was ordered to attend on pain of censure.[2] Just over a fortnight later, however, the Speaker informed the House that Jackson had 'kept out of the way of receiving the order of the house requiring his attendance'.[3] To save 'face', the House then ordered that Jackson be expelled[4] (which was what he wanted).

This insistence on reasonably regular attendance and members' (on the whole) respect for this regulation, indicates an underlying and continuing[5] seriousness in the Assembly's sense of function. There is evidence, too, that the Assembly was making an effort to see itself, and to be seen, as an impartial institution, representative of the whole society, as distinct from being, what it could so easily have become, a closed, self-help co-operative or club for its members. In 1786, for instance, Sir Charles Price, son of the 'Patriot',[6] from a family with possibly the longest Assembly record in the island (a Penn and Venables pedigree), and who, no doubt, felt himself liable to some consideration from the House, applied for a loan to help save his estates. On 20 December the House voted £5,000, to be vested in trustees, 'for the purpose of taking up a mortgage on the Decoy, in the parish of St. Mary, the property of sir Charles Price; the mortgage on the said property to be assigned to the said trustees, in trust, for the security of the public, until the said sum shall be discharged.'[7] The next day an attempt was made to give this proposal general application:

That if any member of this house should, by misfortune or imprudence, be reduced to great distress, and his estate or other property being mortgaged, and the mortgagee threatens to foreclose his mortgage; in that case this house will, on petition, grant him a loan to be vested in trustees, to take assignment of such mortgage, to prevent such member from being turned out of his estate.[8]

This motion was defeated 21–3,[9] although the particular case of the

---

[1] See *JAJ*, VI, 649 of 16 Nov. 1776. He was not returned in the elections for 1787. (See *JAJ*, VIII, 266 of 23 Oct. 1787.)

[2] *JAJ*, X, 321 of 6 Nov. 1799.   [3] ibid., 361 of 23 Nov. 1799.   [4] ibid.

[5] This seriousness and sense of function had been a quality of the Jamaica Assembly since its establishment.

[6] See Cundall, *Historic Jamaica*, pp. 259–64; Metcalf, op. cit., *passim*.

[7] *JAJ*, VIII, 245 of 20 Dec. 1786.   [8] ibid., 246 of 21 Dec.   [9] ibid.

loan to Price was not then affected. But on 25 October of the following year, it was proposed

That the appropriation of public money, by vesting the same in loans to members of this house, is unconstitutional, and of dangerous example, destructive of public confidence, and a breach of trust towards our constituents . . .[1]

This was amended to

That the appropriation of public money, by vesting the same in loans to members of this house, is unconstitutional, and of dangerous example.[2]

Price himself voted in favour of the amendment.[3]

In 1790, 'an act of the English parliament, which passed in the second year (commonly called the first) of the reign of James the first, entitled "An Act for new executions to be sued against any which shall hereafter be delivered out of execution by privilege of parliament, and for discharge of them out of whose custody such person shall be delivered" ', was declared in force in Jamaica.[4] It was a direct result of the Kemeys case.[5] John Gardner Kemeys, member for Portland, had been called to court for debt 'before and at the time of his election as a member for . . . Portland'.[6] He claimed parliamentary privilege but was nevertheless placed in custody by the Provost-Marshal for debt. The Provost-Marshal was able to ignore the plea for parliamentary privilege because, on this occasion, the election was a disputed one. When Kemeys' election was confirmed, the House resolved (i) that he *was* entitled to parliamentary privilege and was therefore to be released from custody; but that (ii) 'the privileges of this house do not extend to an extinction of the rights of creditors'.[7] The Act 31 Geo. III, c. 4 of 1790 followed from this. What the House was demonstrating, for the sake of its own integrity, was that its members could not be expected to claim an infinity of parliamentary privilege. In fact, in 1817, an attempt was made to exclude members who were declared debtors from sitting in the House, but this was decisively defeated.[8]

The Assembly was also increasingly aware, during this period, of the damage being done to its autonomy by the presence, among its

[1] *JAJ*, VIII, 272 of 24 Oct. 1787.   [2] ibid.   [3] ibid.   [4] 31 Geo. III, c. 4.
[5] See *JAJ*, VIII, 180–242 of 14 Nov.–19 Dec. 1786; John Grant, *Notes of Cases adjudged in Jamaica, from May 1774 to December 1787* (Edinburgh, 1794), pp. 284–6, 298–9, 327–8.
[6] *JAJ*, VIII, 596 of 19 Nov. 1790.   [7] ibid.
[8] ibid., XIII, 110–11 of 28 Oct. 1817. The voting was 8 to 25.

members, of judges and persons holding public office of profit under the Crown. As early as 1711 'An act [10 Annae c. 17] to disenable any member of the council, or of the assembly of this island, from acting as commissioner for receiving any public money, raised or to be raised by the governor, council and assembly of this island; and to disenable any such commissioner to be a member of the council, or of this or any future assembly of this island', was passed in Jamaica but disallowed by the British Government. Now, not only the House, but certain sections of the public were pressing for reforms. In 1785, for instance, the freeholders of St. Mary asked: 'what can the good people of this island expect from the determinations of men who hold an interest in contradistinction to theirs, and who, by their acquaintance and influence, get themselves elected members of the assembly?'[1] In 1786 the House had introduced a bill to regulate seats in the Assembly, especially of those holding certain offices,[2] but this had got nowhere. In 1787, a resolution that 'the exercise of legislative power, by persons invested with judicial authority, is unconstitutional'[3] failed by 25 votes to 14 to gain approval, though it was agreed that a committee be appointed 'to prepare and bring in a bill for vacating the seat of any member of [the] house who shall hereafter accept any of the following places or offices, viz.— receiver-general, clerk of the supreme court, clerk of the crown, officers of customs, and naval officer, provost-marshal, secretary of [the] island, register in chancery, or any other place or office of profit in the appointment of the crown or governor of [the] island . . .'.[4] This committee, however, it would appear, never did anything. In 1788, a Bill, using the same words as the first of the 1787 resolutions, was shelved.[5]

In this matter, of course, it was now no longer a simple matter of the Assembly's assertions *vis-à-vis* other local bodies and institutions. The presence of judges and Crown officials in the Assembly was part of the imperial system of control, discussed in Chapter 2. How could the Assembly feel itself, or be seen to be, a truly creole institution as long as these connections and controls existed? The House, in this particular instance, attempted to get around the problem by introducing in 1792 and 1799 a unicameral regulation to make their point:

[1] *JAJ*., VIII, 109 of 22 Nov. 1785.   [2] ibid., 192 of 25 Nov. 1786.
[3] ibid., 292 of 21 Nov. 1787.   [4] ibid., 293 of 21 Nov. 1787.
[5] ibid., 477 of 12 Dec. 1788.

That if any member of this house shall hold private communications with either of the other branches of the legislature, on the subject-matter of questions depending in this house, in the view of influencing their opinions on such questions before they shall come before them in a regular parliamentary course, or shall endeavour surreptitiously to obtain the sentiments either of the commander in chief, or of the members of the council, on such questions, depending in this house, in the view of influencing the debates and proceedings of this house, that this house will proceed with the utmost severity against such member.[1]

That no member . . . holding any office of profit under the crown, either in his own right or in the right of any other person,[2] or executing any such office, either by himself or any substitute or deputy, shall hereafter be allowed to vote in any case wherein any matter shall come in question touching any such office holden or executed, in the manner aforesaid, by such member; but shall previously withdraw, whenever the question shall come to be determined by a division of the house.[3]

Here the right of public officers sitting as elected members was not being challenged, but an attempt was being made to curtail the area of their participation in the business of the House, especially where this impinged on their executive functions. In the event, both these resolutions were defeated: that of 1792 by 14 votes to 9, that of 1799 by 18 votes to 13; those against including the Chief Justice, the Receiver-General and the deputy Provost-Marshal.[4]

By the turn of the century, however, as in so many things in the creole world of Jamaica, there was change. In 1802, collecting constables were excluded from standing as election candidates by the Act of 43 Geo. III, c. 1. In 1804, a bill for the exclusion of the Provost-Marshal was introduced;[5] it passed the House but was unacceptably amended by the Council.[6] In 1811, however, a resolution excluding, in effect, senior public officers from sitting in the Assembly was finally upheld:

That no officer attending on the council or assembly of this island, or whose duty it is to give attendance at, or responsible to, any public board, composed wholly or principally of members of the council or assembly, ought to sit or vote in this house.[7]

[1] *JAJ*, IX, 92–3 of 10 March 1792.
[2] This was a reference to the patent office holders; see p. 13, above.
[3] *JAJ*, X, 376 of 27 Nov. 1799.
[4] See ibid., IX, 93 of 10 March 1792 and X, 376 of 27 Nov. 1799.
[5] ibid., XI, 214 of 22 Nov. 1804.   [6] ibid., 282 of 14 Dec. 1804.
[7] ibid., Vol. XII, 352–3 of 30 Oct. 1811.

By the 1816 elections, most public officers had departed the House: the Chief Justice in 1801,[1] the Receiver-General in 1806,[2] the Solicitor General, C. N. Pallmer, in 1808.[3] George Cuthbert, the Provost-Marshal, was elected for St. Andrew in a by-election in 1804,[4] but went up to the Council in 1808.[5] John Jaques, the Mayor of Kingston, resigned his seat in 1812 for reasons of health.[6] On the other hand, a few judges—J. C. Pownall, two James Stewarts (Trelawny, St. Andrew), John Campbell, Alexander Grant, and J. S. Williams—remained on in the House until the end of the period of this study.[7] A move in 1817 to expel Alexander Aikman, Snr. from the House on the grounds that as Official Printer to the Assembly he was, in fact, a public officer, was defeated by 7 votes to 29.[8] Aikman remained in the Assembly until 1825.[9] But after 1811, as a general rule, public office holders did not sit in the elected chambers of the legislature of Jamaica.

[1] Henckell, the Chief Justice, died in 1801. (See *JAJ*, X, 639 of 8 Dec. 1801.) John Kirby his successor (1802–8) was never a member of the House. His name appears for the first time on the Council lists in 1807. (See Cundall, *Historic Jamaica*, p. xix; *Jamaica Almanack for 1807*, p. 127.) For the rest of the period, all C.J.s sat on the Council.

[2] William Mitchell, Receiver-General (1800–6), resigned his Assembly seat in 1809. (See *JAJ*, XII, 145 of 31 Oct. 1809.) The new Receiver-General, John Young (see C.O. 137/125) sat in neither House of the legislature.

[3] *JAJ*, XII, 3 of 25 Oct. 1808.   [4] ibid., XI, 266 of 11 Dec. 1804.

[5] Roby, op. cit.; *Jamaica Almanack for 1808*.   [6] *JAJ*, XII, 426 of 27 Oct. 1812.

[7] See relevant *JAJ* and *Jamaica Almanacks*.   [8] *JAJ*, XIII, 174 of 4 Dec. 1817.

[9] Cundall, *Press and Printers*, p. 24.

PART TWO

JAMAICA AND THE
AMERICAN REVOLUTION

5

THE AMERICAN CONNECTION

MANY questions, stemming from the Assembly's claim and assumption of internal legislative competence, were still to be raised. But there can be no doubt that from the inception of representative government, Jamaica was seen by its settlers as an English colony, settled by Englishmen, loyal to the Crown if not Parliament, obeying the same laws[1] and enjoying the same rights as their cousins at 'home', with the important proviso, from their point of view, that because of the distance from London, they should, subject to the King's prerogative, tax and govern themselves. This was an attitude shared with Jamaica by the Leeward Islands, Barbados, and the mainland American colonies. Despite regional differences[2] in climate, geography and social development, all these territories had, from the same source, language, religion, and certain cultural assumptions in common.[3] They also shared certain common problems and ex-

---

[1] C.O. 139/5: 'Act declaring the laws of England in force in this island'
Whereas the laws and statutes heretofore made and used in our native country, the Kingdom of England, for the public weal of the same, and all the liberties immunities and privileges contained therein, have ever been of force, and are belonging unto all His Majesty's liege people within this island. . . .

This Act, however, went on to stipulate that only those Acts of Parliament 'naming and relating to [the] island' or accepted 'by common consent of the General Assemblies of [the] island', would in fact be recognized. The Assembly was making a general declaration by reserving to itself particular distinctions. As it turned out, the Lords of Trade and Plantations, on the advice of the Attorney-General, rejected the bill outright on the ground that 'the people of Jamaica have no laws but as are made there and established by His Majesty's authority'. See also *C.S.P.*, 1677–80, nos. 1323, 1347.

[2] See, for example, F. W. Pitman, *The Development of the British West Indies 1700–1763* (New Haven, 1917), 3rd ed., London, 1967, pp. 1–2.

[3] S. Zavala, *The Colonial Period in the History of the New World*, trans. and abridged, M. Savelle (Mexico, 1962), pp. 282–3. A strong case for seeing the American colonies and the West Indies as an entity is also made by L. J. Ragatz in 'The West Indian Approach to the Study of American Colonial History' in a paper for the American Historical Association, 1934 (London, 1935). See also, among others, Richard Pares, *Yankees and Creoles* (London, 1956), p. 2; M. L. Hansen, *The Atlantic Migration, 1607–1860* (Harvard University Press, 1940), New York ed. 1961, p. 41; Bernard Bailyn, *The New England Merchants of the Seventeenth Century* (Cambridge, Mass., 1955), p. 84; F. W. Pitman, 'Slavery on the British West India Plantations in the Eighteenth Century', *Journal of Negro History*, Vol. XI (1926), p. 585. Philip D. Curtin, *Two Jamaicas* (Harvard University Press, 1955), p. 4, refers to 'the South Atlantic System, a regional economic, political, and social order of which Jamaica [was] part'.

periences of 'plantation' settlement and they were all colonies. The tropical and semi-tropical regions of this area relied increasingly on the labour of slaves in the production of their major export staples, the reliance increasing in intensity as one approached the tropics. These regions (and particularly the islands) were intimately connected and increasingly dependent on the northern parts of the area for their food supply and for plantation provisions, while the northern colonies, in turn, relied on the Caribbean for plantation products and orders for slaves which were delivered in North American ships.[1]

As early as 1627, in fact, when John Winthrop dispatched his son, Henry, 'to . . . the Barbethes' (in the first year of its settlement),[2] there had been initiated those commercial partnerships and links between mainland and islands[3] that were to lead to other connections. The New England trade with Barbados, for example, resulted in a postal route from New England to 'Old', via Barbados, that was to be used from 1631 until the War of American Independence.[4] For many American merchants, it became almost *de rigueur* to serve apprenticeships in the West Indies, going as supercargoes from one island to another, getting to know the local merchants, the local market, and the customers.[5] This led to American property holding in the West Indies and vice versa. The Middletons, the Bulls, and the Colletons of South Carolina had plantations in Barbados and Jamaica.[6] Thomas Benson of Jamaica held lands in St. Kitts and Philadelphia.[7]

From these commercial and property ties came, naturally, personal and social relationships as well. Adam Dolmage, Clerk of the Supreme Court of Jamaica in 1805, was a former citizen of New York.[8] John Perry, Assemblyman for St. James (1796–1809), was described by Lt.-Governor Nugent as 'much more an American than a British subject.'[9] Another Assemblyman, Samuel Vaughan, was the son of Samuel Vaughan, a West India London merchant

[1] Ragatz, 'The West Indian Approach', pp. 6–7.
[2] See V. T. Harlow, *A History of Barbados, 1625–1685* (London, 1926), p. 268.
[3] See A. M. Whitson, 'The Outlook of the Continental American Colonies on the British West Indies, 1760–1775', *Political Science Quarterly*, Vol. xlv (1930), no. 1; Pares, *Yankees and Creoles*, p. 8, n.2. The trade was mainly in cattle, fish, timber, wheat, Indian corn, horses, tread-mills for sugar-mills, casks, barrels and staves, mainly from New England, but also (especially corn and horses) from Virginia. (Harlow, op. cit., pp.280–5.) From the Caribbean came sugar, molasses and rum.
[4] Harlow, op. cit., p. 269.   [5] Whitson, 'Outlook', pp. 58–62.
[6] ibid., pp. 62–3.   [7] ibid., p. 62.   [8] *LNJ* (Cundall), 1939 ed., p. xcix.
[9] *LNJ* (Wright), p. 312. The biographical information supplied by Philip Wright for this edition of *LNJ* is mostly from a paper by General Nugent entitled 'Sketch of the characters of certain individuals in the Island of Jamaica, etc., etc., etc.' Nugent Papers, Untyped (1806), no. 807 at the Institute of Jamaica.

who was a friend of George Washington.[1] Vaughan, Snr.'s wife was from Boston.[2] Yet another Jamaican, Philip Livingston, a Kingston merchant and member of the Assembly for Portland,[3] was the eldest son of Philip Livingston, one of the signatories of the American Declaration of Independence.[4] Livingston, Snr., also a merchant, had married in Jamaica while on trading business there.[5] Kingston society read about Charleston in the *Columbian Magazine* (published monthly in Kingston from 1796 to 1800)[6] and in the 'American Intelligence' column of the *Royal Gazette*. Charleston and New York read about Kingston in the *South Carolina* and *New York Gazettes*, respectively.[7] Touring American theatrical companies took in Jamaica as a normal part of their circuit. 'It is possible to draw, if not a straight line, at least a comfortable, meandering curve from Harbour Street, Kingston, to Broadway, New York.'[8] The young Major George Washington accompanied his elder brother, Lawrence, to Barbados in 1751/2. Lawrence was suffering from a pulmonary disease which was proving obstinate. It 'induced him to try the efficacy of a winter within the tropics, in the hope of finding relief'.[9] He was not the only North American who came south for his health.[10] At the same time, there was a steady West Indian trek in the opposite direction for very much the same reason. 'I am afraid', wrote an American doctor from Barbados to his friends in Philadelphia, '. . . you will be obliged to limit emigration from this part of the world, so many [are] now declaring for Philadelphia. . . . I would advise Adam Chart to begin another House directly and call it the Barbados Hotel, putting up for a sign, the worn-out West Indian, dying of a dropsy from intemperate living.'[11]

Naturally, there were also marriages between Yankees and Creoles, and many West Indian families sent their children to school in the northern colonies—especially those who could not afford to send them to England or who already had relatives or close friends

---

[1] P. Wright, op. cit., p. 320. [2] ibid.

[3] 1768, 1770, 1776, 1781. See Feurtado, op. cit., p. 61 and *JAJ*, V, 554 of 11 July 1766; VI, 112 of 8 Nov. 1768; and p. 54, above.

[4] Cundall (*LNJ*), p. 206; E. B. Livingston, *The Livingstones of Livingston Manor* (New York, 1910), pp. 551, 560–1. [5] Livingston, op. cit., p. 560.

[6] See, for instance, 'View of Certain Regulations and Customs, subsisting at Charleston, South Carolina, and in Kingston, Jamaica', *Columbian Magazine*, Vol. II, March 1797, pp. 630–2.

[7] Whitson, 'Outlook', p. 66. [8] R. Wright, op. cit., p. 2.

[9] J. M. Toner, ed., *The Daily Journal of Major George Washington in 1751–52* . . . (Albany, New York, 1892), p. 4.

[10] Whitson, 'Outlook', p. 65. [11] Quoted in Whitson, 'Outlook', p. 65.

on the mainland.[1] It was probably this kind of connection that brought Alexander Hamilton to New York in 1772.[2] In 1772, Dr. Witherspoon published an 'Address to the inhabitants of Jamaica and the West India Islands on behalf of the College of New Jersey',[3] begging for financial help and pointing out that his institution offered an excellent preparatory course for the university. In that same year, Dr. Hugh Williamson issued an appeal to 'The Humane and Liberal Friends of Learning, Religion and Public Virtue in the Island of Jamaica' on behalf of the Academy of New Ark, Delaware.[4] Alexander Hamilton, for instance, went to school in New York, and to the college at Princeton (under Dr. Witherspoon) and Columbia (then King's College).[5] With the Revolution, over 1,270 white American loyalists and more than 4,000 of their slaves sought and obtained refuge in Jamaica.[6] Among these refugees were the printers Alexander Aikman, Snr. and David Douglass who were to become publishers of the *Royal Gazette* and official printers to the Jamaica House of Assembly.[7] Among the slaves were certain Baptists, who as preachers, were to have a considerable effect on the slave population of the island,[8] and who helped form a black cultural bridge (more than ever evident today) between the two areas.

The American Atlantic seaboard and the English Caribbean, constituted, then, by the first half of the eighteenth century, a mutually dependent entity. As John Adams put it:

The commerce of the West India Islands is a part of the American system of commerce. They can neither do without us, nor we without them. The Creator has placed us upon the globe in such a situation, that we have

[1] Whitson, 'Outlook', pp. 63–5; J. I. Cooper, 'The West Indies, Bermuda and the American Mainland Colleges', *JHR*, Vol. II. no. 1 (Dec. 1949), pp. 1–6.

[2] ibid., p. 63, n. 8; *Dictionary of American Biography*, Vol. VIII (London, 1932), p. 171.

[3] ibid., p. 64. This College was later to become Princeton. See R. B. Nye, *The Cultural Life of the New Nation, 1776–1830* (New York, 1960), 1963 ed., p. 35.

[4] ibid., p. 64, n. 4.

[5] John T. Morse, *The Life of Alexander Hamilton* (Boston, 1876), pp. 7–8.

[6] Ragatz, *Fall*, p. 194; *JAJ*, VII, 476 of 19 Oct.; 497 of 2 Nov. 1782; 551 of 13 Feb. 1783; and 23 Geo. III, c. 23 (1782); Wilbur H. Siebert, *The Legacy of the American Revolution to the British West Indies and Bahamas* (Columbus, Ohio, 1913), pp. 14–16.

[7] Cundall, *Press and Printers*, pp. 122–3. Douglass (b. Scotland?, 1720, d. Spanish Town, 1789) had been a printer in Jamaica, but joined the American Company of Comedians and went to North America in 1758 as their manager. He returned to Jamaica and printing in 1775. He was a J.P. for St. Catherine and Master in Ordinary from about 1785. See R. Wright, op. cit., pp. 28, 42, 57–8; *Jamaica Almanack* (1785), p. 66. Aikman became a Member of the Assembly.

[8] See pp. 161–4, 253–5, below.

occasion for each other. We have the means of assisting each other, and politicians and artful contrivances cannot separate us.[1]

By 1760, on the other hand, the northern American colonies had developed into essentially commercial colonies, with a self-supporting agriculture and economy. Industrialization was on the way. The southern states, with a labour force that was part free and part slave, were, as their reliance on slaves increased, beginning to face the 'Caribbean problems' of low productivity, soil exhaustion, underdeveloped technology, and lack of diversification, though with less severity; and during this period, it was still possible to expand into new territory. There was also, on the mainland generally, a considerable development of material, institutional, and artistic culture, based mainly on the towns and cities of these colonies. There was nothing like this in the islands. Jamaica, St. Kitts, Barbados, knew no *Mayflower*, had no Founding Fathers. There was no settlement in Jamaica with the religious base of the Massachusetts Bay Colony or the Pennsylvania Quaker establishments. Nor was there anything in the West Indies comparable to the philanthropic and proprietary aspects of, say, the Georgia and Virginia colonies. Barbados and the Leewards were settled on the initiative of single proprietors (not so surprising when their size is considered). Jamaica started off with major-generals and pirates. Under these conditions (Barbados was a qualified exception) dependants rather than equals were attracted into these colonies. They certainly never developed, like, say, Virginia, a self-conscious, articulate, cohesive social class of proprietor-administrators.

Given the political and diverging cultural development of the colonies, therefore, the question by the 1770s was whether the unity of the area could be maintained. In 1773, the Thirteen American colonies provided an answer. But for Jamaica, this American answer raised other questions. What was Jamaica's place within this Atlantic system? Would and could the island follow the American lead? Could the island, like the Americans, carry the claim to internal legislative competence to its logical conclusion? Was the society potentially revolutionary or was it conservative? And what, if anything, would its burden of slavery and the resulting development of a creole society contribute to whatever the answer might be?

[1] *The Works of John Adams*, ed. C. F. Adams, 10 vols. (Boston, 1856), Vol. VIII, p. 74. Adams (1735–1826), lawyer and politician, became the second President of the United States in 1796.

6

POLITICAL IDEAS

U . S

The Petition of 1774

On 23 December 1774, the Jamaica House of Assembly passed a 'humble petition and memorial' in support of the American colonies during the Stamp Duties crisis with Britain:[1]

We, your majesty's most dutiful and loyal subjects, the assembly of Jamaica, having taken into our consideration the present critical state of the colonies, humbly approach the throne, to assure your majesty of our most dutiful regard to your royal person and family, and our attachment to, and reliance on, our fellow subjects in Great-Britain . . .[2]

The king, here, is head of the Commonwealth to whom all his subjects are loyal. The dispute, which is a colonial American one, is between the American section of this Commonwealth and the British Parliament, not named, but referred to as 'fellow subjects in Great Britain', with whom there is clearly an ambivalent relationship: equality on the one hand ('fellow subjects'); 'attachment' and 'reliance' on the other. Reliance because

weak and feeble as this colony is, from its very small number of white inhabitants, and its peculiar situation, from the encumbrance of more than two hundred thousand slaves, it cannot be supposed that we now intend, or ever could have intended, resistance to Great-Britain . . .[3]

Jamaica, as an island in an international Caribbean sea, was dependent on the protection of the British Navy,[4] and was intestinely vulnerable because of the preponderance of slaves who, in some parts

---

[1] Jamaica was not alone in this. The Grenada, Tobago and Barbados legislatures passed similar resolutions. Bermuda sent delegates to the Congress at Philadelphia and supplied the Americans with arms until British intervention in 1779. The Bahamas also actively supported the Americans. See Burns, op. cit., p. 518; W. Kerr, *Bermuda and the American Revolution, 1760–1783* (Oxford University Press, 1936).

[2] *JAJ*, VI. 569 of 23 Dec. 1774.   [3] ibid.

[4] See Helen J. Crump, *Colonial Admiralty Jurisdiction in the Seventeenth Century* (London, 1931); Richard Pares, *War and Trade in the West Indies, 1739–1763* (Oxford, 1936). For Jamaican admission of this dependence, see for instance, *JAJ*, VIII, 41 of 4 Dec. 1784.

of the island, outnumbered the white population by as much as 29 : 1.[1] But despite these obvious weaknesses, which must have inhibited any bargaining power the colony might have had in this issue, there is no denying the instinctive cultural response to *American* interests and well-being:

we implore your majesty's favourable reception of this our humble petition and memorial, as well on behalf of ourselves and our constituents, the good people of this island, as on behalf of all other your majesty's subjects, the colonists of America, . . . for whom we entreat to be admitted as humble suitors, that we may not, at so important a crisis, be wanting to contribute our sincere and well-meant (however small) endeavours, to heal those disorders which may otherwise terminate in the destruction of the empire.[2]

That this was a cultural and not only a political reaction and appeal for the preservation of unity (the Jamaicans were hoping to *heal* a disordered condition) was, in fact, the basis of the Petition:

That the settlers of the first colonies, but especially those of the elder colonies of North-America, as well as the conquerors of this island, were a part of the English people, in every respect equal to them and possessed of every right and privilege at the time of their emigration, which the people of England were possessed of. . . .[3]

But this claim was important not only from the point of view of the American issue; it was also the idea on which the assertion of local autonomy had been and could be founded. Without true and full local autonomy it would hardly be possible to develop those institutions and that way of life from which a recognizable and articulate society could evolve. But to what extent could this take place as long as the colonists remained colonists?

having been bred, from their infancy, to venerate the name of parliament, a word still dear to the heart of every Briton, and considered as the palladium of liberty, and the great source from whence their own is derived, . . . we received those regulations of trade from our fellow subjects of England and Great-Britain, so advantageous to us, as colonists, as Englishmen, and Britons . . . [but this] did not thereby confer on them a power of legislating for us, far less that of destroying us and our children, by divesting us of all rights and property.[4]

On the break-up of 'the old colonial empire' with the revolt of the continental colonies, Jamaica's petitions to Britain concerning trade

[1] See figures in Orlando Patterson, *The Sociology of Slavery* (London, 1967), p. 56.
[2] *JAJ*, VI, 569.   [3] ibid.   [4] ibid., pp. 569–70.

and the state and prosperity of the island, and later the island's pro-slavery arguments, were also to be based on the above statement with its political implications. But the claim to local autonomy was not, at the time of the American petition, being positively made. It was being expressed in an ambiguous, somewhat negative way. Not Jamaican self-government but Parliamentary tyranny was the issue.

Your petitioners do therefore make this claim and demand from their sovereign ...

The two-handed 'claim' and 'demand' is typical—

that no laws shall be made, and attempted to be forced upon them, injurious to their rights as colonists, Englishmen, or Britons. . . .
    [We are] entitled to your protection and the benefits of the English constitution; the deprivation of which must dissolve that dependence on the parent state, which it is our glory to acknowledge, whilst enjoying those rights under her protection.[1]

Throughout there runs the theme of dependence not independence. Dissolution of *dependence* will mean a change in affection for the parent and a new relationship, but not necessarily a break with the family:

. . . should this bond of union be ever destroyed, and the colonists reduced to consider themselves as tributaries to Great Britain, they must cease to venerate her as an affectionate parent. . . .[2]

It was not until 1807, faced with Parliament's abolition of the Slave Trade, that the Jamaican Assembly was stung into a more positive formulation of its constitutional position; though not, it must still be noted, without the crippling rider and reminder (italicized):

That the legislature of this island has, and ever had, the exclusive and absolute right to enact its own laws, and to regulate entirely its internal government and affairs; that the Imperial parliament hath not, nor hath any other power on earth, . . . (*except his majesty in the instance of disallowing the laws here made*), and that, in support of the dearest rights and liberties of our fellow-subjects, it is our duty, by all constitutional means in our power, to resist the attempt that has been, and every attempt that may be, made to destroy or to abridge that right. . . .[3]

And not until 1815, in the course of a long and careful discourse by John Shand, member for St. John, on the subject of the Parlia-

[1] *JAJ*, VI, p. 570.   [2] ibid.   [3] ibid., XI, 600 of 29 Oct. 1807, my italics.

mentary bill 'for effectually preventing the unlawful importation of slaves . . . ', that an opportunity was made to compare Jamaica's position with the Americans and their War of Independence 'which [had shaken] the empire to its centre and [had] terminated in the loss of its most valuable colonies'.[1] But eventually, as in 1774 and 1807, the tide flowed quite clearly towards conciliation and 'constitutional means' and of course loyalty to the Crown.

While therefore it is clear that the Jamaican Assembly sincerely saw itself in the triple role of defender of British American cultural unity, watchdog of local political autonomy, and spokesman for Jamaican rights and property against encroachments from outside, it is also clear that there was a dichotomy between the Assembly's appearance in this role and its performance in it. It was all very well for Edward Long[2] to say that

The Assembly consider their privileges as derived to them from their constituents; and that they are not concessions from the crown, but the right and inheritance of the people; and that the privileges which they claim are absolutely necessary to support their own proper authority, and to give the people of the colony that protection against arbitrary power, which nothing but a free and independent assembly can give. . . .[3]

To have achieved effective performance in this kind of role, the Assembly would have had to have been representative of a different kind of Jamaica: a Jamaica with revolutionary ideas about its economy, its defence, its self-reliance—about its entire social structure and manner of living. In other words, significant cultural development would have had to have been taking place (as it had been in the American Colonies),[4] for some considerable time before 1774. But it does not appear that Jamaicans had the *will* to have conceived of such a structural re-ordering—quite apart from any consideration of the *means* to make it effective. As the Continental Congress wrote when thanking the Assembly for its part in the dispute with Britain: 'By converting your sugar plantations into fields of grain, you can

---

[1] *JAJ*, XII, 784 of 20 Dec. 1815.   [2] See p. 73, below.
[3] Long, *History*, Vol. I, p. 56.
[4] See, for example, L. B. Wright, *The Cultural Life of the American Colonies, 1603–1763* (New York, 1957); Hansen, op. cit.; C. Eaton, *The Growth of Southern Civilization, 1760–1860* (New York, 1961); Oscar Handlin, *The Americans* (New York, 1963); C. P. Nettels, *The Roots of American Civilization* (New York, 1938; new ed. London, 1963); Eugene Genovese, *The Political Economy of Slavery* (London ed., 1966); Pares, *Merchants and Planters*, esp. pp. 1–13.

supply yourselves with the necessaries of life'.[1] *This* was real independence talk. But in Jamaican terms, such an idea was not even conceivable. Apart from Edward Long, no one in Jamaica seems to have considered the possibility of a self-sufficient agriculture.[2] Equally unthought of was the possibility of opposing Britain with force. The size and inefficiency of the militia made this unthinkable. As the Americans tactfully put it in 1775:

The peculiar situation of your Island forbids your assistance. But we have your good wishes. From the good wishes of the friends of liberty and mankind, we shall always derive consolation.[3]

From this point on, there was to be a real parting of the ways: the Americans to independence; Jamaica into increasing dependence on Britain and on British mercantilist requirements. In being unable to provide more than words and 'good wishes', Jamaica appears not only to have been separated from the British American complex, in connection with which it might well have continued to develop its economic, perhaps even intellectual, prosperity, but also to have lost its one chance of political independence during this period. This is not to say that there were not elements within the island who wanted American-type independence. As late as 1811, Governor Morrison was reporting 'that a party has long existed in [the] Island, whose object is (however improbable under present circumstances) a separation from the control and jurisdiction of the British Government'.[4] But the very existence of such a body at that time served only to underline the oddity of such extreme political thinking.[5] Political thinking in Jamaica, in fact, never went beyond the Whiggish/intellectual formulations of perhaps the two most distinguished 'creole' writers of the period here under consideration —Edward Long, whose *History* was published on the eve of the

---

[1] P. Force, ed. *American Archives* . . . , 6 vols. (Washington, 1837–46), Vol. II, 4th series, col. 1891.

[2] Long, *History*, Vol. I, pp. 435–64.

[3] Force, op. cit., col. 1891.

[4] C.O. 137/131: Morrison to Liverpool, 19 Sept. 1811; quoted in A. L. Murray, op. cit., p. 85.

[5] The group in the Assembly who pushed through the Petition of 1774, were apparently not without support in the island. In September 1781 the then Lt.-Governor was complaining of the aid American naval prisoners had received from their 'Rebel friends in Kingston, of whom there are but too many of influence and property'. (C.O. 137/81; Campbell to Germain, 27 Sept. 1781, quoted in A. L. Murray, op. cit., pp. 46–7.) This was probably the same group (Murray, p. 47), who had, in 1775, circulated copies of Tom Paine's *Common Sense* throughout the island. (C.O. 137/71: Keith to Germain, 27 May 1776.)

American Revolution, and Bryan Edwards, the first edition of whose *History* appeared in 1793.

Edward Long

Edward Long, the fourth son of Samuel Long of Longville, Jamaica, was born in Cornwall, England, in August 1734. He arrived in Jamaica on his father's death in 1757 and remained there until 1769 when ill health made him leave the island. While in Jamaica he was private secretary to the Lt.-Governor Sir Henry Moore and later a judge in the Court of Vice-Admiralty.[1] His connections with Jamaica were not only on his father's side (the Long family had been in Jamaica since 1655).[2] Through his wife, Mary Ballard, the sole heiress of Thomas Ballard, he was connected with the greatest of all Jamaican family aggregations, the Beckford–Ballard–Palmer group. In 1750 this group owned at least 44,670 acres in Jamaica;[3] and as late as 1828 their names still appear among the leading slave and property owners of the country.[4] Long was therefore a man of 'influence and property'. With regard to the institution of slavery and the social hierarchy on which it was based, he held a conservative, even reactionary, almost feudal attitude. People were placed in ranks as God had ordained, and as for the slaves, they were less than animals.[5] But on the question of the possibility of Jamaican independence, Long was perhaps the most radical thinker the island had produced. In a passage quoted earlier,[6] he made the important constitutional point that the authority of the Assembly was derived, not from royal concessions but from the people; that the privileges which it claimed were 'absolutely necessary to support [its] proper authority, and to give the people . . . protection against arbitrary power'. These ideas—essentially seventeenth century in tone— are developed in Long's discussion of 'faction' and the place of the Council in the Constitution:

It has been a commonly-received opinion, that the people of this island are fond of opposition to their governors; that they are . . . discontented, and factious. This notion, artfully disseminated by bad governors and their

[1] *DNB*, Vol. XXXIV, pp. 100–1.
[2] R. M. Howard, *Records and Letters of the Family of the Longs of Longville, Jamaica and Hampton Lodge, Surrey*, 2 vols. (London, 1925), Vol. I, pp. 23–4.
[3] This figure is derived from Add. MS. 12436: 'List of Landholders in Jamaica 1750'.
[4] See *The Jamaica Almanack* (1829), 'Return of Givings-In'.
[5] Long's attitude to slaves is discussed in detail on pp. 181–3, below.
[6] See p. 71, above.

adherents, is extremely unjust. The native spirit of freedom, which distinguishes British subjects beyond most others, is not confined to the mother country; but discovers itself in the remotest parts of her empire, and chiefly in a resistance to acts of oppression, and such unwarrantable measures, as they know, or at least believe, have a certain tendency to abridge them of [their] rights.[1]

He supports his argument that the Council of Jamaica could not possibly be regarded as a House of Peers, either through their own wish or the King's will, by using the Lockean argument that 'The sovereign holds his legislative power originally of the will of each member of society; it is evident no man can confer upon another a right which he has not in himself.'[2] But by 1774 this kind of argument was outworn.[3] It was no longer the sovereign who was the threat, but Parliament. And in basing his argument on constitutionalism, without reference to the final sanction of force, Long rendered his position as constitutionally ineffective as that of the Assembly. What was 'radical' about Long's thinking, however, was not his political ideas *per se*, not his constitutionalism, but the application of these (both in vision and in detail) to what Jamaican society could mean and could achieve, and his conviction that social progress could best be initiated through legislation.[4]

In the first place, he felt certain that Jamaica could provide its own best defence:

Its own permanent inhabitants are unquestionably its most natural, faithful, and active defenders; and, when they become sufficiently numerous to execute this important trust, the maintenance of soldiers must be an unnecessary burthen, and conducive to no honest design.[5]

To increase the population, more white settlers should be encouraged, helped financially, and made to take advantage of existing unused landholdings. Settlement should as far as possible be on the inland highlands (better for health, easier for defence), and to support this, a central town should be built that would be the centre of a system of internal fortification.[6] The sort of men, best qualified for increasing the number of Whites, 'are the sober, frugal, and industrious artificers; together with the poorer farmer and graziers, a hardy useful people, and most fit for occupying the unsettled desarts, and

---

[1] Long, *History*, Vol. I, pp. 39–40.   [2] ibid., p. 186.
[3] See Elsa V. Goveia, *A Study on the Historiography of the British West Indies to the end of the Nineteenth Century* (Mexico, 1956), p. 58.
[4] See, for instance, *History*, Vol. I, pp. 140, 408–11, 416, 440; Vol. II, pp. 37, 333–4.
[5] ibid., Vol. I, p. 69.   [6] ibid., p. 404.

changing the woods and wildernesses into flourishing pastures and plantations.'[1] The dependence on external trade, especially with North America, could be obviated by diversifying the economy, paying attention to coffee, afforestation, cattle, and horses.[2]

The greater abundance there is provided of [meat, poultry, eggs, etc.], the more money will be saved to the island in various ways; and it would consequently grow more populous and thriving, and better able to maintain families; a matter of the utmost concern to all who wish to see it flourish; marriages, the best source of well-peopling it, and from which some men pretend they are at present deterred, from the expensiveness of housekeeping, would be greatly promoted; nor would many useful persons emigrate from the colony, if they could live in it as [cheaply] as in Europe. To live otherwise in an island, so fertile and so capable of affording not only the comforts, but the luxuries of sustenance, in the greatest profusion, is a reproach to industry and policy. . . .[3]

There is a certain Gonzago-like utopianism running through some of Long's pages—as in the passage on marriage, above. But there is no mistaking his instinct and his vision: his suggestions for new approaches to agriculture and to the militia, for instance; and his argument that local law should be the product of local conditions has a modern ring about it:

. . . the municipal laws [of Jamaica] differ, in many respects, from those of the mother country. They should then be judged according to the exigencies, policy, and welfare, of the colony; and not by Westminster-hall authorities, which have relation to other laws, other facts and to a people differently circumstanced. . . . I think, I have observed Westminster-hall practice too fondly extolled and caressed in our court[s]. . . .[4]

Bryan Edwards

The logic of these arguments led to internal self-determination and Bryan Edwards[5] in his *History* said so:

[1] Long, *History*, Vol. II, p. 283.   [2] ibid., Vol. I, p. 402–35.
[3] ibid., Vol. II, p. 37.   [4] ibid., Vol. I, pp. 72–3.
[5] Bryan Edwards (1743–1800), was born in Westbury, Wiltshire. He came to Jamaica at the age of sixteen to live with his uncle Zachary Bayly, Custos of St. Mary, from whom he inherited large properties. Edwards was a member of the Jamaican Assembly (for St. George), 1765–70 and 1771–2 and a member of the Council, 1772–82, when he resigned and went to England. There he stood unsuccessfully for Parliament. He returned to Jamaica in 1787 and resumed his place in the Assembly as a representative for Trelawny, 1787–92, after which he left for England again. This time he was more successful in British politics and sat in the Commons from 1796 until his death. (See Philip Wright, op. cit., p. 297; *DNB*, Vol. XVII, pp. 111–13; Roby, op: cit.; H. E. Vendryes, 'Bryan Edwards, 1743–1800',*JHR*, Vol. i, no. 1 (June 1943), pp. 76–82.

On the whole, subject to the restriction that their trade-laws are not repugnant to those of Great Britain, there are no concerns of a local and provincial nature, to which the authority of the colonial laws does not extend.[1]

The difference between Long and Edwards, the one writing before the American Revolution, the other writing afterwards, both creoles by adoption, friends of each other, both influenced by Lockean ideas of reciprocal responsibility,[2] is that while Long's bogy was the despotism of the King, Edwards recognizes Parliament as the source of authority. Edwards' solution to this 'new' situation (and in this he was nearer than Long to the Americans of 1773)[3] was the idea of an informal federation of equal parliaments with the King as head and centre.

. . . the colonists have legislatures of their own, which are subject to the king of Great Britain, as to their own proper head. The person, who, by the laws of Great Britain, is king of Great Britain, is *their* king; but they owe no allegiance to the lords and commons; to whom they are not subjects, but *fellow* subjects with them to the same sovereign.[4]

It would seem, then, from these elements of thought in Long and Bryan Edwards, and the Assembly's Resolutions of 1807 and 1815 already referred to,[5] that throughout this period there persisted the idea of a possible internally autonomous Jamaica. But just as the Assembly's position was vitiated by its admission of weakness, of military and commercial dependence on Britain, so there was a fatal dichotomy in the loyalties of the two historians under discussion. They were Englishmen, as well as Jamaicans, at a time when it was becoming increasingly difficult to be both. Long, for instance, matched his optimistic vision of Jamaica's possible self-sufficiency with contempt for the island's society, and working on a revision of his *History* during the American War,[6] he made this defence of British mercantilism:

Under this System of policy, our Plantations in the West Indies were formed, and have grown up, and flourished—For it is not to peculiar excellence of Soil, or to extraordinary *skill* that they are indebted for their

[1] Edwards, op. cit., Vol. II, p. 420.   [2] Goveia, *Historiography*, pp. 57, 83.

[3] R. G. Adams, *Political Ideas of the American Revolution* (Durham, North Carolina, 1922), p. 64; Goveia, *Historiography*, p. 83.

[4] Edwards, op. cit., Vol. II, p. 436.   [5] pp. 70–1, above.

[6] This statement is based on internal evidence in Add. MS. 12407. Long's revisions, which were for a second edition of his *History* (which never appeared), contains material for as late as 1799.

Success, but to this *hereditary* preference at the British Market—It is this which has given a Confidence to the Merchant in the Loan of his capital; and to the Planter, in the application of that Loan, to Industry, and Improvement. . . .

And if the eventual benefit of the Nation was the true ground of the Parliamentary regulations . . . which I think we cannot deny . . . and if these regulations have been not only wise in their Object, but beneficent in their Effect; then, we have a right to conclude that they will not be rescinded, or at least, not materially deviated from, except on clear un-equivocal certainty of introducing others in their room, *more wise*, and more *nationally* beneficial.[1]

What Long says, in fact, corresponds to the reality of the situation. The point, however, is that Long, the defender of Jamaican liberties, is now the upholder of traditional British mercantilist policy—the very policy being constantly petitioned against by the Jamaican Assembly—the source, the Jamaicans felt, of their hardship since the American Revolution. Long had also come to recognize by 1779 that it was Parliament that now was the source of real political power. There was thus here a conflict between recognition of British parliamentary authority, and the colonists' claim for local parlia-mentary autonomy. Edwards stresses that the British Parliament should not 'interpose its authority in matters to which the colonial assemblies are sufficiently competent';[2] that these assemblies 'must necessarily be sovereign and supreme within their own jurisdiction; unobstructed by, and independent of all controul from without . . .'.[3] But having made this point, he hastens to add that this in no way tends 'to sovereign and national empire, distinct from, and inde-pendent of, the government of the parent state.'[4] The whole system of British colonial government, he goes on, is based on securing, through the Crown, the just rights and privileges of its colonial subjects.[5] If, under these conditions, the colonists should feel, 'or are in danger of feeling oppression',[6] their best remedy is not in revolt, but in a reliance on, and touching faith in, the constitutional watchfulness of 'big brother' Parliament:

It cannot . . . be denied, that if parliament should be apprised that the just authority of the crown over the colonies has degenerated into tyranny, it is not only their right, but their duty to interpose, even on their own

---

[1] Long, Add. MS. 12407, f. 14 verso–15 verso. Italics in text.
[2] Edwards, op. cit., Vol. II, pp. 424–5.   [3] ibid., pp. 425–7.
[4] ibid., p. 429.   [5] ibid., pp. 429–32.   [6] ibid., p. 433.

account; for it has been well and eloquently said, that whenever the liberties of Great Britain be devoted [sic], it is probable her dissolution will not begin in the centre: *she will feel subjection, like the coldness of death, creeping upon her from her extremities.*[1]

This, however, was an Englishman's argument—an English Parliamentarian's argument. It assumed that the British constitution, as defined in and by the House of Commons, would keep the 'remaining colonies'[2] intact. What Edwards' thinking did not take into account was what would happen if Parliament was not 'apprised' of imperial tyranny; or if, from the point of view of the colonies, Parliament did not appear to see or understand that such tyranny existed. For Edwards, all that mattered was the mystique of constitutional rule and the supremacy of Parliament. But this only led him into an ambivalence of statement—the colonies were to be both equal *and* subordinate:

Justly considering . . . the protection which they receive in the name of the sovereign, *as afforded by the state*, and that the colonies are parts of one great empire, of the various branches of which the king in parliament, is arbiter, controuling and regulating all intercourse with foreign nations, they [the colonists] readily admit that they stand towards the British legislature in the degree of subordination, which implies every authority in the latter, essential to the preservation of the *whole*; and to the maintenance of the relation between a mother-country and her colonies. . . .[3]

So much, then, for the theory of colonial legislative competence. According to (latter day) Long and Bryan Edwards, the island assemblies were—and were not—masters in their own political households. Neither writer provided a theory to resolve this dilemma, and the time was coming when the island colonies would be faced with the need for such a theory. For what would happen if (or when) the British Parliament invaded, 'for the good of the whole', the institution of slavery which the tropical colonists regarded as a property of which they alone had the *right* to dispose? To turn to this, would hardly be adequate:

. . . to the reasons already stated . . . may be added, the utter impossibility that two different legislatures can, at all times, and in the same moment, enforce their authority on the same object, in as much as they may happen to differ in opinion, and in that dilemma, this consequence must follow;

[1] Edwards, op. cit., Vol. II, p. 433; italics in text.
[2] ibid.   [3] ibid., pp. 436-7.

either the British must yield to the provincial, or prevail over it in points, for which, from the practical or constitutional unfitness of the former, the latter was formed.[1]

But this dilemma, as faced by Edwards, was more imaginary than real, because he had already admitted that

the king ... possesses ... the right of disallowing and rejecting all laws and statutes of the colonial assemblies, even after they had received the assent and approbation of his own lieutenant in the colony.[2]

The Assembly, later,[3] was to attempt to get around this fact of colonialism by questioning the competence of Parliament to interfere in the island's affairs. But this was hardly the point, since the King remained inviolate as admitted head of the constitutional structure. *Realpolitik*, after all, is founded on power; on the maxim, as Edwards pointed out, that 'whoever holds the sword will decide upon the question of law'.[4]

[1] Edwards, op. cit., Vol. II, p. 441.   [2] ibid., p. 429.
[3] See pp. 96–100, below.   [4] Edwards, op. cit., Vol. II, p. 432.

7

A CREOLE ECONOMY

THE American Revolution, however, did not only provoke a constitutional reaction in Jamaica. One of its first effects was to make some, at least, realize that the island had to diversify its economy and begin to rely more on local industry if it was to survive the break in trade and supplies from the Thirteen Colonies and the rising costs in freight, insurance, and imports introduced from Britain as a result of the American War.[1] In his *History of Jamaica*, published in the year of the Assembly Petition in support of the Americans, Edward Long had produced a far-reaching and long-term inventory of what needed to be done to make the island more self-sufficient and certainly less dependent on North America. It was a blue print for possible action. 'Arguing in the character of a planter', Long said,

> let me say, that in several respects, it is in our power to lessen our dependence on the North Americans; namely, by importing from Great-Britain and Ireland, many of the commodities with which the North Americans supply us; and by good management, providing many others of them within our own island. Might we not, for example, be supplied from Britain with soap, candles, ham, fish, bacon, cheese . . . *etcetera*, as cheap, in general, as from them? as also with beef, pork, and butter, entirely from Ireland? Corn, in abundance, we may have of our own growth, and lamp oil of our own manufacture, both far cheaper than we can buy of them. How strange, and inexcusable is it, that we should pay so much money every year for their horses, when those of our own breed are so incomparably more beautiful and serviceable! Great quantities of hoops, heading, and shingles, might be provided in the island, were proper methods taken to encourage our own settlers. . . .[2]

Jamaican shingles, he said, were 'five times more durable and secure'. And if shingles were unobtainable, why not use local tiles: 'manu-

[1] For the economic effect of the American Revolution on Jamaica and other parts of the Caribbean, see Richard Pares, *A West India Fortune* (London, 1950), pp. 78, 92–3, 186, 208, 229; David H. H. Makinson, *Barbados, A Study of North American–West Indian Relations, 1739–1789* (The Hague, 1964); J. F. Jameson, 'St. Eustatius in the American Revolution', *American Historical Review*, Vol. VIII (1903), pp. 683–708; Siebert, op. cit.; and Ragatz, *Fall*, pp. 142–203.   [2] Long, *History*, Vol. I, p. 541.

factories of tiles [could be] set on foot in the island, which abounds with excellent clays'.[1] The Spaniards, after all, had used tiles for roofing and this had helped to give their housing its local character.[2] He also saw the restoration of the local cattle industry as essential. This was so important it should be legislated for:

> an act of legislature [is necessary] to encourage the island-breed, and throw gradual restraints upon . . . importation; by which means, beef might possibly, in course of a few years, return to a more moderate price . . . thus might be saved many thousand pounds now paid for foreign salted beef, which is neither so wholesome, nutritious, nor pleasing . . . as fresh meat.[3]

Coffee growing (there was plenty of land and the climate was suitable) should also be encouraged, the woods and flora of the Blue Mountains studied scientifically for their commercial and medicinal possibilities, and above all, white settlement of the interior undertaken not only as a measure of local defence but to help make agricultural diversification and self-reliance possible.[4] But to achieve this goal, Long warned, Jamaicans would have to slough off their conservatism:

> To persevere in errors, because our forefathers did so, is the sure mark of a narrow or indolent soul; not to endeavour to correct them, is equally reprehensible. The opening a liberal communication of remarks and opinions, and selecting such as are distinguished for their seeming rectitude, is a sure method, whereby we may be freed from those restraints which our ancestors imposed, and to which we may have yielded implicitly under the sanction of custom, and long usage.[5]

This warning was necessary. Long knew his creoles. The year after the American crisis, and as a direct response to the new conditions created by it,

> A member in his place, represented to the house [of Assembly], that it is probable, in the present critical situation of affairs, the importation from North-America to this island, of provisions of all sorts of grain, as well as of staves, boards, and other lumber, will be greatly diminished, if not totally interrupted for some time; and therefore moved, that a committee be appointed, to take into consideration . . . what measures ought to be taken to prevent a scarcity of provisions, and what encouragement ought to be given to increase the cultivation and produce thereof, as well as the procuring and manufacturing of staves, boards, and other lumber. . . .[6]

---

[1] Long, *History*, Vol. I, p. 541.   [2] ibid. Vol. II, p. 20.   [3] ibid., p. 37.
[4] ibid., Vol. I, pp. 402–35; Vol. II, pp. 124–7.
[5] ibid., Vol. I, p. 437.   [6] *JAJ*, VI, 574–5 of 1 Nov. 1775.

The result of this was the Act 16 Geo. III, c. 12 of 1775 'to encourage the planting and growth of provisions in the several parishes of [the] island'. 'An act to encourage the taking and curing of fish and turtle, and the making of oil, and procuring salt, and importing the same into [the] island' (16 Geo. III, c. 16), was also passed that year. The next year saw 'An act for encouraging the manufacturing of *agnus castor*, or nut oil' (17 Geo. III, c. 17 of 1776), a bounty to encourage the introduction of buffaloes,[1] and the renewal of the bounty, first introduced in 1773,[2] for the encouragement of coffee production.[3] In 1779, again because of the American Revolution, there is evidence that some attempt was being made to encourage the local cattle industry, in order to supply British troops quartered in the island with fresh meat.[4] In 1783, local cattlemen, petitioning the Assembly for its continued support, said that 'many of them [had], of late years, employed their time, labour and little capitals in establishing pens of breeding stock', with the result that 'new roads of communication [had] been opened, [and] large tracts of wood-land cleared'. This, the cattlemen felt, showed 'a spirit of improvement, which, if not . . . checked, would soon penetrate into the very heart of the country'.[5] In 1780, a bill removing all restrictions to the encouragement of new white would-be settlers was introduced and passed through the House.[6] This was followed in 1782, by an Act (23 Geo. III, c. 23) to encourage loyalist settlement from North America, the Bay of Honduras and the Mosquito Shore.[7] In 1783 it was resolved by a Committee of the House

That it appears . . . to be highly expedient for the welfare of this island, that the proprietors of sugar estates should have the liberty of refining

---

[1] *JAJ*, VI, 676 of 6 Dec. 1776.   [2] ibid., 464 of 26 Nov. 1773.
[3] ibid., 634 of 23 Oct. 1776.   [4] ibid., VII, 146 of 18 Aug. 1779.
[5] ibid., 609 of 21 Nov. 1783.

[6] 21 Geo. III, c. 22. Plans for white settlement are discussed more fully on pp. 86–92, below.

[7] These were British protectorates within Spanish territory on the Caribbean coast of Central America: Honduras on the Yucatan peninsula, the Mosquito Shore, part of Nicaragua. From the early seventeenth century, and probably even earlier, Honduras Bay had become a settlement for English logwood (later mahogany) cutters. English adventurers had also settled along the Mosquito Shore where the Mosquito Indians, a people of mixed Negro and Amerindian descent, had claimed the protection of Charles I. (*C.S.P.*, 1685–8, no. 1624.) Both territories were administered by the Governor of Jamaica from 1744 until 1884 (Honduras) and 1894 (the Mosquito Shore), although by 1810, the local Superintendents there were in direct contact with the British Government. (See Burns, op. cit., pp. 49, 365, 497, 657, 685, 693; D. A. G. Waddell, *British Honduras: A Historical and Contemporary Survey* (London, 1961), pp. 10, n. 17; 52–4.)

their own sugars for exportation to Great-Britain and Ireland, and that application to that effect should be made to his majesty . . .[1]

This was a direct result of the rising British import duties on muscovado sugar.[2] There were already two sugar refineries in Kingston.[3] In 1775, John Russell introduced and had patented by a private bill, his method of 'applying friction wheels to mills for grinding sugar canes'.[4] In 1789, Isaac Lascelles Winn of St. James patented his 'principle of manufacturing sugar, and distilling rum, with a much smaller quantity of fuel' than was necessary hitherto; and James Small, a Clarendon carpenter, patented his 'mills for grinding sugar canes'.[5] In 1790, a private bill was passed to protect John Reeder, Esq., in his 'discovery and invention of a varnish for copper, and his introduction of the discovery of joining the seams of copper, and making the same water-tight without solder'.[6] Daniel Siddon, of Westmoreland, a mason, was protected by a private bill for his 'Method of hanging of coppers, for boiling of cane juice, and manufacturing of sugar', in the same year. Private bills of patent were drawn up for John Ashley and Josias Robbins in 1793, for a 'machine for raising water without friction, to be applied to mills for grinding sugar-canes' (Ashley), and a steam pump (Robbins).[7] In 1800, Thomas Roper of Portland, a planter, had his 'wheels for turning water-mills' patented, and Ezra Waldo Weld received protection for his 'machine for cleansing of clothes, called the New Laver'.[8] In 1785, John Hunter (not a creole), applied to the House for help in manufacturing alkaline salts from wood ash. This ash, he said, was essential in British and Irish linen manufacture, and at the time it was being produced only in North America. He had come to Jamaica to carry out experiments, had set up first in the wrong area because he did not know the country, but now, in Vere, he had made 'trial of almost all the different woods in the island', except the resinous ones, and found that they yielded 'a considerable quantity of salts'. He had been working on the estate of Robert Jackson,[9] a representative in the Assembly for Vere. It is not clear what became of this project, but the same year, Joel Evans, a Kingston merchant, made this petition to the Assembly:

That [he] hath, at a very considerable expence and trouble, erected buildings, enclosed yards, and provided implements and materials necessary for

[1] *JAJ*, VII, 553 of 14 Feb. 1783. [2] Ragatz, *Fall*, p. 164. [3] ibid., p. 16.
[4] 16 Geo. III. [5] 30 Geo. III. [6] 31 Geo. III. [7] 34 Geo. III.
[8] 41 Geo. III. [9] *JAJ*, VIII, 124 of 2 Dec. 1785.

carrying on and bringing to perfection the tanning business in all its branches, in the said town of Kingston, and hath already manufactured sundry sorts of leather, such as, upper and sole leather for shoes and boots, for kitteeren tops, and covering close carriages, for smiths' bellows, for saddlers' use, harness, and white sheep skins for aprons and other uses....[1]

He had, he continued, sold examples of all these various leather products to patrons, who, upon trial, declared them to excel 'any imported hither from other countries'.[2] The House decided to examine Evans' claims, commenting that since the island possessed all the raw material necessary for this industry, and since the product could be produced and sold cheaper than imported leather goods, and since it would give employment to many industrious white people, 'it might . . . be proper to encourage, in its infant state, so useful a manufactory in [the] colony'.[3] In 1786 an attempt to further encourage the local cattle industry by imposing a tax on all imported cattle was introduced,[4] but shelved.[5] That same year, though, it was agreed that the breadfruit should be introduced into the island,[6] (though it did not arrive until 1793)[7]—the climax of a whole series of horticultural improvements: the establishment of Botanical Gardens (1775),[8] the appointment of a Gardens Supervisor (1777),[9] the introduction of the ackee (1778),[10] now one of the island's staple foods, the mango (1782),[11] cinnamon,[12] clove, nutmeg, and black pepper (1788).[13]

This, in outline, was the Jamaican response to the economic imbalance created by the American Revolution. As a response it was local—creole—in character. But how much did it achieve? How far to making the local economy self-sufficient and viable did it go? Here Long's warning about conservatism becomes relevant. All the activity, as outlined above, was considered and remained marginal to sugar production and the imperatives of sugar production; and sugar production not only tied Jamaica firmly to Britain and the dictates of mercantilist policy, but increasingly after 1783,

[1] *JAJ*, VIII,106 of 16 Nov. 1785.   [2] ibid. They were also cheaper.
[3] ibid., 134 of 8 Dec. 1785.   [4] ibid., 242 of 19 Dec. 1786.
[5] ibid., 246 of 21 Dec. 1786.   [6] ibid., 258 of 22 Dec. 1786.
[7] *JAJ*, IX, 247–8 of 27 Nov. 1793.
[8] ibid., VI, 597 of 30 Nov. 1775. An earlier Garden purchased from Huddesley Baker of St. Andrew in 1773, failed. (19 Geo. III, c. 17 of 23 Dec. 1778; *Laws*, Vol. II, pp. 236–7.)
[9] Dr. Thomas Clarke. See *JAJ*, VIII, 602 of 1 Dec. 1790; Cundall, *Historic Jamaica*, p. 26.
[10] Cundall, *Historic Jamaica*, p. 25.   [11] ibid., and Edwards, op. cit., Vol. I, p. 257.
[12] Edwards, op. cit., Vol. I, p. 257.   [13] Cundall, *Historic Jamaica*, pp. 25–6.

to the whims and needs of the British consumer. Rising British taxes
on West Indian sugar meant a rising cost of sugar, a consequential
fall in demand for it in Britain and a consideration there, of alternative sources of supply.[1] Nor, in Jamaica itself, were the planters
prepared to divert effort from sugar production into growing food
and providing supplies. Instead, they wanted to retain and have
reassumed the trade links with the American colonies. It might
have been possible, for instance, as Long had suggested, that local
woods be used for staves, etc., but as a petition from the parish of
St. George pointed out in 1784, rather reiteratively,

the staves of this country are infinitely heavier than the red oaks of America;
and there being only a certain given tare allowed at the custom-house at
London, all that the hogshead weighs above that, freight and a duty is
paid for, at the same rate as if it was actually sugar, . . . which additional
grievance to the sugar-planter is occasioned by the loss of their usual
supply of red oak staves from America; an evil they patiently submitted to,
during the war, in hopes it would only be . . . temporary . . . but are now
told by their factors in London, that they have no remedy; but that of
sending home to them for Hamburgh staves, which would make the remedy
as bad as the disease. . . .[2]

Petitions of a similar nature came in from Vere, St. David, St.
Dorothy, St. John, St. Thomas-in-the-Vale, St. Ann, St. Mary,
St. Andrew and St. Thomas-in-the-East.[3] Trade with Canada and
Nova Scotia—the proposed British alternative—was rejected as
unsuitable and too expensive. The planters wanted the restoration
of the old links, the proved intercourse. Deprived of American
trade, the Assembly informed His Majesty that

in all probability, such planters who have it in their power, will emigrate,
with their families and slaves, to happier countries; and those who cannot,
as honest men, take this step, of which the number is great, must remain
unhappy spectators of their properties mouldering into ruin, themselves
and families reduced to indigence and want. . . .[4]

Nor was the situation helped by bountiful Nature. Hurricanes hit
the island in 1780, 1781, 1784, 1785, and 1786—that of 1780 being
one of the most devastating in West Indian history.[5] This was

[1] *JAJ*, VIII, 661 of 5 March 1791.   [2] ibid., 59 of 14 Dec. 1784.
[3] ibid., 28–30 of 25 and 26 Nov.; 37–8 of 2 Dec.; 43–4 of 4 Dec. and 467 of 7 Dec.
1784.   [4] ibid., 41 of 4 Dec. 1784.
[5] Maxwell Hall, 'The Jamaica Hurricane of October 3, 1780', *Quarterly Journal of the
Royal Meteorological Society*, vol. xliii (1917), no. 182, pp. 221–5; *Notes of Hurricanes*,
p. 4.

followed by a severe drought which persisted until 1787. It was estimated that between 15,000[1] and 24,000 slaves[2] 'PERISHED OF FAMINE OR OF DISEASES CONTRACTED BY SCANTY AND UNWHOLESOME DIET'.[3] This, too, the planters attributed to the loss of American trade.[4] Of the projects for local diversification of the economy, in fact, only coffee, which enjoyed a golden period from about 1788 to about 1813,[5] and which is discussed in more detail below,[6] and the horticultural activities centring around the breadfruit came to anything. (These activities petered out when the Liguanea Gardens were sold in 1810.)[7] The sugar refining scheme wilted under prohibitive British taxes on colonially refined sugar.[8]

But perhaps the most important factor in the attempt to rehabilitate the Jamaican economy was the failure to encourage white settlement. An Act of 1776,[9] repealing 'part of an act entitled "An explanatory act for the further encouraging the settling the parish of Portland..."', described nicely what, in the eyes of the Assembly, would have been an ideal situation:

[That] the governor . . . shall grant to every person willing to become a settler . . . [in Portland], a quantity of land, not exceeding five hundred acres, in proportion to the number of negroes and white men they are willing and ready to put thereon, and perfect the settlement thereof, and also a lot of land in the town of Titchfield;[10] . . . with a condition or proviso . . . That every person, so patenting any parcel of land, shall be obliged to build and erect a house on such lot in the said town within nine months from the date of such his patent, and to maintain and repair the same; and to keep one white person actually residing thereon, at the least, for and during the term of three years . . .; and also to begin and carry on a settlement on his said land, in proportion to the number of acres in it. . . .[11]

In 1781, even more generous terms were offered;[12] but up to the end of the period of this study, the parish of Portland remained largely unsettled.[13]

[1] Edwards, op. cit., Vol. II, p. 515.
[2] Minute Book: The Honourable Committee of Correspondence, Minute of 9 March 1814.   [3] Edwards, op. cit., Vol. II, p. 515. See also *JAJ*, VIII, 429 of 12 Nov. 1788.
[4] Committee of Correspondence, as for n. 2, above.
[5] See *R.G.*, XXXIII (1811), no. 45, p. 10 and XXXV (1813), 11, 17.
[6] See pp. 147–8.   [7] 51 Geo. III, c. 30 of 1810.   [8] Ragatz, *Fall*, p. 16.
[9] 17 Geo. III, c. 26 of 21 Dec. 1776.   [10] See Map I.
[11] *Laws*, Vol. II, pp. 211–12. Some versions of this Act read 'six months' and 'four years' and specify 'white persons'.   [12] See 21 Geo. III, c. 22 of 12 Jan. 1781.
[13] As late as 1863, the parish of Portland had only 8,540 registered inhabitants. Port Royal, St. David, St. George, St. Dorothy, and St. John all had under 10,000. (*Handbook of Jamaica for 1883*, p. 65.)

In 1797, a different line was taken:

... that in case any master, owner, or possessor, of slaves and stock, shall, at his proper cost and charges, import into this island any family of white persons, of which one member, at least, shall be capable of serving, and become actually enrolled, in the militia of this island, within three months after their arrival ...; or shall settle any poor white family now living, or which may hereafter reside, in this island, by granting them a lease of land for a term of years, not less than twenty-one years, or for life, or any greater estate in such land, without any rent reserved (save and except the quit-rents to his majesty ...) in the proportion of thirty acres of land for the husband, fifteen acres for the wife, and seven acres for each child, with a house thereon in good habitable condition, and two acres thereof cleared and planted with provisions, for each member of such family; and shall pay or cause to be paid to them ... the sum of £15 *per* head *per annum* ..., shall be entitled to have each and every member of such family admitted and allowed to save deficiency for him or her [according to certain proportions as set out].[1]

This clause, proposed as an amendment, was ordered to be printed (100 copies) and circulated to members for consideration and discussion.[2] But as nothing appears to have come of it, perhaps it suffered the same fate as an earlier attempt to encourage family life by a tax on bachelors.[3]

In 1798 it was proposed that the 2,000 British troops to be sent to the island as a result of the war with France, should be enlisted on a long-term (five-year) basis, with the option of a further three to five years on payment of a bounty to them and a grant of land— 'small settlements in the interior parts.'[4] This long-term employment of white troops, the Assembly felt, allowing them time to become inured to the climate and offering the opportunity to set themselves up after service as small landed gentlemen in the island, was the only way to provide the country with a stable and permanent defence, and add 'to the population and militia of the island.'[5] It was a sensible and realistic plan, a justification of the argument that only the local people, in a colonial situation, really know what is best for them, given the chance to express their ideas. Enlistment, the House

---

[1] *JAJ*, X, 65–6 of 16 Dec. 1797.   [2] ibid., p. 65.
[3] 'from 21 years and upwards'. *JAJ*, VI, 661 of 27 Nov. 1776. The Kingston Vestry Minutes throw some light on the small number of families in the island with figures for 1788, showing the proportion of free white male to free white female as standing at 4:1. There were 4,793 free white males in Kingston in 1788, compared to 1,746 free white women. (Kingston Vestry Minutes for 28 Feb. 1788.)
[4] *JAJ*, X, 135 of 8 Nov. 1798.   [5] ibid., 279 of 7 March 1799.

also pointed out, should be staggered over the five-year period involved.[1] The local legislators were so pleased with this plan and so optimistic that it would succeed, that they asked the British Government

> That it [be] perfectly understood that the engagement, which pledges this country to provide for the whole expence of these two thousand men, will be completed *as soon as the whole of the non-commissioned officers and privates shall be provided with settlements in the interior. . . .*[2]

In the event, this plan was hardly given a chance to succeed. When the troops arrived, they found that not even the barrack accommodation promised them had been provided.[3] But there was still hope. The Committee of Public Works, inspecting the Army barracks at Stony Hill in 1800 reported:

> That twenty-five non-commissioned officers and fifty-six privates have . . . built huts for themselves, which your committee visited with great satisfaction, as an earnest of what their industry will produce when they come to be settled in the interior of the country. . . .[4]

Above all, the Assembly still hoped that the soldiers would settle as family men:

> . . . out of six hundred and fifty-one non-commissioned officers and privates [at Stony Hill], there are only thirty-nine who have wives with them in Jamaica; but your committee find that twenty-two non-commissioned officers and privates have wives in Europe, whom they are anxious to have here; the more so, as they now understand that they are to be settled in the interior of the country.[5]

But by 1802 the Assembly was refusing to pay for the subsistence of British troops in the island[6] and the plan fell through.

Jamaica, therefore, never solved the problem of attracting and gaining a sizeable body of small-settlers to help with its economy and defence. The American and French (St. Domingue) Revolutions did supply, however, a certain number of émigrés. Nine hundred adult (white) Americans and 378 children arrived at Port Royal in January 1783 after the British surrender at Charleston,[7] and in

---

[1] 'His Majesty's ministers must easily perceive the evil that would result . . . should the periods of enlistment expire at one and the same time. . . .' (*JAJ*, X, 284 of 12 March, 1799.) [2] *JAJ*, X, 284 of 12 March 1799, my italics.
[3] See the Report of the Inquiry conducted by Army Officers into the State of the Barracks: *JAJ*, X, 358–60 of 22 Nov. 1799.
[4] *JAJ*, X, 457 of 7 Feb. 1800.   [5] ibid.   [6] ibid., 671–3 of 21 June 1802.
[7] Ragatz, *Fall*, p. 194.

1798/9, some 1,200 'Frenchmen' were to come from St. Domingue.[1] The Rev. G. W. Bridges,[2] always anxious and willing to support the forces of tradition and 'civilization' in the creole/slave society of his adoption, said of the American immigrants generally:

... several of these emigrating royalists settled in this island, bringing with them fixed principles, and faithful slaves, who were much further advanced in the scale of civilised society than the plantation negroes, amongst whom they were here dispersed, and over whom their example soon spread its beneficial influence.[3]

In 1782, apart from the civilians, there were two groups of loyal American forces in Jamaica: the Duke of Cumberland's Regiment under the command of the Right Hon. Lord Charles Montagu, and Col. Odell's corps of Loyal American Rangers, which included the Black Carolina Corps.[4] These troops (the white ones) wanted to settle in Jamaica. Their behaviour, they claimed, entitled them 'to the name of good citizens as well as soldiers.'[5] But the Assembly was not at all happy about them. It told the Governor that no money was available 'for any more troops than are already provided for.'[6] Eventually, however, the white troops were compensated with grants of lands.[7] After considerable argument between the Military and the Jamaicans, the Black Carolinas were 'removed to [the] Leeward [Islands] command'.[8]

But the real problem was in dealing with the American refugee civilians. The British Government, like Bridges later, saw the arrival of these American loyalists as a welcome stiffening to Jamaican society. 'With proper encouragement', the Governor told the House, '[these refugees] must prove a great accession of strength to the

[1] Bridges, op. cit., Vol. I, p. 505.

[2] The Rev. G. W. Bridges, an Englishman, came to Jamaica in 1816. He was rector of Manchester (1817–23) and while there was also made a magistrate and assistant judge of the Court of Common Pleas (1820). He was rector of St. Ann (1823–37) after which he returned to England. Apart from his *Annals*, he published several other pro-slavery works, including *A Voice from Jamaica* (1823), *Dreams of Dulocracy* (1824), *Emancipation unmask'd . . .* (1835) and a *Statistical History of the Parish of Manchester . . .* (1824). (See Cundall, *Historic Jamaica*, pp. 299, 372; *R.G.*, XLII (1820), 37, 19; Ragatz, *Guide*, pp. 194, 599.)

[3] Bridges, op. cit., Vol. I, p. 507.

[4] Cundall, *Historic Jamaica*, pp. 226–7; *JAJ*, VII, 535 of 18 Dec. 1782. For details of the Black Carolinas and the British units in the Caribbean see A. B. Ellis, *The History of the First West India Regiment* (London, 1885); Caulfeild, op. cit., and G. Tylden, 'The West India Regiments, 1795–1927' in *Journal of the Society for Army Historical Research*, Vol. xi.

[5] *JAJ*, VII, 535 of 18 Dec. 1782.   [6] ibid., 559 of 20 Feb. 1783.

[7] Cundall, *Historic Jamaica*, op. cit., p. 226.   [8] A. B. Ellis, op. cit., p. 51.

country.'¹ The Assembly agreed. The Americans would 'meet with every favour and encouragement to which good policy, and their sufferings, give them so just a claim.'² Early the next year, a bill was drawn up³

to exempt from taxes, for a limited time, such of his majesty's subjects of North-America, as, from motives of loyalty, have been, or shall be obliged to relinquish or abandon their possessions in that country, and take refuge in this island, with intent to settle here.⁴

But how was this 'settlement' managed? What kind of land had been appropriated for these refugees? According to Patrick Grant, a surveyor, between 14 February 1783 and November 1784 28,040 acres of (morass) land had been divided into '183 separate parcels' for use by the Americans.⁵

Q. Are you acquainted with the lands and swamps laid out for the loyalists in St. Elizabeth, by Mr. Grant?
    . . .
Q. Are you of opinion that there is a quantity of dry land interspersed among the waters, sufficient to make 183 comfortable settlements . . . ?
    . . .
Q. Are you of opinion that any living creature, besides fish, frogs,⁶ Dutchmen, and amphibious animals, can exist in the district . . . ?
A. He thinks not.
Q. Are you of opinion that this spot . . . can be drained, so as to make it useful for the habitation of man . . . ?
A. He does not think it possible to drain it, but at a very great expence . . .⁷

In other words, having made their gesture of sympathy to the American refugees, Jamaicans were not really prepared to spend money for permanent hospitality on them. Although the Assembly was aware of the need for increased white settlement, it did not really have in mind the kind of settler the Americans represented—tough, go-

¹ *JAJ*, VII, 476 of 29 Oct. 1782.   ² ibid., 479 of 2 Nov. 1782.
³ 23 Geo. III, c. 23 of 1783.   ⁴ *JAJ*, VII, 544 of 11 Feb. 1783.
⁵ ibid., VIII, 22 of 13 Nov. 1784.
⁶ Was this an intentional pun? One *hopes* so, although there is no evidence in the *Journals* of this kind of levity. One of the first Americans to inspect the swamps with a view to settlement was a Mr. Robert Frogg. (*JAJ*, VIII, 148 of 16 Dec. 1785.)
⁷ George Murray, surveyor and member of the Assembly, before a House Investigating Committee: *JAJ*, VIII, 82–3 of 21 Dec. 1784.

ahead planters and merchants. Too many creole vested interests were involved. As Patrick Grant, the surveyor, said:

a few interested persons, who have properties in the neighbourhood of the morass, in the dry seasons of the year, take the benefit of the morass and turn their cattle therein, and are desirous of preventing the loyalists from settling there.[1]

A colleague of his, Grant went on, had been 'instructed to give every opposition' to the settlement of the area, 'and that he was determined so to do.'[2]

Equally unhappy about the American influx were the merchants who dominated the Kingston Vestry. In 1784, they complained about seventy American housekeepers (i.e. householders) 'who are refugees and who, by that circumstance, are exonerated of all parochial taxes, although many of them are apparently wealthy, and practise commerce to a considerable extent'.[3] In December 1786, there was another memorandum from the Kingston Vestry before the House. The population of Kingston was increasing, trade was declining because of restrictions on American trade and heavier British taxes on Jamaican exports, and there were more and more poor people in the town, which was a burden on the parish. The situation was being aggravated, the vestrymen continued, 'by the multitude of loyalists who have taken refuge' in Kingston 'under the encouragement and sanction' of the Act of 1783, which though acknowledged to be wise, was still 'severely felt' by the petitioners.[4] The trouble, really, was this: as far as the Jamaicans were concerned, the American refugees were either too rich and successful, or too poor and burdensome:

. . . some of the opulent and industrious practise commerce, and exercise their trades with peculiar advantages, occupying houses and stores in valuable situations, and other visible property, which were formerly productive of relief to the poor, but now wholly lost to the [vestry], as sources of parochial impost. . . .

[On the other hand, many of the loyalists are] extremely indigent and wholly supported at the expence of the parish, whilst some others of them are rivalling the petitioners in the little trade they have left, and, in their successes, are enjoying an immunity from all taxation.[5]

[1] *JAJ*, VIII, 148 of 16 Dec. 1785.   [2] ibid.
[3] ibid., 32 of 30 Nov. 1784.   [4] ibid., 202 of 1 Dec. 1786.   [5] ibid.

There was not much, though, that could be done about this situation short of repealing the 1783 Act. This was attempted in 1785 after a petition from the Kingston Vestry which complained that

> as there are upwards of eighty houses in the said town now occupied [by Americans] paying no taxes whatever; many of whom are very well able so to do, reaping all the benefits of commerce in common with the other inhabitants, whose burdens are increased by so much taxable property being possessed by these people. . . .[1]

the tax holiday should be rescinded. But although the House decided to bring in a Bill for the repeal of the Act, it was lost on the first reading.[2]

The opportunity offered, then, by the American Revolution, in its dislocation of traditional American/Caribbean economic connections, was not taken full advantage of by Jamaica. The island's sugar planters remained conservative; and how could they, under eighteenth-century West Indian conditions of instability and incalculability do, otherwise than stick to what they knew and continue to harvest their precarious, though often substantial, profits from that? Besides, as long as the island remained a colony within the mercantilist system, the British Government would, in any case, be unwilling to see a change of structure within its economy—an economy 'fixed', too, by a tremendous capital expenditure on slaves. Yet, there might have been greater efforts made to 'creolize' the economy, especially when it is realized that of all the British islands, Jamaica was the only one which maintained any significant diversification during the period of this study.[3] A little planned effort might have gone a long way. But in Jamaica there seemed to be little interest in soils, manures, terracing, etc.; nor was there a learned Agricultural Society concerned with studying and discussing local problems.[4]

In 1796, though, Bryan Higgins, a distinguished London physician

---

[1] *JAJ*, VIII, 138 of 13 Dec. 1785.

[2] ibid., 150 of 17 Dec. 1785. Complaints about wealthy Americans persist until 1787. (See *JAJ*, VIII, 502–3 of 27 Nov.) The French refugees from St. Domingue were even less welcome because of their connection with the republican French Revolution and the black slave revolt in that island.

[3] See Ragatz, *Fall*, p. 38.

[4] According to Long (Vol. I, p. 436), such a Society had been started in 1767, but after a few publications, had disappeared. See also, Stewart, *View*, p. 115, and [J. Stewart], *An Account of Jamaica and its Inhabitants* (London, 1808), pp. 113–14. The Cornwall Agricultural Society, started sometime around 1808, had disappeared by 1823.

and doctor, was engaged by the West India Interest of that city to go
to Jamaica to direct experimental work connected with the improvement of sugar and rum production, 'whereby the sugar may be made
whiter, purer, and more valuable, intrinsically, and the rum . . . more
grateful, salubrious, and valuable'.[1] Higgins arrived in May 1796,
but it was not until December that his presence was 'approved' by the
Assembly, it being agreed, then, that he was not, 'in any shape, to be
regarded as a needy adventurer, or idle projector'.[2] On the contrary,
there was 'reason to believe that the specific services proposed [by the
doctor] would, if effected, produce solid advantages to [the] island,
in the manufacture of the principal staples'.[3] Committees were
appointed in the three counties 'to attend doctor Higgins in his
operations', and he was offered £500 currency a quarter.[4] He
remained five years in the island, during which time he experimented
with and introduced, mainly on the Constant-Spring estate in
Liguanea,[5] several new ways of hanging coppers and clarifiers (used
in the process of sugar boiling and the distillation of spirits). He also
studied the relationship of the soil to the quality of cane produced in
it. These findings were published in his *Observations and advices for
the improvement of the manufacture of Muscovado Sugar and Rum.*[6]
Copies of this work were dutifully purchased by most planters; but
very few, apparently, adopted his methods, and experiments along
the lines recommended by him were discontinued after his departure.[7]
James[8] Stewart, who had lived for more than twenty years in Jamaica,
summed up the situation when he said:

Agriculture, though practically well understood in this island, is very little
cultivated as a science. . . . There was either a disinclination to the toil of
scientific study, or a want of talent, or both. . . . And yet, considering
the great variety and value of the products of this island, there are few

[1] *JAJ*, IX, 551 of 15 Nov. 1796.   [2] ibid., 584 of 29 Nov. 1796.   [3] ibid.
[4] ibid.   [5] ibid., X, 555 of 4 March; 576–7 of 13 March 1801.
[6] Published in four parts at St. Iago de la Vega: 1797, 1800, 1801, 1803, and in
The Columbian Magazine (Kingston, 1798), Vols. 3–5, *passim.*
[7] Ragatz, *Guide* p. 299. Higgins left the island, rather reluctantly, it appears, because
of age and ill health. (*JAJ*, X, 576 of 13 March 1801.)
[8] There is some confusion as to whether this should be John, as listed in Ragatz's
Guide (p. 234) or James. The title page of *A view of the past and present state . . . of
Jamaica* (1823), in fact, reads J. Stewart. *An account of Jamaica* (1808), is written by
'A Gentleman, Long Resident in the West Indies', but is clearly an earlier version of
View. A James Stewart (of Trelawny), almost certainly the member of Assembly for
Trelawny, 1794–1820, wrote *A Brief Account of the Present State of the Negroes in
Jamaica* (Bath, 1792), and from internal evidence would appear to be the author of the
other two books.

countries that present a more ample and interesting field for inquiry on this subject. . . . [1]

Because of its conservative attachment to the American connection, in other words, alternative sources of supply, within the island, were never seriously explored. The island continued to look 'overseas'. The result, after American Independence, was an increased Jamaican dependence on Britain. But Britain was geographically distant and the relationship with the 'Mother Country' was constitutionally and necessarily different from what it had been with the Americans. In this sense, the American Revolution caused a certain isolating of Jamaica from immediate contact with centres of lively culture—the journey to Britain was long[2] and was not undertaken lightly; when one left Jamaica for Britain it was often 'for good' or at least for an extended stay. Contact with the American seaboard had been easier,[3] visits more casual. It does not follow, though, that the break with America, caused by the Revolution, was the most important single factor in the decline of the Jamaican economy after 1774. Since 1763 the American/Caribbean balance had been tilting, more and more steeply, in favour of the Americans[4] and the developing French islands. The Jamaican/West Indian decline was also connected with the role played (perforce) by colonies within the European mercantilist and imperialist framework. Wars, gluts of plantation products on the world market, were as important as anything else in the overall decline, as well as the inability of a slave-based economy to react quickly to change, to reflect economic and social versatility.[5] What is significant, though, is that the Jamaicans, culturally and traditionally connected with the North American colonies, saw their decline (certainly until the second decade of the nineteenth century),[6]

[1] Stewart, *View*, pp. 115–16.
[2] The Nugents took sixty-six days (25 May–29 July 1881) to reach Jamaica. Mrs. Nugent left for England on 28 July 1885, reaching Weymouth in thirty-eight days. (See *LNJ*.) 'Monk' Lewis did his first Gravesend–Black River journey in fifty days (11 Nov. 1815–1 Jan. 1816), his second in eighty days (5 Nov. 1817– 24 Jan. 1818). His return to England in 1816 took sixty-two days sailing (1 April–1 June). (See M. G. Lewis, *Journal of a West India Proprietor, kept during a residence in the island of Jamaica* (London, 1834).) Lewis died at sea while returning to England in 1818.
[3] The run from Jamaica was six weeks at the most. (See R. Wright, op. cit., pp. 1–2.)
[4] See Elsa V. Goveia, *Slave Society in the British Leeward Islands at the End of the Eighteenth Century* (Yale University Press, 1965), pp. 1–22.
[5] This is the main argument of Genovese, op. cit., with regard to the American South. It holds good for Jamaica also.
[6] The Jamaican attitude to the United States changed with the war of 1812–14. See, for example, *R.G.*, XXXV (1812), 37, 17: 'We are happy to learn that a subscription has been set on foot in this city [Kingston] and in Spanish Town, for the relief of the inhabitants of the British North-American colonies, who have suffered great losses and

always devolving on the break with them. Twenty years after American Independence, with the islands faced with the possibility of competition from the East Indies, the Jamaican planters were still expressing themselves in this way:

. . . the expence of carrying on plantations in the West-India islands, augmented lately by many local causes, increased indirectly by every impost on the British manufacturer, and directly by duties levied on the exports for our own use and consumption, leave no room for fair competition with those who shall embark in the cultivation of sugar in the East-Indies, unfettered by these disadvantages, and with power to send their produce, direct to any market, in foreign vessels; . . . this expence has been greatly enhanced by the restrictions on our intercourse with the United States of North-America, not only without benefit to the mother-country, but to her manifest injury when viewed in all its consequences: That the articles supplied are of prime and indispensable necessity is admitted; that they cannot be furnished by the united kingdom of Great-Britain and Ireland, or any dependency of the empire, is evinced by twenty years experience; that they cannot be transported in British bottoms, at least during war, is equally evident; yet the planters of this island are restrained from paying for what they cannot forego, by bartering a small part of the commodities they possess, and are drained of specie wanted for common circulation, and of large quantities of bullion, which would centre in Great-Britain; whilst the cultivation of their staples is cramped, and the quantity of what would be sent to the mother-country, in more favourable circumstances, most probably diminished. . . .[1]

privations by the invasion of the Americans . . .', and 'We are as averse as even Administration could wish to giving encouragement to the Agriculture or Shipping of the United States, and will concur readily in any permanent measures to exclude them from the West Indies at a general peace' (Minutes of the Hon. Committee of Correspondence: 9 March 1814). But the economic dependence continued: 'but if it were believed that the bulk of the inhabitants of the Island were in danger of suffering for want of Subsistence We cannot think that Government would refuse to invite a temporary supply from every quarter, Nothing more is asked for, nothing further expected . . .' (Minutes, 9 March 1814).

[1] *JAJ*, XI, 156 of 15 Dec. 1803.

8

JAMAICA: COLONIAL OR CREOLE ?

Political

As things stood, then, Jamaica was unable, unlike the Americans, to claim and take independence in 1774. In one sense there was no desire for this—the island was apparently satisfied with its measure of legislative autonomy. On the other hand, certainly on the evidence of the state of its economy, the island could hardly have taken and certainly not have maintained—as a white-dominated society—a constitutionally independent stance in the 1770s, even if it had wanted to. Besides, Britain clearly reserved the right, as Edwards admitted, to intervene in the affairs of the island. The King was determined 'in no way to recede from His Right on this Important Point'.[1] This right of intervention and the willingness to use it was, needless to say, crucial to the constitutional development of the colony *qua* colony. As long as the Mother Country could *enforce* this right, the territory remained a colony; unless, that is, it was *granted* some other status—a development still beyond the horizons of this study. But this right of intervention, from the point of view of a *creole* society, as Jamaica also was, was to be even more important to the development of the island; because it meant that the 'Establishment' of the white élite, fostered and protected by the Assembly, could, if it was felt necessary, be interfered with from outside. Constitutional politics, in other words, could affect the social development of the island; in fact, was part of that social development in a very intimate way. This was why it was essential for the whites, through their Assembly, to prevent, restrict, or as a last line of defence, moderate, the British Government's right of intervention in its internal affairs. As long as colony and Mother Country saw eye to eye on the question of slavery— the vital heart of Jamaica—all might be well. But if there were external changes . . . ? It was therefore important to establish the island's right to complete internal legislative competence; and it is here that the paucity of creole constitutional theory, as expressed by people like Long and Bryan Edwards (see pp. 73–9, above),

[1] C.O. 138/44, Draft to Manchester, 19 March 1810.

becomes apparent. The Assembly's main arguments on this point were as follows:

That this house hath, as the representative of the people of this island, all the privileges that the house of commons hath as the representative of the people of Great-Britain; and that any instruction from the king and his ministry can neither abridge or annihilate the privileges of the representative body of the people of this island.[1]

That the inhabitants of this colony, unhappily situated at so remote a distance from Great-Britain, and thereby deprived, in many cases, of the means of laying their grievances at the foot of the throne, . . . have no defence against the abuse of power, and the tyranny and oppression of ill governors, but in the frequent meetings and freedom of their assemblies . . .[2]

The committee [reporting on the state of the island], in the course of [their] inquiries, have seen, with the deepest distress and anxiety of mind, that there are reasons to fear that the House of Commons may be induced, by men of great authority, to renew the doctrine of a right in the British parliament to legislate for and tax the colonies. The committee dare not venture to state to the house the case wherein it was proposed to legislate for the colonies; for, if made public here, it might have the most fatal consequences. . . . [But] the committee are of opinion, that it is absolutely necessary, on this occasion, to declare in the most solemn manner, that the colonists are entitled to the same rights and liberties, within the colonies, that the subjects born in England are within the realm; that they have the indefeasible right of giving and granting their own money, and of legislating for themselves; that it is the indispensable duty of the assembly of Jamaica to maintain, to the utmost of their power, in perfect consistence with the truest loyalty to the crown, the just privileges of the colonists; and that they will oppose, in every constitutional manner, any attempt to deprive them of such rights and privileges, though they most fervently pray that such an attempt may never be made. . . .[3]

The last quoted statement was an early response to House of Commons' activity over the Slave Trade. With the actual abolition of the Trade, the argument, now based firmly on the right of and to internal legislation, is repeated:

. . . the act contains clauses foreign to the avowed purposes of the law, which are calculated to establish measures of internal regulation, subversive of the local rights and legislative authority of this island.[4]

---

[1] *The Privileges of the Island of Jamaica Vindicated*, p. 101 (1810 ed.).
[2] *JAJ*, VI, 294 of 15 Nov. 1770.   [3] ibid., IX, 147–8 of 23 Nov. 1792.
[4] ibid., XI, 598 of 27 Oct. 1807.

[the act has] an internal and unjust operation by interfering with and being subversive of laws, which are to regulate the internal government of the colony, the enacting of which has long and uniformly been asserted by this island, and recognized by the parent state.[1]

The following year, the point about internal self-competence was again repeated:

your committee think themselves bound to warn the house and the country of the necessity of maintaining unimpaired the exclusive right of the colonial legislature to legislate internally for the island.[2]

But the fact that on this occasion the resolution was defeated by twenty votes to sixteen,[3] a majority of members being more keen on conciliation with Britain in the hope of gaining some compensation for the losses envisaged as a result of Abolition, indicates once again the limitations imposed by the Assembly on its own arguments— not to mention the bankruptcy and cultural myopia of the arguments. The real concern should not have been with legislative competence at all, but with social reform; not with 'states' rights, but with civil liberty; not with property, but with people. Perhaps the white creole Jamaicans subconsciously recognized the culturally reactionary nature of their claims and arguments, and this may, in part at least, account for their failure, once again, to push their constitutional arguments to their logical conclusions. In any case, this failure (inability, or lack of desire) indicated the existence, within the Jamaican mind, of a dichotomy between argument and sanction, wish and reality, colonial and creole. The choice before the Assembly was, in fact, a simple one. The material terms in which they stated their predicament made it easy for them. In the face of the British attack on what was, in effect, the whole structure of white-dominated society, should the Assembly hope for concessions through appeasement, or should it stand on the unilateral assumptions of its own internal legislative competence?

The answer, as it turned out, was appeasement. This is illustrated by the defeat of the committee resolutions of 1808 on the question of Abolition. In 1809, the British Government 'encroached' again; this time by reviving its right to suspend Jamaican legislation—in

---

[1] *JAJ*, XI, 598 of 27 Oct. 1807.   [2] ibid., XII, 27 of 16 Nov. 1808.
[3] ibid., 28 of 16 Nov. 1808.

this instance, a Consolidated Slave Act of that year.[1] The Assembly's first reaction was prompt and firm. 'The present momentous question', it declared, '[involves] nothing less than [our] existence'.[2] A long report, reviewing Jamaica's constitutional position from the beginning of civil government in the colony, was presented to the House and the Act of 1728 was referred to as 'the Magna Charta of Jamaica'.[3] When, the next month, the royal disallowance of local religious legislation came before the House, the old no-taxation-without-proper-satisfaction argument was resurrected:

That if the board of trade or his majesty's ministers can prescribe or limit the objects of internal policy on which this house shall or shall not legislate, no vestige remains of the free constitution established by our ancestors, and it will not be expedient to exercise the invidious power of imposing taxes, if we are to be divested of the functions which render that power supportable to our constituents. . . .[4]

The strength of feeling in the House on this occasion may be gauged from the heavy defeat—28 votes to 4—of a conciliatory resolution, 'trusting to [his majesty's] gracious interposition for redress'.[5] To save the situation, the Governor dissolved the Assembly.[6] When the House reassembled, however, there was no more violent language and the legislators, in fact, were co-operative.[7] But the dichotomous symptoms were there: anger; cooling off. By the time the Parliamentary attack on slavery itself developed, the Assembly had run out of ammunition. Continuing economic decline, increasing fear of slave revolts, especially after the Maroon War at home and the Haitian Republic next door, had taken their toll. Nevertheless, the committee report of 20 December 1815,[8] on the question of possible Emancipation, produced, for the first time, some new arguments. Bryan Edwards' view of the British Parliament as *primus inter pares*,[9] was rejected:

Your committee must assert, that as British subjects we are, as our birthright, entitled to British freedom: We shall resort to no abstract principles or fine drawn theories of equality;[10] but we do claim the same privileges, immunities, and franchises within this island, which are enjoyed by our

---

[1] C.O. 138/44, Draft to Manchester, 19 March 1810.
[2] *JAJ*, XII, 172 of 16 Nov. 1809.   [3] ibid., 169 of 16 Nov. 1809.
[4] ibid., 241 of 13 Dec. 1809.   [5] ibid.
[6] ibid., 242 of 14 Dec. 1809.   [7] See ibid., 253 of 9 Nov. 1810.
[8] *JAJ*, XII, 781–825 of 20 Dec. 1815.   [9] See p. 76, above.
[10] Cf. Edwards, op. cit., Vol. II, pp. 436–7.

fellow-subjects within the body of the realm, particularly the right to consent by our representatives to the laws, by which our property, liberty, and lives are to be regulated, abridged, and disposed of.[1]

This was a claim to full legislative autonomy. These were 'inherent rights' . . . 'which his majesty could not confer or take away',[2] nor could they be transferred 'to the House of Commons of Great Britain'.[3] But up to this point, despite the forceful language, it could be argued, as A. L. Murray does, that here was nothing more than the old arguments, 'ineffective except in the courtroom'.[4] But embedded in the rhetoric was a significant *creole* point:

> In the exercise of these powers and privileges, it became the duty of the general assembly of Jamaica to enact such laws as were called for *by the new and peculiar circumstances of their constituents. . . .*[5]

Here, at last, perhaps, was a peg from which to hang a whole new series of constitutional arguments, the beginning of a (white) creole political philosophy in defence of their peculiar institution. But such a theory never developed. Instead, the planters settled for compensation.

So much then for the notion of Jamaican legislative competence. It takes the story back to the Assembly Resolution of 1774 and the American reply. Claims made by colonial 'Britons' against Britain, in British constitutional terms, would remain meaningless unless the claimants, like the Americans, were willing to break with the whole structure of British colonial culture, and if, in its place, they had evolved, or were evolving, an alternative cultural tradition, based upon the realities of their situation and environment. Anything less than this created a dichotomy of thought, action, and attitude which finally weakened the possibility of action.

Jamaica found itself in this position in 1774 when the island's relationship to a wider (American) cultural complex was in question. In 1807, when it was a question, as they saw it, of defending their own internal structure, the (white) Jamaicans' ambivalence of attitude and their cultural dependence on the Mother Country again defeated them. At every step, it seems, the creatively 'creole' elements of the society were being rendered ineffective by the more reactionary 'colonial'.

[1] *JAJ*, XII, 782.   [2] ibid.   [3] ibid., p. 783.
[4] A. L. Murray, op. cit., p. 38.   [5] *JAJ*, XII, 782–3, my italics.

What this study is concerned with, therefore, is determining how far this colonial status (and the mentality that went with it) affected the process of creolization. Was the failure of political action, the failure to make the economy viable, in locally autonomous terms, a result of colonialism, a failure of the creole society, or (as was more likely) a combination of the two? If the latter, how much of one and how much of the other? After all, all Jamaican creoles were colonials, but it does not follow that all colonials in Jamaica were creolized. The assumption is, of course, that the social process of creolization, since it created, by its very nature (as will be discussed later), a way of life essentially different from the metropolitan model, would tend to make for the creation of attitudes which in their evolution would alter the very nature of colonial dependence. This was certainly the case with the Americans. But why was it not so also with the Jamaicans? Can 'creole' in this study's terms, be identified with stability, with change, or with both? If with both, did this result in some kind of creative friction, or merely in the kind of ambivalence we have already examined as a cultural attribute of 'colonial'? We must now, therefore, examine Jamaica's infrastructure. What was society like within the island; how did it interrelate; what were the views and attitudes both to themselves and to each other, of the various sections of the society? Was the dichotomy already described related only to Jamaica's 'external' (colonial) relationship with the Mother Country; or was the external dichotomy a reflection of a deeper cleavage—of attitude and action—within the society itself?

PART THREE
THE SOCIETY

9

handwritten: Demographic

WHITES

> The inhabitants of this colony consist of four classes; whites, free people
> of colour having special privileges granted by private acts, free people of
> colour not possessing such privileges, and slaves . . . all these classes, when
> employed in the public service, have, as far as it has been practicable, been
> kept separate.[1]

THIS, from the Assembly itself, was an 'official' admission of basic
social divisions, though one could hardly have expected it to have
been otherwise. Slave societies, though to varying degrees,[2] are
naturally divisive; and Jamaican society, built up by Englishmen still
retaining, in the seventeenth century, many of their medieval feudal
instincts, conformed to pattern. What this study is concerned with,
however, is determining how far these divisions contributed to,
or militated against, the process of creolization within the society.
It will be convenient, in the first place, to treat each class separately,
as suggested in the Assembly statement.

The white population of the island increased from about 18,000 in
1786[3] to approximately 30,000 in 1807.[4] It appears to have remained at
about this figure for the rest of our period, even perhaps declining.[5]

'White' in this context means people from Europe or of patently
unmixed European descent—in Jamaica, mainly English, Scots,
and Irish. There was also a small but wealthy settlement of Portuguese
Jews, especially in Kingston. These Jews had first arrived during the
Spanish occupation of the island and by 1730 numbered about
900.[6] They were legally, politically, and, to some extent, socially dis-
criminated against because of their religion,[7] but counted as white.

[1] *JAJ*, IX, 647 of 28 July 1797.

[2] See Smith, *Plural Society*, pp. 116–61: 'Slavery and Emancipation in Two Societies';
David Brion Davis, *The Problem of Slavery in Western Culture* (Cornell University
Press, 1966).   [3] Long, *History*, Vol. I, p. 377.

[4] Renny, op. cit., p. 127.   [5] Until 1831.

[6] Add. MS. 12419, f. 74; Jacob A. P. M. Andrade, *A Record of the Jews in Jamaica
from the English Conquest to the Present Time* (Kingston, 1941), pp. 15–26.

[7] See C. H. Wesley, 'The Emancipation of the Free Coloured Population in the
British Empire', *Journal of Negro History*, Vol. XIX (1934), no. 2, p. 139. By 1844, the
white population had fallen to 15,776. The 1861 Census recorded it as 13,819.

The Royal Administrators

The first convenient sub-division[1] of whites in Jamaica was that of the Royal administrators: the Governor with his entourage at Spanish Town, the Admiral in charge of the Jamaica Station at Port Royal, the officer commanding the armed forces in Kingston. This group represented Jamaican dependence on British power and was (technically at any rate) symbolic of British culture. The King's Birthday celebrations and the visits of Prince William Henry in 1783 and 1788[2] underlined this. No creoles ever held the posts of Admiral or General during the period of this study. Between 1726 and 1767, four creoles acted as Governor of the colony, but after 1770 none did, except George Cuthbert briefly in 1832 and 1834.[3]

The contribution of this British administrative élite to the development of Jamaican society was minimal; though the Army, through its desire to use armed black troops to help in the defence of the island,[4] and the rank and file's virile need of (black) female company near them in their camps,[5] made a not insignificant contribution to social integration. Because of their 'outsider' attitudes, at least two senior Army officers ran foul of the Establishment.[6] Maj.-General Walpole fought and won the campaign against the Maroons (1795/6) with great skill but without the bloodthirstiness urged on him by the Governor and many in the Assembly. He was clearly unhappy about the use of Cuban bloodhounds against his adversaries, sympathized with the Maroons' hope for new cultivable lands (one of the causes of the war was growing Maroon dissatisfaction with their allotments)[7] and entered into a gentleman's agreement with them against their possible transportation.[8] His refusal of a Sword of Honour from the

[1] Professor Goveia points out in her study of the Leewards (*Slave Society*, pp. 205, 213, 314–15), that there was, despite the stratification, an unconscious sense of solidarity among all classes of whites in slave society. They were all, because of their colour, members of the élite. This was less markedly the case in Jamaica—a much larger single territory: 30,000 whites compared with the Leeward Islands' less than 9,000 at the end of the eighteenth century. (See *Slave Society*, p. 203.)

[2] See *JAJ*, VII, 550, 551, of 13, 14 Feb. 1783; VIII, 455, of 25 Nov. 1788.

[3] See Metcalf, op. cit.; Cundall, *Historic Jamaica*, pp. 51, 55, 139, 167, 217, 249.

[4] 'A deliberate arming of bondsmen to defend their masters marks the opening of a new epoch in interracial relations in the Caribbean.' (Ragatz, *Fall*, p. 33.) British policy ref. black troops is discussed in Caulfeild, op. cit., pp. 28–37; A. B. Ellis, op. cit., pp. 3–4, 83–4; John Hunter, *Observations on the diseases of the army in Jamaica and the best means of preserving the health of Europeans in that climate* (London, 1788), pp. 269–73; Add. MS. 12411: 'General Dalling's Plan for the Security and Defense of Jamaica' (1781); King's MS. 214; J. W. Fortescue, *A History of the British Army*, Vol. IV (London, 1915), pp. 542, 543.   [5] See *RG*, XXXV, 47, 17 of 20 Nov. 1813.

[6] To this may be added the case (1818) of Sir Home Popham, the naval Commander-in-Chief, who entertained the black Ambassadors from Haiti. (See pp. 35–6, above.)   [7] See pp. 248–50, below.   [8] See *JAJ*, IX, 437, 457–68 of 2, 23 March 1796.

Assembly (it broke or rather ignored his agreement with the
Maroons) was symbolic of his alienation from creole standards.[1]
Even the liberal Bryan Edwards mentions the incident in his *History*
with 'great concern'.[2] In 1808, Maj.-General Carmichael refused to
co-operate with the Assembly in a witch-hunt against mutineers in
the black 2nd West India Regiment.[3] This led to yet another constitutional dispute and Carmichael's removal.[4] But Walpole and
Carmichael were exceptions. They could not have survived within the
System. The society could not have tolerated the kind of dissenter
that they were. It could not have done so and remained the same.
Protest, disagreement (and this is still very much so today) had to be
censored out of the body politic. The result was that the island was
bereft of the sort of active social criticism which it feared and from
which, paradoxically, it might have benefited.

The Admirals, for their part, seemed mainly concerned with
looking out to sea—from Port Royal and Port Henderson—as they
had to be until the end of the Napoleonic wars. But they were
enormously popular—no doubt because of their dramatic roles as
protectors of the island. It was a long and distinguished tradition:
Morgan, Benbow, Vernon, Ogle, Rodney, Parker, Nelson. By far the
most popular was Rodney who, by defeating de Grasse at the Battle
of the Saints on 12 April 1782, is supposed, as every Jamaican school-
boy learns, to have saved the island. 12 April became a day of
national celebration and Rodney something of a cult figure. The
House of Assembly voted £1,000 to have 'the most eminent artist in
England . . . prepare an elegant marble statue . . ., with a handsome
pedestal to the same'.[5] This, executed in the Mother Country by
John Bacon,[6] arrived in the guise of a Roman general in January
1790—all twenty tons of it.[7] After a 19 to 19 division in the Assembly

[1] On the other hand, how does one interpret this: Walpole to Balcarres, Old Maroon
Town, 24 Dec. 1795: 'If I might give you an opinion, it should be that they [the
Maroons] should be settled near Spanish-Town, or some other of the large towns in the
low lands: The access to spirits will soon decrease their numbers, and destroy that
hardy constitution which is nourished by an healthy mountainous situation' (*JAJ*, IX,
437 of 2 March 1796). Walpole perhaps respected the Maroons as fighters but despised
them as blacks. This love/hate relationship, which is a feature of the colonial situation,
has been discussed by O. Mannoni in *Psychologie de la Colonisation* (Paris, 1950),
trans. *Prospero and Caliban* (New York, 1956), and is revealed, from the colonial's
point of view, in Franz Fanon, *Peau Noire, Masques Blancs* (Paris, 1952). For details of
Walpole's ambivalence, see A. E. Furness, 'The Maroon War of 1795', *JHR*, Vol. V
(1965), no. 2, pp. 40–9.   [2] Edwards, op. cit., Vol. I, p. 576.
[3] See *JAJ*, XII, 36 of 17 Nov.; 56 of 29 Nov. 1808; 60 of 25 April 1809.
[4] C.O. 138/44/2, 12, 16: Castlereagh to Manchester, 20 Feb. 1809.
[5] *JAJ*, VII, 559 of 20 Feb. 1783.   [6] English sculptor, 1740–99.
[7] *Daily Advertiser*, 5 Jan. 1790.

as to whether it should be placed in Kingston or Spanish Town, it was finally decided by the casting vote of the Speaker that it should go to Spanish Town.[1]

Nor was this all. There were fireworks displays depicting the Battle of the Saints, with 'the report of the guns heard, the destruction of some of the enemy's vessels, the agitation of the seas, [and] in short, every circumstance attending that celebrated action'.[2] Meanwhile, an American theatre group was presenting in Kingston a 'Miscellaneous Entertainment' (August 1790) which was to conclude

with a Transparent likeness of the Gallant Lord Rodney, descending from the Clouds, supported by Victory and Britannia, and accompanied by the Brave Admirals and Officers who supported him on the Memorable 12th of April 1782 . . .[3]

By 1817, however, the Rodney enthusiasm seems to have cooled, though 'A Lover of my Country' could still write to the Editor of the *Royal Gazette*:

Sir,

In all ages and countries a particular reverence and regard has always been paid to the Monuments of departed Heroes and benefactors to their country.

On a late visit to Spanish-Town it was with pain that I observed the decayed appearance and mutilated state of the Triumphal Dome and Statue [of Rodney].

I am not sufficiently acquainted with the items of public expenditure to be able to say if there is any provision made by the House of Assembly towards defraying the expence of keeping this ornament to the country in repair. . . .[4]

But the Memorial had already cost the island over £30,000,[5] and there was no response to the patriot.

Of the Governors, Dalling (1772–4, 1777–81), Campbell (1781–4), both advocated the use of black troops to help with the island's defence.[6] Sir Eyre Coote (1806–8) directed his demonic energies (he went mad in 1815)[7] into reforming and streamlining the colony's

---

[1] *Daily Advertiser*, 27 March 1790. Actually there were two motions: (1) that the statue should stand in Kingston, defeated by the Speaker's vote; (2) that it should be placed in Spanish Town, passed 17 to 21.
[2] Quoted in R. Wright, op. cit., p. 293, from *R.G.*   [3] ibid., pp. 287–8.
[4] *R.G.*, XXXIX (1817), 41, 23.   [5] £30,918. (Cundall, *Historic Jamaica*, p. 121.)
[6] See n. 1, p. 26, and n. 4, p. 106, above.   [7] See Wright, *LNJ*, p. 293.

administration and especially its militia,[1] a job started by his predecessor Lt.-General George Nugent (1801–6), whose contribution to our understanding of creole society is his 'Sketch of the Characters of certain Individuals in the Island of Jamaica';[2] and his wife's more celebrated *Journal*.[3]

But like the Admirals, the Governors (mainly military men), did not contribute very much of lasting cultural value to the society.[4] This was perhaps because (like the rest of the administrative élite), they were never resident in the island (and could not expect to be, under the conditions of colonial service) for any real length of time, so that they never really came to know the island intimately.[5] The Duke of Manchester had eleven years in Jamaica, but in two spells (1808–11; 1813–21). Alured Clarke (1784–90) and the Earl of Balcarres (1795–1801) had six years each, and so had Dalling, in two instalments (1772–4, 1777–81). But the average gubernatorial appointment within our period lasted for about three and a half years —not quite long enough to settle down. Of the six-year stayers, only Dalling, with his 'Plan for the Security and Defense of Jamaica',[6] appears to have contributed anything beyond the routine of duty. In fact, if Maria Nugent's comments on Lord Balcarres are anything to go by, it is doubtful whether the average Jamaican Governor *had* anything to contribute:

I wish Lord B. would wash his hands, and use a nail-brush, for the black edges of his nails really make me sick. He has, besides, an extraordinary propensity to dip his fingers into every dish. Yesterday he absolutely helped himself to some fricassée with his dirty finger and thumb.[7]

I must not omit to mention . . . an extraordinary pet of Lord B's, which makes its appearance every day in the dining-room. It is a little black pig, that goes grunting about to every one for a tit-bit. . . .[8]

[1] See p. 30, above.   [2] See p. 64, n. 9, above.

[3] *A Journal of a voyage to, and residence in, the island of Jamaica, from 1801 to 1805, and of subsequent events in England from 1805 to 1811*, by Maria, Lady Nugent, first appeared, privately printed in London in 1839, five years after her death. (See Ragatz *Guide*, p. 231; Wright, *LNJ*, p. ix.)

[4] H. P. Jacob's rehabilitatory effort on 'The Earl of Effingham' (*Sunday Gleaner*, 3, 10, 17 May 1970) does not alter this assessment. Effingham arrived in 1790 and was dead by 1791.

[5] F. W. N. Bayley, *Four years' residence in the West Indies, during the years 1826–1829* (London, 1833), p. 236. For conditions of and in the Colonial Service, see, among others, H. R. G. Greaves, *The Civil Service in the Changing State* (London, 1947); Henry L. Hall, *The Colonial Office; A History* (London, 1937); Charles Jeffries, *The Colonial Empire and its Civil Service* (Cambridge University Press, 1938).

[6] Loc. cit., n. 4, p. 106, above.   [7] *LNJ* (Wright), 31 July 1801, p. 11.

[8] ibid., p. 12.

We drove to Lord B's Penn. Never was there such a scene of dirt and discomfort. Lord B. was in a sad fright, thinking that we should expect a breakfast. However, upon his Secretary's whispering me, that there was one whole tea-cup and saucer and a half, we declared our intention of returning to the King's House. . . .[1]

It must be borne in mind that Balcarres was enjoying (?) the status of bachelor,[2] that he was the Nugents' immediate predecessor in office and had a title to boot—something which Maria Nugent devoutly wished for her husband.[3] Mrs. Nugent was also quite prissy:

Left alone part of the morning, with Major Gould, who entertained me with an account of Lord B.s *domestic* conduct, and his menage here altogether. Never was there a more profligate and disgusting scene, and I really think he must have been more than half mad. I was glad to get to my own room, and employ my time more profitably than in listening to such horrid details.[4]

Middle class Mrs. Francis Brodbelt, on the other hand (her husband was Physician to the Spanish Town Jail), no doubt impressed with his aura of peerage, 'could scarcely keep [her] Eyes from him'[5] when she first dined in his company. 'There is', she informed her daughter, 'a very great resemblance in him to the King!'[6] But this was when the Earl had just arrived; before, that is, in Maria Nugent's estimation, he had gone 'creole'.

In like manner, the Duke of Manchester, 'one of the finest and handsomest men of his time',[7] became a 'good type of the traditional Jamaica grandee—a hard drinker, a hard rider, a reckless gambler and a begetter of numerous brown-skinned illegitimate progeny'.[8] Sixteen years after he left Jamaica, 'five of his bastards were at school in Kingston'.[9]

The Nugents, by contrast, were very much a family group, and were active socially: breakfasts, dinners and dances, entertaining Government officials, Army and Naval officers, a few merchants, the

---

[1] *LNJ* (Wright), 10 Aug. 1801, p.15.
[2] Alexander, 6th Earl of Balcarres, was married in 1780 and had four sons and two daughters; but the Countess Elizabeth, his wife, did not go out with him to the Caribbean. See *DNB*; A. W. Lindsay, *Lives of the Lindsays; or a memoir of the houses of Crawford and Balcarres*, 3 vols. (London, 1849, 1858), Vol. II, pp. 345, 358, 367.
[3] Wright, *LNJ*, pp. 256, 260, 269, and especially pp. 188, n. 1, 266, n. 1.
[4] ibid., 7 Nov. 1801, p. 38.   [5] *Letters to Jane*, 4 May 1795; p. 105.
[6] ibid., 17 May 1795; p. 110   [7] Quoted in *DNB*, Vol. XIII, p. 722.
[8] Sydney H. Olivier, *Jamaica the Blessed Island* (London, 1936), pp. 91–2.
[9] ibid., p. 92, note 1.

legislators of Spanish Town; and their wives making royal 'pro-
gresses' over the countryside. What is noticeable, however, is that
they do not appear to have had any 'friends of the family'. Visitors
came to the General on business. He had little time, according to
his wife's account, to relax. She herself had one or two female
acquaintances from among the Spanish Town wives, but nothing
intimate. There were three, possibly four, relatives in the island—
Lt. Noble of the 67th Regiment, a distant relative of Mrs. Nugent;
her own brother, Downes Skinner, who arrived in Jamaica in 1802
to take up appointment as Captain of Fort George, Port Antonio
and Collector of Customs, Savanna-la-Mar (he died in December
of the same year); John Nugent, a relative of the Governor; and
Nelly Nugent, housekeeper of Simon Taylor's Golden Grove estate
in St. Thomas-in-the-East, who claimed she was.[1] The only one of
these relatives the Nugents saw much of, however, was John, who
was a teacher at Wolmer's Free School.[2] Unlike Balcarres and Manchester, the Nugents were clearly upholders of British culture and
tradition. They were critical of creole departures from the 'established' norm then, though they did nothing themselves to upset the
local *status quo*.

The Merchants

The merchants (as distinct from shopkeepers and retailers),[3]
were among the richest people in Jamaica, the very wealthiest
deserting the island in 'West Indian style' for Britain where they
formed the core of the powerful West India Interest. The Jamaica
Coffee House, the first headquarters of this body in London, was
functioning as early as 1674,[4] forming a coalition with other West
Indian and American mercantile interests, but keeping separate
from the planters (who had their own Planters' Club),[5] until 1781
when, as another adjustment to the American Revolution, the
Society of West India Planters and Merchants was formed.[6]

This coalition reflected changes in the West Indian economy.
In the pre-sugar days, planters had found it possible to conduct their
own trade with overseas markets. From the 1740s, with sugar exports

[1] *LNJ* (Wright), p. 68.

[2] ibid., pp. 209, 212, 309.   [3] Long, *History*, Vol. I, pp. 575, 577.

[4] Lillian Penson, *The Colonial Agents of the British West Indies* (London, 1924),
p. 181.   [5] ibid., pp. 189–91.

[6] ibid., pp. 205–7. Meetings of merchants and planters had actually started in 1775;
see West India Committee Minutes, West India Merchants, Vol. 1, April 1769–April
1779 (W.I. Committee Library, London), Minutes of 3 Jan. 1775.

and the white population rising, and a corresponding rise in the import of slaves and plantation equipment, planters found it increasingly difficult to carry out and finance these operations themselves, and came to rely more and more on the credit and operational facilities provided by the merchants.[1] These facilities were the *raison d'être* of, if not the only reason for, absenteeism. It was simply more convenient for those merchants (and planters) who were doing well to move to London—the governmental and banking seat of the Empire. Here it was possible, through influence in and on Parliament, to secure favourable trade legislation for West Indian sugar (the Sugar Act of 1764, for example),[2] and to raise loans from British banks; though, as Pares has suggested, the major part of the financing of the West Indian trade and economy probably came from West Indians themselves.[3] With the American Revolution, however, the economic balance of the British New World was permanently disturbed, and there was a sharp decline in West Indian prosperity. This, plus the naturally growing personal relationships between merchants and planters, and the need for a common front,[4] resulted in the coalition already referred to.

In the islands this decline, except in Jamaica and Barbados, affected the mercantile community. There was a steady fall in numbers.[5] Some merchants emigrated to Britain. Others remained in the islands, but turned their talents to attorneyship and commissioneering for estates.[6] They were ceasing to be specialists. Merchants and factors in the Mother Country—and local big-time planters—were beginning to carry the risks of the trade.

In Jamaica, however, this kind of break-down was not taking place, mainly because the merchants of Kingston were still closely connected with the Spanish trade[7] and the North American commercial complex. In the years 1769–71, according to Edward Long,[8] some 700 ships, representing 75,000 tons of shipping, cleared Jamaican ports; and 725 ships were cleared—460 from Kingston alone—in 1774.[9] The inward/outward figures for ships through Jamaican ports for the year beginning September 1783 were as follows:

[1] Pares, *Merchants and Planters*, pp. 47–9.
[2] See Ragatz, *Fall*, p. 53.
[3] Pares, *Merchants and Planters*, p. 50.
[4] Lillian Penson, 'The London West India Interest in the Eighteenth Century', *English Historical Review*, Vol. XXXVI (1921), no. 142, pp. 378–81.
[5] Pares, *Merchants and Planters*, p. 33.   [6] ibid., p. 78, n. 57.   [7] ibid., p. 33.
[8] Add. MS. 12412, f. 31.   [9] ibid.

Kingston	687
Montego Bay	187
Savanna-la-Mar	55
Port Antonio	38
Lucea	20
Total	987 ships[1]

In 1787 (Bryan Edwards' figures),[2] 474 ships, representing some 86,000 tons of shipping, cleared Jamaican ports. In 1803, according to Dallas,[3] Jamaica owned 400 ships valued at £1,500,000 and employing 9,000 seamen. The total tonnage of vessels trading to and around the island between September 1807 and September 1808 was well over 170,000 tons.[4] By 1815, this figure was almost 188,000 tons.[5] 121,444 hogsheads of sugar, 52,409 puncheons of rum, 6,529 bags of pimento and 29,528,273 lb. of coffee, among other products, were exported in 1807–8.[6] In 1814–15, 118,767 hogsheads of sugar, 52,996 puncheons of rum, 27,386 bags of pimento and 27,362,742 lb. of coffee, among other products, were exported.[7] No matter what the 'groans of Jamaica' about economic decline and commercial neglect, therefore, it is quite clear that the island's trade continued to prosper in the post-1774 period. The real question was: who made and kept the profits?

Kingston was very much a merchants' town. 126 merchants appeared on the Kingston Vestry Jurors' list in 1784,[8] 167 in 1805,[9] and 135 in 1819.[10] The 135 merchants in the 1819 list made up almost half of the entire rota. There were 141 other occupations listed; but even here, seventeen of these had mercantile connections.[11] 298 of the 420 occupations listed in 1805 were mercantile. As early as 1745, the Kingston Vestry had ordered

That the Pew Commonly known by the Name of the Merchants Pew and the next Adjoining Pew to the Northward be kept Separate for the use of the Merchants and Officers and that no Other Person be admitted to Sett there.[12]

[1] *P.P.*, Vol. LXVIIa. *Accounts and Papers* (9) 1785; nos. 113–19.
[2] Edwards, op cit , Vol. I, p. 285.   [3] Dallas, op. cit., Vol. I, p. cv.
[4] *JAJ*, XII, 42 of 22 Nov. 1808.   [5] ibid., 716 of 14 Nov. 1815.
[6] ibid., 42 of 22 Nov. 1808.   [7] ibid., 716 of 14 Nov. 1815.
[8] Kingston Vestry Proceedings, 1781–8; Minute for 6 Jan. 1784.
[9] K.C.C. Minutes 1795–1805; 24 April 1805.
[10] ibid., 1815–20; 22 March 1819.
[11] Vendue master, ship-carpenter, shipwright, sailmaker, etc.
[12] Kingston Vestry Minutes, 1744–9; 19 July 1745.

The merchants also had their own Association, situated in the Kingston Coffee House, and in 1794 'appropriated the large hall upstairs and room adjoining, where a REGULAR Marine Intelligence [was] kept, and a very excellent Spy Glass for [the use of merchants and ships' captains]'.[1] There was also the Old South-Sea House near the Customs, on Port Royal Street,[2] and in 1817, the more elaborate Kingston Commercial Rooms were opened at the corner of Harbour and Orange Streets:[3]

The Subscribers[4] are induced, from the very liberal encouragement they have met with from several Commercial Members of this Community . . . to establish in this City, by subscription, a place for the greater dispatch and convenience of transacting Mercantile Affairs, and whatever is connected with them. . . .

The Rooms will be fitted up with every requisite convenience, viz. Pens, Ink, Paper, and a Drawer, with lock and key. . . .[5]

Relevant publications, including all local newspapers, the *London Times*, Liverpool, Bristol, Glasgow, Irish and American journals, Current Prices, Army and Navy Gazettes, and 'all Shipping Lists that can be procured', were to be available.

The Rooms will be provided with every Map and Chart relative to the trade of this island; Publications on Insurance and all other Works that may be deemed useful to the Establishment.

Books will be kept regularly for the following purposes, viz.
  1. To announce all Arrivals.
  2. To announce all Departures.
  3. All Public Sales of Produce, Provisions, etc.
  4. The Arrival and Departure of Packets, and Vessels of War carrying Letter Bags.[6]

Arrival and departure of packets were naturally of considerable concern to the merchants, and the records are full of requests from Kingston merchants to the Governor to delay sailing of these ships.[7] Maria Nugent, just arrived in Jamaica and anxious to get letters sent home, noted in her diary for 8 August 1801, for instance:

---

[1] *R.G.*, XVI (1794), 5, 20.   [2] See n. 4, p. 269, below.
[3] ibid., XXXIX (1819), 20, 24.   [4] Absalom and Thompson.
[5] *R.G.*, XXXIX, 20, 24.   [6] ibid.
[7] See, for example, *LNJ* (Wright), p. 203, 21 May 1804.

Begin letters to England at 6 o'clock, but find that, at the request of the merchants, General N. had ordered the packet to be delayed, till the 17th....[1]

The Rooms were to be open from seven in the morning until four in the afternoon, except when a packet arrived, when they would remain open until seven in the evening. Refreshments would be supplied 'at the Tavern prices'.[2] The subscriptions proposed for these facilities were as follows:

A subscriber	£10. 13s. 4d. per annum
A Firm with 2 partners	£16. 0s. 0d. „ „
A Firm with 3 partners	£21. 6s. 8d. „ „
A Subscriber outside Kingston	£ 5. 6s. 8d. „ „
Transients in Kingston more than 3 months	£ 5. 6s. 8d. „ „[3]

These Rooms, it was pointed out, would not only be of benefit to merchants:

The Landed Proprietor and the Planting Attorney will also derive considerable advantage from such an Establishment, during their occasional visits in Kingston; at one view they would see what Vessels are for Sale, Freight or Charter, and thereby regulate the shipment of their Produce, should Shipping be scarce in the Ports to which their Properties may be contiguous; and to those, whose professional pursuits cannot strictly be termed Mercantile, though all, more or less, are connected with Commerce in this island, it is presumed select Company, and a multiplicity of English Publications, embracing every political party, will prove a sufficient inducement for their patronage and support.[4]

The resident Jamaican merchants, according to Stewart,[5] were either 'dry-good merchants, provision merchants, [or] lumber merchants, though one man sometimes deals in all those articles'. In the nineteenth century, there was a tendency for these merchants to combine in firms; Donaldson and Forbes; Atkinson and Hanbury; Hibbert, Taylor and Markland; Willis and Waterhouse.[6] The most famous of all Kingston's merchants was perhaps John Wolmer,

[1] *LNJ* (Wright), p. 14.   [2] *R.G.*, XXXIX, 20, 24.   [3] ibid., XL (1818), 36, 13.
[4] ibid., XXXIX, 20, 24.   [5] Stewart, *View*, p. 199.
[6] These names are mentioned in Wright's edition of *LNJ*.

though technically he was not a merchant at all, but a goldsmith or moneylender, who died in Kingston in June 1729. His fame derives from the fact that he was one of the few of this class who left anything for posterity—£2,360 in his will for the foundation of a Free School.[1] The school (Wolmer's) was established in 1736,[2] but did not get going properly until 1774–6 when the Assembly stepped in with a £2,000 grant and plans for the reorganization of its trustees.[3] Wolmer himself seems to have been forgotten until 1787 when an anonymous correspondent to *The Essayist* for 6 January 1787, pointed out that it was 'extraordinary that one of the best benefactors of this town, the late Mr. Wolmer, should lie undistinguished, and without a stone to mark the place of his interment',[4] and suggested raising funds for a monument by means of a Concert of Music. This suggestion was taken up by the Vestry[5] and a monument was erected three years later.[6]

In the mid-eighteenth century, most of Kingston's wealthiest merchants appeared still to live in the heart of the city. It was here that John Bull built Bull House on North Street, Jasper Hall built Jasper Hall on High Holborn Street, and Thomas Hibbert, of one of the wealthiest of Jamaican mercantile families, built Hibbert House (now used by Government) on Duke Street.[7] But even by this time, the wealthy Kingston merchants were moving out of town and becoming landowners. John Bull had a coffee estate at Sheldon in the Blue mountains and Thomas Hibbert owned Agualta Vale in St. Mary.[8] Those who did not become landowners on a big scale also moved out of the hot town into the higher suburbs (as they still do today), where it is cooler, quieter and healthier:

The merchants, from their pens in the country, or the higher part of the town, go down to their stores or shops in kittereens (single horse chairs) about seven in the morning. Having breakfasted, they generally get a second breakfast at eleven, and dine at four or five, when all business is

[1] See John Wolmer's Will dated 15 July 1729 in Wolmer's Old Minute Book, 1736–1826, 2 vols; Institute of Jamaica, MS. 97; Proceedings, 24 June, 1736.

[2] 9 Geo. II, c. 6 of 15 May 1736.

[3] *JAJ*, VI, 520 of 4 Nov. 1774; 661 of 27 Nov. 1776.   [4] Add. MS. 12414, f. 42.

[5] Kingston Vestry Proceedings, 1781–8; Minutes nos. 299, 300 of 22 Oct. 1788.

[6] 'The monument in memory of Mr. Wolmer, who founded our free-school . . . arrived in one of the ships, and will shortly be put up in the South aisle [of the Kingston Parish Church]' (*Daily Advertiser*, 8 June 1790).

[7] See Cundall, *Historic Jamaica*, pp. 179, 180; T. A. L. Concannon, 'Houses of Jamaica', *Jamaica Journal* (Kingston, 1967), Vol. I, no. 1, p. 37. The house was used as Military H.Q. from 1814 to 1872.

[8] Cundall, *Historic Jamaica*, pp. 179–81, 265–6.

ended for the day, . . . and if no public diversion is going forward, retire to bed at eight or nine, after having supped upon tea.[1]

The merchants as a group (though wealth could and did create exceptions)[2] were looked down upon by 'gentlemen'[3]—in keeping with the still existing British prejudice against 'commerce'. Those who were invited to King's House during General Nugent's regime, for instance, usually came there on business, especially to discuss St. Domingue affairs.[4] But the merchants had their own social organization in Kingston, in addition to the Commercial Rooms, based on Ranelagh House, Vauxhall, Harmony-Hall, the Kingston Theatre, and their 'assemblies' at Half-way Tree.[5] With their contacts, occupations, and concerns, they contributed significantly not only to the running and efficiency of the Kingston Vestry—the development of the Kingston police and fire service,[6] for instance, owed a great deal to them and their natural desire to safeguard their inflammable warehouses and their property—but also to the cosmopolitan nature of the town.

The Planters

While we were at breakfast, I saw a column of negroes at some distance coming towards the house, with things upon their heads, which I could not well distinguish; but the master of the penn taking his spy-glass (with one of which most balconies and piazzas are furnished) he told me that it was only a *trunk-fleet*. . . .

A dozen or more negroes, men and women, are dispatched in the morning, long before day, their heads charged with band-boxes, bundles and heavy trunks, containing the most considerable part of the wardrobe of the visitors:—under this load the poor creatures trudge twelve, fifteen, and

[1] Peter Marsden, *An account of the island of Jamaica, with reflections on the treatment, occupation, and provisions of the slaves. To which is added a description of the animal and vegetable productions of the island* (Newcastle, 1788), pp. 6–7. See also Stewart, *View*, p. 28 and E. Montule, *A voyage to North America, and the West Indies, in 1817* (London 1821), p. 44.
[2] See, for instance, Long, *History*, Vol. I, p. 575.
[3] See the comments on William Bolt's status, on p. 49, above.
[4] See *LNJ* (Wright), pp. 15, 33, 298, 301 and entries for 10 Jan., 29 April, 24 June 1802; 28 May, 19 July, 27 Aug., 1803; 27 Jan. 1804, among others.
[5] See Gardner, op. cit., p. 168; *The Jamaica Mercury*, Vol. I, no. 12 for July 1779. Ranelagh House, Vauxhall, and Harmony-Hall were taverns.
[6] Serious efforts to establish an efficient police (or Town Guard) and fire service began in 1781. See *JAJ* VII, 402 of 7 Nov. 1781; Kingston Vestry Proceedings 1781–8, Minutes for 11, 18 Oct., 24 Dec. 1781; 7, 14 Jan. 1782. The Town Guard was legally recognized by 25 Geo. III, c. 14 of 1784.

sometimes twenty, and five-and-twenty miles, to prepare the toilet for their mistresses, whose arrival they are in time to announce. . . .

An hour after the arrival of the *trunk-fleet*, I perceived something like another fleet, which I soon found to be the lady herself and her family proceeding to Prospect Penn in journey array.

It was a procession of several horses in a strait line one after the other: it is a rule that the gentlemen should ride before the ladies; so first came young Chewquid, the heir, next Bob Chewquid, then Mrs. Chewquid; after her rode her eldest daughter, then two more daughters on horseback; then three negro boys on mules, then stout negro men a-foot carrying young children.—The ladies wore white and green hats, under which white handkerchiefs were pinned round their faces, meeting over their noses— this is the usual precaution for preventing the sun from blistering the skin. —The gentlemen wore white handkerchiefs, under the fore part of their hats, and rode in long trowsers, made of Russia sheeting, the little children were also pinned up, and all the company had umbrellas.

Most of the horses were American, and of course what are here called pacers: they have a shuffling gait, that gives a very slight and easy motion to the rider—but the eldest son rode a fine stallion, bred in the country, that no English jockey would have been ashamed to mount.

At last the procession arrives before the piazza, all puffing for breath and half stiffled with their handkerchiefs. After the first how-dees were over, the ladies were shewn to their bedchambers, and the gentlemen took chairs in the piazza.

The manner in which the last seat themselves, would strike you on the first view as ludicrous.—They draw their chairs to the railing of the piazza, and fixing themselves nearly upon the end of their back bones, they elevate their feet into the air upon the highest rail above their heads. . . .

The gentlemen were no sooner seated, than one of them gave a shrill whistle, by the help of his fingers, and immediately a negro boy came running in: as soon as he made his appearance, the gentleman, who had whistled, cried (rather laconically, I thought) 'Fire!'—upon which the boy went out as fast as he had entered, and returned in a minute with a bit of wood burning at one end. By this time the tobacco pouches were all opened, segars prepared, and each with his scissars had clipped the ends: the negro then presented the fire all round, the tobacco was lighted, and I walked off.[1]

This passage has been quoted at length because it describes, with a novelist's sense of timing, a moment in the life of the plantocracy,

[1] Anon., *A Short Journey in the West Indies* 2 vols. (London, 1790), Vol. II, pp. 26– 34. Stewart, *View*, pp. 212–13, also describes a progress and visitation.

and because, also, three of the main characteristics of planter life in Jamaica: its medieval quality (the procession and the fact that it was a 'progress' from one estate or home to another, for an extended stay of hospitality); its American 'frontier' quality (the easy loping horses, the feet up on the verandah) and its 'creoleness' (the presence of the slaves and their place in the pattern), come out very clearly.

There was certainly much that was medievally feudal about the life and social attitudes of the planters,[1] and at least one West Indian historian[2] has suggested the need for a re-examination of West Indian slave societies in the light of what we know about medieval times. As Bridges put it:

The negro slave-code, which, until lately, governed the labouring classes of Jamaica, was originally copied from that of Barbadoes; and the legislature of that colony resorted, for a precedent, to the ancient villeinage laws, then scarcely extinct on British ground. They copied thence the principles which ruled, and the severity which characterised, the feudal system under the Saxon government.[3]

The Statute Against Vagabonds (with branding, iron collar, use of the word 'slave', etc.) was passed in 1553, 'not seventy years', Bridges points out, 'prior to the settlement of Barbadoes',[4] and as late as 1574, British slaves were being 'manumised, under a commission from Queen Elizabeth';[5] therefore

The early settlers in the West Indies might be expected to carry with them, as they did, those ancient prejudices in favour of the villeinage system, which coincided with their ideas of the active government, and necessary restraint, of wild Africans....[6]

But Bridges' point is only a constitutional/legal one. Medieval feudal attitudes went much deeper than this. In the first place, as in medieval Europe, here were the wide-open spaces of an agrarian economy. The units of this economy were the estates or plantations, with their self-contained and dependent labour forces, and their

---

[1] See Long, *History*, Vol. II, p. 485; Thomas Southey, *Chronological History of the West Indies*, 3 vols. (London, 1827), Vol. II, pp. 197–8.
[2] Douglas Hall, 'Slaves and Slavery in the British West Indies', *Social and Economic Studies*, Vol. xi (1962), no. 4, p. 312, n. 22.
[3] Bridges, op. cit., Vol. I, p. 507.   [4] ibid.   [5] ibid., p. 508.
[6] ibid. See also Viola F. Barnes, 'Land Tenure in English Colonial Charters of the Seventeenth Century' in *Essays in Colonial History Presented to Charles McLean Andrews by his Students* (New Haven, 1931), pp. 4–40; Pitman, *The Development of the British West Indies*, p. 102; James Stephen, *The Slavery of the British West India Colonies delineated*, 2 vols. (London, 1824, 1830), Vol. I, pp. 18–22.

strictly observed ranks of precedence and control. When in 1785, for instance, the Assembly proposed in a Bill that the Chief Justice and a committee of judges, rather than the Crown (Governor) should be responsible for appointing judges, the freeholders of St. Catherine protested that this would 'reduce the people . . . to be dependent on, at most, their equals; *the meanest of vassalage*'.[1] In 1815, as intelligent a person as the Hon. James Stewart, Assembly representative for Trelawny, in giving evidence against Chief Justice Lewis (Lewis was being arraigned for corruption), said that he knew Lewis had 'some sinister designs of his own'

because I saw in the panel for the July Cornwall assize . . . the names of several gentlemen placed low in such panel, and instead of having their description of esquire, . . . they are designated as planters, and . . . I saw the names of several gentlemen placed at the head of the panel entitled esquires, . . . who . . . were men of inferior conditions in life.[2]

As in medieval Europe, although of course there were exceptions, there was little possibility of mobility within the various ranks of society, and those persons and social groups, such as merchants and free people of colour, for instance, who were not directly a part of the planting structure, had difficulty in finding a 'place'.[3] (The merchants, as in late medieval Europe,[4] got around this because of their wealth and their intermarriage into the planting society, or by becoming planters themselves.)

The plantations

For the beginning of our period, Edward Long[5] provides the following record of Jamaican plantations:

Sugar estates	680
Cotton works	110
Pimento walks	100
Ginger plantations	30
Breeding pens	500

[1] *JAJ*, VIII, 114 of 25 Nov. 1785, my italics.
[2] ibid., XII, 771 of 14 Dec. 1815.
[3] Many novels of the period, especially *Montgomery* (see n. 7, p. 124, below), illustrate this. See also Jacobs, 'Elletson', pp. 57, 67; but cf. pp. 137–8, below.
[4] See, for example, V. F. Rörig, *The Medieval Town* (1932, trans. London, 1967). For a discussion of feudalism as a world system, see *Feudalism in History*, ed. R. Coulborn (Princeton University Press, 1956). A full examination of the relationship between slavery and serfdom is in Davis, op. cit., esp. Ch. 2. One planter, the Barbadian Joshua Steele, actually made plans to convert his slave plantations to a copyhold manorial system. See William Dickson, *Mitigation of Slavery. Part I, Letters and Papers of the late Hon. J. Steele . . .* (London, 1814), pp. 95–6. Steele lived in Barbados, 1773–90.
[5] *History*, Vol. I, pp. 495–6.

Polinks[1] and provision places	600
Coffee plantations	150
Indigo works	8

In 1820[2] there were 5,349 properties in Jamaica. Of these, 1,189 contained over 100 slaves or head of stock or both. Those, however, that could be considered really big estates (over 500 slaves or 650 head of stock)[3] were:

		slaves	stock	owner
Worthy Park	(St. John)	514		Sir Rose Price
Bushy Park	(St. Dorothy)	673		William Mitchell
Rio Magno	(St. Thomas-in-the-Vale)		661	Sir Alex Grant
Parnassus	(Clarendon)	585		James Dawkins
Rhymesbury			673	Lord Dudley and Ward
Moreland	(Vere)	612		James Mitchell
Martin's Hill	(Manchester)		697	Earl of Balcarres
Grier Park	(St. Ann)		720	Hamilton Brown
Dornock	(St. Ann)		662	R. H. Gordon
Greenfield	(St. Ann)		766	Thomas Hynes
Soho	(St. Ann)		818	John Moncrieffe estate
Golden Grove	(St. Thomas-in-the-East)	717		Chaloner Archdeckne
Holland	(St. Thomas-in-the-East)	600		G. W. Taylor
Lyssons	(St. Thomas-in-the-East)	516		Simon Taylor (heirs of)
Albion	(St. David)	512		Robert Hibbert
Gibraltar	(St. George)	598		Wentworth Bayly
Fort George Pen	(St. George)		1,006	John Ellis
Spring Garden	(St. George)	616		Grossett, Schaw and Son
Hampstead	(St. Elizabeth)		678	Thomas Smith
Goshen	(St. Elizabeth)		1,590	F. G. Smyth
Carysfort	(Westmoreland)		851	Ann C. Storer
Paradise	(Westmoreland)		745	John Wedderburn
Old Hope	(Westmoreland)		933	Martin Williams
Ramble Pen	(Hanover)		661	Wm. Hudson (heirs of)
Burnt-Ground	(Hanover)		731	James Haughton James
Knockalva	(Hanover)		1,031	Neil Malcolm
Green Park	(Trelawny)	551		Edward Atherton
Orange Valley	(Trelawny)	646		H. N. Jarrett[4]

[1] Sometimes spelt 'polinck', a small farm or provision plantation usually in the mountains. See p. 133, below. For history and derivation of the word, see F. G. Cassidy and R. B. Le Page, *Dictionary of Jamaican English* (Cambridge University Press, 1967).

[2] These figures are derived from *The Jamaica Almanack for 1821*, 'Givings-In for the March Quarter, 1820', pp. 3–134.

[3] Bryan Edwards (op. cit., Vol. II, p.295) considered a 250-slave estate the lowest optimum. U. B. Phillips, *American Negro Slavery. A survey of the supply, employment, and control of negro labour as determined by the plantation regime* (New York, 1918), p. 50, calculated that 180 slaves would have been found on an average Jamaican sugar estate.   [4] *The Jamaica Almanack for 1821*.

The parishes with the highest concentration of estates were:

	+ 100 slaves/stock	+ 300 slaves/stock
St. Ann	121	30
Trelawny	98	24
St. Thomas-in-the-East	98	18
St. Mary	97	31
St. James	90	20
Hanover	88	22
St. Elizabeth	83	31
Westmoreland	74	32[1]

Of the 5,349 properties, 562 were probably specialized sugar estates,[2] 155 pens, and 452 complex estates, containing both sugar estates and pens. There were perhaps about 771 coffee or other estates.[3] The other 3,409 properties had few slaves and/or stock. When it is realized that this cultivated area (1,740,000 acres in 1789)[4] represented only one-quarter of the island's 4 million acres, of which 3¾ million was cultivable,[5] the full force of the *frontier* nature of Jamaican society becomes apparent. 80,000 acres in St. Elizabeth and 100,000 acres in St. James were 'waste' in 1768.[6] The situation had not appreciably improved by the end of the period. The total acreage under cultivation in 1820 was just over 2,222,000.[7]

Houses

This frontier situation partly accounts for the style of living reported by many contemporary observers. Edward Long in the 1770s said that

It is but of late, that the planters have paid much attention to elegance in their habitations: their general rule was, to build what they called a *make-shift*; so that it was not unusual to see a plantation adorned with a very expensive set of works, of brick or stone, well-executed; and the owner residing in a miserable, thatched hovel, hastily put together with wattles and plaister, damp, unwholesome, and infested with every species of vermin. [Few] of the inhabitants are curious in the decorations of their apartments: the halls are seldom adorned with any thing better than a large

[1] *The Jamaica Almanack for 1821.*

[2] This figure is arrived at by counting properties of 100 or more slaves as sugar estates. Judging from Long's 1774 figure, above, this total does not seem unreasonable. The Long, Fuller, Chisholme Evidence before the House of Commons Investigation Committee gave the number of sugar estates in 1789 as 1,060. See P.P., Vol. LXXXIV *Accounts and Papers*, 1789 (29), Part III, A. No. 51 and Add. MS 18273 f. 94. But smaller, non-specialist estates were probably included in its estimate.

[3] There were 686 coffee estates in 1800. See *JAJ*, XII, 796 of 20 Dec. 1815.

[4] Edwards, op. cit., Vol. I, p. 248.

[5] See ibid., pp. 247–8.   [6] Long, *History*, Vol. II, p. 191, 213.

[7] *Jamaica Almanack for 1821*, p. 136.

pier-glass or two, a few prints, or maps: the greatest expence is bestowed upon the arch of the principal hall, which is generally of mahogany....[1]

Bryan Edwards said:

There are some peculiarities in the habits of life of the White Inhabitants, which cannot fail to catch the eye of an European newly arrived; one of which is the contrast between the general plenty and magnificence of their tables (at least in Jamaica) and the meanness of their houses and apartments; it being no uncommon thing to find, at the country habitations of the planters, a splendid side-board loaded with plate, and the choicest wines, a table covered with the finest damask, and a dinner of perhaps sixteen or twenty covers; and all this in a hovel not superior to an English barn.[2]

Maria Nugent, on her visits to country estates during her residence in Jamaica, made similar comments, though she found exceptions: 'King' Mitchell's house at Bushy Park, for instance.[3] Monk Lewis, when he arrived from England to visit his Cornwall estate in 1816 found his house 'frightful to look at, but very clean and comfortable on the inside'.[4] In fact, his impressions were, on the whole, more favourable than Governor Nugent's wife's:

The houses here are generally built and arranged according to one and the same model. My own is of wood, partly raised upon pillars; it consists of a single floor: a long gallery, called a piazza, terminated at each end by a square room, runs the whole length of the house. On each side of the piazza is a range of bed-rooms, and the porticoes of the two fronts form two more rooms, with balustrades, and flights of steps descending to the lawn. The whole house is virandoed with shifting Venetian blinds to admit air; except that one of the end rooms has sash-windows on account of the rains, which, when they arrive, are so heavy, and shift with the wind so suddenly from one side to the other, that all the blinds are obliged to be kept closed....[5]

[1] Long, *History*, Vol. II, p. 22.

[2] Edwards, op. cit., Vol. II, pp. 9–10, footnote. Turner's vision of the American frontier and its effect on the process of *mestizo* creolization may be recalled here. 'The frontier is the line of most rapid and effective Americanization. The wilderness masters the colonist. It finds him a European in dress, industries, tools, modes of travel and thought. It takes him from the railroad car and puts him in the birch canoe. It strips off the garments of civilization and arrays him in the hunting shirt and the moccasin. It puts him in the log cabin of the Cherokee and Iroquois and runs an Indian palisade around him. . . . He must accept the conditions which [the frontier] furnishes, or perish . . . the outcome, is not the old Europe . . . here is a new product that is American.' (Frederick Jackson Turner, *The Frontier in American History* (New York, 1920), 1962 ed., pp. 3–4.)

[3] *LNJ* (Wright), pp. 55–6.   [4] Lewis, op. cit., (1929 ed.), p. 62.

[5] ibid., pp. 77–8.

Edward Long, despite his general strictures, was quite enthusiastic about the Pinnocks' house in Half-way Tree:

[The] chief ornament [of Half-way Tree] is a very magnificent house, erected here a few years since by Mr. Pinnock; which may vie, in the elegance of design, and excellence of workmanship, with many of the best country-seats in England. The stone used about this fabrick was brought from the Hope river-course: it is far more beautiful than the Portland [stone], and of a closer and finer grain. The mahogany-work and ornaments within have been justly admired for their singular beauty, being, as I am informed, selected with great expence.[1]

The Palmers' house (Rose Hall) near Montego Bay,[2] built about 1760,[3] Sir Charles Price's house, "The Decoy", in St. Mary,[4] Chief Justice Fearon's house and library,[5] the Great House of Rhimesbury estate,[6] Citron Vale,[7] Marlborough House in the Manchester Hills near Spur Tree, Cardiff Hall in St. Ann, Arcadia, Bryan Castle and Good Hope in Trelawny[8] were also, among many others, excellent examples of local building standards and are evidence of a creole style, a Jamaican 'vernacular'[9] and indicate that considerable effort was being made, the popular traditional view to the contrary, to 'civilize the wilderness'.

A flight of stone steps, with iron balustrades, on which run beautiful twining or creeping plants. . . , leads the visitor up to the front door, and he is immediately ushered into a spacious hall, of the form of a cross, extending the whole length and breadth of the house. This large hall is characteristic of all Jamaica houses; it forms the principal sitting room; and, from its shape, admits the cooling breeze to sweep through it, whenever there is a breath of air. The two square areas formed by one side of the cross are filled by bedrooms; but with these exceptions the whole of the

---

[1] Long, *History*, Vol. II, p. 124.
[2] Gardner, op. cit., p. 166.
[3] Concannon, op. cit., p. 36.
[4] ibid.; Gardner, op. cit., p. 166; Frank Cundall, *A Brief History of the Parish Church of St. Andrew in Jamaica* (Kingston, 1931), p. 66.
[5] Gardner, op. cit., p. 166.
[6] Marsden, op. cit., pp. 16–17.
[7] For a description of this in 1812, see Anon., *Montgomery: or the West Indian Adventurer*, 3 vols. (Kingston, 1812–13), Vol. II, pp. 217–19. *Montgomery* is one of the first novels written about domestic West Indian life and appears to have been the first published in the West Indies. See my 'Creative Literature of the British West Indies during the period of Slavery', in *Savacou*, Vol. I, no. 1 (1970), pp. 46–73.
[8] Concannon, op. cit., p. 36; *LNJ* (Wright), p. 83.
[9] See A. W. Acworth, *Buildings of Architectural or Historic Interest in the British West Indies* (H.M.S.O., London, 1951), p. 5.

sides and ends of the hall are either occupied by windows, or open, and
furnished with jalousies, a broad sort of transverse Venetian blinds, which
freely admit the air while they exclude the glare of light. . . .

BELLEVUE, KINGSTON JAMAICA. (c.1765)

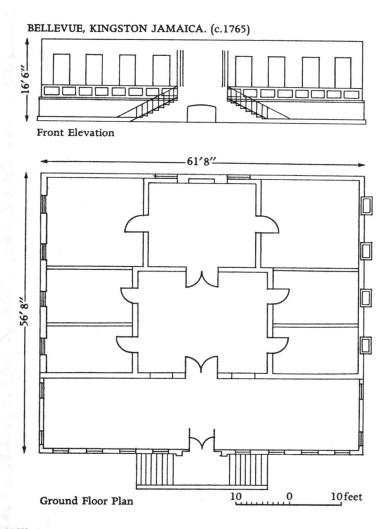

Front Elevation

Ground Floor Plan

A. W. ACWORTH, *Treasure in the Caribbean: A First Study of Georgian Buildings in
the West Indies* (London, 1949), p. 10.

This large and cool apartment is furnished with sofas, ottomans, tables, chairs, etc., not differing from ours; but there is no fire places, nor any carpet. Instead of the latter the floor is made of the most beautiful of the native woods, in the selection of which much taste is displayed, as also in the arrangement, so that the various colours of the wood may harmonise or contrast well with each other. Mahogany, green-heart, bread nut, and blood-heart are among the trees whose timber is employed for floors. Great hardness is an indispensable requisite in the wood used, and capability of receiving a high polish, which is given and maintained with great labour. Scarcely anything surprises an European more than to tread on floors as beautifully polished as the finest tables of our drawing rooms . . .[1]

Gosse was at Phoenix Park (Westmoreland) during the 1840s, but his description holds good for many of the better-kept Great Houses of our period. It was here, in these material arrangements; in the shaping of the physical environment—Great Houses, aqueducts, bridges, roads, churches, public buildings and monuments, burial grounds, forts, and schools—that the white contribution to the island's cultural development lay. A listing of some of these structures, built during our period, will help indicate the scope and nature of this achievement.[2]

[1] Phillip H. Gosse, *A Naturalist's Sojourn in Jamaica* [1844–5] (London, 1851), pp. 156–7. For a modern novelist's description, see John Hearne, *Stranger at the Gate* (London, 1956), pp. 12–13, 15.

[2] Sources used in the list that follows include, Cundall, *Historic Jamaica*; Philip Wright and Paul F. White, *Exploring Jamaica* . . . (London, 1969); R. Bickell, *The West Indies as they are: or a real picture of slaving: but more particularly as it exists in the island of Jamaica* (London, 1825); Concannon, op. cit.; Inez Knibb Sibley, *The Baptists in Jamaica* (Kingston, 1965); Thomas Dancer, *Some Observations respecting the Botanical Garden* (Kingston, 1804); Alan Eyre, *The Botanic Gardens of Jamaica* (London, 1966); *Laws*; *JAJ*; *R.G.*; *Jamaica Mercury*; Kingston Vestry Minutes; *LNJ*; J. H. Buchner, *The Moravians in Jamaica. History of the Mission of the United Brethren's Church to the Negroes in the Island of Jamaica from the year 1754 to 1854* (London, 1854); Andrade, op. cit.; Francis X. Delany, *A History of the Catholic Church in Jamaica, BWI, 1494 to 1929* (New York, 1930). Ray Fremmer, *Daily Gleaner*, 12, 26 May 1970, R. Wright, op. cit.

For an inventory of the island's public and historical structures, see 'List of Public Monuments in Jamaica', issued by the Jamaica Information Service, *Sunday Gleaner*, 19 June 1966, p. 20.

For descriptions of Jamaican and West Indian architecture, see A. W. Acworth, *Treasure in the Caribbean: A First Study of Georgian Buildings in the British West Indies* (London, 1949), pp. 5–12; 'Georgian Architecture in the British West Indies', *The Connoiseur Yearbook* (London, 1953), pp. 39–44; A. J. May, 'The Architecture of the West Indies', *West India Committee Circular* (1933), 48 (899) 16 March, 105–7; 48 (900) 30 March, 125–6; 48 (901) 13 April, 147–8; 48 (902) 27 April, 167–8; 48 (904) 25 May, 207–8; 48 (905) 8 June, 227–9; Frank Cundall, 'Architecture in Jamaica', stencil (W.I. Ref. Lib. Institute of Jamaica) [Kingston, n.d.].

Forts

Port Henderson	(Healthshire[1] Hills, St. Cath.)	c. 1770
Rodney's Look-out	(Healthshire Hills, St. Cath.)	1771–4
Keith Hall Barracks	(St. Catherine)	c. 1774–7
St. Ann's Bay Fort	(St. Ann)	1777
Fort Dundas	(Rio Bueno, Trelawny)	1778
Fort Columbus	(Dry Harbour, St. Ann)	c. 1783
Fort Haldane	(Oracabessa/Port Maria, St. Ann)	c. 1789
Up Park Camp Barracks	(Kingston/St. Andrew)	c. 1793
Stony Hill Barracks	(St. Catherine)	1799
Windsor Fort	(St. Ann)	1803
Fort Balcarres, Falmouth	(Trelawny)	1803[2]
Fort Nugent	(St. Andrew)	1805

Public Buildings and Monuments

King's House, Spanish Town		1762
Rodney Memorial		1796
Montego Bay Town Hall	(2nd building)	1804
Falmouth Barracks		1804, 1812
Falmouth Court House		1814–17
St. Mary Court House	(Port Maria)	1820

Aqueducts

Wag Water to Constant Spring (built by Daniel Moore)	1770

Bridges

Rio Cobre (wood)	1775–6
Rio Bueno	1782–9
Rio Cobre (stone)	1794
Milk River to Bath	1797–8
Spanish Town (iron)	1801[3]
Black River	1810
Yallahs River	1812–13
Montego River	1813–14
Rio Magno	1816

Burial Grounds

Jewish Cemetery, Montego Bay		c. 1770
Jewish Cemetery (Elletson Road)		1787
Wesleyan Methodist Cemetery	(Windward/Elletson Road)	1791
Spring Path		1794
Baptist Cemetery	(Windward Road)	1801

Churches, Chapels, Synagogues

Hanover Parish Church, Lucea	c. 1770
St. James Parish Church, Montego Bay	1775–82
Baptist Church, Kingston	1783
Church of England, Montego Bay	1789

[1] Or Hellshire. See F. Seal Coon, 'How healthy is "Hell"?', *Daily Gleaner*, 30 Oct. 1969, p. 3.

[2] Built about 1774, when the town of Falmouth was founded; renamed Balcarres in honour of the then Governor, and transferred from centre of town to present site near the Court House. (Fremmer, 'Fort Balcarres', *Daily Gleaner*, 12 May 1970, p. 3.)

[3] This is said to be the first cast-iron, and possibly the oldest iron bridge in the Americas. (See Wright and White, op. cit., p. 234.)

Jewish Synagogue, Kingston[1]	1789
Baptist Chapel, Crooked Spring, St. James	1791
Roman Catholic Chapel, Kingston[1]	c. 1796–9
Jewish Synagogue, Spanish Town[1]	1796
Trelawny Parish Church, Falmouth	1796
Westmoreland Parish Church, Savanna-la-Mar	1796–9
Scots Kirk, Kingston	1814
Trelawny Baptist Chapel, Falmouth	1814
Irwin Hall Moravian Church, St. James	1815
St. Catherine Baptist, Spanish Town	1819
Methodist Chapel, Kingston	c. 1820
Manchester Parish Church, Mandeville	c. 1820
New Eden Moravian Church, St. Elizabeth	1820

Hospitals

Public Hospital, Kingston	1776
Military Hospital, Kingston	1779
Slave Hospital, Kingston	1779
Jamaica Spa	1790
Negro Hospital, Half-Way Tree	1812
Marine Hospital, Savanna-la-Mar	1812
Marine Hospital, Montego Bay	1817
Naval Hospital, Port Royal	1819

Botanical Gardens

Spring Garden, Gordon Town	1770
Enfield, St. Andrew	1774
Bath, St. Thomas-in-the-East	1776–9

Schools/Public

Rusea's, Lucea	1777
Titchfield, Portland	1785
Jamaica Free School, Walton Pen	1806

Private Buildings/Great Houses

Golden Grove, St. Thomas-in-the-East	1770–80
Montpelier, St. James	c. 1775
Hampden, St. James	1779
Arcadia Pen, Trelawny	c. 1785
Cardiff Hall, St. Ann	1790s
Chippenham Park, St. Ann	c. 1791
Bryan Castle, Trelawny	1793
Marlborough House, Spur Tree Hill	1795
Minard, St. Ann	c. 1810
Greenwood House, St. James	c. 1810
Auchindown House, St. Elizabeth	c. 1810
Barrett Hall, St. James	c. 1810

Theatres

Spanish Town	1776
Montego Bay	c. 1777
Theatre Royal, Kingston	c. 1800

[1] The Synagogues served the small but very active Jewish communities in Kingston and Spanish Town; the Roman Catholic Chapel the small resident French and Spanish trading community in Kingston and, after 1799, the St. Domingue refugees.

The most significant material contribution of the planters to creole society, however, was the pen and the sugar estate.[1]

Sugar Estates—General

There were, in fact, two kinds of sugar estate: the so-called 'dry weather' estates and the 'planting estates'.[2] The 'dry weather' estates were situated on the coastland and called 'dry weather' perhaps because the rainfall was appreciably lower on the coast than in the hills. On these coastal plains the soil was clayey, intermixed with sandy spaces. These estates yielded the steadiest returns—about $2\frac{1}{2}$ tons per acre[3]—and were relatively convenient *vis-à-vis* the shipping ports. Because of the sand, light rains evaporated quickly and left the canes dry. Heavy rains, on the other hand, tended to settle in pools in the clayey soil, rotting the shoots.[4] But the nature of the soil allowed 'dry weather' canes to grow again from their stumps ('ratoon') and so saved considerable labour.

The 'planting estates' were situated on higher ground—the expansion of the frontier—inland. Here the black mould soil, 'accumulated perhaps from rotten vegetable substances',[5] made for brilliant first crops. But the rocky base of this soil resulted in rapid soil exhaustion. Jamaica does not have the wide fecund valleys of, say, St. Lucia, Trinidad, or St. Domingue and not more than two crops could be expected from any one planting.

Because of the nature of these estates, the plough was never effectively used in Jamaica, though the conservative nature of the creole planters must also be taken into account.[6] The clay soils of the dry weather estates made ploughing slow and difficult; the rock-based soil of the planting estates could be costly on the implement and,

as it often happens . . . there is not a blacksmith's shop within fifteen miles to repair the plough when out of order, and they [the planters] look to immediate labour so as not to admit of any delay, by which the ordinary plantation work might be kept back. . . .[7]

'Monk' Lewis wrote in 1818, rather wistfully, that the plough had

[1] For the distribution of these, see James Robertson, *Map of the County of Cornwall in the island of Jamaica, constructed from actual surveys, under the authority of the Hon. House of Assembly* . . . (London, 1804); *Map of the County of Middlesex* . . . (London, 1804); *Map of the County of Surrey* . . . (London, 1804).

[2] See Benjamin M'Mahon, *Jamaica Plantership* (London, 1839), pp. 247–50.

[3] See R. C. Dallas, op. cit., Vol. I, p. xc. [4] Long, *History*, Vol. I, pp. 352–3.

[5] ibid. [6] See, for instance, Beckford, *Account*, Vol. II, p. 204.

[7] William Fitzmaurice, *P.P.*, Vol. XCII, *Accounts and Papers* 1790–1 (34), no. 745, pp. 225–6.

been introduced 'completely successfully' in several parts of the island; on his own well-managed estates, however,

the awkwardness, and still more the obstinacy, of the few negroes, whose services were indispensable, was not to be overcome; they broke plough after plough, and ruined beast after beast, till the attempt was abandoned in despair.[1]

There was also a noticeable lack of experiment with manures;[2] and the absence of local agricultural societies has already been mentioned.[3]

This failure to improve their farming methods has been advanced on a wide front in criticism of the planters; they were concerned with 'pushing' their estates[4]—the soil and their slaves—in their single-minded dedication to the export of sugar for profit. Looking for explanations of this 'failure', it has been generally held that absenteeism was to blame. Had planters remained resident, it is argued, instead of making for England and handing their properties over to the clumsy mercies of attorneys and overseers, things would have been more efficient, more humane, certainly different.[5] This may well be so, though keeping in mind the purpose of the Jamaican economy and the colony's frontier psychology, it is very much to be doubted. Besides, the actual number of *permanent* absentee proprietors throughout the entire slave period, has not been firmly determined. Patterson, for instance,[6] points out that though only one-sixth of Jamaica's proprietors were absentees in 1774, it was this one-sixth who owned most of the property and slaves in the island. The 1820 property figures reveal that one-fifth of the island's proprietors owned most of the slaves and acres in the island. Yet some of the very largest holders[7]—Price, the Mitchells, Grant, Dawkins, Archdeckne, the Taylors, Bayly, Ellis, Storer, Wedderburn, James,

[1] Lewis, op. cit. (1929 ed.), p. 272. For Beckford's despair of the plough, see Beckford, *Account*, Vol. II, pp. 202–3.

[2] Beckford, *Account*, Vol. II, p. 195. Fuller, Long, and Chisholme discussed the kind of manures used in the island in P.P. Vol. LXXXIV, *Account and Papers*, 1789 (29), Part III, A. no. 51.   [3] Page 92, above.

[4] Stewart, *View*, p. 186.

[5] See, for example, Dr. Harrison, *P.P.* as n. 5, p. 129, above; *R.G.*, XL (1818), 45, 26; Thomas Roughley, *The Jamaica planters' guide; or, a system for planting and managing a sugar estate or other plantations in that island and throughout the British West Indies in general . . .* (London, 1823), *passim*, but esp. Ch. 1; Ragatz, *Fall*, Ch. 2; *Absentee Landlordism in the British Caribbean, 1750–1833* (London, 1931); Patterson, op. cit., pp. 33–51.

[6] Patterson, op. cit., pp. 36–8.   [7] See pp. 40, 121, above.

Shand—appear to have been in the island.[1] Even admitting the high proportion of absentees, it does not necessarily follow that had there been fewer of them, they would have been more efficient than their professional substitutes, the attorneys.[2] When William Beckford returned to Jamaica with his wife in 1774 (he was born in the island in 1744 but went to England for his education)[3] he railed against the negligence of his attorneys and set out to reform his estates.[4] But in 1781 his mortgage stood at £25,000[5] (he had first taken it out in 1777), and he went back to Britain after thirteen years in Jamaica to be seized as a debtor.[6] He was a casualty not simply of absenteeism but of the economic imbalance following the American Revolution, the victim of rising British duties on sugar, the rising cost of living, the devastating hurricanes of 1780, 1781, 1784, 1785, and 1786, drought, famine, the unprecedented loss in slaves due to these, 'the villany of others'[7] and his own managerial inefficiency.[8]

Sugar Estates: Layout and Output

Jamaican sugar estates varied from about 300 to 3,000 acres in size,[9] and a 900-acre estate was considered average.[10] On a typical 'average' estate, there was the proprietor's or Great House—the residence of the owner or, if he was absent, of the overseer. Conveniently near was the accommodation, often quite makeshift, for the other white personnel—the book-keeper or book-keepers (usually two),[11] the distiller, mason, carpenter, blacksmith, cooper, wheelwright. The numbers of these depended on the size of the estate, and from about the middle of the eighteenth century, black artisans increasingly replaced indentured whites in these skilled crafts.[12] A few of the very largest estates had a resident (white) doctor.[13]

[1] *Jamaica Almanack* for . . . 1821, 'Return of Givings-In for the March Quarter, 1820', Feurtado, op. cit.; John Roby, *Members; Members of the Assembly for the Parish of St. James* (Montego Bay, 1837).

[2] For a critical look at the commonly held views of absenteeism, see Douglas Hall, 'Absentee-Proprietorship in the British West Indies, to about 1850', Vol. iv (1964), pp. 22–6. For a picture of a professional attorney in action, see pp. 140–2, below.

[3] See *Alumni Oxonienses*.

[4] See R. B. Sheridan, 'Planter and Historian: The Career of William Beckford of Jamaica and England, 1744–1799', Vol. iv (1964), p. 56.

[5] ibid.   [6] See, *A Short Journey in the West Indies*, Vol. II, p. 144.

[7] ibid., p. 140. Gilbert Mathison (op. cit., pp. 99–100) made the same complaint in 1808.   [8] Sheridan, op. cit., pp. 55–8.

[9] See J. Wedderburn, P.P., Vol. LXXXVII, *Accounts and Papers*, 1790–1 (29), no. (7), p. 378.

[10] See Edwards, op. cit. (1793 ed.), Vol. II, pp. 250, 251; Ragatz, *Fall*, p. 37.

[11] Marsden, op. cit., pp. 20, 22.   [12] See Sheridan, op. cit., p. 52.

[13] Beckford, *Account*, Vol. II, p. 379.

Other estates shared one between them.[1] The domestic slaves (butler, coachman, postilion, cooks, waiting-men and maids, house-cleaners, washer-women, seamstresses) were also often housed within this compound which usually stood on high ground overlooking the estate. Further away (it varied with the size of the estate, but on the average half a mile away—'not so far removed as to be beyond the sight of the overseer',[2] were the Negro (field slaves') quarters. Forming a third complex were the industrial buildings—the sugar mill (water, cattle, wind), the boiling and curing houses, the distillery, the blacksmith's and carpenters' sheds and the trash houses. There was also a cattle yard and poultry pen. Separate from all these was the Negro hospital or 'hot house',[3] which apart from sick slaves, provided 'accommodation' for plantation runaways.

Surrounding the buildings were the estate lands. One-third of the total acreage was usually occupied by the sugar cane, another third by pasture and kitchen-gardens. The rest was woodland or waste—the former a source of fuel, timber, and since unlike St. Kitts, for instance,[4] rotation was not practised, possible ground for expansion.

The cane-land was divided into fields of various extent and shape, according to the terrain. Intervals of about twenty feet were left between each field for the convenience of carriage, and each field in Jamaica was enclosed and protected by stone walls, logwood hedges or mounds of earth planted with a prickly penguin shrub.[5] Each acre of cane contained about 3,500 cane holes, three and a half feet square, and it was calculated[6] that forty slaves could dig an acre in a day. Output from the estimated 200,000 acres in use rose from 69,451 hogsheads (exported) in 1772 to 80,000 in 1792, to 129,544 in 1802 (reflecting the introduction of Bourbon cane in 1799); and then began to decline: 105,283 hogsheads in 1812, 88,551 in 1822.[7]

The estate pastures were planted with sweet and sour orange,

---

[1] Marsden, op. cit., p. 18.   [2] Beckford, *Account*, Vol. II, p. 20.

[3] For detailed descriptions of estate lay-outs see, among others, Marsden, op. cit., pp. 16–38; Beckford, *Account*, Vol. II, pp. 27–34; R. C. Dallas, op. cit., Vol. I, pp. xciii–iv; Patterson, op. cit., pp. 53–6.

[4] See Long, Add. MS. 12413.

[5] Stewart, *View*, pp. 106–7.

[6] See Moreton, op. cit., pp. 43–4.

[7] Cumper, op. cit., p. 41. See also Noel Deerr, *The History of Sugar*, 2 vols. (London, 1949), Vol. I, p. 198. A hogshead (cask of 52½ imperial gallons) varied in weight from 12 to 18 cwt. See the *Shorter Oxford English Dictionary*; Herbert C. Bell, 'The West India Trade before the American Revolution', *American Historical Review*, Vol. XXII (1916–17), p. 272; Edwards, op. cit., Vol. II, p. 245; Douglas Hall, *Free Jamaica* (Yale University Press, 1959), p. 282, n. 1.

lemon, and lime trees. If the pastures were also pens,[1] they were naturally quite extensive. On the Rhimesbury pen in Clarendon, there were often (the reference is to 1784), 'a thousand head of cattle in charge of the overseer, a vast quantity of swine, poultry of all kinds, and flocks of sheep and goats, which are all numbered at set times, to prevent their being stolen. . . .'[2]

The estate kitchen-gardens and/or provision grounds, which supplied the whites with food, were situated near the Great House. Peas, beans, sweet potatoes, cassava, peppers, pine-apples, pumpkins, cucumbers and ochro were grown here, and after 1792,[3] the breadfruit also. Poultry and meat were available from the pens, though these were heavily supplemented by imported beef, pork, herring, butter (salt or rancid),[4] and flour.[5] Fresh fish—Jew-fish, hog-fish, mud-fish, snappers, god-dammies, groupers and grunts[6] among them—came up to the estates twice a week for the whites.[7] Salt-fish was issued at regular intervals to the slaves.[8]

The estate slaves also had their kitchen-gardens—small ones—behind their huts, where they grew plantain, ackee, ochro, various 'ground provisions' (yam, eddoe), mangoes, oranges, shaddock, etc.[9] They were also allowed to keep hogs and poultry, though if the hogs broke into the cane-pieces, they could be shot by command of the overseer.[10] But the main provision grounds of the slaves, certainly on the 'planting estates', were the 'polincks'—areas in the hills up to ten miles[11] from their houses, which they cleared and tended themselves. These polincks were required by law, the first Act to this effect being passed in 1678. It stipulated that proprietors should, under penalty, provide 'one acre of ground well planted in provision for every five Negroes and so proportionately for a greater or lesser number. . . .'[12]

[1] Also spelt 'penns'; cattle farms. See Cassidy and Le Page, op. cit.

[2] Marsden, op, cit., p. 17.

[3] See p. 84, above.   [4] R.G., XXXVIII (1806), 25, 10.

[5] See Moreton, op. cit., p. 79; Marsden, op. cit., p. 13.

[6] Lewis, op. cit. (1834 ed.), p. 104.   [7] Marsden, op. cit., p. 24.

[8] Edwards, op. cit., Vol. II, p. 159 says that this allowance was weekly.

[9] Alexander Barclay, A practical view of the present state of slavery in the West Indies (London, 1826), pp. 313–4. The dates of introduction into Jamaica of some of these plants are mentioned on p. 84, above.   [10] Marsden, op. cit., p. 18.

[11] Thomas Cooper, Facts illustrative of the condition of the negro slaves in Jamaica (London, 1824), p. 5. The distance of the polincks would depend of course on the location of suitable land. The planters would hardly want their slaves travelling or straying too far afield. The 1781 Act defining runaways (see Acts . . . 1770-1783, No. 91, p. 264), gave eight miles as the limit a slave could travel without 'a Ticket, or other Permit to pass'; though enforcement of this depended on the local planter.

[12] C.O. 139/5/5. The statutory number of slaves per acre of provision ground fluctuated during the period of this study. By 22 Geo. III, c. 17 of 1781 and 29 Geo. III, c. 2

The Rhimesbury estate, according to Marsden,[1] allowed its slaves one acre each.

The shape and positioning of all the buildings and areas described above, were aspects of the function of the estate. There was nothing chance or haphazard here. The organization of this complex was even more impressive. The cycle of the seasons and the nature of the cane dictated where and how it should be planted, nurtured and harvested. Weeding time, planting, cutting the cane, its conversion to sugar and transport to the wharves, were regular and unvarying activities which made their mark on the social activities and psychology of all concerned and played an essential part in their creolization. There was unquestionably considerable maltreatment of and brutality practised against the slaves within this specialized society. The slaves retaliated in ways that will be discussed later. There was also considerable inefficiency and carelessness on these estates. But they functioned always towards the purpose for which they were designed—as the export figures of Jamaican sugar attest. The successful realization and maintenance of this function was the planters' contribution to creole society.

of 1788, the proportion was given as four slaves per acre. 32 Geo. III, c. 24 of 1791 placed the figure at ten slaves per acre of provision ground, and so it remained for the rest of the period.

[1] Op. cit., p. 18.

10

OTHER WHITES

Other Whites

From the constant complaints about absenteeism, from the continuing (and unsuccessful) attempts of the Jamaican legislature and administration to encourage white settlement,[1] from the remarks of visitors about the shortage of white women and lack of family life, the impression has been formed that Jamaica was almost exclusively a planter society—or rather an *absentee* planter society, with no 'yeoman' or lower-middle class backbone. Closer examination, however, reveals a different picture. There were some 30,000 whites in Jamaica in 1820 of whom only about 1,189 were men of property.[2] An allowance for rich merchants and the families of both, would put this 'upper class' at something around 6,000 whites. This leaves 24,000 other whites of whom not more than 5,000, after the middle of the eighteenth century, would have been servants (calculating, in a slave society that relied mainly on black and coloured domestics, one white servant per very rich family.[3] There were also 3,000 British troops permanently stationed in Jamaica from 1773.[4] Whether these were included in contemporary population returns is not clear. Governor Lyttleton included white troops in his 1764 figures[5] and so did Long in his *History*.[6] On the other hand, the Vestry returns, on which the Assembly returns were based, did not include British troops. Depending, therefore, on whether soldiers are included or not, there are still between 18,000 and 24,000 whites to be accounted for in Jamaica—the majority of this section of the population.

[1] See pp. 86–92, above.

[2] This figure is based on the estimates made on p. 121, above.

[3] Long's figure for 1768 was 5,983 white servants, calculating these at one-third of the total white population. (*History*, Vol. I, p. 377.) His figure for 1787 was 5,000. (Add. MS. 12414, f. 23.)

[4] C.O. 142/33, 'Subsistence of Jamaica Troops', Minute dated 6 Feb. 1829, initialled JFS.

[5] See *JAJ*, I, Appendix, p. 50.

[6] Vol. I, p. 378. Wesley (op. cit., p. 140) calculates that of the 28,800 whites in 1826, 400 were 'rich', 5,500 were 'fair', and 22,900 were 'absolutely poor'.

Who then were these 18,000/24,000, what did they do and what did they contribute to the society?

There was, in the first place, the white population of the towns— small merchants, lawyers, doctors, parsons and preachers, teachers, organists, clerks, tavern keepers, hostel keepers, police and night watchmen, fire-engine drivers and maintenance men, beadles, collecting constables, midwives, nurses, druggists, iron founders, masons, lumber measurers, lime-sellers, gunsmiths, brickmakers, brick-layers, cabinet-makers, milliners, plumbers, seamstresses, carpenters, cooks, pedlars, printers, saddlers, butchers, black-smiths, gardeners, tailors, butlers, upholsterers, shipwrights, coopers, silversmiths, goldsmiths, coppersmiths, watchmakers and repairers, painters, pilots, shoemakers, sailmakers, wharfingers, vendue-masters (auctioneers), stationers, hairdressers, staymakers, joiners, bakers, coachmakers, dyers, etc.[1] The wealthiest of these—Government printers like Aikman and John Lunan—served in the Assembly.[2] A wealthy goldsmith like Wolmer would have reached the Vestry.[3] So probably did many lawyers, saddlers, watchmakers and tailors—a group that did particularly well in the island.[4] The rest served on juries, helped with parochial administration and turned out for militia duty. The most numerous of this group were the shopkeepers—dealing mainly in dry-good, provisions, lumber, wine, and liquor.

The retail store-keeper's shop, or *store*, as it is called, contains a strange medley of all sorts of articles. In one part of it may be a customer bargaining for a cheese, a ham, a pound of tea, or a dozen of wine or porter; in another, a gentleman may be fitting himself with a pair of boots or a hat, or cheapening a saddle; while a party of ladies, elsewhere, are trying on bonnets, gloves, etc., selecting ribbons, laces, and other fancy articles, or culling some valuable articles of jewellery.[5]

Many of these retailers were Jews. The Kingston Vestry Poll Tax returns show them concentrated in Peter's Lane, Orange Street, White Street, and Tower Street. In 1770, thirty-six of the thirty-

---

[1] The list is taken from the Kingston Vestry Jury Lists in the Kingston Vestry/Common Council records.

[2] See p. 42, above.

[3] Many of these goldsmiths, according to Mr. H. P. Jacobs, to whom I am indebted for this information, were probably brokers connected with the slave trade, like Wolmer (see pp. 115–16, above). Wolmer, himself, does not appear to have been a vestryman.

[4] See Stewart, *View*, p. 201.   [5] ibid., pp. 199–200.

seven houses in Peter's Lane were owned by Jews.[1] They sold at more moderate prices than Christian dealers, 'but their goods [were] generally of an inferior description.'[2] But whether Jew or Gentile, *all* the local shopkeepers collected 100 per cent profits, according to Stewart, though bad debts pulled these gains down by 50 per cent.[3] The liquor shops did a roaring trade, especially in the sea-port towns of the island. In Kingston alone, in 1787, there were 270 rum-shops.[4] In the ten years 1770–80, £8,000 was paid out by the owners of these shops for liquor licences—three-quarters of the total sum coming from Kingston.[5]

Clerks

All merchant houses, the larger shops, and lawyers' offices, had their clerks—usually bachelors earning between £150 and £200 per annum. They slept on the premises or had to find their own accommodation. Board and lodging in a creditable house cost about £80 sterling:

and as constant washing, and the destructive method black women take of beating and rubbing the clothes with stones and stumps of grass to save the expence of soap, wears them amazing fast, it will require yearly, if he has not brought a good stock of shirts, neck-cloths, breeches, waistcoats, coats and stockings from home, about £30: add to this £20 for two cloth coats, two hats, twelve pair of shoes, hair-ribband and hair-dressing, and £12 for washing, [and the whole amounts] to £142 ...[6]

These bachelors were the local bucks, the fashionable Brummels of Kingston and the larger towns, frequenters of the taverns and theatre. They were also the most 'upwardly mobile' members of society, especially the rich merchants' clerks:

If a poor young man serves a merchant three or four years so as to gain his favour, he may get letters of credit, and be put into business for himself; or if he be clever at business he may be taken into partnership, and in time his friend and benefactor may go to Europe for the benefit of his health, whereby he is intrusted with the conducting of all the business, and has a glorious opportunity of becoming a great man ...; or if a young man is sober, keen, and active, he may push himself into credit, get bargains at vendue, ... and in time ... make some money, get credit, and

[1] Kingston Vestry Minutes 1769–70, Parish Tax Returns for 1770, pp. 304–50.
[2] Stewart, *View*, p. 200.   [3] ibid., pp. 125–6.
[4] Kingston Vestry Proceedings 1781–8; Minute no. 209 for 6 Sept. 1787.
[5] See Gardner, op. cit., p. 163.   [6] Moreton, op. cit., p. 98.

Other Whites

turn merchant; indeed any huckster or grog-shop keeper' with care, industry, and a little roguery, will make money fast. . . .¹

Country Whites

In the country districts, the *petit blancs* consisted of estate staff (professional attorneys, overseers, book-keepers, machine operators, and maintenance men), housekeepers, doctors, preachers, and parsons, a few teachers, pedlars, tavern keepers, toll gate keepers, stone masons, millwrights, land surveyors, land attorneys, postmasters and mistresses, coastal shipping captains and owners, pilots, etc. After the 1780 hurricane, the following smallholders in Hanover and Westmoreland applied for Government aid.²

mechanic	1
'business in the mercantile line'	3
widow	7
poor women	5
dry.goods business shopkeeper	2
tavern keeper	2
nurse	1
small farmer/settler	6
carpenter	3
journeyman blacksmith	3
taylor	2
clerk	2
blacksmith	2
'gentleman'	1
butcher	1
mason	1
cooper	1
book-keeper	1
canoe-man	1

The wealthiest of these—small planters, small merchants, land attorneys and surveyors, estate attorneys—sat on the vestries. The rest, as in the towns, served on juries and in the militia. Householders in the out-parishes relied heavily on pedlars for their dry-goods and imported provisions, though the better-off imported direct from England.³ The number of stores was growing, however, especially in the more settled areas of the country parishes,⁴ but as a class, the shopkeepers remained below the line. In the hills outside Montego Bay, for instance, were 'all the gentlemen's houses, or those not immediately shopkeepers'.⁵

¹ Moreton, op. cit., pp. 99–100.   ² *JAJ*, VII, 486–97 of 12 Nov. 1782.
³ Gardner, op. cit., p. 163.
⁴ See, for instance, the advertisement of John Sibbit and Co. (Clarendon) dated 6 Dec. 1793 in *R.G.*, XVI, 1, 23.   ⁵ *LNJ* (Wright), p. 88.

Estate attorneys

The attorney . . . is the chief manager of the plantations; he is paid by the owner, who appoints him at home [i.e. in England] according to agreement: his business is to see that every thing is in order and properly conducted; and if any complaints are made by the negroes, the remedy lies in him.[1]

There were, in fact, two sorts of estate managers: 'six per cent attornies, and salaried attornies'.[2] A really big attorney, with charge of some fifteen to twenty plantations, was a nabob in his own right, with a yearly income of from £8,000 to £10,000. Such a man often became a proprietor himself. More usual, however, was the attorney in charge of five or six plantations, who had to travel up to seventy miles between estates.[3] It was after 1809, when most estates in Jamaica began reforming themselves and attorneys were confined to a few manageable properties, that the fixed salary made its appearance.[4]

In general, attorneys were rather harshly described in contemporary accounts. They were reputed to have a favourite black or mulatto girl on every estate, which the overseers were obliged 'to pamper and indulge like goddesses'.[5] When an attorney visited a plantation, wrote Moreton, who had himself been a book-keeper in Jamaica,[6]

he commonly invites a few dissipated gentlemen to spend a few days with him; he sends wines and other necessaries previously; the only duty he does, is, to take a ride in the cool of the morning or evening with the manager [overseer] along the pleasant walks or intervals, or round some of the cane pieces.[7]

'He is followed about the country', said Beckford,

with a retinue of carriages, of servants, and of horses, which shake the ground as they thunder along; and when he arrives upon the plantation, the command goes forth, to catch and kill; the table is covered with profusion, and few are suffered to go empty . . . away . . .[8]

This may well have been the case, though it should be noted that Moreton had a rather prurient eye for detail[9] and Beckford (see p. 131, above) had no reason to love his attorneys. A good attorney,

---

[1] Marsden, op. cit., pp. 19–20.   [2] Dallas, op. cit., Vol. II, p. 359.
[3] *Montgomery*, Vol. II, pp. 43–4.
[4] Stewart, *View*, pp. 184–8.   [5] Moreton, op. cit., p. 77.   [6] ibid., p. 9.
[7] ibid., p. 77.   [8] Beckford, *Account*, Vol. II, p. 366.
[9] See op. cit., pp. 120–1, 126–7, 129–32.

Otter White[s]

as Niniam Jeffreys said in evidence before the House of Commons in 1790, was one 'who could send home the greatest quantity of sugar'.[1] This, despite the details of their private lives, was their function, and this is what they did. Wynter, Edward Long's attorney in Jamaica, is a case in point:

11 January, 1779
Since my last we have been *very dry* in Clarendon and the young Canes were suffering much, but on 29th last month came on a very fine rain in the mountains. Some few showers have fallen since, at L[ong] Valley and at present the Canes look tolerable. We shall get up hill about the 14th.

9 March 1779
. . . continued dry weather at L. Valley which has done very great damage both to the canes of this crop and the young Canes—Our water near gone. repairing the Cattle mill. last years rum all sold.

1st April 1779
Much might be saved in the [Corn] supplies, provided proper use was made of the great crops of Corn annually raised at L. Valley but I never go to y Estate without seeing 5 or 6 horses belonging to — and his partner, eating large quantities of Corn, which had better be applied to fatning hogs for y use of the Estate. . . .

27 May 1779
[Bought] 6 young men last month. the *Rains though* late in May will certainly do much good to *the next Crop*; they really suffered from the dry weather. Not a puncheon of Rum yet sold of this Crop.

30 May 1779
I have not seen a better May Season for many years.

9 July 1779
I have directed the overseer at L. Valley to plant the Bambu cane in different parts of the Estate, I shall see that this is not neglected.
    The frequent floods in May & June did much damage to the Guttering. Several times it carried away some parts of it, which retarded the getting off the Crop, and obliged [us] to work the Cattle Mill. I shall set about repairing the Gutter in the best manner our situation will admit of. . . .

27 July 1779
The Weather very dry in most parts of the Island & in Clarendon much so. No higher price than 2/4 is yet given for Rum. about 40 acres Cane holes dug. I *see clearly we shall require more aid in the holing business.*

[1] *P.P.*, Vol. LXXXVIII, *Accounts and Papers*, 1790 (30), p. 234.

20 November 1779
The Season now favourable. Were rather dry in Octb. but much rain has fallen in this month; indeed we have had no communication with any part of the Country for several days, owing *to the great rains,* which will no doubt *put the time of cutting the canes a little more distant than if the rains had fallen in Octb.*

When I was last in L. Valley the Estate was going on very well. but as Negroes and White people having been taken off during Martial law, had certainly put it back; I was therefore obliged to *hire a Jobber* to *assist the plantation Negroes in holing.*

13 January 1780
On the 10th instant the Mill was put about. I have seen a sample of the Sugar which is made, & it is good—But the *Weather,* is and *has been dry for* some time past. The Expenses incurred during last Martial law, amount to near £90,000. The present Deficiency is £39 which is triple [what it was] and the poll Tax on negroes 7/6 p. head. punchn. Staves and heading £55 . . . and Hhd. Staves at £40 & every Article of Supply for plantations at a most exorbitant price.

4 April 1780
I feel exceedingly for what you will suffer in your crop, by the long continuance of *Dry weather,* we have had, and still have. my last was 13th Jany, since which *we have not had any* rain at L. Valley (12 weeks). In Octb. last I thought the prospect for the crop a very good one: I did expect 300 Hhds. but the *dry weather* has baffled all my hopes; & *I see clearly the Crop will* be just . . . *of 200 hhds.* The Sugars I think are as good as those of last year. shall ship 160 hhds. by y first fleet to sail 21 May. . . .

The Seasons are the only cause which prevents me from making good crops at L. Valley. Were I to say that for these five years past, the Seasons are not so good in Clarendon as they were before that time, it might look as if I was endeavouring to find out an excuse for a short crop, which might proceed from some other cause than the want of Seasons, but it is really so with me.

The crops in general will be short this year.—present price of rum 2/9, but the market dull.

13 May 1780
160 Hhds shipt in the Fleet. Since my last very fine rains at L. Valley, which have recovered the young plants very much. have finished crop. shall be able to put in a good plant for 1782—

. . . [given] *some help in the holing by Job*; it will enable us to enlarge the plant & save our Negroes some hard labour.—

This crop is *206* hhds. dont think the crop of rum will be great as the sugars *are fine*, and gave but *little molasses*. some of rum sent to Market has sold for 2/9 & 3/–. which is the present price.

2nd June 1780
57 hhds. Sugar remain. To be shipt on the Nancy . . . have not had May rains. but only some *partial showers* in the mountains, which have *kept the Canes from burning*. . . .
 Shall soon set to dig cane holes. . . .[1]

Estate personnel

These were the overseers, book-keepers, 'mechanics' and, in some cases, the plantation doctor and housekeeper.

Overseers, on salaries of from £140 to £200 (on some of the larger estates, £300),[2] lived on the plantations with a small domestic staff of slaves of their own, supplied by the proprietor. The more industrious reared sheep, swine and poultry for themselves and their book-keepers.[3] Their job was the day-to-day management of the estate: supervising the book-keepers, dismissing them if necessary, taking care of all stock and stores, distributing clothing and food to the slaves, ordering their daily work, inspecting it, punishing the delinquent, visiting the sick slaves (he had to be something of a quack)[4] and investigating cases of malingering and sabotage. On absentee plantations, the overseer was master of the place. It was he who appointed the housekeepers and entertained travellers. He was professional to the core, having usually worked his way up from mechanic or book-keeper.[5] Since there was 'a prevailing Objection against the employing of married Men, on the Supposition that their Families use more Sugar, and keep more Attendants about the House than Bachelors',[6] and since many a potential bridegroom found the idea of a blushing English rose in the tropics an unobtainable—often inconvenient[7]—luxury. Overseers and the white estate personnel

---

[1] Wynter to Long, Add. MS. 12412, p. 19–20 verso. Italics in text.
[2] Stewart, *View*, p. 194.   [3] Moreton, op. cit., p. 79.   [4] ibid., p. 80.
[5] ibid., Stewart, *View*, p. 194.
[6] P.P., Vol. LXXXIV, *Accounts and Papers* 1789 (29). Part III, Rev. James Ramsay, 'Further Evidence received by the Committee respecting the Treatment of Slaves in the West Indies.'
[7] 'As to marrying, he imagines there are many objections to that—if he be in the planting line, he cannot get a situation as a married man—and if he be engaged in mercantile affairs, he is afraid that he cannot support it, by driving a Carriage and keeping up such an equipage as some others do. And besides he can live in whoredom for a few years till he accumulates a fortune, and he can then leave his brown family and return home. . . . [Such] a general prejudice exists against the ladies of our complexion, especially on the estates, that it is but here and there [that] a married overseer . . . can be met with, whilst a poor book-keeper or tradesman on an estate must not think of

generally, soon found it suited their needs and the situation, more often than not, to acquire a black or coloured mistress or 'house-keeper'—useful women whose role in the subtle control of plantation slaves should not be underestimated.

The book-keeper's job was not so much keeping books as looking after the plantation small stock.[1] It was the poultry book rather than the account book that was his first responsibility. 'He must', said Moreton, 'every morning enter in his book the number of each [fowl] that are with egg, least the stock-house woman deceives him'.[2] When the hens inevitably produced their eggs, each one had to be dated. The sheep, goats, and swine had to be regularly inspected for sores and vermin.

About eight o'clock the book-keeper goes to breakfast, and afterwards gives out necessaries for dinner, and hastens to the field 'till twelve, at which time he returns—he dines about one o'clock—he sits at the foot of the table opposite the overseer. When the bell is rung to order the slaves [back] to work, [he departs again and] returns about five or six o'clock to see the stock fed, and is kept constantly busy about one thing or another till past eight. . . .[3]

It was also the book-keeper's business to see to the safe transport of the estate sugars and rum to the wharves, and to check the hogs-heads and puncheons as they were stored aboard ship.[4] For all this, they earned between £20 and £30 a year in the middle of the eighteenth century, from £50 to £80 after.[5] In other words, they, too, were little more than slaves to the system. In the first year in the island, if they survived, their money went on the purchase of the indispensable horse—worth the money for convenience sake and even more for the sake of prestige—no white man worth his colour walked.[6] In the second year, most of his money went on doctor's

such a thing at all. . . .' (John Shipman, 'Thoughts on the Present State of Religion among the Negroes in Jamaica'; loc. cit., n. 6, p. 263, below.) This (again), though the traditional picture of marriage in Jamaica, is not necessarily the complete one. On a casual count, from a single source, the following figures were obtained. 1794: 68 marriages; 1813: 63 marriages; 1815: 84 marriages; 1820: 68 marriages (*R.G.*, XVI, XXXV, XXXVII, XLII).

[1] Stewart, *View*, p. 189.   [2] Moreton, op. cit., p. 95.   [3] ibid., p. 96.
[4] Marsden, op. cit., p. 21.
[5] Beckford, *Account*, Vol. II, p. 379; Stewart, *View*, p. 194.
[6] 'Here are none of the substantial inhabitants who do not keep their coach or chariot with four or six horses. The shop-keepers have their two-wheel chaises, or kittereens; and they who cannot afford a carriage, even to the poorest free Negro, will not be with-out a saddle-horse or two.' (Long, *History*, Vol. II, p. 33.) See also Stewart, *View*, p. 210; WMMS. *Notices*, Vol. II, p. 168.

bills, and in the third year, thanks perhaps to these, money could at last be spent with the merchant and the tailor.[1] But it was a hard life as most of the accounts confirm. Many 'fed and inflamed by sickly Hope's delusive dreams' (the fine phrase is from Moreton),[2] shone bravely on for a little time, then '[went] off in a stink, like the snuff of a candle'.[3]

The estate 'mechanics' (distillers, carpenters, masons, coopers, etc.) were much better off because they were specialists. The quality of rum, to take one example, depended on the distiller's skill. The fabric and machinery of the sugar factories depended on the millwrights, carpenters, and masons. Until the 1780s, most of these had been indentured artisans,[4] though even then they received higher salaries than book-keepers (£50–£100 per annum compared with £20–30).[5] But by the beginning of the nineteenth century, plantation skills like carpentry and masonry were increasingly practised by craftsmen acting as entrepreneurs in their own right, making their services available to clients outside the plantations. 'There is so constant a demand for their services', Stewart wrote in 1823,

that nothing but the most glaring misconduct can occasion them to be long out of employment. The profession of a master coppersmith and plumber, if he has ten or twelve slaves brought up to the business, and a white or brown journeyman to attend them, is one of the most lucrative in the island; as, even with that small establishment, and constant employment, he may make from £3,000 to £4,000 per annum....[6]

Doctors

There was no shortage of these in Jamaica. In 1770, in St. Ann, eleven practitioners of physic and surgery appeared on the Jurors' List for the March Quarter.[7] Twenty-four doctors are listed in the Kingston Parish Tax Returns for the same year.[8] The Kingston Medical Society, started in 1791, could claim eighteen members in 1796.[9] According to Curtin,[10] there were 300 doctors in the island in 1833.

As a group, the profession appears to have been respected and was

[1] Moreton, op. cit., p. 97.   [2] ibid., p. 91.   [3] ibid.
[4] See Beckford, *Account*, Vol. II, p. 379.   [5] ibid.   [6] Stewart, *View*, p. 195.
[7] St. Ann Vestry Orders, 1767–90; Minute for 28 March 1770. This was an exceptional year, however. In 1777, no doctors appeared on the Jury List; in 1789 and 1790, there were only three doctors on the list. (See Minutes 28 March 1777, 13 Feb. 1789, 27 Feb. 1790.)
[8] Kingston Vestry Minutes, 1769–70, Parish Tax Returns for 1770.
[9] *Jamaica Almanack* for 1796, p. 107.   [10] *Two Jamaicas*, p. 48.

respectable. Professional standards were at least competent. Doctors were helpful, reliable and often (given the state of sanitation, public health ideas, medical science,[1] and 'the quick march of death in [the] climate'),[2] ingenious:

N. E. Van Eckhout, M.D. informs his Friends and the Public that he has removed from King-Street to Princess-Street, . . . and . . . continues to practise with success the application of the Medical Power of the GALVANO-VOLTAIC ELECTRICITY to the cure of various Chronical and Nervous Affections, which have before been deemed incurable. The principal Diseases, in the cure of which he has succeeded, are Palsy in general; Epileptic Fits; Locked Jaw, or Tetanus; Rheumatics . . ., Weakness of the Sight; Defect of it and Blindness . . .; partial or total Deafness, or Buzzing Noise in the Ear; Weakness of the Arms, Heads [*sic*], or Legs; Chronical Sore Throat; Recent and Chronical Head Aches; Hysteric and Hypochondriacal Affections; Obstruction of the Liver and Spleen, and Glands in general; Pain in the Articulations, with or without swelling; long and obstinate Intermittent Fevers, that have resisted every medical assistance.[3]

In addition to physics, doctors like N. E. Van Eckhout were not above using herbal remedies; as a grateful patient testified in a letter to the editor of the *Royal Gazette*:[4]

Sir,
Having observed some time ago in one of the daily papers a cure, in a consumptive cough, effected by the infusion of a wood called Alcornoque,[5] and feeling afflicted in that way, I made application to D[r]. Van Eckhout, who had the same in his possession. From a severe cold, which increased into a spitting of blood and obnoxious matter, and at last caused a restlessness . . . , I thought fit to try this infusion of Alcornoque, in the use of which for about 18 days I felt a remarkable decrease of spitting, and at last a perfect recovery of rest, being now able to lie in any position, which for three months before I could not do. . . .

Besides the local whites, these doctors looked after the slaves on the plantations; indeed, some of the larger plantations had their own resident doctor. Others shared a doctor between them,[6] not a very satisfactory arrangement for the slaves, since 'at a sickly period',[7]

[1] See Ch. 18, below. [2] K.C.C. Minutes, 1815–20; 23 Nov. 1818.
[3] *R.G.*, XXXV, 6, 24, dated Kingston, 6 Feb. 1813.
[4] ibid., 49, 5, in a letter dated 10 Nov. 1813. [5] The American corn-oak.
[6] See p. 132, above. [7] Stewart, *View*, p. 196.

strict medical attention to all patients was impossible. This helps to explain the high slave mortality in the island. The doctor's fee per slave was 6s. 8d., the proprietor paying, in addition, for the medicine. The usual charge for a visit to a white patient was £1 6s. 8d.—not unreasonable, but the cost of imported medicine was high; according to Stewart,[1] 2000 per cent of the prime cost.

Small Settlers

The most numerous and important group of 'other' whites in Jamaica, were the smallholders and pen-keepers. These were the people that the Government, since 35 Charles II, c. 3 of 1683 had been trying to encourage to settle the island. Within the period of this study (as discussed on pp. 86–92, above), the Assembly was very much involved with this problem of settlement, especially in the parishes of Portland and Trelawny—the areas of sparsest white population and dominated, until 1796, in the interior parts, by fear of the Maroons. By 'small settlers' the Jamaica Government had in mind resident cultivators on not more than 500 acres of land per white man.[2] Jamaica was not very successful at these efforts in terms of numbers and acres cultivated (the Assembly calculated that there were only 4,000 settlers in this category in 1792),[3] but their contribution to the society was not negligible.[4] Jamaica, alone of the British West Indian islands during the period of slavery, was able to maintain, to some degree, at any rate, a diversified economy[5]—a diversification due mainly to the activity of smallholders on cattle, plantain, ginger, pimento, coconut, and coffee estates and holdings. Some, the 'jobbers', set up in supplying slave labour to estates that needed help with holing, cutting, or transporting cane. Country parishes increasingly relied on these jobbers to supply slaves for road work and repair.

These small settlers were the true 'pioneers' of the island; and they were not all men either. For instance, during a debate in 1813, certain sympathetic Assemblymen pointed out that the Deficiency Law (an old Jamaican statute imposing fines on landholders if a certain proportion of whites to blacks was not maintained on their properties or premises) was

[1] *View*, p. 196.   [2] See 17 Geo. III, c. 26 of 21 Dec. 1776.
[3] *JAJ*, IX, 147 of 23 Nov. 1792.
[4] See, for example, *JAJ*, VII, 374 of 13 July 1781.
[5] See F. W. Pitman, 'The Settlement and Financing of British West India Plantations in the Eighteenth Century', *Essays in Colonial History*, op. cit., p. 253; Ragatz, *Fall*, p. 38.

peculiarly oppressive to white females possessing small properties, the whole income of [which] barely yield[ed] a sufficient sum to defray the expence of a white overseer, for whom they would be compelled to maintain a separate establishment on their properties, as it could not reasonably be expected that a female could introduce a single man to reside in the same dwelling with her.[1]

But it was, naturally, mainly a man's world. John Cole of St. Ann took up

several parcels of land in an uncultivated neighbourhood [in his parish], known by the name of Tingley's Valley, far distant from any settlement, and . . . with much trouble, expence, and industry, opened and planted about 200 acres . . . in provisions and Guinea-grass. . . .[2]

He also made a ten-mile road 'at much labour and expence [and] encouraged several others to patent lands in that neighbourhood, and to begin settlements upon the same'.[3] But the most important, certainly the most independent, of these small settlers were the coffee planters. In

a certain part of the interior mountains in the parish of St. George, commencing northwardly, at the mouth of Bautima river, where the new road from Swift-river to Silver-Hill begins [are] about twenty-two coffee-settlements, most of them new ones, and whose number are yearly increasing.[4]

The above was typical of a development taking place all over the island. Coffee had been introduced in 1728[5] but it was not until 1773 that it was officially encouraged. In that year, the Assembly offered a premium of £100 to 'the person who shall produce to a committee of the house, in the session of Assembly to be held in November, 1774, a quantity not less than [1 cwt.] of coffee, the produce of his own land. . . .'[6] There were then about 150 coffee plantations on the island.[7] The advantage of coffee planting, as those who took it up were to discover, was that it required relatively little labour.[8] One slave could look after an acre and a half and the average coffee plantation employed between fifty and seventy slaves.[9] Coffee plants would yield, on suitable soil, 300 lb. per acre in the second year, 500 lb. in their third, and from 600–700 lb. in the fourth year of cultivation,[10] and growers were receiving on the British

[1] Reported in *R.G.*, XXXV (1813), 48, 18.   [2] *JAJ*, VIII, 203 of 1 Dec. 1786.
[3] *JAJ*, VIII, 203 of 1 Dec. 1786.   [4] ibid., X, 609 of 17 Nov. 1801.
[5] *Jamaica Almanac for 1815*, p. 135.   [6] *JAJ*, VI, 464 of 26 Nov. 1773.
[7] Long, *History*, Vol. I, p. 496.
[8] Benjamin Moseley, *A Treatise Concerning the Properties and Effects of Coffee* (London, 1785), 5th ed., 1792, p. v.
[9] See *JAJ*, XII, 796–7 of 20 Dec. 1815.   [10] ibid.

market from 77*s*. to 95*s*. per cwt. in 1793/4 and from 185–96*s*. per cwt. in 1799.[1] As a result of the local encouragement, which was a direct result of a shilling-in-the-pound reduction in British excise duties in 1783,[2] plus the further boost given by the closing of the St. Domingue market as a result of the Revolution there (1790),[3] there was a steady increase in the number of coffee plantations. Compared to the 150 in 1774, there were 607 in 1792, employing 21,000 slaves[4] and 686 in 1799, employing 34,000 slaves.[5] Exports jumped from 654,700 lb. in 1773[6] to 1,603,000 lb. in 1791, 11 million lb. in 1800, and to 25 million lb. by 1810;[7] and though, because of the recovery of St. Domingue and Bonaparte's exclusion of British coffee from the European market, merchants felt that the boom was over,[8] production still averaged over 24 million lb. in 1815 and 22 million lb. in 1820.[9]

A typical 'pioneer' coffee plantation, worth, say 10–15,000 lb. of beans, along with a small pen of twelve cattle, in Trelawny, in the 1790s (within striking distance of the Maroons) consisted of the mansion house, coffee store, coffee kiln, pulping-mill and water-mill for cleaning the coffee, twelve 'negro houses' for seventy negroes, plus forty-five acres of provision grounds exclusive of polincks.[10] A more 'settled' small planter, growing, say, plantain and pimento, lived in a dwelling house forty-two feet by thirty-two feet, floored with cedar, tamarind or mahogany and covered with cypress shingles. This house would have four bedrooms, a hall, a front and back piazza, with kitchen, toilets, stable, offices and perhaps a pigeon-house nearby. The pimento walk would be of about 120 acres, the plantation walk about ten acres, with about ten acres of provisions (corn and cassava).[11]

Pens, even quite small ones, could be much more elaborate affairs. Some smallholders, like John Lamond in 1779, coming up in the world, could not afford to buy one of these outright. He started off by renting Castile Fort Pen (445 acres, between Port Royal and Kingston) for £220 per annum. He, however, purchased all the stock

[1] Ragatz, *Fall*, p. 206.   [2] Edwards, op. cit., Vol. II, pp. 339–40.
[3] Stewart, *View*, p. 119.   [4] *JAJ*, IX, 146 of 23 Nov. 1792.
[5] ibid., XII, 796–7 of 20 Dec. 1815.
[6] William Young, *The West-India Common-place Book, compiled from parliamentary and official documents, showing the interest of Great Britain in the sugar colonies* (London, 1807), p. 15.
[7] *JAJ*, XII, 796–7 of 20 Dec. 1815.   [8] See *R.G.*, XXXIII (1811), 44, 9.
[9] *JAJ*, XII. 796–7; Stewart, *View*, p. 118.
[10] Taken from a list of losses suffered by two coffee planters after a Maroon attack in 1795; *JAJ*, IX, 534 of 2 Nov. 1796.
[11] See *JAJ*, VII, 489, 491 of 12 Nov. 1782; IX, 550–1 of 15 Nov. 1796.

on the pen, amounting to several hundred pounds. There was a storehouse 'annexed' to the pen, a corn field, some valuable woodland, and a wharf.[1] To get his produce to Kingston (meat, corn, dairy products), Lamond found that the most convenient route (this was a common mode of transport at the time), was across the bay, by water. He therefore made use of the pen's wharf, and bought a number of sailing craft. This led him into trading in cordwood, white-lime and stone (to be sold as ballast to ships in Kingston harbour). Unfortunately, during the martial law in force early in 1779, the militia took possession of Castile Fort Pen, and

converted it into a fortification and encampment; the cattle pen was destroyed, the fences were spoiled; prodigious havock was made of the cord-wood . . .; the cornfield was changed into a parade . . . and his store-house and wharf were appropriated to the use of the public; all the lignum-vitae and bastard cedar trees were hewed down, and dragged out of the pastures. . . . One pasture particularly, wherein grew many cashew trees, which were the only shelter for the sheep in the rainy seasons, was so destroyed, by lopping the trees, and the fences so broken, as rendered it useless for that purpose. . . .[2]

This was the problem facing many small settlers. Although the Government was interested in settlement and was willing, to a limited extent at any rate, to help encourage it, the small planters themselves had no say in the legislature or on the vestries and therefore had no way (except through petitions) of influencing the authorities to their needs. The case of Castile Fort Pen is only one example. Small settlers on One-Eye estate in St. Elizabeth, to take another case, were unable to continue settlement because of attacks from runaway slaves in the area. They petitioned, without success, for soldiers to be settled near One-Eye as a deterrent.[3] But the most scandalous case of Establishment callousness *vis-à-vis* smallholders' welfare followed the 1780 hurricane which devasted the parishes of Westmoreland, Hanover, and St. James. The British House of Commons voted £40,000 to assist with rehabilitation in these parishes.[4] But the spate of complaints from small settlers concerning the administration of

---

[1] A fair proportion of Lamond's estate, given the Castile Fort area, would have been simply waste, scrub.

[2] *JAJ*, VII, 202 of 11 Dec. 1779.

[3] ibid., X, 253 of 20 Feb. 1799. For an account of the Assembly's plan to have British soldiers settle in the island as small proprietors, see pp. 87–8, above.

[4] See *JAJ*, VII, 366 of 5 July 1781, which contains a Whitehall, Treasury-Chambers Order, dated 16 Feb. 1781.

this fund in Jamaica, indicates that the purpose for which it had been provided was being misinterpreted; certainly the money was being misdirected.

That the . . . commissioners, little regarding the benevolent and charitable purposes of the trust reposed in them, have made most partial and inadequate allotments of the trust-money. . . . And the petitioners do ascribe the injuries done to themselves and others, in this respect, to the too extended plan of distribution strangely assumed by the said commissioners, according to which, very many persons of rank, figure, and fortune, in the community, have been permitted to receive, as objects of charity, [larger] proportions of the said trust-money [than they ought to have had].[1]

Alexander Mylne of Hanover, a mason, applied to the commission, received for answer 'that as he was a young man (though near fifty years old) they thought he was no object.'[2]

The Savanna-la-Mar shopkeepers complained that

The planters undoubtedly suffered much; their canes were injured, their provisions mostly destroyed, and their buildings blown down; but the materials, and their other effects remained on the spot, and they were possessed of abundant resources to repair their losses; whereas the unfortunate inhabitants of Savanna-la-Mar, whose situation in the dire calamity affording them no shelter, were swept away by the torrent, with their houses, slaves, apparel, furniture, and money, a few only escaping the tremendous and general wreck.[3]

It is surprising, indeed, that in the teeth of depredations from Maroons, from runaway and rebellious slaves, from the weather, from the Establishment, that the Jamaican small settlers were able to contribute as much as they did to the island's economy. With more luck and more encouragement from Government they might have achieved even more. They were the pioneers of a frontier society, but unlike their American cousins, they were not able to respond properly and fully to its challenge. Had they been able to do so, they might have enriched, perhaps even transformed, the creole society of which (despite their numbers) they were so marginally a part. But they remained scattered, separate, without any consciousness of themselves as a group. The result, after 1815, was their steady decline, leaving only the sentiment of what might have been.

[1] *JAJ.*, VII, 486 of 12 Nov. 1782.   [2] ibid., 494.   [3] ibid., 488.

11

BLACKS

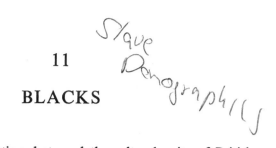

THE American Revolution destroyed the cultural unity of British America, isolating Jamaica and throwing the island back upon its own resources. The response to this new situation was positive but limited because of the basic constitutional and military weakness of the territory, and because, as a specialist sugar producing colony, there was no real attempt, or apparent need, to diversify the internal economy and make the island self-sufficient. Even within the context of British mercantilism this might have been achieved, had it been possible to obtain a sufficient number of independent white settlers, or to utilize the large non-white population of the island towards this end. The difficulty here was that most of the non-white population were slaves—either African or of African descent—and regarded legally and to a large extent socially, as *things*, human machines, while the free coloured population (approximately 40,000 in 1820)[1] was excluded from effective participation in the life of the island until 1830.[2]

Slavery in Jamaica

As in the Americas generally, West African Negro slaves were imported into Jamaica to labour on the plantations—in Jamaica's case, mainly on the sugar plantations. Significant importation began in 1703 and by 1775, nearly 500,000 had already been absorbed into the island.[3] It is estimated that there were 167,000 slaves in the colony in 1768.[4] By the end of the period of this study, the figure had risen to 339,000.[5] Of the 250,000–255,000 in the island in 1790/91, about

[1] This figure is arrived at from the discussion in Duncker, op. cit., pp. 1–10. 'Coloured' in this context means people of mixed African and European descent.

[2] Duncker, op. cit., p. 37.

[3] See 'account of the number of negroes imported into this island from Africa, since the year 1702 . . .', *JAJ*, VI, 598 of 30 Nov. 1775. Some of these were re-exported to North America and elsewhere. In 1788, Henry Shirley put the then total import figure at 676, 276. (*JAJ*, VIII, 429 of 12 Nov. 1788.)

[4] Long, *History*, Vol. I, p. 58.

[5] *JAJ*, XIII, 507 of 9 Dec. 1820. Total imports into Jamaica are estimated at 747,500; into the British Caribbean as a whole 1,665,000. See Philip D. Curtin, *The Atlantic Slave Trade: A Census* (University of Wisconsin Press, 1969), p. 268.

three-fifths were employed on sugar plantations,[1] concentrated in the parishes of Trelawny, St. Thomas-in-the-East, St. Mary, St. James, Hanover, Westmoreland, Clarendon, St. Ann, St. Elizabeth, Vere, St. Andrew, and St. Thomas-in-the-Vale, in descending order of density.[2] In the parish of St. David, slaves outnumbered whites by as much as 29 : 1 in 1793.[3] The average slave/white ratio for the island as a whole was just under 10 : 1 throughout the period of this study:[4]

	slaves	whites
1768	166,914	17,000[5]
1785	229,000	25,000[6]
1787	c. 237,000	23,800[7]
1790	255,700	c. 23,000[8]
1791	250,000	30,000[9]
1805	280,000	28,000[10]
1807	c. 260,000	c. 30,000[11]
1820	339,287	35,000[12]

These slaves may be divided for convenience into five main functional groups: field slaves, mechanics, domestic slaves, 'jobbing' or hired slaves, tradesmen and 'professionals'. Runaways, rebels, and freed slaves formed another category, and within the slave groups, there were also distinctions based on colour (black, brown, yellow, ash) and on whether the slave was African or creole.

The Field Slaves

These made up the great mass of the slave population, 160,000 out of a total 220,000 in 1787, according to Long;[13] 140,000 out of the total of 250,000 reported by Coke in 1791.[14] Their work routine has

[1] Phillips, *Negro Slavery*, p. 50; Coke, *History*, Vol. I, p. 369.
[2] *JAJ*, IX, 425 of 17 Dec. 1795. Compare this with the table on p. 122, above.
[3] St. David Vestry Minutes, 1793–1800: Deficiency Tax Returns, December Quarter 1793.
[4] In Barbados (1790), the white/slave ratio was just under 1 : 4; in Antigua, 1 : 18; in St. Domingue, 1 : 16. (Edwards, op. cit., Vol. II, p. 2; Vol. III, pp. 2, 12.) Barry Higman, using the 'Returns of Registrations of Slaves, 1832', at the Jamaica Archives, Spanish Town, places the Jamaica white/slave all-island ratio in 1832 at 1:19·83, and the rural ratio at 1:26·06; the white population figures being derived from the 1844 Census. St. David then had a ratio of 1:42·97 and St. Thomas-in-the-East a ratio of 1:47·97. (Barry Higman, 'Some Demographic Characteristics of Slavery in Jamaica, c. 1832', U.W.I., Dept. of History, Postgraduate Seminar Paper, March 1969, [Appendix], p. 2.)
[5] Stewart, *View*, p. 24.   [6] Moreton, op. cit., p. 38.
[7] Add. MS. 12431 f. 224.   [8] Beckford, *Account*, Vol. I, p. xxix.
[9] Edwards, op. cit., Vol. I, p. 284; Vol. II, p. 2.   [10] Young, op. cit., p. 3.
[11] Renny, op. cit., p. 127.   [12] *JAJ*, XIII, 507; Stewart, *View*, p. 36.
[13] Add. MS. 12414 f. 23.
[14] Coke, *History*, Vol. I, p. 369. For Coke, see p. 208, n. 6, below.

been well described in contemporary and modern accounts,[1] and will not be repeated here.

On a well-run estate, it was said,[2] 60 per cent of the field slaves would be effective as and for labour at any given time. This was true, say, for the Prices' estate at Worthy Park in St. John where, in 1789, seventy-nine of the 119 field slaves (66 per cent) were unequivocally recorded as 'able'.[3] But a picture of the economic wastage involved in the System begins to emerge when the *total* slave population at Worthy Park is considered. In 1787, only 157 of the 306 slaves there (51 per cent) were 'able';[4] and in 1789, only 112 out of 310—36 per cent.[5] Seventy women (47 able) as compared to 29 male 'specialists' (20 able) were in the fields in 1789. Twenty other men doubled as field slaves and boilers, wainmen, etc.; and there were 28 watchmen, all old, infirm and/or sickly.[6] Jobbing gangs had to be hired.[7] Here was 'built-in obsolescence' with a vengeance. Some small Government properties were little more than asylums. Of the sixteen slaves at the Botanical Gardens in 1799, six were like the Worthy Park watchmen, either old or lame and diseased.[8] In 1796, on the Government Mountain (the Governor's 'retreat'), there were eleven working men and five unfit ones; six working women and seven unfit.[9] (Soon after the revelation of this, the 'retreat', at the Governor's suggestion, was sold and £2,000 per annum added to his salary instead.[10]

[1] See, for example, Marsden, op. cit., pp. 28–30, 35–8; Moreton, op. cit., pp. 146–52; Wm. Fitzmaurice and Dr. Harrison in *P.P.*, XCII (34), no. 745, pp. 47, 217–21; Edwards, op. cit., Vol. II, pp. 245–75; H. T. De la Beche, *Notes on the present condition of the negroes in Jamaica* (London, 1825), pp. 4–8; U. B. Phillips, 'A Jamaica Slave Plantation', *American Hist. Review*, vol. XIX, no. 3 (April 1914), pp. 543–58; Patterson, op. cit., pp. 65–9.
[2] See *R.G.*, XXXVIII (1816), 27, 10. In St. Kitts (May 1801) the figure for one well-run estate was 80 per cent. See Clement Caines, *Letters on the Cultivation of the Otaheite Cane . . .* (London, 1801), table facing p. 246.
[3] 'A General List of the Negroes on and belonging to the Worthy Park Plantation taken the 1st January, 1789', Worthy Park Plantation Register, 1787–91, MS. Worthy Park Estate, Lluidas Vale, Jamaica. Phillips's 'A Jamaica Slave Plantation' makes use of a second Worthy Park Register (1791–1811) which came into his possession at a New York auction and is now in the Library of Congress. (Phillips, p. 544, n. 1; Ragatz, *Guide*, p. 26.) No photostat or microfilm copies of this document are yet available in Jamaica. Two English researchers, however, have recently completed a study of Worthy Park, initiated by the Estate as part of its tricentenary celebrations. See Michael Craton and James Walvin, *A Jamaican Plantation: the History of Worthy Park, 1670–1970* (London, 1970). For the period of slavery, it is critical of much of Phillips's use and interpretation of material. The 1787–91 Register is soon to be transferred to the Jamaica Archives. 'The General List' for 1789 is included in this text as Appendix III.
[4] 'A General List of the Negroes on and belonging to the Worthy Park Plantation taken on the 1st January, 1787', as at n. 3, above. [5] See Appendix III.
[6] ibid. [7] Worthy Park Plantation Register, op. cit., *passim*.
[8] *JAJ*, X, 285 of 12 March 1799. [9] ibid., IX, 486 of 12 April 1796.
[10] ibid., 508–9 of 23 April 1796.

The annual plantation slave decrease was calculated by Bryan Edwards to be $2\frac{1}{2}$ per cent per annum in 1789.[1] Robert Hibbert, in Evidence before the House of Commons in 1790, claimed the decrease to be 5 per cent per annum, with a compensatory increase, by births, of 2 per cent.[2] The optimum working life of an able-bodied male slave was estimated, on the average, as being seven years.[3]

Before the Abolition of the Trade (1807), the approximate purchase price of a 'new' male slave was between £50 and £70. Healthy females cost between £50 and £60, as did a youth approaching manhood ('man-boys'). Children (under fourteens) fetched from £40 to £60, if African.[4] Prices for creole slaves were about 20 per cent higher.[5] Children were valuable, obviously, because they could be more flexibly trained and successfully adapted than adults. Prices for all categories rose steadily throughout the period;[6] steeply after 1807. James Stewart,[8] writing just before 1823, put the value of an able field slave at £180. Bickell,[9] writing in 1825, quotes £140.[10] 'Seasoned' slaves were of course valued much higher. Some field slaves at the Botanical Gardens, for instance, fetched from £100 to £200 in 1799.[11] On the other hand, old lame and/or diseased slaves were valued at £60 to £20[12] and one exasperated owner put the value of his slave, Pompey, who was not only very old and infirm, but had 'been runaway for upwards of 10 years' and had been sentenced to transportation, at a microscopic $7\frac{1}{2}d$.[13]

Long estimated the average annual cost of maintaining a field slave (in the 1780s) at about £12 sterling. This included food, clothing, medicine, poll tax, and insurance.[14]

Mechanics

These were the skilled workers (usually black or coloured creoles) who had steadily replaced white indentured labour during the

[1] Speech to the Free Conference between the Assembly and Council, Spanish Town 10 Nov. 1789, reported in the *Daily Advertiser*, 22 Jan. 1790.
[2] Robert Hibbert, *P.P.*, LXXXVII (29), p. 368.
[3] Wm. Fitzmaurice, *P.P.*, XCII (34), no. 745, p. 222; Frank Tannenbaum, *Slave and Citizen, the Negro in the Americas* (New York, 1947), p. 36.
[4] Edwards, op. cit., Vol. II, p. 154; *P.P.*, LXXXIV (26), Part III, Jamaica, A. No. 29
[5] ibid.
[6] See Ragatz, *Fall*, pp. 130, 191; Phillips, *Negro Slavery*, p. 365.
[7] Phillips, *Negro Slavery*, p. 400; *R.G.*, *passim*.   [8] *View*, p. 116.
[9] The Rev. R. Bickell, author of *The West Indies as they are* (loc. cit., n. 2, p. 126) was a curate in Kingston and later in Port Royal towards the very end of the period of this study.   [10] Bickell, op. cit., p. 245.
[11] *JAJ*, X, 285 of 12 March 1799.   [12] ibid.   [13] *R.G.*, XXV, 18, 9.
[14] Add.MS. 12404 f. 405; letter to Lord Wakingham, 15 March 1787.

eighteenth century. On the plantations, these men maintained the sugar works: carpenters, millwrights, coppersmiths, wheelwrights, coopers, sawyers, distillers, boilers, blacksmiths, bricklayers, to whom may be added other specialists like head-drivers, mule-men, cattle-men and midwives. The jobs of watchmen and 'governesses' went to superannuated males and females respectively. There was also an 'official' known as the 'Jumper' or 'Johnny Jumper', who was employed, according to evidence before the House of Commons in May 1790,[1] to whip the delinquent or intransigent.

The most valuable slaves in this category (that is, those on whom the highest valuation was placed by the owners) were the carpenters, millwrights and coppersmiths (valued in 1789 at £140 to £300 currency), followed by coopers, sawyers, distillers and midwives at £120 to £200. Head-drivers, (according to the House of Commons evidence)[2] were worth only between £120 to £150, but they no doubt made up for this in social prestige (*vis-à-vis* the field slaves) and through special clothing and drink allowances.[3]

Perhaps the most skilful slave on an estate was the Head Boiler, who had to know how the cane had been raised and treated, its species, the kind of soil it had grown in, whether it had been arrowed, bored or rat-eaten. Knowledge of this kind would determine the juice's tempering with lime, how long it would have to boil, and hence the quality of the sugar.[4]

Master mechanics like carpenters, coopers, masons and coppersmiths had perhaps the greatest amount of freedom on sugar plantations, as (especially before the Abolition of the Slave Trade), they were encouraged to 'job' off the estate and pay the planter a weekly sum.[5]

Domestic Slaves

This group was regarded by most slaves and masters as being in a more 'honourable' position than the field slaves.[6] Poor Ned, a mulatto stable boy, a domestic, was in 1790, because of some misdemeanour, 'stripped of his livery, *degraded to a field negro*, and for six months dug cane-holes, weeded and cut down the crop. . . .'[7]

[1] *P.P.*, Vol. LXXXVIII (30), pp. 246, 374.
[2] *P.P.*, as for n. 9, p. 154, above.   [3] De la Beche, op. cit., pp. 10–12.
[4] Pitman, 'Slavery', p. 598; Roughley, op. cit., pp. 85–6.   [5] Lewis, op. cit., p. 200.
[6] See William Beckford, *Remarks upon the situation of negroes in Jamaica, impartially made from a local experience of nearly thirteen years in that island* (London, 1788), p. 13.
[7] '. . . with a fifty pound weight fastened to his body'. *A Short Journey*, Vol. II, p. 74, my italics.

A similar disgrace befell the Pinnocks' 'House Wench', Rose.[1] A high proportion of these slaves were coloured, which perhaps also gave them status in the unfree hierarchy, though in *Marly* a black slave tells a coloured one: 'You brown man hab no country— Only de neger and de buckra hab country.'[2] On the other hand, because of their proximity to the masters (and mistresses) domestic slaves were probably less personally independent than field slaves and what is more, could be subject if they were so unfortunate, to the sadistic whims and devices of their frustrated owners. As one witness told the House of Commons Inquiry of 1790/1:

... I have heard many of them say, that they would rather continue under the hardship of the field, than be what is there called a House Negro; and here I will give an instance of one person, at whose house I was boarded about six months. He was a doctor, who treated his Field Slaves ill, but I had an opportunity of seeing how his domestics were treated daily. A boy that waited on him, he made no more of knocking down than if he had been a piece of wood. ... [There] were two house wenches he served in the same manner. One evening one of them had either broken a plate, or spilt a cup of tea, which raised his passion so much, that he took a hammer and a tenpenny nail, and nailed one of her ears to a bullet-tree post. ... We went to bed, and left her standing there; in the morning we found she was gone, having torn the head of the nail through her ear. As soon as the Doctor knew, he dispatched a man, who brought her again, and when I came to breakfast about eight o'clock, I found he had given her a very severe whipping. His fury did not stop here; he had taken a pair of large scissors and clipt both her ears off close to her head, and she was set picking seeds out of cotton, amongst three or four more that had been emaciated by his cruelties till they were fit for nothing else.[3]

On smaller plantations, if not the treatment, certainly the distinction between field and house slave might have sometimes been less clear—the slave working in or about the house when young, moving to the field in his prime, and returning to the house as his back cracked and he became weaker. On larger estates, however, where specialization was necessary, this happened more rarely.[4]

Peter Marsden (writing, however, after only one year's experience of living on a plantation),[5] regarded the presence of domestic slaves

[1] Pinnock, Diary, 7 Aug. 1777.   [2] *Marly*, p. 94.
[3] Henry Coor, *P.P.*, XCII no. 745, pp. (34), 91–2. The Evidence contains several more such instances.
[4] For a recent imaginative reconstruction of slave labour (in the American South see William Styron, *The Confessions of Nat Turner* (London ed. 1968).
[5] See Marsden, op. cit., p. 1 of Advertisement.

as a positive danger.[1] He was perhaps in dread of being poisoned. This was a not unreasonable anxiety, considering the slaves' skill in this matter and the opportunities open to them to give it practice.

I attended the Slave Court, where a negro was tried for sheep-stealing, and a black servant girl for attempting to poison her master. . . . The latter was a girl of fifteen, called Minetta: she acknowledged the having infused corrosive sublimate in some brandy and water; but asserted that she had taken it from the medicine chest without knowing it to be poison, and had given it to her master at her grandmother's desire. This account was evidently a fabrication. . . . She [had] stood by the bed to see her master drink the poison; witnessed his agonies without one expression of surprise or pity . . .[2]

A neighbouring gentleman, as I hear, has now three negroes in prison, all domestics, and one of them grown grey in his service, for poisoning him with corrosive sublimate; his brother was actually killed by similar means. . . . Another agent, who appears to be in high favour with the negroes whom he now governs, was obliged to quit an estate, from the frequent attempts to poison him; and a person against whom there is no sort of charge [of] tyranny, after being brought to the doors of death by a cup of coffee, only escaped a second time by his civility, in giving the beverage, prepared for himself, to two young book-keepers, to both of whom it proved fatal. . . .[3]

Eliza, belonging to Mr. John Williams, of the parish of St. Thomas in the East, carpenter, found guilty of having administered night-shade and other poisonous drugs to her master, by mixing the same in his coffee. . . .[4]

In 1776, a committee of the Assembly reported that it could not 'reflect, without horror, upon the late attempt at Montego-Bay, of poisoning the market, by making use of arsenic; a circumstance impossible to guard against';[5] and observed, 'with concern, the careless manner in which that pernicious drug is kept in almost every apothecary's shop'.[6] But this was a slave conspiracy, not domestic action. What is surprising is that potions were not more widely and systematically used by house slaves—despite the cases cited above— against their masters. In fact, many deaths from 'poisoning' were probably not from poisoning at all. When 'Monk' Lewis, for instance, had thought some more about Minetta's case, he added that 'as [her master had] lived intemperately, the whole blame . . . must not be laid upon the poison'.[7] In any case, the slaves poisoned each other

[1] See Marsden, op. cit., p. 2 of Advertisement.   [2] Lewis op. cit. (1929 ed.), p. 149.
[3] ibid., p. 126.   [4] R.G., XXXV (1813), 4, 17.
[5] See JAJ, VI, 693 of 17 Dec. 1776.   [6] ibid.   [7] Lewis, op. cit. (1929 ed.), p. 327.

more often than they poisoned their masters. This was usually attributed by whites to the influence of *obeah*[1]—though again it is probable that this was, in many instances, merely an accepted way of explaining away a death.

Marsden notwithstanding, the whites, on the whole, did not appear to fear death by slaves' drugs as much as might have been expected. Domestic slaves, in fact, contributed significantly to the integration of the black/white creole society. Many of them, according to the Rev. Dr. Coke, could read.[2] Many of the females were often kept as mistresses, and were 'exceedingly faithful and useful in overlooking the others in their master's absence'.[3] Long found them 'orderly and obedient'[4] and held that they conceived 'an attachment to the families they serve, far stronger than may be expected from the ordinary white domestics'.[5] This is borne out in the letters to Jane Brodbelt written to her in England from Jamaica:[6]

October 12th, 1788
Tabby [Marshall] presents her respects and is pleased you liked the Guava marmalade.[7]

July 12th, 1789
Your good dry nurse Tabby sends her warmest wishes to you and your sister.[8]

March 1st, 1793
Mama has got another little girl . . . Marshall is her Nurse, she tells you how dee.[9]

April 14th, 1793
Marshall is nursing Mrs. Gardner Millward's little Girl, they are both of them at this Minute seated down quite close to my Chair. . . .[10]

May 15th, 1794
John and Frances Millward, with your old favorite Marshall, are to sail for England in the *Simon Taylor*. . . .[11]

---

[1] See Lewis, op. cit. (1929 ed.), pp. 291–2; *R.G.*, XXXVI (1814), 17, 9. For an excellent treatment of the subject, covering the French and British islands, see Monica Schuler, 'Slave Resistance and Rebellion in the Caribbean during the Eighteenth Century'; unpublished paper, Dept. of History, University of the West Indies, Mona, Jamaica (n.d. [1966]), pp. 27–36; and Lucien Peytraud, *L'esclavage aux Antilles françaises avant 1789* (Paris, 1897), pp. 315–22.
[2] Thomas Coke, *Statement of the receipts and disbursements for the support of the missions established by the Methodist society for the instruction and conversion of the negroes in the West Indies* (London, 1794), p. 16, footnote.
[3] Marsden, op. cit., p. 8.   [4] Long, *History*, Vol. II, p. 282.
[5] ibid., pp. 282–3.   [6] *Letters to Jane*, op. cit.   [7] ibid., p. 11.
[8] ibid., p. 20.   [9] ibid., p. 55.   [10] ibid., p. 57.   [11] ibid., p. 83.

October 12th, 1794
Marshall's second trip to England has no doubt made her *quite* the English-woman.[1]

March 8th, 1795
I am distressed on account of Marshall, who you say 'left Gravesend the beginning of November', for as she was placed altogether under the directions of the Captain, I can have no doubt of her having been on board the Ship from the time of Her first sailing, as those Gentlemen are Seldom indulgent to Servants in general, but less so to those of her complexion.[2]

May 4th, 1795
Poor Marshall was truly happy to return to Us . . . [3]

James Pinnock[4] however, was not so lucky to get his man-servant back after leaving Jamaica:

October 12th, 1790
My Slave Charles Bobbie, who had lived with me in the greatest Confidence for 14 years, hearing me speak of returning to Jamaica if there was a War, ran away to Town. Had him taken up . . . put on board a press Tender [and taken before the Marshall].

November 18
. . . sincerely as I believe repenting of his Folly, he was taken into Service again.[5]

But in 1793, returning to Britain after a tour of Europe:

September 5
My negroe Charles Bobbie ran away and engaged himself as cook on board HM's frigate the *Leda*. . . .[6]

Jobbing and Hired Slaves

These were of two types. The first type were labourers kept specially by small white settlers (as already discussed),[7] to be hired out to plantations to do, or assist with, particularly heavy labour-consuming jobs like digging cane holes or weeding or transporting sugar to the ports, or hired out to the vestries to act as road-making

---

[1] *Letters to Jane*, op. cit., p. 96.   [2] ibid., p. 104.   [3] ibid., p. 105.
[4] James Pinnock was a member of an old, wealthy, influential and very well connected Jamaican family. His father, Thomas, who died in 1758, was at one time Receiver-General. His brother Phillip, was Chief Justice (1755–6), Speaker of the House of Assembly from 1768–70 and from 1775–6. James was educated at Westminster and Trinity Hall, Cambridge, and Lincoln's Inn. He became Advocate-General in Jamaica in 1787. He died in London in 1811. (See Add. MS. 33316; Metcalf, op. cit., pp. 118, 130, 144; Cundall, *Historic Jamaica* p. xvii; *Alumni Cantabrigienses*.)
[5] Add. MS. 33316.   [6] ibid.   [7] See p. 146, above.

or road repair gangs. This labour was worth, in the last twenty years of the period of this study, 2s. 6d. a day, or 15s. a week for general plantation work; 3s. 6d. to 4s. a day for road work, and 5s. a day for digging cane holes[1]—the most arduous of plantation tasks. The other type of hired-out slave was skilled: the plantation mechanics already referred to, gardeners, waiting-boys 'who can dress Gentlemen's hair' (two in 1794 were to be hired out at 32s. 6d. per month each),[2] horse-boys, coachmen, washerwomen, sempstresses, tailors, and prostitutes.

The question of slave prostitution came up before the House of Commons Inquiry into the Slave Trade in 1790–1, when a Lt. Davison, for one, admitted that it was 'a very common thing' 'for Female Slaves to be let out by their Owners for purposes of prostitution'.[3] On 20 November 1813, Col. Hamilton, Commanding Officer at Fort Augusta, the Army barracks near Kingston, because of the frequent taking-up of Negro girls from about the camp, had the following notice inserted in the newspapers:

> The Commanding Officer of Fort-Augusta, being desirous to prevent as much as possible Runaway Negro Women from being permitted to remain in or about the Fort, thinks it necessary to acquaint those persons, who are in the habit of granting passes to their Women Slaves, to resort to the Garrison, that after the present month, every Woman found there, who cannot produce a regular pass, countersigned by a Magistrate, will be taken up, and forwarded to one of the Workhouses.[4]

In other words, only authorized prostitutes—i.e. those with *owners*— were to be allowed in. One must not, however, become too 'moral' about this. As Bryan Edwards reminded his readers, prostitution was not as flagrant as it was in the cities of Europe,[5] and in a slave society, it was only natural that many of the prostitutes would be slaves.[6]

Tradesmen and 'Professionals'

From the point of view of the future development of the society, and also as individuals contributing to the development of creolization, this category of slave was perhaps the most important. In fact, many in this category were not slaves at all, and many that were, did not appear to recognize their servile status. Carpenters, semp-

[1] Bickell, op. cit., pp. 243–4.   [2] *R.G.*, XVI, 5, 4.   [3] *P.P.*, Vol. XCII (34), p. 183.
[4] *R.G.*, XXXV, 47, 24.   [5] Edwards, op. cit., Vol. II (1793 ed.), p. 23.
[6] Cf. Patterson (op. cit., pp. 160–2) who, following Moreton, makes too much, I think, of the 'problem'.

stresses and master mechanics feature prominently in this group, as did (especially in the towns) higglers.

The very scanty supply [of provisions] lately brought to this city [Kingston] ... is chiefly intercepted and bought up by negro and mulatto higglers of the town, principally slaves, and many, no doubt, runaways, before it reaches the proper and legal market-place; and these locusts thereby levy a contribution of 75 to 100 *per cent* in profit upon the inhabitants, and at the same time defraud the industrious and praise-worthy planters of small properties, the mountain gardeners, and the industrious slaves. ...

The greater part of the supply of country provisions and vegetables for this market come in by the north road; and as the demand for Up-Park Camp is pretty large, the higglers of this city go beyond that distance; and, indeed, even to the bottom of the mountains, to meet the country negroes coming down.[1]

Another group of independent slaves were the fishermen, seamen, boatmen, pilots, and canoe-men. The Kingston/Port Royal canoe men in the 1820s earned 2s. 6d. a week for 'pulling a large canoe with six or eight persons in it, three or four times a day from Kingston to Port Royal and back (and vice versa), a distance of six miles'.[2] There were also slave woodsmen, guides, 'shots' (hunters), firemen (in the towns) and rat-catchers. There seem to have been large quantities of these rodents in Jamaica during the period of this study, both in town and country. One of the book-keepers' jobs was noting in their books the number of rats captured and killed.[3] On one large estate, where records were kept, 40–50,000 of these 'noxious animals' were destroyed in a year, 'independent of those killed by poison'.[4] Rat-catchers were therefore very much in demand, the more so as one needed to have a gift for the job. An expert could capture 60 to 100 rats in a week, using 'a wooden trap of his own making, with as much effect as the best steel-spring trap'.[5]

Because slaves doing these kinds of work were indispensable and worked, on the whole, very much in isolation, they were more or less independent of a master. Many runaways were to be found in this category, carrying on their lives in virtual freedom:

---

[1] *R.G.*, XXXVIII, 29, 18.

[2] Bickell, op. cit., p. 88. This was good earning by prevailing scales. In the West India Regiment, for instance, black privates earned 6s. 9d. a day in 1796, white privates one shilling (A. B. Ellis, op. cit., pp. 5, 84). The canoe fares were probably shared between owner and canoe-man. If this was so, the 2s. 6d. a week could represent the slave's 'take-home' earnings.

[3] See *Marly*, p. 51.

[4] *The Jamaica Magazine* (Kingston, 1812), Vol. II, no. 9, p. 296.   [5] ibid.

RAN AWAY

ADAM, a creole, a fisherman by trade, much pitted in the face with the small pox, short and well made, and will attempt to pass for free; being a great smatterer in religious topics, has been lately converted by Parson Lisle, and is always preaching or praying: he was seen on board a ship this morning, going to Old Harbour, and no doubt will sail out with her when she is completely loaded. . . .[1]

Equally significant were the black and/or slave preachers, doctors and obeah-men. Whether as Christian or pagan, European or African trained or inspired, these men were almost entirely independent of white control and contributed enormously to the physical and psychological well-being of the slave population and therefore to the health of the society as a whole. Slave doctors usually confined their work to their own particular plantation. A good obeah-man would have influence throughout the district. These obeah-men (and women) received a great deal of attention from the white legislators of the island, especially after the (Tacky) slave rebellion of 1760 which was said to have been inspired by them:

And in order to prevent the many Mischiefs that may hereafter arise from the wicked Art of Negroes, going under the Appellation of Obeah Men and Women, pretending to have Communication with the Devil and other evil spirits, whereby the weak and superstitious are deluded into a Belief of their having full Power to exempt them, whilst under their Protection, from any Evils that might otherwise happen: Be it therefore enacted . . . , That from and after the First Day of June [1760], any Negro or other Slave, who shall pretend to any supernatural Power, and be detected in making use of any Blood, Feathers, Parrots Beaks, Dogs Teeth, Alligators Teeth, broken Bottles, Grave Dirt, Rum, Egg-shells or any other Materials relative to the Practice of Obeah or Witchcraft, in order to delude and impose on the Minds of others, shall upon Conviction thereof, before two Magistrates and three Freeholders, suffer Death or Transportation. . . .[2]

With the influx of American Baptist slaves or freed slaves into Jamaica as a result of the American Revolution,[3] the *public* leadership of a large mass of the slaves shifted from obeah-men to black preachers—evidence, certainly, of creolization, since it was now an element of the white man's religion that was being used by the slaves for their own spiritual purposes, though the extent to which the

[1] *Daily Advertiser*, 24 Dec. 1790.
[2] 1 Geo. III, c. 22; Act 24 of 1760, clause x, *Acts of Assembly* (1769), Vol. I, p. 55.
[3] See p. 66, above.

majority of slaves made any real distinction between obeah-men[1] and black (Christian) preachers, cannot be determined. Certainly these black preachers were not always recognized as acceptable *Christian* ministers by the white missionaries.[2] Moses Baker, the Black Baptist ex-slave from New York, had in 1814, at Flamstead, in St. James, a congregation of some 500,[3] and claimed 3,000 followers throughout the island.[4] He was prohibited from preaching under the Slave Preaching Act of 1806, but continued as an itinerant to the end of his life.[5] George Lewis, another Black Baptist, came to Jamaica from Virginia as a slave, but was allowed by his owner, a Miss Valentine of Kingston, 'upon his paying her a certain sum every month, to traverse the country as a pedlar; and [she gave] him a ticket of leave to this effect. He travelled frequently in the parishes of Manchester and St. Elizabeth . . . [and was soon] so well known among the slaves, that they assembled round him at night wherever he went'.[6] The same may be said of George Liele (the 'Parson Lisle' referred to in the Runaway Notice quoted above),[7] the first Black Baptist in Jamaica,[8] and George Gibb, an ex-slave married to a slave woman.[9] Like the obeah-man, this kind of Negro was seen as a real threat by the white power structure and gave the Establishment considerable cause for alarm.

Friday one JOHN GILBERT, a black Preacher, was brought to the Workhouse in this town [Kingston], under a commitment from the magistrates of St. George, by whom he is sentenced to two months hard labour. The practices of this black Itinerant among the negroes on various properties to which he has introduced himself, under pretence of instructing them in religious duties, have occasioned much mischief, and given very serious cause for alarm. It appears, by affidavit, that among other

[1] See Anon., *Hamel, The Obeah Man*, 2 vols. (London, 1827).

[2] See, for example, *A narrative of recent events connected with the Baptist Mission in this island, comprising also a sketch of the mission, from its commencement, in 1814, to the end of 1831* (Kingston, 1833), p. 3.

[3] 'John Rowe's Journal in Jamaica', 31 Dec. 1813 to 23 June 1814, in *Periodical Accounts relative to the Baptist Missionary Society* (Bristol, 1816), pp. 502–5.

[4] *The Baptist Annual Register, 1801–1802* (London, n.d.), p. 1146.

[5] *The Baptist Magazine* (1815), (London, 1815), pp. 168–9. An account of Baker's arrival (1783) and settlement in Jamaica, and his establishment of a Baptist community on Adelphi estate in St. James, told partly in his own words, is in John Clarke, *Memorials of Baptist Missionaries in Jamaica* (London, 1869), pp. 18–30.

[6] Buchner, op. cit., p. 48.   [7] P. 162.

[8] See, *Baptist Annual Register, 1798–1801* (London, n.d.), pp. 332, 333, 335; F. A. Cox, *History of the Baptist Missionary Society from 1792 to 1842*. 2 vols. (London, 1842), Vol. II, pp. 12–16; Clarke *Memorials*, pp. 10–11; *R.G.*, XVI, 14, 23.

[9] Clarke, *Memorials*, p. 16. This fact is mentioned because it was unusual in Jamaican society. Gibb, in fact, was twice married. His first wife had been a woman of colour.

pernicious doctrine, he strenuously insisted on the necessity of the negroes fasting at least one day in the week, when fowls, hogs, etc., were put into the hands of their teacher, as an expiatory sacrifice; and that no work whatever, either for themselves or owners, should be done on the Sabbath. The consequence of this was, that the Slaves, particularly on one estate, became, from fasting, spiritless, sick and emaciated; and being deprived of the produce of their own grounds by the prohibition of Sunday's labour, were driven to the shameful and casual recourse of plundering the property of their neighbours, to save themselves from perishing by famine. . . .[1]

African and Creole Slaves

Apart from the groupings described in the foregoing (not all of which were consciously recognized as such in the society), there were two general categories which slave owners used to distinguish what they regarded as two different kinds of Negroes. Creole slaves were those born into the society; African slaves were imported. These latter were further divided into 'old' and 'new', depending on the length of time they had been in bondage in the island.

It is not possible to provide a picture of population ratios for creole and African slaves for the entire slave period, as early statistics made no distinction between the two groups; and even within the period of this study, figures reveal significant discrepancies. In 1789, the Assembly calculated that Africans made up 25 per cent of the slave force. Ten years after the abolition of the slave trade, however, the available figures indicate that Africans made up 36 per cent of the slave population.[2] The Parish Returns for St. James (1817), in fact, give an even higher ratio: Africans, 9,150; Creoles, 16,627.[3] The figures for twelve plantations in 1817 and 1820 were as shown on page 165. In other words, in spite of considerable variation on individual estates, African slaves made up and continued to make up, until the end of our period, a significant proportion of the black population of the island.

The whites, for their part, preferred creole slaves for a variety of reasons and valued them at three times the price of African or 'salt-water Negroes' ('Guinea-birds'). In the first place, since creole slaves were indigenes, they came, as it were, ready-made and already seasoned. On the whole, they were regarded as having accepted their

---

[1] *Daily Advertiser*, 30 Aug. 1790.
[2] See *P.P.*, 1831–2, Vol. XX, Reports from Committees (16): Minutes of Evidence taken before the Select Committee on Slavery, p. 521, A. 7937.
[3] In *R.G.*, XLII, 46, 22.

	1817		1820	
	African	Creole	African	Creole
Orange Valley (Trel.)	142	473	119	520
Linton Park (Trel.)	142	163	137	169
Fontabelle and Southfield (Trel.)	261	317	235	314
Hopewell (St. Mary)	110	305	90	326
Llanrummy (St. Mary)	252	190	231	207
Fountain, etc. (Clar.)	165	223	153	217
Whitney (Clar.)	5	248	5	261
Bogue (St. Eliz.)	3	368	3	381
Hampstead (St. Eliz.)	203	137	191	141
Lyssons (St. Thos. E.)	229	297	213	299
Hector's River (St. Thos. E.)	76	305	61	316
Golden Vale (Portland)	176	299	160	320

(*P.P.*, 1831–2, Vol. XX (16), Appendix (A), pp. 566, 568.)

condition. 'The characters of creole negroes', William Beckford asserted, with thirteen years' Jamaican experience behind him,

are widely different, and in many instances may serve as a faithful contrast [to those of new negroes. New] negroes, although they seem to be cheerful upon their arrival in the colonies,[1] are apparently heavy in body and mind. . . . They have not the least idea of personal delicacy, or shame. . . .[2]

And, he added, 'The creoles are not from nature, but example, somewhat more decent.'[3] In other words, the creoles had the advantage of contact with 'civilization'—an advantage denied the 'Guinea-birds' in their homeland.

These Africans, indeed, were seen to be proud and recalcitrant ('heavy'), with a propensity to abscond as soon as opportunity presented itself—usually very soon after arrival. Besides, unlike many creole slaves who 'ran away' merely to another town or district and continued, if unofficially, as functioning members of the society,[4] African slaves tended to take to the hills, forming gangs of aggressive marauders or organizing themselves into self-contained Maroon-like communities. Those on the plantations tended to become focal points for 'seditions and mutinies'.[5] Because of this difference in

[1] As Bryan Edwards put it: 'They display . . ., on being brought to market, very few signs of lamentation for their past, or of apprehension for their future condition; but wearied out with confinement at sea, commonly express great eagerness to be sold; presenting themselves, when the buyers are few, with chearfulness and alacrity for selection. . . .' (Edwards, op. cit., Vol. II (1801 ed.), p. 153.) From the slave's own point of view, needless to say, it was not as simple as this. There was terror, relief, renewed apprehension and finally an adjustment—or not—depending on circumstances and the psycho-physical make-up of the sufferer concerned. See, *The Interesting Narrative of the Life of Olaudah Equiano or Gustavus Vassa the African*. Written by Himself. 2 vols. (London, 1789); abridged and edited by Paul Edwards (London, 1967), pp. 30–2.   [2] Beckford, *Remarks*, p. 88.   [3] ibid.
[4] See pp. 192–201, below.   [5] Long, *History*, Vol. II, p. 444.

psychological orientation,[1] the Africans tended to despise the creole slaves[2] (though this was mutual),[3] and at times of crisis—for example during the widespread slave unrest during and after the second Maroon War—tended to be openly hostile to creoles.[4]

Physically, also, African Negroes appeared different from creoles in that (with many) their teeth were filed, they had tribal marks on face and sometimes on body; their women wore their hair in plaits or combed into rolls or toupees, while some of the men shaved their heads in stripes.[5] For Long, they were less attractive than creoles in 'shape, feature and complexion'.[6] Apart from a few brilliant exceptions (usually youngsters) they had not the same kind of command of the masters' language that the creoles enjoyed, and they were great 'obeah men'.

It was from this group, however, that a real cultural contribution to creole society could have come, since they had a cultural inheritance of their own[7] which could (had conditions been different) been available for the benefit of the whole society, and a sense of continuity that was lacking in black creoles.

On my return to the West Indies [in 1785], I was surprised [wrote Bryan Edwards] to find the old-established Negroes, when young people newly arrived from Africa, were sent among them, request, as a particular instance of favour and indulgence to themselves, the revival and continuance of the ancient system [of receiving newcomers]; assuring me they had the means of supporting the strangers without difficulty. Many who thus applied, proposed each of them to adopt one of their young country-folks in the room of children they had lost by death, or had been deprived of in Africa; others, because they wished, like the patriarchs of old, to see their sons take to themselves wives from their own nation and kindred; and all of them, I presume, because, among other considerations, *they expected to revive and retrace in the conversation of their new visitors, the remembrance and ideas of past pleasures and scenes of their youth.* The strangers too were best pleased with this arrangement, and ever afterwards considered themselves as the adopted children of those by whom they were thus protected, calling them parents, and venerating them as such. . . .[8]

---

[1] See *Laws*, III, p. 362.   [2] Long, *History*, Vol. II, p. 410.   [3] ibid., p. 420.

[4] See C.O. 137/100: Balcarres to Portland, 30 July 1798.

[5] Anon., 'Characteristic Traits of the Creolian and African Negroes in the Island, etc., etc.,' in *The Columbian Magazine*, Vol. II, April 1797, p. 700; and p. 233, below.

[6] Long, *History*, Vol. II, p. 410   [7] See Chapter 15, below.

[8] Edwards, op. cit., Vol. II (1801 ed.), p. 155, my italics. The more usual view of this relationship was that the 'old' Negroes imposed a tyranny on the newcomers. See, for example, *The Diary of the Rev. William Jones, 1777-1821*, ed. O. F. Christie (London, 1929), pp. 38-9.

12

THE (FREE) PEOPLE OF COLOUR

THE offspring of white-black unions in the Americas were placed on an elaborate ladder of skin colouring. In *Marly*,[1] for instance, we find the following gradations:

Sambo:	child of mulatto and negro
Mulatto:	child of white man and negress
Quadroon:	child of mulatto woman and white man
Mustee:	child of quadroon [or pure Amerindian] by white man
Mustiphini:	child of mustee and white man
Quintroon:	child of mustiphini and white man
Octoroon:	child of quintroon and white man.

The Spaniards, with even more sophistication, accounted for, and named, combinations such as *saltatras* (mulatto/quadroon), *tente-enel-ayre* (quadroon/mustee) and givero (sambo Indian/sambo mulatto).[2] Even mulattoes were further sub-divided into *pardo*, *prieto*, *obscuro*, etc. In all, some 128 gradations were apparently possible.[3] As Long put it, referring to the Dutch,

They add drops of pure water to a single drop of dusky liquor, until it becomes tolerably pellucid. But this needs the apposition of such a multitude of drops, that, to apply the experiment by analogy to the human race, twenty or thirty generations, perhaps, would hardly be sufficient to discharge the stain.[4]

On this argument, in Jamaica, the 'stain' could be discharged much quicker. The most commonly observed distinctions were sambo, mulatto, mustee, and octoroon. Legally, all coloured people were 'mulatto' and this 'corruption of blood'[5] was visited upon 'not the

[1] Op. cit., p. 183, footnote.
[2] Long, *History*, Vol. II, p. 261. *El tente en el aire* (literally, suspended), was the term given to a colour that showed neither 'progress' nor 'retrogression'.
[3] See Charles Wagley and Marvin Harris, *Minorities in the New World* (New York, 1958), pp. 106–7, footnote, also G. A. Beltràn, 'Races in 17th Century Mexico', *Phylon*, vi (1945), no. 3; Irene Diggs, 'Color in Colonial Spanish America', *Journal of Negro History*, Vol. xxxviii (1953) no. 4, pp. 403–7; Marvin Harris, *Patterns of Race in the Americas* (New York, 1964), pp. 54–62.
[4] Long, *History*, Vol. II, p. 261.   [5] *JAJ*, III, 123 of 30 March 1733.

sins of the fathers but the misfortunes of the mothers'[1] unto the third and fourth generation of intermixture from the Negro ancestor exclusive.[2] An octoroon was therefore legally white and so automatically free in Jamaica and the British West Indies.[3]

Numbers

Professor G. W. Roberts,[4] using census figures, estimates that the average rate of increase of Jamaica's coloured population between 1844 (68,500) and 1861, was 1 per cent. Mrs. Duncker, accepting this percentage for the end of the period of her study, places the coloured population in 1830 at 59,797 of which about 15,000 were slave and 44,000 free.[5] Assuming that Professor Roberts' 1 per cent would apply for the period of this present study as well,[6] the number of coloured people in Jamaica in 1774 might be estimated at 23,000, with about 4,000 of these free (accepting Long's figure),[7] rising to 10,000 including free blacks in 1793 (accepting Bryan Edwards' figure).[8] Dallas estimates the same figure for 1803.[9] Stewart's 1823 figure is 35,000 free coloured[10] out of a possible 50,000 coloureds. This leaves 15,000 coloured slaves in 1823, which tallies with Mrs. Duncker's figures for 1830.[11]

These figures, it must be stressed, cannot be taken as reliable as there are no reliable figures for this period. Mrs. Duncker discusses this thoroughly on pages 1–10 of her study. They may, however, be taken as an indication of the steady rise of the coloured population in the island.

[1] Michael Hanley to Bathurst, 22 Sept. 1823, quoted in Duncker, op. cit., p. 20, n. 1.
[2] See Edwards, op. cit. (1793 ed.), Vol. II, p. 16.
[3] In fact, all grades above mustee were in this category.   [4] Op. cit., p. 39.
[5] Duncker, op. cit., p. 9. Mrs. Duncker's study was found invaluable in the preparation of this chapter.
[6] It would probably have been higher, since black/white sexual mixing no doubt declined sharply after Emancipation as the male whites lost their right of control over the bodies of black women. On the other hand, of course, the post-Emancipation fertility rate might have risen.
[7] Long, *History*, Vol. II, p. 337.
[8] Edwards, op. cit. (1793 ed.), Vol. II, p. 2.
[9] Dallas, op. cit., Vol. I, p. cxi.   [10] Stewart, *View*, p. 36.
[11] Barry Higman disagrees with this. 'Working from the slave side of the problem I reckon roughly 10% of the slaves were coloured in 1832, that is 31,000. Certainly both sides of the question are difficult ground, but the slave registers give a sounder statistical base than do the estimates of free-coloured. I would argue that something in the order of 25,000 coloured slaves for 1820 would be a better estimate—and I assume . . . that they had a better rate of survival than the slave population as a whole (since they were all creole and less subject to field labour), so that the estimate is on the conservative side' (Higman, Private Communication, 17 March 1969). In his paper, Higman (op. cit., p. 17) places the 1832 coloured slave population even higher—at 39,000, or about 12 per cent of the total.

Distribution

The free coloureds lived mainly in the towns: Kingston, Port Royal, Spanish Town, St. Ann's Bay, Montego Bay; in the parish of Manchester (created 1814), 'where mixed blood was a characteristic of the whole population';[1] and along Parratee Bay, east of Black River, in St. Elizabeth.[2] Kingston had by far the largest concentration of coloureds, with about 1,200 reported there in the years between 1774 and 1793,[3] 3,500 in 1807,[4] 6,719 in 1814 and 7,064 in 1819.[5] Spanish Town came next with 1,056[6] (including some 380 free blacks)[7] in the early 1770s, rising to about 1,530 in 1796.[8] One hundred and twenty-four coloured names were 'given in' to the St. Ann Vestry in 1806, sixty-three of whom were women.[9] The 1807 figures drop to fifty-nine, including twenty-two women.[10] This might indicate a 'floating' free coloured population in this area; more likely it reflects inefficiency in record keeping and collation. (The Assembly was constantly reprimanding vestries for failure to send in statistics.)[11] A small parish like St. David recorded only fourteen free people of colour in 1785.[12] But Beckford, for the 1790s, claimed that there was an average of 500 free coloured and blacks per parish.[13]

Restrictions

Of the (approximate) 35,000 free people of colour in 1820, some would have been born free as mustiphini and octoroons. A high proportion would have been born free as the children of freed mothers. The rest would have acquired their freedom through petitions to the

[1] Duncker, op. cit., p. 10. Higman queries this. The 1832 *slave* figures 'show Manchester to have [had] a below average percentage of coloured slaves'. (Private communication, 17 March 1969.)   [2] Long, *History*, Vol. II, p. 186.

[3] See ibid., p. 103; Moreton, op. cit., p. 34.   [4] Renny, op. cit., p. 103.

[5] [Gerad Tikasingh], 'A Method for Estimating the Free Coloured Population of Jamaica', unpublished paper, U.W.I., Dept. of History, Staff/Graduate Seminar [1967], p. 15.

[6] ibid., p. 14. Long (*History*, Vol. II, p. 28) says 800.

[7] Tikasingh, op. cit., p. 16.   [8] ibid., p. 14.

[9] St. Ann Vestry Proceedings 1800–9, 7 July 1806, 248–9.

[10] ibid., 13 July 1807, f. 292.

[11] See, for example, *JAJ*, VI, 457 of 18 Nov. 1773 (returns for free coloureds); VIII, 169 of 24 Dec. 1785 and 543 of 16 Dec. 1788 (Free Schools returns); XII, 794 of 20 Dec. 1815 and 57 Geo. III, c. 15 of 11 Dec. 1816 (returns of slaves); and pp. 271–2, below. The inadequacy of several Vestry records is also commented on by Duncker, op. cit., pp. 7 and 8.

[12] St. David Vestry Minutes, 1785–93: Giving-in List, 2 April 1785, f. 13. Free Negro and Indian are included in this return.

[13] Beckford, *Account*, Vol. II, p. 324. The same estimate is given by Bryan Edwards in *JAJ*, VIII, 429 of 12 Nov. 1788.

Free Black

legislature for private declaratory acts of manumission, presented by white or free coloured sponsors. Persons thus freed, however, had no civil rights *per se*. Their names had to be registered at the local vestries (until 1823) and they were issued (until 1813), with Certificates of Freedom,[1] valid for seven years,[2] which they could not travel without, and, according to Long,[3] the poorer members of this group[4] had to wear 'a blue cross on the right shoulder, on pain of imprisonment'— the badge of freedom.[5] Freed people of colour and blacks (the law of Jamaica made no distinction) were also restricted, until 1813, by the Act 2 Geo. III, c. 8 of 19 December 1761, from inheriting more than £2,000 currency or worth of property. Until 1796[6] they could not give evidence in court even in cases involving themselves[7] and not until 1813[8] could they appear in cases involving white men. Even the limited liberties granted were not as generous as they appeared. Attested certificates of baptism into the Anglican church had to be produced before appearance in court was possible, and all cases were tried before all-white judges and juries. Of especial hardship to coloured employers and owners of slaves was the legislation of 1772[9] which took away their right to save 'deficiency'[10] themselves. Coloured proprietors with more than ten slaves were legally obliged after this legislation to employ one white man per every ten slaves or pay a fine accordingly. This was not only expensive, but as a group of free coloureds put it in 1773, those

who do hire or employ such white men, are obliged to submit themselves to the humour of every white man they so employ, who oftentimes take advantage of the situation of the [coloured employer's] not being on an equal footing with them, and treat [them] with great incivility.[11]

Despite concessions in 1794, 1809, 1812, and 1813,[12] however, the

[1] See 1 Geo. III, c. 22 of 1760.   [2] See 2 Geo. III, c. 10 of 1761.
[3] *History*, Vol. II, p. 321.
[4] Those without at least a ten-slave settlement. (Long, as n. 3, above.)
[5] See Act 64 of 1717 in *Acts of Assembly* Vol. 1 (1769), p. 116. Long, however, is the only writer who mentions the cross as being actually worn. The Assembly admitted in 1788 that the law was very seldom complied with, many of the free negroes considering the badge rather as a token of disgrace, than a mark of distinction. (*JAJ*, VIII, 429 of 12 Nov. 1788. See also C.O. 137/91, Report of the Assembly by Bryan Edwards on the condition of the free people of colour, 16 May 1793.)
[6] 36 Geo. III, c. 23 of 25 March 1796.
[7] An act of 1748 (21 Geo. II, c. 7) had already granted this, but it distinguished between coloureds with and without special privileges.
[8] 54 Geo. III, c. 19.   [9] See *JAJ*, VI, 467 of 27 Nov. 1773.
[10] See p. 146, above, for an explanation of this term.
[11] *JAJ*, VI, 467 of 27 Nov. 1773.
[12] See 35 Geo. III, c. 15 (1794); 50 Geo. III, c. 18 (1809); 53 Geo. III, c. 27 (1812); 54 Geo. III, c. 20 (1813).

generality of free coloureds (and free blacks) were not able to save their own deficiency until 1830.[1]

Nor were these the only restrictions against this class. Free coloureds could not normally vote for either local or Assembly elections,[2] and they were excluded from holding office.[3] They could not of course run for election into the Assembly, and even though they had to bear arms in the militia (and by 1796[4] were outnumbering whites in this organization in several parishes)[5] they were excluded from the cavalry (it was too precious a status symbol) and could not rise above the rank of sergeant in the foot militia.

Privileges

Within this framework, however, it was possible to be given special privileges. Petitioners, again sponsored by white men or other free persons of colour, could apply for concessions, usually on the ground that they were baptized Anglican Christians, had considerable property or were at least comfortably well off, and (quite often if males) had received their education abroad—all of which placed them slightly higher in the scale than ordinary people of their caste. These petitioners would be granted, through private acts, the rights of persons born of white parents 'with certain restrictions', these restrictions varying with the individual, though never allowing them to sit in the legislature or hold government office.[6]

That the petitioner hath caused all his . . . natural children to be baptized, educated, and instructed, in the principles of the Christian religion, and intends bringing them up in a respectable manner, and to bestow on them such fortunes as to raise them above the common level of people of colour. . .

That, by the unfortunate circumstances of their births, they are subject and liable to the same rules of government, and to the same pains and penalties, as free negroes and mulattoes are, who have no education.

The petitioner therefore humbly prays, that the house will be pleased to give leave to bring in a bill, for the granting unto . . . the before-mentioned children, the like privileges as have been hitherto granted to persons under the same circumstances.[7]

[1] See Duncker, op. cit., pp. 88–93.
[2] 'It is the opinion of this committee, that mulattoes have no right to vote in the election of any member to serve in any assembly.' (JAJ, II, 531 of 1 Oct. 1725.)
[3] See 10 Annae c. 4 of 1711.   [4] See JAJ, IX, 650 of 1 August 1797.
[5] See p. 29, n. 2, above.   [6] Long, History, Vol. II, p. 246.
[7] JAJ, VII, 537 of 18 Dec. 1782.

Some petitioners in addition to their spiritual education and worldly achievements, felt also that their moral conduct distinguished them from the common herd. Eleanor Thomas told the legislators that she and her sister Juliet had 'conducted themselves in a more decent and creditable manner than persons of their complexion in general. . . .'[1] This was a not uncommon form of argument. Between 1772 and 1796, at least sixty-seven petitions involving 512 free coloured (and one only free black)[2] had passed before the Assembly. Of those involved, 176 were mulattoes, 245 quadroons, and 90 mustees.[3]

Activity

Not all privileged free coloureds, however, relied on their privileges alone to see them through life. John Swaby, a white planter, left his estates of Montpelier and New River (in St. Elizabeth) to his mulatto son James, by will, in 1826.[4] The *Jamaica Almanack* for 1828 records James Swaby as possessed of 217 slaves and 331 head of stock. He had also been to Charterhouse and held a commission as a lieutenant in the British Army.[5] People like Swaby became planters. The free coloureds in Manchester and St. Elizabeth, on the other hand, owned and worked more modest lands—small pens and coffee plantations.[6] Along swampy Parratee Bay they fished or bred poultry.[7] Many of them were overseers,[8] book-keepers, and (in the towns) artisans, clerks, tradesmen, wharfingers, collecting constables, schoolmasters, druggists, tavern keepers, grog-shop proprietors. Dugald Clarke (or Clark), a mulatto, 'the reputed son of Robert Clark, of the parish of Hanover, esquire' had[9] by great study and application made himself thoroughly acquainted with the mathematics, and the principles of mechanics in general, in order to render himself useful to the public'.[10] In 1771, he applied 'the powers of the machine commonly called a fire or steam engine, to the working of his new-constructed sugar-mills'.[11] In 1787 he was at it again: 'by

---

[1] *JAJ*, IX, 169 of 4 Dec. 1792. [2] ibid., VIII, 405 of 4 Oct. 1788.
[3] References, from *JAJ*, Vols. VI–IX and *Laws*. Vols. II–III, are too extensive to cite here.
[4] Duncker, op. cit., pp. 42–3. [5] ibid., p. 42.
[6] ibid., p. 161, n. 1. [7] Long, *History*, Vol. II, p. 186.
[8] This was unusual, because under the Deficiency Laws, free coloureds were normally supposed to employ white men to run their estates. This created the erroneous impression that the people of colour *preferred* white overseers. (See Duncker, op. cit., pp. 30, 31, 89; *The Cornwall Gazette* (Falmouth), I, 30, 232 of 25 Nov. 1823.) But there were some brown overseers. One was killed in 1798 by Cuffee, the runaway slave rebel leader. (See C.O. 137/100: Falmouth, 15 July 1798; Patty's [slave] evidence.)
[9] Duncker, op. cit., pp. 90–1, taken from Deficiency petitions to Vestries.
[10] *JAJ*, VI, 381, 382 of 14 Dec. 1771. [11] ibid., 367 of 3 Dec. 1771.

great pains, study, and labour, [he had] invented various methods of applying the power and motion of the waves, to the freeing vessels at sea of water . . .'.[1] This same contrivance, he claimed, 'which may save ships when under sail, or in storms, from sinking, will also, in calm weather, where no anchorage is to be had, prevent them from drifting . . .'.[2] This seemed, to say the least, rather vague and fanciful. But Clarke obtained £100 from the Assembly 'in full compensation for the models of [the] sundry discoveries and inventions by him exhibited at different times to the house'.[3]

More typical, perhaps, were the more solid coloured (and black) master workmen like Daniel Saa, of Spanish Town, who started work as a mason on the Rectory there in 1809 and by 1833 was rich enough to buy it;[4] Hardy, a brown skin mason of Kingston, who built the Presbyterian Kirk, and his darker son who built the Methodist Chapel.[5] As a group, these coloureds and blacks were steadily taking the place of the lower and middle-class whites in the towns, in the mechanical trades, and in jobs like piloting boats around the coast. In 1816, the law forbidding 'any negro, mulatto or other free person of colour, whether of free condition or not', to act as a master pilot, was repealed.[6]

The steady rise of the free coloured population and the defensive reaction of the white population is dramatically suggested in the admission figures (average numbers) for Wolmer's Free School for the period 1814–37.[7]

	white	coloured
1814	87	0
1815	111	3
1816	129	25
1817	146	36
1818	155	38
1819	136	57
1820	116	78
1821	118	122
1822	93	167
1823	97	187
1824	94	196

[1] *JAJ*, VIII, 278 of 27 Oct. 1787.   [2] ibid.
[3] ibid., 353 of 27 Dec. 1787.   [4] Duncker, op. cit., p. 99.
[5] Bickell, op. cit., p. 208. Clarke, like de Bundo (pp. 199–200, below), was an extraordinary person. He died in a debtor's gaol in Kingston, appointing in his will the Hon. Charles James Fox and William Wilberforce, among others, his executors. (*Columbian Magazine*, Vol. V, p. 254, of Sept. 1798.)
[6] See 56 Geo. III, c. 28.
[7] J. A. Thome and J. H. Kimball, *Emancipation in the West Indies. A Six Months' Tour in Antigua, Barbadoes, and Jamaica in the year 1837* (New York, 1838), p. 87.

Free Black

	white	coloured
1825	89	185
1826	93	176
1827	92	156
1828	88	152
1829	79	192
1830	88	194
1831	88	315
1832	90	360
1833	93	411
1834	81	420
1835	85	425
1836	78	428
1837	72	430

In other words, as the school became flooded with coloureds, white parents (unless there was an overall decline in the numbers of their children, which is unlikely at this time) probably removed their children to private, still segregated schools, of which there were several in the town.[1] Examination of school admission lists throughout the West Indies even up to the years following the Second World War would, more than likely, reveal a similar pattern.

Position in Society

These middle-class mechanical and professional coloureds who were making their way in the white world were, however, only a fraction of the whole.[2] In a society that was not designed for them and did not really recognize them (or at least did so very reluctantly), the 'lower' class of free coloured suffered. Mrs. Carmichael, speaking of St. Vincent, said that the coloured domestic slave was ten times richer and more comfortable than the ordinary free person of colour.[3] Mrs. Duncker, quoting Manchester to Bathurst,[4] says that the people of colour did not pay in taxes one thirty-fourth of what the white inhabitants paid. 'So near the borderline of poverty did many of [them] live that quite often they were buried at expense of their church.'[5]

On the estates, however, where their colour counted in relation to

[1] See advertisements in the *Royal Gazette* for the period of this study.

[2] Free coloured women (those who worked), went in for retail trading, selling 'Ribbons, silks, laces and gauzes', and some of them did a 'little genteel and skilled laundering'. Others kept lodging houses of varying classifications of repute. (See Duncker, op. cit., p. 85; Mrs. A. C. Carmichael, *Domestic manners and social condition of the white, coloured and negro population of the West Indies*, 2 vols. (London, 1833), Vol. I, p. 79.)

[3] Carmichael, op. cit., Vol. I, p. 80.   [4] 23 Dec. 1823; Duncker, op. cit., p. 76.

[5] Duncker, op. cit., p. 213.

the black slaves and in its propinquity of blood to the white masters, things were better. A very high proportion of domestic slaves were coloured,[1] and many of these were mistresses to estate owners, attorneys, overseers, and the white plantation staff generally. Their children, if slaves, in 'Monk' Lewis' experience, were 'always honoured by their fellows with the title of Miss. My mulatto house-maid is always called "Miss Polly" by her fellow-servant Phillis.'[2] It was 'considered inhuman that the child of a white man should be reduced to the same state as that of a negro',[3] and for their part, 'no freed or unfreed Mulatto ever wished to relapse into the Negro'.[4]

---

[1] See *Marly*, p. 95 and p. 156, above. [2] Lewis, op. cit. (1929 ed.), p. 143.
[3] *Marly*, pp. 94–5. [4] Long, *History*, Vol. II, p. 332.

ATTITUDES OF WHITES
TO NON-WHITES

THIS then, in outline, was the black and coloured population of Jamaica, which the white creoles utilized but generally failed to recognize as distinctive, legal, even social, personalities. This failure of recognition resulted in a crucial weakening of Jamaican society as a whole. Edward Long, in spite of his strong racialist views, saw this—visionary creole that he was—though his thoughts were only of the coloured section of the non-white population:

I can foresee no mischief that can arise from the enfranchisement of every Mulatto child.... The retrieving them from profound ignorance, affording them instruction in Christian morals, and obliging them to serve a regular apprenticeship to artificers and tradesmen, would make them orderly subjects, and faithful defenders of the country.[1]

With all this, however, Long still did not give enough credit, for instance, to the industry and proven skills of the coloureds.[2] If he could have had his way, he would have banned sexual relations between white and black altogether and would have had Jamaica peopled by a race of 'pure' whites:

[It would be far better if in Jamaica] the white men ... would abate of their infatuated attachments to black woman, and, instead of being 'grac'd with a *yellow offspring not their own*', perform the duty incumbent on every good citizen, by raising in honourable wedlock a race of unadulterated beings.[3]

But this sexuo-racial endogamy, for better or for worse, was apparently not possible in Jamaica, and as a coloured population appeared, so did the stereotypes:

The Mulattos are, in general, well-shaped, and the women well-featured. They seem to partake more of the white than the black. Their hair has a natural curl; in some it resembles the Negroe fleece; but, in general, it is

[1] Long, *History*, Vol. II, p. 333.   [2] See pp. 173–5, above.
[3] Long, *History*, Vol. II, p. 327.

of a tolerable length. The girls arrive very early at the age of puberty; and, from the time of their being about twenty-five, they decline very fast, till at length they grow horribly ugly. They are lascivious; yet considering their want of instruction, their behaviour in public is remarkably decent; and they affect a modesty which they do not feel. They are lively and sensible, and pay religious attention to the cleanliness of their persons: at the same time, they are ridiculously vain, haughty, and irascible. . . .

Some few of them have intermarried here with those of their own complexion; but such matches have generally been defective and barren. They seem in this respect to be actually of the mule-kind, and not so capable of producing from one another as from commerce with a distinct White or Black.[1]

I think it is Long who asserts, that two mulattos will never have children; but, as far as the most positive assurances can go, since my arrival in Jamaica, I have reason to believe the contrary, and that mulattoes breed together just as well as blacks and whites; but they are almost universally weak and effeminate persons, and thus their children are very difficult to rear. . . .[2]

mulatto women . . . [are] constantly liable to miscarry, and subject to a thousand little complaints, colds, coughs, etc.[3]

On a sugar estate one black is considered as more than equal to two mulattoes. Beautiful as are their forms in general, and easy and graceful as are their movements (which, indeed, appear to me so striking, that they cannot fail to excite the admiration of any one who has ever looked with delight on statues), still the women of colour are deficient in one of the most requisite points of female beauty. . . . Young or old, I have not yet seen such a thing as a *bosom*.[4]

As for Mongrel women, though the daughters of rich men, and though possessed of slaves and estates, they never think of marriage; their delicacy is such, for they are extremely proud, vain and ignorant, that they despise men of their own colour; and though they have their amorous desires abundantly gratified by them and black men secretly, they will not avow these connections.[5]

It would be considered an indeniable stain in the character of a white man to enter into a matrimonial bondage with one of them; he would be despised in the community, and excluded from all society on that account.[6]

[1] Long, *History*, Vol. II, p. 335.   [2] Lewis, op. cit., (1929 ed.), pp. 94–5.
[3] *LNJ* (Wright), p. 69.   [4] Lewis, op. cit. (1929 ed.), p. 95.
[5] Moreton, op. cit., pp. 124–5.   [6] ibid., p. 125.

As the coloured population grew and acquired property, as sons were acknowledged and even sent to England for their education and on return began gently but steadily pressing for more social, economic, civil even political liberty, two other white attitudes began to express themselves—jealousy[1] and the feeling that these people should be 'kept in their place' for the general good of the body politic (i.e. of the whites):

That it hath ever been an essential part of the constitution of Jamaica, supported by laws wisely framed for that purpose, to preserve a marked distinction between the white inhabitants and the people of colour and free blacks. . . .[2]

Besides, the argument went on, like the Jews, the coloureds in Jamaica were 'under no civil disabilities whatever'. They had '*merely* [the emphasis is mine] been excluded from political power'.[3] The assumption, as far as the white Establishment was concerned, was that despite efforts on their behalf, the moral, if not physical, nature of the coloureds ('mongrels') remained suspect, possibly even corrupt:

Supposing that these great changes[4] may work the moral effects which are expected by enlightened men, in the character of the coloured population it may at a future period be fit to review their condition, but nothing short of gross ignorance or deliberate malice could allege that everything has not been conceded which could be bestowed . . . with safety to the country or utility to this class of its inhabitants *in the actual state of their minds and faculties*. . . .[5]

But attitudes and stereotypes used by Jamaican whites in face of the coloured population were fragile compared to those elaborate masks of thought they used (and were forced to use), confronted by the mass of slavery. To say though, that these constructions were exclusively fashioned by slavery would be too easy an answer. Slavery, as seen within the terms of this study, was an institution of the society. But no white creole, it must be realized, ever thought in terms of slavery in the abstract. Slavery meant the workers on the

---

[1] See Duncker, op. cit., p. 125, quoting the Rev. Thomas Cooper.

[2] *JAJ*, XII, 531 of 25 Nov. 1830, Petition of the city and parish of Kingston against the proposed Act of 1813 granting further privileges to people of colour and free blacks.

[3] The Hon. Committee of Correspondence, Minute Book, 1794–1821; 22 Dec. 1815.

[4] See p. 172, above.   [5] As for n. 3, above; my italics.

plantation, the higglers in the sandy streets of Kingston,[1] black men and women making noise in the market. Even more than the Assembly, here (but less consciously so) was an institution that had 'encroached' until it had become almost completely identified with the society in which it was rooted. If the Assembly had established itself within the period of this study, as the head, arms, and legs of the body politic, slavery was certainly its back, guts, and thighs. White attitudes to slaves and to slavery were therefore, in a subtle, intimate manner, also white attitudes and sentiments about themselves. They simply looked into a black mirror of subordinate flesh. White treatment of their slaves was in a way that was to have its own consequences later on in time, white treatment of themselves; for the health of the slaves and of their social world was inextricably related to the health of the whites and of the society as a whole. As Douglas Hall has put it, 'the essential and unanswerable problem . . . was that although the slaves were accounted as capital equipment, they were people, and their masters were torn by conflict between these two views of their property'.[2]

But even when seen as people, what sort of people were slaves in the island seen to be? Many writers of verse, for example, perhaps feeling the then fashionable urge to express 'fine feelings' and certainly influenced by contemporary models in England, saw their slaves through the sentimental eyes of neo-classic or rural romanticism. Isaac Teale, for one, saw his 'Sable Venus' in this way:

> Her skin excell'd the raven plume,
> Her breath the fragrant orange bloom,
>   Her eye the tropick beam:
> Soft was her lip as silken down,
> And mild her look as ev'ning sun
>   That gilds the COBRE stream.[3]

In the anonymous *Jamaica*, written in 1776, the slaves, after 'In field or household' passing 'the toilsome day'

---

[1] See, for instance, George Pinckard, *Notes on the West Indies, . . . including observations . . . relating to the Creoles and Slaves of the Western Colonies, and the Indians of South America* . . ., 3 vols. (London, 1806); 2nd ed., 2 vols. (London, 1816), Vol. 2, pp. 369, 371.

[2] Hall, 'Slaves and Slavery', p. 309.

[3] In Edwards, op. cit., Vol. II, p. 35, without attribution to Teale. 'Cobre stream' is the Rio Cobre, near Spanish Town.

> ... spend the night in mirth-enlivening play:
> With pipe and tabor woo their sable loves,
> In sad remembrance of their native groves;
> Or, deck'd in white, attend the vocal halls,
> And Afric postures teach in Indian balls.[1]

The Rev. William Jones, who went out to Jamaica as a tutor to Thomas Harrison,[2] the Attorney-General's family in 1778–9 also saw the slaves as a happy lot:

> 'Tis my real opinion that they are the happiest, most contented Inhabitants the Island can boast of. . . . Their life is far happier than any labouring Man's in England. After their return from daily labour they have no Wife, no numerous Family stunning their Ears with the pressing Calls of Want. . . . Their Children, as soon as they are born, are taken care of. If they are really sick or hurt by any mishap, no concern is wanting. . . .[3]

Everything, in other words, was taken care of by Good God-Father Planter, Jones claimed, in the conventional accents of the time,[4] though there is no evidence in his diary that he even visited a slave plantation, far less one of the slave's huts. White liberals, on the other hand, felt that 'The character of the negro slaves [was] no doubt deteriorated by the nature of their condition. They [had] . . . good qualities mingled with their bad ones.'[5] Renny admitted that 'The Negroes, especially the Creols, so far from being slow of comprehension, [were] uncommonly acute and penetrating', though, he was careful to add, 'this observation applies chiefly to those, who have been much in the company of the white inhabitants.'[6] Charles Campbell, a Scottish Jack of many trades, who had once been an overseer in Jamaica before becoming a surgeon back home, and whose life (threatened by yellow fever in the West Indies) had been saved through the devotion of a negro woman,[7] gave much more generous credit:

---

[1] *Jamaica, a poem, in three parts . . .* (London, 1777), p. 23.

[2] Harrison was Attorney-General, 1769–84. (See Cundall, *Historic Jamaica*, p. xix.)

[3] *The Diary of the Rev. William Jones*, pp. 27–8.

[4] See F. W. Sypher, *Guinea's Captive Kings* (Chapel Hill, 1942); the same author's 'The West Indian as a "Character" in the Eighteenth Century', *Studies in Philology*, Vol. XXXVI (1939), pp. 503–20; Elsa Goveia, *Historiography*, pp. 52–107; Philip D. Curtin, *The Image of Africa. British Ideas and Action, 1780–1850* (University of Wisconsin Press, 1964), London ed. 1965.

[5] Stewart, *View*, p. 249.   [6] Renny, op. cit., p. 172.

[7] Ragatz, *Guide*, p. 220; Charles Campbell, *Memoirs of Charles Campbell, at present prisoner in the jail of Glasgow, including his adventures as a seaman and as an overseer in the West Indies* (Glasgow, 1828), p. 9.

The slavish condition of the Negroes, and the total absence of moral and religious instruction, is a sufficient excuse for their ignorance. They know nothing about religion, and yet they have more piety than their masters. They are not so deficient in intellectual energy, as is sometimes asserted. A West Indian slave is every whit as rational a creature as a Scots peasant or mechanic, and tinged with less vulgarity.[1]

But the general and overwhelming assumption was that slaves, if human, were of a different *genus*; that they were lazy, lying, profligate, promiscuous, cowardly, savage, debased, tyrannical to their own people, ugly, and demonstrably inferior to whites.[2] The rationale of this assumption of white superiority and black inferiority was magisterially expressed by Edward Long in his *History of Jamaica*. With medieval confidence in rank and a social hierarchy set out, ready-made, by Nature,[3] Long declared that

The freedom of philosophic enquiry may still proceed to extirpate old prejudices, and display more and more . . . the beautiful gradation, order, and harmony, which pervade the whole series of created beings on this globe.[4]

Within this created order, in Jamaica, were

three ranks of men [white, mulatto and black], dependent on each other, and rising in a proper climax of subordination, in which the Whites would hold the highest place.[5]

Or, as he put in a quatrain:[6]

> The general *order*, since the whole began,
> Is kept in *nature*, and is kept in *man*.
> *Order* is heaven's first law; and, this confest,
> *Some are*, and *must be*, *greater* than the rest.

[1] Campbell, op. cit., p. 19.

[2] For a random sample of these conceptions see Long, *History*, II, pp. 320–485; *Diary of William Jones*, pp. 38–9; *P.P.*, Vol. XCII (34), no. 745, p. 203; Benjamin Moseley, *A treatise on tropical diseases, on military operations, and on the climate of the West Indies* (London, 1787), 1803 ed., pp. 115–16, 119–20, 492–3; Lewis, op. cit. (1929 ed.), p. 111 ('unless a negroe has an interest in telling the truth, he always lies—in order to keep his tongue in practice.'); John Williamson, *Medical and miscellaneous observations relative to the West India islands*, 2 vols. (Edinburgh, 1817). Vol. II, pp. 199–200; Montule, op. cit., pp. 43–4 ('Their features it is true, are not prepossessing in our eyes: but does not each of their senses perfectly fulfil its functions?'); Bickell, op. cit., p. 94; John Shipman, Dr. Stewart West in WMMS Archives, Box B. 1, West Indies.

[3] For a monograph on this, see Arthur Lovejoy, *The Great Chain of Being* (London, 1936). Lovejoy, however, does not include Long in his discussion. Long's theories were, at the time, widely accepted and continued to influence racialist thinking until well into the nineteenth century. See Curtin, *The Image of Africa*, pp. 43–5; J. C. Greene, 'The American Debate on the Negro's Place in Nature, 1780–1815', *Journal of the History of Ideas*, Vol. XV (1954), pp. 386–8.

[4] Long, *History*, Vol. II, p. 337.   [5] ibid., p. 333.   [6] ibid., p. 485.

From this, it was not too difficult to reach the conclusion 'that the White and the Negroe are two distinct species'.[1] Falling back upon his 'knowledge' of certain African tribes, Long was able to describe, with utter candour, the exact nature of the Negro 'species':

In many respects they [the Hottentots] are more like beasts than men; their complexion is dark, they are short and thick-set; their noses flat, like those of a Dutch dog; their lips very thick and big; their teeth exceedingly white, but very long, and ill set, some of them sticking out of their mouths like boars tusks. . . .[2] Their hearing is remarkably quick; their faculties of smell and taste are truly bestial, nor less so their commerce with the other sex; in these acts they are libidinous and shameless as monkies, or baboons.[3]

It was in fact the monkey tribe (ape, baboon, orang-outang) that Long finally settled on as the aptest analogue for the Negro, with sometimes the ape, sometimes the Negro, having the edge, but never really with very much to choose between them.

That the oran-outang and some races of black men are very nearly allied, is, I think, more than probable. . . . [They (the orang-outangs) do not] seem at all inferior in the intellectual faculties to many of the Negroe race; with some of whom, it is credible that they have the most intimate connexion and consanguinity.[4]

Indeed, he did not think 'that an oran-outang husband would be any dishonour to an Hottentot female'.[5]

Being therefore so intimately bestial, it followed that the Negro was also cannibal:

. . why should we doubt but that the same ravenous savage, who can feast on the roasted quarters of an ape (that *mock-man*), would be not less delighted with the sight of a loin or buttock of human flesh, prepared in the same manner?[6]

From this African savagery, the poor carnivorous blacks were rescued into New World slavery. But even in the sunny Caribbean the trait persisted. On 6 November 1790, the white creoles read in the *Daily Advertiser* that

This evening a Negro lately purchased at a slave sale and employed on Shortwood estate in Liguanea, went to the hut of another Negro with intent to steal some fowles, which he was carrying away when a child threatened to tell his father, the thief seized the poor infant, and stopping

[1] Long, *History* Vol. II, p. 336.   [2] ibid., pp. 364–5.   [3] ibid., p. 383.
[4] ibid., pp. 365, 370.   [5] ibid., p. 364.   [6] ibid., p. 382.

his mouth with dirt, severed the head from his body, which he carried into a cane piece with intent, it is thought, to devour.[1]

Under the burden of all this evidence, it was only natural that white creoles would be prejudiced against Negroes and seek to keep them apart (in the South African sense of that word). '[In] whatever light white people may view them', declared one of the characters in *Marly*,

there is, I must confess, an involuntary feeling apparently implanted in the breasts of white men by nature herself, that black men are a race distinct and inferior to those whom providence has blessed with a fair complexion. This distinction of colour forms, indeed, such an impassable boundary between these two races of mankind, that it would seem to countenance the general supposition that Providence, in the wise dispensation of earthly affairs, has formed them to be hewers of wood and drawers of water to those of the favoured caste distinguished by complexions less dark.[2]

Which is a more roundabout way of saying what Long so succinctly expressed when he declared that black and white were 'two tinctures which nature has dissociated, like oil and vinegar'.[3] This notion of white superiority was accepted by all whites and (tacitly at least) by the mass of the slave population. This notion, in fact, gave sanction to the coercive whip- and fire-power of the whites. They could use the notion, because of its basic *moral* intention. Negroes were slaves in the New World for their own good. '[A] good mind', Bryan Edwards assured himself,

may honestly derive some degree of consolation, in considering that all such of the wretched victims as were slaves in Africa, are, by being sold to the Whites, removed to a situation infinitely more desirable, even in its worst state, than that of the best and most favoured slaves in their native country.[4]

This 'opinion of their Superiority', shared by all ranks of the society, as the Kingston Common Council pointed out, was 'essential . . . for preserving the dominion of the few over the many'.[5]

[1] *Daily Advertiser*, 6 Nov. 1790.   [2] *Marly*, p. 215.
[3] Long, *History*, Vol. II, p. 332.
[4] Edwards, op. cit., Vol. II, p.128. Edwards' view should be compared with more recent discussions of African slavery in Africa; for instance, N. R. Bennett, 'Christian and Negro Slavery in Eighteenth Century North Africa', *Journal of African History*, Vol. I (1960), no. 1, pp. 65–82; Smith, 'Slavery and Emancipation'. These studies, however, deal with areas outside the accepted New World supply regions which were not, on the whole, Muslim, as the Bennett/Smith areas are. For the West Coast see Walter Rodney, *A History of the Upper Guinea Coast, 1545–1800* (Oxford University Press, 1970); 'African Slavery and forms of social oppression on the Upper Guinea Coast in the context of the Atlantic Slave Trade', *Journal of African History* (1966), no. 3, pp. 431–43.   [5] K.C.C. Minutes, 1803–15; 22 Aug. 1808.

Whether it followed from this that the blacks accepted the white concept of black inferiority it is not possible to establish, mainly because of the absence of direct slave testimony on the subject. It is difficult, though, to see how slavery would have been possible in the Americas if the slaves as a group had not somehow agreed to play the role assigned to them in the drama. Creole slaves—especially that is, those born into the system—were more than likely, through a kind of emotional osmosis, to have absorbed prevailing Establishment ideas about themselves. At the First Conference of the Caribbean Artists Movement held at the University of Kent in September 1967, Professor Elsa Goveia, referring to her work on the Leeward Islands' slave society (loc. cit., p. 94, above), said: 'I have tried to point out that this integrating factor which affects the society as a whole, *is the acceptance of the inferiority of Negroes to whites.*'[1] The general preference given to coloured slaves within the period of this study and the apparent deference to them by darker slaves,[2] plus the evidence of a continuing 'white bias' throughout the Caribbean[3] and indeed the New World as a whole,[4] tends to lend support to this view. On the other hand, there are only two references[5] in the material examined in the preparation of this study which offer any indication of a sense of Negro-held views of their own inferiority.

They believed [wrote Phillippo][6] that at the creation of the world there were both a *white* and a *black* progenitor, and that the black was originally

[1] Elsa Goveia, 'The Caribbean: Socio-Cultural Framework', *Caribbean Artists Movement Newsletter*, No. 4 (August/September 1967), p. 4. Italics in text.

[2] 'The difference of colour, which had offended Nicholas so much in Psyche's child ["Oh, massa!" answered Nicholas, "the child is not my own, that is certain; it is a black man's child"] is a fault which no mulatto will pardon; nor can the separation of castes in India be more rigidly observed, than that of complexional shades among the Creoles. My black page, Cubina, is married: I told him that I hoped he had married a pretty woman; why had he not married Mary Wiggins? [see p. 198, below], "Oh massa, me black, Mary Wiggins sambo; that not allowed".' (Lewis, op. cit. (1929 ed.) pp. 73–4.)

[3] See F. Henriques, *Family and Colour in Jamaica* (London, 1953); Lloyd Braithwaite, 'Social Stratification in Trinidad: A Preliminary Analysis', *Social and Economic Studies*, Vol. II (1953), nos. 2, 3; R. T. Smith, *The Negro Family in British Guiana* (London, 1956), pp. 191–203; Errol L. Miller, 'Body Image, Physical Beauty and Colour among Jamaican Adolescents', *SES*, Vol. xviii (1969), no. 1, pp. 72–89.

[4] A useful short study is Harris, *Patterns of Race in the Americas*. See also Wagley and Harris, op. cit.; Irene Diggs, op. cit.; Oracy Nogueira, 'Skin Colour and Social Class' in *Plantation Systems*, pp. 164–83; Herbert S. Klein, *Slavery in the Americas: A Comparative Study of Virginia and Cuba* (Oxford University Press, 1967), pp. 254–64; Carl N. Degler, 'Slavery and the Genesis of American Race Prejudice', *Comparative Studies in Society and History*, Vol. ii (1959).

[5] See B. M. Senior, *Jamaica as it was, as it is, and as it may be . . .* (London, 1835), p. 45; J. M. Phillippo, *Jamaica: its past and present state* (London, 1843), pp. 188–9.

[6] Op. cit., pp. 188–9. Phillippo, A Baptist missionary, went out to Jamaica in 1823 and worked in the island for twenty years.

the favourite. To try their dispositions, the Almighty let down two boxes
from Heaven, of unequal dimensions, of which the black man had the
preference of choice. Influenced by his propensity to greediness, he chose
the largest, and the smaller one consequently fell to the share of the white.
'Buckra box,' the black people are represented as saying, 'was full up
wid pen, paper, and whip, and negers, wid hoe and bill, and hoe and bill
for neger to dis day.'

But even this is not so much acceptance of inferiority, as an ironic
explanation of reality, as in the blues.[1] The inferiority principle,
really, can only be accepted if it is assumed that the blacks had no
autonomous attitudes and traditions of their own. The material in
Chapter 15 (below) suggests that they had. From this base, many
slaves resisted European ideas and practices:

such is the ignorance, obstinacy, and inattention of negroes, so little
regard have they for each other, and so averse are they to executing the
directions of white people, when repugnant to their own prejudices. . . .[2]

these people are universally known to claim a right of disposing of themselves . . . according to their own will and pleasure, without any controul
from their master. . . .'[3]

Professor Goveia's concern, however, was with the larger issue of
social control. Here, from one view of the evidence, such as it is, it
would appear that she is right in stressing that the superiority/
inferiority principle, co-ordinated with psychological reactions to
colour, was (and is) a means of ensuring the stability of West Indian
society.[4] It must be pointed out at the same time, however, that the
presence and acceptance of these principles also weakened (as to a
large extent it still does) the society.

It weakened the society because the logic of the argument of
natural Negro inferiority in a society governed by a small white élite,
led to legal and social apartheid—though virile white males allowed
themselves important sexual exceptions to this rule. Plantation slaves
lived apart from white quarters in their own 'villages' and could not

[1] A great deal has been written on the subject in recent years. The best study, since it
is literary, socio-cultural, historical, and is written from 'inside', is LeRoi Jones, *Blues
People: Negro Music in White America* (New York, 1963).
[2] James Chisholme of Clarendon, a former member of the Assembly, on birth
customs of the slaves; *JAJ*, VIII, 434 of 12 Nov. 1788.
[3] Dr. Quier on polygamy; *JAJ*, VIII, 434.
[4] For a discussion of this in other contexts see Max Gluckman, 'The Peace in the
Feud', in *Custom and Conflict in Africa* (Oxford, 1956); Jacques J. Maquet, *The
Premise of Inequality in Ruanda* (trans., Oxford University Press, 1961).

move beyond certain statutory limits without a ticket.[1] In the towns there were Negro ghettoes. All non-whites, both slave and free, were legally discouraged from the social activity of drinking in rum-shops,[2] from riding ('furiously') along the streets, and from coming into intimate contact with whites.[3]

The legally sanctioned second-class citizenship of the free coloureds has already been discussed.[4] Coloured children, within the period of this study, had very little share in the island's public and charitable educational system. In 1793, the Trustees of Wolmer's Free School in Kingston were wondering 'how far it may be right to allow such descriptions of persons [on to] the foundation'.[5] They were not admitted (with the results indicated), until 1815.[6] Before this, the only vestry that appeared to be at all catering for coloured children, was St. Ann's, where there was a fairly high concentration of free coloureds, but even here there were restrictions:

That no more than four Children of Colour shall be received in the Free School under Mr. Prescot and that no one shall be hereafter received above the age of eight years which reception shall be always in open Vestry, that each Child of Colour born in lawful wedlock be hereafter discharged from the free School on attaining the age of fifteen years. . . .[7]

Even this limited generosity did not last. On 28 March 1800, the Vestrymen resolved that 'none but white children be admitted' to the free school,[8] thus reasserting the 'apartheid' principle.

The result was that blacks had their own social life in town and on plantation, the wealthy free coloureds had theirs, mainly in the large towns,[9] and the whites had theirs. With the exception of the theatre, coloured people, not to mention black, did not appear at public entertainment designed for the whites. Once, at a dance in Spanish Town, two educated but coloured (illegitimate) sons of no less a personage than the Chief Justice, were thrown out by a white objector on the grounds of colour, not bastardy.[10] This was not an

[1] Even to bathe in the sea, slaves needed a ticket. (See *R.G.*, XVI, 26, 24.)
[2] See, for example, Kingston Vestry Proceedings, 1781–8; Order No. 59 of 17 Jan. 1781.
[3] See 28 Geo. III, c. 5, section 25 of 22 Dec. 1787, for instance. Parallels here with white attitudes and action in Southern Africa suggest and present themselves. See, for example, Boris Gussman, *Out in the Mid-day Sun* (London, 1962); C. A. Rogers and C. Frantz, *Racial Themes in Southern Rhodesia: The Attitudes and Behaviour of the White Population* (Yale University Press, 1962).   [4] Pp. 170ff, above.
[5] Wolmer's Old Minute Book, Trustee's Meeting 12 March 1798.
[6] P. 173, above.   [7] St. Ann Vestry Proceedings, 1791–1800, 28 March 1791, p. 215.
[8] ibid., 28 March 1800, p. 259.
[9] Stewart, *View*, pp. 329–30; Lewis, op. cit., p.171.   [10] Bickell, p. 226.

isolated example of this kind of social prejudice.[1] The system operated in the churches (except the Baptists') as well. The Kingston Common Council's Resolution of 31 May 1813 is typical:

That in future the pews in the East and North Isles [*sic*] . . . excepting the North West corner Pew be exclusively appropriated to the White Inhabitants and the said Corner pew with the remaining pews and the Organ loft for all other of the Inhabitants.[2]

'Instead of encouraging their Attendances on public worship' the Rev. William Jones remarked apropos of this situation,

those Negroes, Mulattoes, etc., who are free, & frequently come to Church, are look'd upon & talk'd of with such Contempt and Disrespect, as if it were a place never design'd for them, and all are desirous of seats as distant as possible from them.[3]

Similar attitudes and arrangements were to be found in the only other place of indoor public gathering—the theatre.[4] As in church, the whites sat as far away as possible from 'the others' who, as a sign of their second-class status were, perhaps quite fairly, asked to pay second-class prices for their tickets. At Montego Bay, at a gymnastic display at the theatre there in 1791, white ladies and gentlemen paid entrance fees of 5s. each, 'Children and People of Colour' paid 3s. 4d.[5] When whites paid 13s. 4d. for a box, free coloureds were asked to pay 11s. 4d.[6] At the theatre in Spanish Town, the free coloureds sat in the upper boxes or gallery. Whites were forbidden to sit in these areas.[7] Sometimes there were separate performances for white and coloured:

An Artist lately arrived from the city of Augsburg in Germany, begs to inform the Ladies and Gentleman [of Kingston] that he exhibits many curious exercises by living Birds as performed before the Emperor of Germany, and His Most Christian Majesty Lewis the XVI and other European Courts. . . .

He also performs with little dogs. Admittance 3s. 4d. each.   *Only white*

---

[1] For other examples, see *Marly*, p.191; Phillippo, op. cit., p. 148; *Negro Slavery or, a view of some of the more prominent features of that state of society as it exists in the United States of America and in the colonies of the West Indies, especially in Jamaica* (London, 1823), pp.24–8; Renny, p. 190, n.; Bickell, pp. 225–6 also gives other examples besides that given in the text.
[2] K.C.C. Minutes, 1803–15, 31 May, 1813.   [3] *Dairy of William Jones*, p.19.
[4] There was a theatre in Kingston, Spanish Town, and Montego Bay.
[5] R. Wright, op. cit., p. 295.   [6] ibid., p. 319.
[7] *St. Iago de la Vega Gazette*, No. 5, Additional Postscript, 27 Jan.–3 Feb. 1816.

persons will be admitted to the above performance. Tomorrow he intends exhibiting to persons of colour.[1]

In 1785, Jonathan James, a free quadroon of St. Elizabeth, applied to the Assembly[2] and obtained,[3] special privileges, including permission to inherit property, for his two children and three grand-children, apparently all quadroons. Eleven years later one of those grandchildren did a remarkable thing. In 1796, the Assembly received a petition 'of John James, Junior, of the parish of St. Elizabeth, free quadroon man, in behalf of himself and of his children . . . lawfully begotten in wedlock, on the body of Anna Bonella James, *a white woman . . .*'.[4] What is even more remarkable, given the prevail-ing winds of the time, is that this was not the only case of 'mixed' marriage during this period of slavery. John's brother, Jonathan, married Elizabeth Keene—apparently, like Anna Bonella, pure white—in 1799. Yet another James boy, Edward, had married Anne Keene (probably Elizabeth's sister) in 1781. Anne, however, was only 'reputedly' white. But the marriage was by banns. A female James married a white man in 1802. In the parish of St. Elizabeth alone, in the period 1780–1815, there were no less than fourteen such mar-riages: white men to coloured women; white women to coloured men:

1781 (4 Feb.)	Edward James and Anne Keene, reputed white. By banns.
1781 (4 March)	Barnet Russell, Jnr. (reputed white) and Sarah Cooper. By banns.
1785 (28 April)	Benjamin Sims, reputed a Mestizo, and Margaret Berry, white. By banns.
1789 (11 Oct.)	William Owens, reputed a Quadroon, and Martha Taylor, a white woman. By banns.
1792 (11 July)	Edward Sinclair, reputed a Mestizo, and Susanna Harriott, a white woman. By banns.
1793 (18 Feb.)	Edward Taylor, a white man, and Elizabeth Ann Bennet [coloured]. By banns.
1793 (28 May)	Thomas Keenes, a white man, and Jane Simines, a free Quadroon. By licence.
[1796	John James, Jnr., a free Quadroon, and Anna Bonella, white.]
1799 (11 July)	Jonathan James, a free Quadroon, and Elizabeth Keene, a white woman. By licence.

---

[1] *Daily Advertiser*, 18 Feb. 1790.   [2] *JAJ*, VIII, 100–1 of 8 Nov. 1785.
[3] ibid., 106 of 17 Nov. 1785.   [4] ibid., IX, 546–7 of 12 Nov. 1796, my italics.

1800 (19 March)	Geo. David Harriott, a Mestizo, and Mary Goodfellows, a white woman. By banns.
1802 (10 Feb.)	John Russell, a white man, and Elizabeth James, a Mestizo. By banns.
1804 (6 April)	John James, Jnr., a free Quadroon, and Martha Cole, a white woman. By banns.
1806 (6 Nov.)	John Grant and Rebecca Malcolm of Burnt Savannah, deemed as white by laws. By banns.
1813 (21 Dec.)	James Mahon of the Parish of Vere, and Eliza Ann Chambers, Spinster (a free Quadroon).[1]

This evidence suggests that the 'apartheid' system was not, perhaps, as rigidly applied at this important personal level as the stereotype of the situation would lead one to expect. There should really have been no marriages of this kind. But more research will have to be done before a clear and possibly new outline presents itself. St. Elizabeth, indeed, may have been exceptional. But why? Who were the Jameses that so many of them married whites; and who were the whites that they married? How were the marriages received? Although Kingston contained the largest number of coloureds, no mixed marriages are reported from that municipality.[2] The Spanish Town records for this sphere and time are not available, so we cannot tell what went on there. In St. Ann, Robert Cunningham, white, married Jeannett Williams, mulatto, on 1 February 1794;[3] and on 21 February 1820, John Gale Scott, a free coloured of Clarendon, married Janet Mary Lowe, of the same parish, who was not specified as being coloured. She was simply designated 'Spinster'.[4] Two other doubtful cases occur in these two parishes: Thomas Bayley to Margaret; and T. G. Donaldson, a free mulatto, to Rachael Wright Priddie, 'a free person'.[5]

There were clearly, then, patches of society in which privileged

[1] St. Elizabeth Parish Register: Baptisms, Marriages, Burials, 1707–1820. MS., Government Archives, Spanish Town.

[2] Kingston: Register of Marriages, 1713–1814. MS., Government Archives, Spanish Town.

[3] St. Ann: Register of Baptisms, Marriages and Burials, 1790–1813. MS., Government Archives, Spanish Town.

[4] Clarendon: Register of Baptisms (1804–19), Marriages (1805–34), Burials (1805–30), MS., Government Archives, Spanish Town.

[5] See St. Ann and Clarendon Registers, as above. Other Registers consulted were St. Catherine: Register of Baptisms, Marriages and Burials, 1693–1836, which does not include Spanish Town; Register of Marriages (St. Thomas-in-the-Vale), 1816–37; St. James: Register of Marriages and Baptisms, 1774–1809. The St. Elizabeth Register is the only one consulted which divided marriages into white and non-white entries. This was stopped after March 1815.

free coloureds were in legal sexual contact with at least a certain class
of white. There are also, from time to time, oblique signals which
suggest that there was perhaps more black male/white female illicit
sexual contact than (again) the stereotype of the situation indicates.[1]
Public expressions of custom said one thing; but there is, for example,
the strange poem written presumably by 'Monk' Lewis and included
in his *Journal*:[2]

> Peter, Peter was a black boy;
>   Peter him pull foot[3] one day:
> Buckra[4] girl, him Peter's joy;
>   Lilly white girl entice him away.
>
> Fye, Missy Sally, fye on you!
> Poor Blacky Peter why undo?
> Oh! Peter, Peter was a bad boy;
> Peter was a runaway . . .
>
> 'Missy, you cheeks so red, so white;
> Missy, you eyes like diamond shine!
> Missy, you Massa's sole delight,
>   And Lilly Sally, him was mine!
> Him say—"Come, Peter, mid me go!"—
> Could me refuse him? Could me say "no"!—
> Poor Peter—"no" him could no say!
> So Peter, Peter ran away!'—
>
> Him Missy him pray; him Massa so kind
>   Was moved by him prayer, and to Peter him say:
>   'Well boy, for this once I forgive you!—but mind!
>   With the buckra girls you no more go away!
> Though fair without, they're foul within;
> Their heart is black, though white their skin.
> Then Peter, Peter with me stay;
> Peter no more run away!'—

On the face of it, this is no more than a proletarian 'La Belle Dame
Sans Merci', pedestrianly performed. But taken in conjunction with
the James case, and with this, from the Rev. William Jones, one

---

[1] For a discussion of this from a Southern American Negro's point of view, see
Calvin Hernton, *Sex and Racism in America* (New York, 1965).
[2] Op. cit. (1929 ed.), pp. 105–6.   [3] To 'pull foot': to run away.
[4] Buckra or backra, from the Efik *mbakara*, means white man or master. 'Him', as
in West African pidgin, is used in Jamaican speech in place of all the standard English
third person forms, irrespective of number or gender. (See Cassidy and Le Page, op.
cit., p. 225.)

senses, again, the great living gap, in the society being considered, between the stereotyped attitude (and expectation) and the possible reality:

He [an Overseer] mentioned many instances of Ladies & Gentlemen in the Island of respectable appearance & who pass for *Boccrahs*, tho' only two or three removes from a *sooty descent* on the Father's or Mother's side. That single, or even married, Planters, Pen-keepers, etc., have mulattoe base Children, is not the wonder of a moment; but I now heard of more than one or two *white* Ladies, within his Knowledge, & cited by name, who had, tho' married, borne Children of Negroes.[1]

With this background, as another Reverend discovered, 'One would imagine that the people of colour, being most of them immediately descended from white fathers, and brought up in the same house with them, would be treated with more consideration; but such is the pride and jealousy of the colonists against any having the least tinge in them, that however worthy, wealthy, or well educated they may be, the males are deprived of most privileges, and shut out from all trusts and offices; and the females, however fair and chaste . . . are not allowed to marry the lowest white man.'[2]

This, despite the exceptions suggested above, was Established creole procedure. When it came to blacks, of course, the protocol was infinitely more rigid. Once, early in her Jamaica sojourn, Mrs. Nugent nearly precipitated a major social crisis at a little country dance.

I began the ball with an old Negro man. The gentlemen each selected a partner, according to rank, by age or service, and we all danced. However, I was not aware how much I shocked the Misses Murphy by doing this; for I did exactly the same as I would have done at a servants' hall birthday in England. They told me, afterwards, that they were nearly fainting, and could hardly forbear shedding a flood of tears, at such an unusual and extraordinary sight; for in this country, and among slaves, it was necessary to keep up so much more distant respect.[3]

The future Lady Nugent was not properly aware, it seems, of the 'oil and vinegar' principle. One of the island's earliest Acts 'for the better order and government of slaves',[4] declared (of the slaves) '*Their children stand in the parents situation.*' That rubric appeared in the margin of all slave laws that were to follow. The slave could make no social advancement, or own property, being himself

[1] *Diary of William Jones*, p. 33, 9 July 1778.   [2] Bickell, op. cit., pp. 113–14.
[3] *LNJ* (Cundall), p. 204.   [4] 8 William III, c. 11 of 1796.

property[1] (by custom, though, his provision grounds were 'his' to use); he did not even possess the right of self-defence, except against another slave. In law and custom a Negro was presumed to be a slave until he could prove otherwise.[2] There was no way in which he could legally disprove the whites' assumption of his inferiority. Where social custom or legal enactment failed to keep him in his place, force could be applied—summary justice, transportation, the chain gang, 'the peal of the whip'.[3] It was this social separation and this necessary coercion that sapped the potential strength of the society, inducing in the white masters an almost organic fear of the slave masses—'the intestine enemy', as the Assembly named it; and induced a form of self-enslavement—managerial, sexual, and domestic—from which they could not escape.

The mistress of a family, where there is a crowd of black and brown servants, has a more difficult and painful duty to perform than can well be conceived; they are often so refractory, vicious, and indolent, that, in managing such a household, she is perhaps, in effect, a greater slave than any of them.[4]

[1] See Elsa Goveia, 'The West Indian Slave Laws of the Eighteenth Century' *Revista de ciencias sociales*, IV (1960), pp. 83–6.

[2] '. . . in the W. Indies, the complexion of the Slave is a real distinction which will always work strongly on popular prejudice; and even on those who make, as well as those who administer the laws. Hitherto, at least, both prejudices and laws (at least in vulgar intendment) presume that every black man is, or ought to be, a Slave.' (William Dickson, *Mitigation of Slavery*, p. 512. See also Southey, op. cit., Vol. III, pp. 388, 469 and 520.)

[3] 'In the mornings, as I frequently passed through the plantations, the overseers were generally setting their Slaves to work, which was mostly attended with *loud peals of whipping* (I make use of that word, on account of the sound which the whip makes at every stroke, that you may hear it at a great distance).' (Henry Coor, *P.P.*, Vol. XCII 34), no. 745, p. 69.)

[4] Stewart, *View*, p. 172. 20–30 servants in a (substantial) planter household was 'nothing unusual'. Long provides (*History*, Vol. II, p. 281) the following inventory: 1 butler, 2 footmen or waiting men, 1 coachman, 1 postillion, 1 helper, 1 cook, 1 assistant, 1 key or storekeeper, 1 waiting maid, 3 house-cleaners, 3 washer-women, 4 sempstresses, plus nurses and assistants.

COLOURED AND BLACK ACTION
AND REACTION IN WHITE SOCIETY

BUT if the slave system enslaved the whites, it damaged the free and unfree non-white even more. These elements of the population appear, in general, not only to have accepted the white stereotypes of themselves, they seem to have acted (self-fulfilling the 'prophecy'), within these images of themselves. 'Monk' Lewis's personal slave, Cubina, *did* appear to be intellectually slow. It took half an hour to make him understand that the Christmas holidays came at Christmas, and even afterwards 'he always hesitated, and answered, at haphazard, "July" or "October"'.[1] Jenny, one of Lewis's field slaves, really seemed *not* to like work, and damaged herself in order to avoid doing it.[2] Mulatto girls *did* seem to prefer white men and some of them had children from several. Frances Sadler, a quadroon, had four children surnamed Cunningham, Laing, and Sadler.[3] Judith Hutt, a free mulatto woman, had two Davidsons, two Millwards and two Laings.[4] Grace Robertson, a quadroon woman, had a Stiles, a Thornhill, two Gibbses, and a Swainson; all mustees.[5] All were destined for an English education. This is not to say that Cubina was a moron, Jenny bestial, the coloured girls licentious—in fact, a majority of the petitions to the Assembly respecting their children suggest, on the whole, very stable relationships, though these, of course, were the better-off liaisons. But it illustrates how easy it was to confirm the stereotype. Creole society was stable because the unprivileged and underprivileged within it conformed to the system, its divisions, and its restrictions. 'The whole slave system began as a coercive one, but developed into a system of consent.'[6]

The role of the free coloured within this environment should not be underestimated. They were, for one thing, loyal to the Establishment,

[1] Lewis, op. cit. (1929 ed.), p. 324.   [2] ibid., p.168.
[3] *JAJ*, VI, 519–20 of 3 Nov. 1774. She had two from Sadler.
[4] ibid. VII, 21 of 26 Nov. 1777.   [5] ibid. VIII, 496 of 27 Oct. 1789.
[6] Schuler, op. cit., p. 9.

and were *seen* to be so.[1] In 1814, 'Most of the inhabitants of colour evinced their loyalty and gratification at the triumph over the enemy [Napoleon] by private entertainments in different parts of the city' of Kingston.[2] The year before, they had told the Governor's Secretary that they were quite happy about the 'moderate and consistent' plans of improvement that were under consideration for them. Any 'specific claims or pretensions on their part would be highly unbecoming'.[3] In 1816 and 1817, after a section of the free coloureds had, in fact, pressed for additional liberties, reaction came in from Kingston and St. James. Addressing the Assembly the Kingstonians said that

fully assured of the justice and liberality which have ever distinguished your Hon. House, [we] beg leave to approach [you] for the purpose of expressing [our] sincere gratitude for the benefits which were conferred on the Free People of Colour in the Sessions of the year 1813, and likewise to assure you that [we] are firmly attached to the Constituted Authorities of this island, and ever will be devoted to his Majesty's Government, and the security of [our] native country.[4]

The petition from the radicals, they felt,

originated more from error than any latent desire of disturbing the peace and good order of Society.[5]

They lamented

with unfeigned sorrow that any part of their body should, by precipitancy and indiscretion, have claimed an extension of privileges, insomuch as to have incurred the displeasure of [the] honourable house.[6]

The St. James memorial of 1817 solemnly disclaimed 'the most distant intention of being presumptuous or inconsistent with their duty and obedience to the legislature'.[7]

But the 'radical' element among the free coloured was not without significance or effect. They served at least to make necessary acts

---

[1] See, for instance, Edwards (1793 ed.), Vol. II, p.21; Dallas,op. cit., Vol. I, p. cxiii; II, p. 457; Renny, op. cit., p. 189; *St. Iago de la Vega Gazette*, Vol. LIX, no. 45, 6 Nov. 1813.

[2] *R.G.*, XXXVI, 6, 17.   [3] See Duncker, op. cit., p. 181.

[4] *R.G.*, XXXVIII, 49, 23 of 30 Nov. 1816.   [5] ibid.

[6] *JAJ*, XIII, 64 of 29 Nov. 1816.

[7] *JAJ*, XIII, 138 of 18 Nov. 1817. The Methodist missionaries, though of course it was in their interest to do so, confirmed this free coloured loyalty. See, for instance, Ratcliffe's Journal, 28 May 1819, Methodist *Missionary Notices*, Vol. II, pp. 153–4. The free coloureds, as a group, tended to prefer and support the Methodist Mission. Duncker, op. cit., p. 138.)

of protest. In 1805, for example, 'An unfortunate man of colour was brought into Spanish Town . . . to be tried for mutiny.'[1] He was Thomas Roper,[2] a sergeant in the militia. He had abused his colonel, *and white people in general*.[3] This had 'a most serious effect; among the men of his company' (no doubt mostly coloured),[4] 'in particular'.[5] He was fined £4,000 and condemned, at the age of 60, to two years' solitary confinement. His business was ruined.[6] But Roper was a solitary, no doubt exasperated, protester who just could not understand why his first-class accomplishment should be constantly equated with second-class status. Around 1813, however, there appears evidence of much more general unrest among certain sections of the free coloured, especially in Kingston. In fact, the alleviatory legislation of 1813, allowing free people of colour to give evidence in all cases and permitting them once again to inherit unlimited property, may well have been partly, at least, due to pressures on Government from the coloureds themselves. There had been a petition for an extension of privileges, especially to be allowed to give evidence in court, from 2,400 coloured signatories in 1813[7] while the Act was being considered in the House. The *Royal Gazette* admitted that with the exception of Barbados and Jamaica, this privilege had been conceded in the other islands—in Grenada, 'for full 50 years'.[8] In June of that same year,

. . . a young man of colour named Martin Halhead, from Spanish-Town, was brought before the Sitting Magistrates, charged with having acted in a most indecorous way in the Church the preceding day, by forcibly violating a regulation of the Corporate Body, and resisting one of the Magistrates in the execution of his duty. While a relation of the facts was going on, he behaved several times in a very intemperate manner, when he was advised to be more cautious, and conduct himself with the necessary decorum; notwithstanding which he became more outrageous, and apparently set the Court at defiance, upon which the Magistrates ordered the Constables . . . to take him into custody.[9]

Nor was this all. When Halhead was being taken away, 'another young man of colour, named Alexander Polson, insisted that he

---

[1] *LNJ* (Wright), p. 237; 31 May 1805.   [2] Wright (*LNJ*), p. 239, n.
[3] *LNJ* (Wright), p. 237, my italics.
[4] In 1805, there were 274 coloured and 176 white militiamen in the St. Catherine Regiment. (*JAJ*, XI, 310 of 4 July 1805.) In Spanish Town itself, where Roper probably served, the proportion of coloureds would most likely have been even higher.
[5] *LNJ* (Wright), p. 237   [6] *LNJ* (Wright), p. 239, n.
[7] *R.G.*, XXXV, 45, 17 of 6 Nov. 1813.   [8] ibid., 46, 18.
[9] ibid., 25, 17 of 19 June 1813.

should not be . . ., as he would become his bail'.[1] Both of them were gaoled.[2] But it indicated a certain restlessness—a perturbation of the stereotype. That same month, another young coloured man was fined for discharging a firearm 'within a certain distance of the city'[3] contrary to the police laws.[4] In April 1815, Martin Halhead was in action again, this time at the head of a group of coloureds protesting against the colour bar at the Kingston Theatre:

On Wednesday evening last week, at the opening of the Theatre of this City for the present season, a mob, composed of persons of colour, assembled on the Parade, and committed many violent outrages, by pelting the house with brick-bats, hissing at females and others who wished to attend the performance, and pulling down the steps leading to the Upper Boxes, etc. A very respectable Magistrate of this city, in his endeavours to quell the riot, received several very severe blows and wounds on his head, and it was deemed requisite to call out the assistance of a military guard from the Barracks, when some of the rioters were taken into custody. . . .[5]

The riot had, apparently, 'originated in a paper which was industriously handed about, and received numerous signatures'.[6] Later, the full picture came to light: certain free people of colour were picketing outside the Kingston Theatre because of a rumour of new colour bar restrictions there. They were collecting signatures from coloureds who had agreed or were agreeing to boycott the Theatre.[7] This was certainly not the kind of behaviour expected of the stereotype. As the Presiding Justice of the Court of Quarter Sessions for Kingston said:

The Court must express its astonishment, that so great an outrage should have been committed by a class of people, who have so recently been favoured by the Legislature by the great privileges, which, placing them in a more elevated state in the community, called for that improvement in their manners as would shew them to have been worthy of the state in which they have been placed. . . .[8]

Two of the accused were ordered into the pillory, but escaped, thanks to the intervention of the Governor.[9]

The next year saw the Petition to the Assembly for further rights and privileges.[10] This petition pressed for coloured representation

[1] *R.G.*, XXXV, 25, 17 of 19 June 1813.   [2] ibid.   [3] ibid.
[4] See, for example, 35 Geo. III, c. 18 of 1794.   [5] *R.G.*, XXXVII, 15, 17.
[6] ibid.   [7] ibid., 20, 17.   [8] ibid., 20, 18.   [9] ibid., 21, 17.
[10] See p. 194, above.

on juries, for the repeal of the Deficiency Law as it affected coloureds and free blacks. It stressed that legal discrimination against free people of colour, born in the United Kingdom of Great Britain and Ireland and whose right of freedom could not be doubted, should be abolished and that the regulations requiring local free coloureds to obtain certificates of baptism from the rectors of the several parishes before they could qualify for certain privileges, should be done away with, especially since many rectors had *not* kept records of baptism, which meant that they had to be rebaptized, which they were unwilling to do, as it was contrary to the Protestant faith. They also objected, in general terms, 'to the humiliating system of exclusion and reproach, which those laws generate and keep alive in this their native land'.[1] This was unfair, they felt, not only because they formed 'so great a proportion of the population of the island', but also because they contributed 'so largely to the resources and contingencies thereof'.[2] The reference to 'their native land' is interesting, the hint at their economic bargaining power significant. But this petition went even further. It dared to raise and rattle that fundamentally radical (and most recently American) bogy: no taxation without representation:

That your petitioners have ever borne an equal share in all taxes and contributions, without deriving an equal benefit in return, with the white population, and have on all emergencies come forward with cheerfulness and promptitude to devote their lives and property in the service of their king and country; notwithstanding such services, your petitioners with the deepest sorrow have to state, that they are in great degradation and contempt, and are still excluded from the just rights and privileges of white subjects, to which your petitioners must ever consider themselves as a free people entitled:

That your petitioners humbly submit to your honourable house, that as 'taxation and representation' have ever been considered constitutionally 'as inseparable', your petitioners should be permitted to claim such rights in general. . . .[3]

This was the kind of phraseology that the white élite could not afford to accept; nor could the Uncle Tom coloureds, who, remaining true to everyone's picture of them, came to the aid of the Establishment.

---

[1] *JAJ*, XIII, 37 of 19 Nov. 1816.   [2] ibid.   [3] ibid.

Slave attitudes

But by now things were changing. The free coloureds, as a group (except the Toms referred to above), realized that they had to 'get themselves [closer] together', if they hoped to reach anywhere. Organizers from Kingston were sent out to the country areas, 'either to form or to inspire and stimulate local groups. Officials from these groups would . . . visit Kingston from time to time to report on their activities as well as to be informed of latest developments.'[1] By 1823, the Kingston group had come out into the open;[2] militants were threatening to withhold their service in the militia during martial law;[3] and the Governor (Manchester) was forced to marvel at the industry displayed by the protest movement in imagining grievances and seeking redress for them.[4]

The position of the slaves made their reaction at once easier and more difficult. It was easier because since they knew they had no legal stake in the system, indeed hardly a human one, they could quite easily and unregretfully attempt to subvert it. More difficult because as 'invisible men', it was almost impossible to give their protests social and therefore meaningful effect. Perhaps only 'Monk' Lewis's Mary Wiggins was ever really *seen* by a white man, though, even with her, romantical elements creep in (not too surprising with the author of *The Monk* and *Tales of Wonder*):

. . . I really think [wrote Lewis in his *Journal*] that her form and features were the most *statue-like* that I ever met with: her complexion had no yellow in it, and yet was not brown enough to be dark—it was more of an ash-dove colour than anything else; her teeth were admirable, both for colour and shape; her eyes equally mild and bright; and her face merely broad enough to give it all possible softness and grandness of contour: her air and countenance would have suited Yarico; but she reminded me most of Grassini [a contralto of the period] in 'La Vergine del Sole', only that Mary Wiggins was a thousand times more beautiful, and that, instead of a white robe, she wore a mixed dress of brown, white, and dead yellow, which harmonised excellently well with her complexion; while one of her beautiful arms was thrown across her brow to shade her eyes, and a profusion of rings on her fingers glittered in the sunbeams. Mary Wiggins and an old Cotton-tree are the most picturesque objects that I have seen for these twenty years.[5]

[1] Campbell, 'Edward Jordan', p. 103.
[2] C.O. 137/175, Minutes of the Colonial Committee, Montego Bay, 15 Feb. 1823.
[3] C.O. 137/154, Manchester to Bathurst, 22 Dec. 1823.   [4] ibid.
[5] Lewis (1929 ed.), pp. 66–7. The white stereotype of the black female form was more or less as follows:
'In walking they agitate their frame much more than we do, the women particularly.'

Augustus Frederick Horatio, Prince de Bundo, 'an elderly black man' who appeared in 1816, was an even more remarkable person. He was, he claimed, son of 'a Turkish merchant, formerly a Mahometan, who married in London his mother, a Cherokee Indian Princess. His grandfather was High Priest of Bundo, in Africa, and it was through him that he claimed his title of Prince de Bundo. . . .'[1] He was born at Staines, in England, went to Eton at the age of seven, and left there at sixteen for various colleges on the continent of Europe. He returned to England in 1776 or 1777 and went to 'Oxford College' for four years, entered the University where he did his B.A. in sixteen months; then 'was ordained a Priest of the English Church by the Bishop of Derry'.[2] He travelled over the Continent and 'was well received at the different Courts',[3] married a Polish Princess, the daughter of Prince Morowski, and received a dowry with her in lands, castles and £3,500 a year.

After he quitted Poland he returned to England, and was handsomely received by the Prince Regent, with whom he was on the most intimate and friendly footing, having received from him a general invitation to visit at all times, of which he availed himself, particularly at Brighton. The Prince introduced him to the Queen, and the rest of the Royal Family, who were all kind and attentive to him. His Royal Highness, in person, stood Godfather for [his] eldest son, who is Leader of the Prince's private Chamber Music, and he has another son also in his service. At the particular solicitation of the Regent, he was introduced at the British Court, *on horseback*, in the costume of a Mahometan. He frequently attended the Court Balls, but being *a Clergyman* he never *danced*. . . .[4]

Later adventures brought him to the West Indies in his brig the *Isabella* (250 tons) 'registered at Lloyd's but . . . not insured there'.[5] He was shipwrecked in the Caribbean, and finally reached Jamaica

A negro wench is little esteemed by the men without a peculiar motion which they generally contrive to give their posteriors, which must, as well as the hips, be prominent to be graceful with them. When Nature has denied a swell to the muscles constituting these parts, they employ artificial means to supply what they consider a necessary roundness. [However, an] early acquaintance and unlimited intercourse with the men, operate strongly against the women; their breasts from a remarkable fullness, soon begin to droop, and after suckling a few children, lose that springiness in the fibres which support them, and they at length hang two loose flaccid dugs, sometimes of such enormous extent, that mothers who tie their children on their backs, can throw them over their shoulders for the child to suck. [A similar belief obtains among some Europeans in Africa with regard to African women.]

'When they go abroad bare-breasted, and have occasion to run, their breasts yield to the least motion, and are flung about in every direction, unless they confine them with their hands.' (*Columbian Magazine*, Vol. II (April 1797), pp. 699–700.)

[1] *R.G.*, XXXVIII, 43, 21 of 19–26 Oct. 1816.
[2] idid.   [3] ibid.   [4] ibid.; italics in text.   [5] ibid.

via Havana and Antigua. On 2 September 1816, there appeared his Notice in the Press, petitioning 'the Most Honourable the Mayor, and the Respectable Corporation of the Island of Jamaica' for 'Succor'.[1]

De Bundo, needless to say, was a fantastic. What is even more fantastic is that the authorities took him seriously enough to have him examined—not by what would have then passed for a psychiatrist—but by the magistrates:

This noble personage yesterday underwent another examination before the Sitting Magistrates, when he dwindled from his high rank into a *Knight of the Thimble*, being by trade a tailor. According to his own confession, made to a Gentleman now here . . . he is a native of Barbados, where he was born a slave, and, being considered a smart fellow, was sent home as servant to one of his master's sons, and during his residence in England, learned to read and write. . . .[2]

As a matter of fact, the 'true story' of de Bundo, if, that is, the magistrates ever really got the true story, was in a way even more remarkable than his tale. In the first place he had learned to read and write, and not only that, but could clearly employ his gifts and learning 'artistically'. When his young Massa had completed his studies and was about to return to the abundant tropics, de Bundo decided to decamp and remain in England as a free man. He got himself a wig of lank black hair and passed himself off as a Lascar.[3]

After a year (in custody) in Kingston, he was shipped back via the Admiral in one of the Navy transports, as 'an improper person to remain in [the] Island'.[4] No doubt the 'fact' that he was intimately acquainted with 'that *worthy Saint*, Mr. Wilberforce'[5] with whom he dined on Tuesdays, Thursdays, and Fridays, had had its effect. But the real point is that de Bundo, on intimate terms with royalty, de Bundo the successful, de Bundo on *horseback*, was a violation of the stereotype. De Bundo had made himself *visible*.[6]

This kind of fantasy, skill, and cunning were essential if black men were to make any kind of impression within their slave society. Dr. Patterson in his *Sociology of Slavery*[7] has described, for Jamaica,

[1] *R.G.*, XXXVIII, 43, 21 of 19–26 Oct 1816.   [2] ibid.   [3] ibid.
[4] K.C.C. Minutes, 1815–20; 27 Jan. 1817.
[5] *R.G.*, XXXVIII, 43 of 26 Oct. 1816. Italics in text.
[6] De Bundo's story, strange as it may seem, was probably a compendium of Negro experience in Europe during the 'Age of Enlightenment'. Ibrahim Petrovich Hannibal, for instance, educated by Peter the Great, became a Lt.-General of Artillery and married a Russian noblewoman. One of their great-grandchildren was Alexander Pushkin.
[7] Patterson, op. cit., pp. 174–81.

what he calls the 'Quashee' personality trait; an 'evasive, indefinable, somewhat disguised and ambiguous quality'.[1] Quashee was 'crafty, artful, plausible; not often grateful for small services; but frequently deceitful and over-reaching'.[2] De Bundo was a super-Quashee. It was a way of reacting against the system, a form of devious protest.

Another way of protesting was to run away. Monica Schuler, who has done a study of runaways in the Caribbean during the eighteenth century,[3] states that in Jamaica, between 1 in 10 and 1 in 15 of all slaves were runaways or had been runaways, and that there were about 100,000 fugitive slaves in the island fastnesses in 1798.[4] Given a slave population of 291,801, according to the poll tax returns of 1799,[5] this figure seems wildly unrealistic. Miss Schuler's only authority for this figure appears to have been the *Handbook of Jamaica for 1882*,[6] which does not reveal the sources of this statement. Even 30,000 runaways (1 : 10) seems a rather high figure. Bridges[7] estimated 20,000 for 1827. The *Jamaica Mercury* had advertisements for 495 runaways for the period 1 May 1779–1 April 1780.[8] The total listed in the *Royal Gazette* for 1794 was 253,[9] but this figure does not include those listed as being already taken up and in custody in the various workhouses. If the workhouse figures are included, the total (Dr. Patterson's calculation), is 1,075.[10] For 1803, again using the *Royal Gazette*, U. B. Phillips' figure is 1,721.[11] The *Royal Gazette* figure for 1813 is 1,460 runaways.[12] These figures establish, at least, a consistent pattern of expectation, even though very few plantation (field) slaves are listed in the newspaper advertisements. The one official return of runaways for this period, that for 1819 in the *Journals* of the Assembly, records 2,555 runaways.[13] Assuming, then, that this figure represents one-third of the total

[1] Patterson, op. cit., p.175, See also the similar 'Sambo' personality trait described by Stanley M. Elkins in *Slavery: A Problem in American Institutional and Intellectual Life* (University of Chicago Press, 1959), New York ed. 1963, pp. 82–7, 130–3, 227–9; and the comments on this by Arnold Sio in *Social and Economic Studies*, Vol. XVI (1967), no. 3, pp. 342–3.

[2] Stewart, *Account*, p. 234.   [3] Loc. cit., p. 158, n. 1, above.
[4] Schuler, op. cit., p. 124.   [5] *JAJ*, X, 464 of 11 Feb. 1800.
[6] Op. cit., p. 112.   [7] Op. cit., Vol. II, p. 348 and footnote.
[8] *Jamaica Mercury and Kingston Weekly Advertiser*, Vols. I and II.
[9] *R.G.*, XVI (1794), 1–52.
[10] Patterson, op. cit., p. 262. It is not possible to say, however, how Dr. Patterson treated the workhouse returns. Many of the same names occur again and again in the various advertisements. Since the slaves had no surnames, this makes it difficult to avoid duplication; or at least makes it difficult for one to be sure whether or not duplication is occurring.
[11] Phillips, 'A Jamaica Slave Plantation', p. 555.
[12] Patterson, op. cit., p. 262.   [13] *JAJ*, XIII, 375 of 30 Nov. 1819.

number of runaways,[1] the average figure per year might be placed at some 8,000, with accumulations from year to year bringing the figure to about 10,000.

As figures are so unreliable or unavailable, it hardly seems worth-while using them or attempting to draw conclusions from them, but it is important to try to obtain a picture of the scale of running away in Jamaica, if we are to understand intimately how the slaves responded to their situation. There is a crucial difference between having 10,000, 30,000 not to mention 100,000 runaways in a society dominated by only 30,000 whites. The figure 10,000 may be cor-roborated on the following (uncertain) ground. There was an average of seven runaways per year on the Worthy Park plantation between 1792 and 1797.[2] The Worthy Park records for 1787–91,[3] support this. Taking seven runaways on an estate of over 300 slaves as typical, five for other sugar estates, two for pens and coffee planta-tions, and one per year from other settlements and properties, a total of 10,389 runaways per year—for what this is worth—is obtained.

But what is important about runaways, within the terms of this study, is not only how many there were, but the descriptions of them—how they were *seen*. Running away made them visible. Gloster, for instance, had a 'full Beard, large broad Lips, speaks thick and fast, is brow-legged [*sic*] and has the Marks of a large Sore, not perfectly cured, on the lowest Part of his left Leg. He had on when he went away, a Pair of black Breeches and a Check Shirt'.[4] Susanna Baker, a sambo woman, had 'a black mark, like a fried sprat, on one of her elbows, and all her teeth broken by fighting'.[5] Adrian, a black creole six-footer, a carpenter by trade, was 'very well made', but 'pitted with the small-pox in the face'. He was very sensible, had a Roman nose, spoke good English and whistled remarkably well, besides dressing very neatly. 'He is supposed to be harboured about the lower end of St. Ann's, or the upper part of Trelawny, as he was very much attached to a wench on Rio-Bueno estate'.[6] Phibe had a 'remarkable large belly owing to some disorder' and 'may pass herself as being with child'.[7] Flood, a slim twenty-five year old Negro carpenter, had 'good features, and bad feet'.[8] Mary, a Mandingo,

---

[1] This assumption is frankly arbitrary. The returns may have been less or more accurate than expected. There is no way of knowing. On the evidence available, however, and supplied in the text, the assumption seems reasonable.

[2] Phillips, 'Plantation', pp. 554–5.   [3] Worthy Park Plantation Register, *passim*.

[4] *Jamaica Mercury*, Vol. I, no. 3, 8–15 May 1779, p. 32.

[5] *R.G.*, XXXIII (1811), 30, 24.   [6] ibid., XV (1793), 13, 8.

[7] ibid., XVI (1794), 1, 15.   [8] ibid., XXXV (1813), 44, 24.

short and thick, had 'very full breasts, small eyes and her Teeth [had] been filed'.[1] Hannibal, a six-foot new Negro, with filed teeth, had no brand marks, 'but the mark of a wound from a lance on each side below his ribs'.[2] Billy, aged 17, was, like so many runaways, 'very artful and capable of telling a most plausible tale'. He had been sent to Kingston with letters and had not been heard of since.[3] The same thing happened with Angis, a Coromantee cook, who 'was sent to town with a basket, money, etc., to buy things at the market'.[4] Romeo, on the other hand, 'by trade an upholsterer', was one of those slaves clearly allowed a considerable amount of freedom of movement, the arrangement being that he would share a certain proportion of his wages with his owner. In February 1794, however, 'he sent home his wages' as usual, but did not himself make his appearance.[5] Peggy was similarly out earning for her employer. When she did not return, Eve (they were both young creoles) was sent to bring her home. Neither of them returned.[6]

Some of these runaways were seen openly, travelling about, often higgling. Venus, a 'tall, slim, wench' was 'seen repeatedly going to and from Kingston, and is supposed to be harboured at Dawkin's Caymanas, where she has a husband'.[7] Billy, a 'yellow' 19-year-old blacksmith, with a sore on the right leg and a scar on his head, 'wearing blue Pantaloons and a sailor's blue Jacket' (blue was the predominant colour among the slave population), 'was seen on the Spanish-Town road . . . with a basket of greens, in company with a black woman, supposed to be a higgler, going to Spanish Town'.[8] It was the same with Susanna Baker (she of the fried sprat on the elbow and the broken teeth).[9] She had been 'frequently seen with a brown woman, named Gibby Serjeant, in Wood-Alley', carrying about needles for sale.[10] Rene, a 22-year old French creole girl, 'stout made, large mouth, fine teeth, flat nose', and who spoke good English, kept 'a Working-School for Negro Children either at Falmouth or Montego-Bay'.[11] In fact, in the sample of 430 individual advertisements collected for this study, sixteen runaways were known to be working elsewhere and thirty-seven, at least, were seen travelling about.[12]

[1] *Jamaica Mercury*, Vol. I, no. 8, June 1779.   [2] *R.G.*, XV, 14, 6.
[3] *Jamaica Mercury*, 1 Jan. 1780.   [4] *R.G.*, XVI, 8, 20.   [5] ibid.
[6] *R.G.*, XVI, 8, 20   [7] ibid., 14, 20.   [8] ibid., XXXV, 45, 22.
[9] P. 202, above.   [10] *R.G.*, XXXIII (1811), 30, 24.
[11] ibid., XXXV, 23, 24.
[12] The runaway advertisements for this study were collected from the *Jamaica Mercury*, Vol. I (1779), nos. 3, 8, 20, 34, and 35, Vol. II (1780), nos. 36–49; the *Jamaica Gazette* (Kingston), 25 March 1775, Vol. III (1781), nos. 136, 743; *Daily Advertiser* for

Rebellion

Many descriptions suggest that some slaves had quite a flair for clothes, Jemmy, for instance, carried with him

> a blue coatee with plated buttons, striped yellow, a white cotton and worsted jacket, with sleeves of the same, both nankeen and Russia-drab breeches, and a kind of purple and white bordered waistcoat.[1]

Figaro, a Congo, 'decamped with 160 dollars and the dozen French handkerchiefs belonging to his owner'.[2] But none of these could beat Prudence, Dick's wife. Dick was an Ibo, who spoke very little English. He was very black, had a bushy head, stood 5 feet 5 inches, was branded, had 'lost the nail and a small bit of the thumb of the right hand' and had 'country marks plain on his breast'. He was 'a good negro'

> until he got acquainted with PRUDENCE his wife, who likewise ranaway with him. She is of the Eboe country, yellow complexion, round chubby face, goggle eyes, has lost several of her front teeth: [is] short, lively and active, a great thief, speaks quick and pretty good English, is one of (the black Parson) Lyle's congregation.
>
> . . . she is capable of great deception, and almost every word she lards with please God . . . had on and took with her a white shift and blue petticoat, small black hat, white woolen great coat, two almost new blankets and sundry wearing apparel, two wooden bowls, knives and forks, spoons and an iron pot, etc.[3]

She was in every sense prudent:

> She was purchased from Mrs. Sarah Osborn, about Christmas last, and has been nine and twenty years in the town of Kingston, and when she left it, *secreted a quantity of her clothes with some of her tribe.* . . .[4]

This husband and wife combination also suggests that the slaves' sense of family was not always as disorganized as some contemporary and modern accounts suggest.[5] Evidence from the runaway advertisements, in fact, confirms to some extent the statement from the Jamaica

1790; *R.G.*, Vol. II (1780); nos. 50, 56; XV (1793); XVI (1794); XXXIII (1811); XXXIV (1812); XXXV (1813); XXXVI (1814); XXXVII (1815).
  Workhouse runaway lists were examined in *R.G.* XXXI (1809) 30; XXXIV, 52; XXXV, 52; XLI (1819), 41, 46; St. Ann Vestry Proceedings, 1817–23, August 1818.
  General runaway returns from *JAJ*, XIII, 375 of 30 Nov. 1819; *R.G.*,XLI, 50, 21.
  [1] *R.G.*, XV, 8, 17. [2] ibid., XVI, 8, 20.
  [3] *R.G.*, XVI, 36, 19. [4] ibid., my italics.
  [5] See, for example, Edwards, op. cit., Vol. II, p. 97; Richard Watson, *A defense of the Wesleyan Methodist missions in the West Indies . . . with facts and anecdotes illustrative of the moral state of the slaves, and of the operation of missions* (London, 1817), pp. 28–9; Patterson, op. cit., p. 167.

Rebellion

Committee of Council to British Parliamentary Commission of Inquiry (designed, however, to give a favourable account of slavery to its critics), that though there was no legal marriage, the slaves cohabited by mutual consent, and though they separated occasionally 'without much Ceremony', they frequently lived and grew old together, and a 'strong Family Attachment [prevailed] amongst them. . . .'[1] Among the sample 430 runaways, 16 were recorded as having wives or husbands, 12 had mothers, aunts, sisters, brothers or other relatives, 7 had lovers or other connections. A few would turn to their 'shipmates'—old cronies, with whom the experience of the Middle Passage had been shared.[2] Lewis remarked how several slaves entreated him 'to negotiate the purchase of some relation or friend belonging to another estate, with whom they were anxious to be re-united'.[3] Owners (within the 430 sample) claimed to know the definite whereabouts of forty-four of the runaways and guessed at the probable harbouring place of another seventy.

It was clear, too, that runaways enjoyed if not the support, at least the connivance, of the mass of the black population. 'It rarely happened that the slaves betrayed the confidence of a runaway, except he were base enough to rob their provision grounds, or insult their women'.[4] The Maroons (though they made money, by treaty, out of catching runaways), the soldiers at the various camps in and around Kingston especially, the sailors at Port Royal, fishermen, a few white men and even some free coloureds, also often helped them:

Mountain has a second time effected his escape from the workhouse. At midnight, he rapped at the window of a small shop kept by a female of colour, begged and obtained a draught of water, and even then was hand-cuffed. He has not been seen since.[5]

Finally, it should be noted that most of the runaways advertised for were simply not 'labour machines', 'animate chattels',[6] and that few of them conformed, even within the narrow limits of the news-paper advertisements, to white stereotypes of slaves and Negroes. Nearly all those advertised for were persons of skill and talent—useful members of society—from the masons, coachmen, seamstresses, pilots, sailors, fishermen, bakers, barbers, butlers, cooks, postillions,

[1] *P.P.*, Vol. LXXXIV (26), 1789, Part III, Jamaica, A. No. 14.
[2] See *R.G.*, XVI, 20, Edwards, op. cit., Vol. II, p. 94, among others.
[3] Lewis, op. cit (1929 ed.), p. 98.
[4] J. B. Vernon, *Early recollections of Jamaica* . . . (London, 1848), p. 28.
[5] *R.G.*, XVI, 18, 23.   [6] Styron, op. cit., p. 21.

to the violin-playing carpenter brothers, Davy and William.[1] The point these runaways were making—implicitly and perhaps unconsciously—was that because of their talents as individual *persons*, they had a right to their freedom.

But there were other ways of reacting against the system and the stereotype, apart from running away. Within the system itself, for instance, there was a reluctance to bear children.[2] This apparent infertility was put down by several writers of the time to polygamy,[3] sexual promiscuity,[4] and disease, much of it venereal.[5] Whether these writers were right or how far they were right, cannot be determined. But there was evidence of deliberate and widespread abortion practices,[6] and it was believed that some slave women practised infanticide.[7] Lock-jaw,[8] pneumonia,[9] malnutrition (especially the shortage of easily digestible protein in the infants' diet),[10] as well as the male/female imbalance[11] and the living and medical conditions generally, must also have been factors. 'I really believe', 'Monk' Lewis said, indicating how far a white 'liberal' view of black humanity went within this period, 'that negresses can produce children at pleasure; but where they are barren, it is just as hens will frequently

[1] *R.G.*, XXXV, 22, 24.

[2] See *The Jamaica Magazine*, Vol. IV (Dec. 1813), no. 6, p. 891.

[3] See, for instance, Charles Leslie, *A New History of Jamaica from the Earliest Accounts to the Taking of Porto Bello by Vice Admiral Vernon. In Thirteen Letters from a Gentleman to his friend* (London, 1740), p. 312; Long, *History*, Vol. II, pp. 435–6.

[4] Long, *History*, Vol. II, p. 436; Edwards, op. cit., Vol. II, p. 176; John Williamson, op. cit., Vol. II, pp. 199–200; Dr. Quier, *P.P.*, LXXXIV (26), 1789, Jamaica Evidence. Appendix No. 8.

[5] ibid., p. 436; Edwards, op. cit., Vol. II, p. 155; *Jamaica Magazine*, as n. 2, above; De la Beche, op. cit., p. 18; Dr. Quier as n. 8, p. 201, above.

[6] Abbé Raynal, *Histoire philosophique et politique des établissements et du commerce des européens dans les deux Indes*, 4 vols. (Amsterdam, 1770). First English ed., 4 vols., London, 1776; Vol. III, p. 452.

[7] Tetanus. See Drs. Chisholme and Anderson, *P.P.*, Vol. LXXXIV (26), 1789, Jamaica Evidence, Appendix, nos. 6 and 7; Benjamin Moseley, *Tropical Diseases*, (1789 ed.), pp. 463–519; *JAJ*, XII, 795 of 20 Dec. 1815.

[9] See Long, *History*, Vol. II, p. 435.

[10] There was a shortage of fish and meat, despite the rations and the allowance made for some slaves to keep pigs and poultry. (See Coor, Cook, Fitzmaurice, *P.P.*, Vol. XCII (34), 1790–1, no. 745, pp. 95, 189, 205, 210, 229.) William Beckford claimed the slaves' main dish was pottage (*Remarks*) (London, 1788), p. 63; Edwards (op. cit., Vol. I, p. 255), stresses the amount of plantain bread that was eaten; Lewis, op. cit. (1929 ed.), p. 94, makes the point about the diet's vegetable nature. Fish and meat provide the best protein intake for growing children and are considered richest for mother's milk.

[11] 'upon some estates there are five men to one woman' (Long, *History*, Vol. II, p. 435). See also Pares, *Merchants and Planters*, pp. 39, 82 n. 11. The male/female gap closed steadily after 1807 until by 1820 (see figures on p. 207) there was a slight excess of slave women.

not lay eggs on shipboard, because they do not like their situation.'[1]
But the fact remains that the production or survival of new-born
slaves was low. 'Monk' Lewis was told by the wife of one of his
slaves that

she had had fifteen children, had taken the utmost care of them, and yet
had now but two alive: she said, indeed, fifteen at the first, but she afterwards corrected herself, and explained that she had had 'twelve whole
children and three half ones'; by which she meant miscarriages.[2]

In fact, towards the end of the period of this study and beyond, to the
years immediately preceding Emancipation, the total slave population of Jamaica (and of the West Indies generally) was actually
declining:

	male	*female*	*total*
1817	173,319	172,831	346,150
1820	170,466	171,916	342,382
1823	166,595	169,658	336,253
1826	162,726	168,393	331,119
1829	158,254	164,167	322,421[3]

After Emancipation, the black birth-rate started to rise and continued
to rise steadily throughout the rest of the century.[4]

Malingering[5] was another way of protesting. Stewart was in no
doubt that some Negro mothers 'wilfully infected their children with
yaws that they [the children] might be released for a time from
labour'.[6] And even if the slaves *were* only 'labouring machines', they
were nevertheless very much aware of their economic value:

When they are severely corrected, they will tell their Masters, *if you killee
me, you lose Negroe*, sensible that their Labour is their Master's Riches.[7]

And Charles Campbell relates the following story:

'Who planted the cane?' said a slave to me one day, when I checked him
for [stealing] a lump of sugar: 'Who nourished its growth? was it not the
poor Negro? Negro man work all day in the hot sun; he toil through mud

[1] Lewis, op. cit., p. 82. See also, *P.P.*, XCII (34), 1790–1, no. 745, *passim*; and Patterson, op. cit., pp. 104–12, who provides a useful summary of conditions.
[2] Lewis, op. cit., p. 111.
[3] *P.P.*, Vol. XXXVI (2), 1833, no. 473, p. 2; 'Returns of Slaves'.
[4] Roberts, op. cit., p. 42.
[5] For sample list of malingerers, see *JAJ*, VII, 160 of 10 Sept. 1779; for examples, see
Lewis, op. cit. (1929 ed.), p. 168.
[6] Stewart, *View*, pp. 303–4. Italics in text.
[7] Anon. *The Importance of Jamaica to Great Britain considered* (London, n.d.),
p. 19.

and rain. He have hunger and wet all day, cold all night, yet he plant the cane, he watch over him, he cut him down, carry him to the mill, he make sugar. Shall Buckra man, who do nothing, eat all; and poor Negro man, who do all dem tings, starve?'[1]

Always, he said, the slaves 'eyed their own degradation with just but silent indignation'.[2] In *Marly*, there is an incident that took place after an overseer had punished a whole gang of slaves (men and women) indiscriminately, because some of them had come to work late.

The negroes said very little, but the moment the Busha's back was turned to go away, the whole line commenced singing in a general chorus, as if they regarded him not, 'I don't care a damn, oh! I don't care a damn, oh!' and this must have sounded in his ears for at least five minutes, before he could get beyond the reach of hearing.[3]

Renny reported hearing slaves in Kingston in 1799 singing:

> One, two, tree,
> All de same;
> Black, white, brown,
> All de same:
> All de same.
> One, two, tree . . .[4]

This kind of democratic reaction was all the more significant in view of that other Revolution that was having a profound effect on Jamaican society—that of Toussaint L'Ouverture's Haiti. In the light of that holocaust (as white Jamaicans would have termed it), every slave was now *seen* as a possible assassin. 'We met a horrid looking black man', Maria Nugent wrote in her *Journal* on 2 April 1805,

who passed us several times, without making any bow, although I recollected him as one of the boatmen of the canoe we used to go out in. . . . He was then very humble, but tonight he only grinned, and gave us a sort of fierce look, that struck me with a terror I could not shake off.[5]

The missionaries, despite their basic paternalism, also helped to foster this democratic and self-assertive reaction among both free coloureds and free and unfree blacks. The free coloureds, since the establishment of the first Methodist mission in Kingston in 1789,[6]

[1] Campbell, op. cit., p. 19.   [2] ibid.
[3] *Marly*, p. 104.   [4] Renny, op. cit., p. 241 n. (p).   [5] *LNJ* (Wright), p. 227.
[6] See Thomas Coke, *A Journal of the Rev. Dr. Coke's Visit to Jamaica and his Third Tour on the Continent of America* (London, 1789), pp. 2–4. Coke, an Episcopalian

had tended to support this Church.[1] Methodist congregations,
though supervised by ministers, were, as in Britain, to a large
extent controlled by leaders, stewards, exhorters and local preachers
and by committees composed of these officers—most of whom were
coloured. It was not long before these committees were making their
presence felt. In 1807, one of the missionaries, Mr. Bradneck,
who, it seems, resented the assumptions of his committee, was
accused at a District General Meeting of exhibiting 'bad temper'
and—worst of all, of having an eye for the girls. Poor Mr. Bradneck
was suspended by his local committee—an action which must have
given a group of people with little other institutional authority to
boast of, a great deal of satisfaction. In the end, Bradneck was
saved, and reinstated on the authority of Dr. Coke in London,
thanks to the intervention of one of those typical and very formidable
Methodist ladies—Mary Smith[2] a white creole—who supplied Coke
with her version of the affair:

. . . one circumstance which I intended to mention . . . relating to Women is
that of Mr. B's Foot being in a young woman's lap. Mr. Burn our Leader
from Manchioneel was in the House and Room with Mr. Bradneck when
the Shoe and Stocking was taken off to search for a Cheger, and Mr.
Burn declared in the meeting and to me afterwards in private that Mr. B's
foot was on a Table the whole time. . . .[3]

By 1814, the coloured leaders and stewards were encroaching even
further in their bid for greater control of the mission. On 31 March

clergyman, joined John Wesley in 1776. In 1784, he drew up a missionary plan and was
sent to America by Wesley that same year. He set out again for America (Nova
Scotia) in 1786, but was driven to Antigua by a storm. He spent a year there, consoli-
dating the Methodist Church already established by the Speaker of the Antigua Assembly. The Wesleyan Methodist Missionary Society was set up under his chairmanship
in 1789—the year of his third American tour and his first visit to Jamaica. Coke
visited Jamaica four times in all: 1789, 1791, 1792, 1793. (See Ragatz, *Guide*, pp. 348–9;
Gardner, op. cit., pp. 345–6; Peter Duncan, *A Narrative of the Wesleyan Mission to
Jamaica* (London, 1849), pp. 7–10, Thomas Coke, *An account of the rise, progress, and
present state of the Methodist missions* (London, 1804); *Extracts of the journals of five
visits to America* (London, 1793).

[1] See Duncker, op. cit., pp. 134–8; Coke, *History*, Vol. I, pp. 425, 432.

[2] Mary Ann Able Smith was born in the United States and came to Jamaica as a
result of the Revolution; she with eight others, are held to be the first Methodists in
Jamaica. When at the annual district meeting of January 1822, it was reported that
the increase of members was upwards of 600, and that the whole number on the island
amounted to nearly 8,000, Mrs. Smith, then very frail, 'raised her hands to heaven,
and with streaming eyes expressed her gratitude to God for what he had spared her to
witness. "I was once," she said, "one of eight, but God has permitted me to live to see
the little one become a thousand".' (Thus, Duncan, op. cit., pp. 11–12.)

[3] Mary Smith to Coke, letter dated Kingston, 15 August 1807 in WMMS Archives;
Letters 1803–1813, f. 249.

they sent off a joint letter to the Mission Committee in London (Mary A. A. Smith headed the signatories), setting out the state of 'the Methodist Society in this place'[1] and suggesting that a particular minister (Mr. Fish) of whom they were fond, should be sent back to Jamaica as being the most suitable man of God for the job in the island. But things had gone even further than that, as missionary Wiggins explained to the London Committee in a letter dated earlier that same month.[2] 'They insist', Wiggins complained,

first, upon revising the society receipts in the Leaders Meetings, and upon keeping both the Money and the Books locked up in their chest. . . . They refused to advance me any sum of money to enable me to open the Spanish Town meeting. . . . They insist, in short, in being the sole Judges of what is, or is not wanting for the Society's use, and of the quantity, quality, price etc. . . . I wanted them to advance money sometime ago to repair the roof of this Chapel, when Shingles were cheap, but they would not. I wanted them to advance what would have purchased the House in Spanish Town . . . when I could have had it for one 6th of its value, but they would not. . . . [How] am I to manage . . . ? If I propose to a quarterly or leaders meeting to deprive them of affairs, they will overreach the judgement and work themselves into the affections of the leaders (. . . mostly women all of whom are Brown and Black but one).[3]

The Blacks, in their own way, found similar ways to self-expression and protest through the church organizations they, on the whole, preferred—the Black Baptist and Baptist chapels and meetings, led, paradoxically, but after all quite reasonably, by those slaves best equipped to do so—the drivers.[4] Mary Reckord, in her study, 'Missionary Activity in Jamaica before Emancipation',[5] sums up the effect of these churches on the slave population in this way:

The slaves expressed their political interests in the religious groups which developed outside the mission churches. [These] groups represented a form of sectarianism which mingled the slaves' African religious beliefs, the Negro Baptist tradition established by George Liele and his followers, and mission Christianity. . . .

[These] groups reflected primarily the slaves' religious interests, and

[1] Mary Smith to Coke, WI. Letter Box. Letter dated Methodist Chapel, Kingston, Jamaica, 31 March 1814.
[2] ibid., WI. Letter Box 1814–15, pp. 147 ff. Wiggins to Methodist Mission Committee, Kingston, 10 March 1814.
[3] ibid., pp. 147 ff.
[4] *A Narrative of recent events*, pp. ix–x.
[5] Unpublished Ph.D. Thesis, University of London, 1964.

mingled Christianity with traditional African forms to produce a style of worship which satisfied more completely than mission services their emotional needs. [Moreover], freed from the supervision of the missionaries and their emphasis on conformity and obedience, the slaves were also able to express their political interests and use religion to sanction their hopes. This tendency was strengthened by the fact that, although the weekly market and occasions such as funerals and dances provided them with social contacts, religious meetings were the only form of organized activity current among them.[1] Such meetings therefore became a natural focal point for all of the slave's interests not served by estate organisation.[2]

The 'political interests' of these groups, Dr. Reckord argues, were primarily and constantly in freedom. Two Black Baptists were sent to trial at Black River in 1816, accused of fomenting rebellion.[3] To make matters worse, it was also believed that a black 'Frenchman' from St. Domingue was in on the proceedings.[4] When brought to trial, and for singing (according to 'Monk' Lewis, though the song as reported does not read very authentically):

Oh me good friend, Mr. Wilberforce, make we free!
God Almighty thank ye! God Almighty thank ye!
    God Almighty, make we free!
Buckra in this country no make we free:
What Negro for to do? What Negro for to do?
    Take force by force! Take force by force![5]

the leader of this conspiracy (an Ibo) insisted that (again this is Lewis' account),

He had sung no songs but such as his brown priest had assured him were approved of by John the Baptist . . . [who] was a friend to the negroes, and had got his head in a pan.[6]

The logical step, obviously, was revolution. But before this and its nature is discussed, it will be necessary to examine, at least in outline, some aspects of the culture of the slave population.

---

[1] But cf. pp. 227–8, below.
[2] Reckord, op. cit., pp. 198–201.   [3] ibid., p. 201.
[4] Lewis, op. cit. (1929 ed.), pp. 185–6.   [5] ibid., p. 186.   [6] ibid., p. 187.

15

THE 'FOLK' CULTURE
OF THE SLAVES

THE vast majority of Jamaica's slaves came from West Africa. No attempt will be made in this study, to enter the argument about African 'survivals', 'retentions', 'adaptations' and so on,[1] within creole society. But the habits, customs, and ways of life of the slaves in Jamaica, derived from West Africa, will be seen in this context as a 'folk' culture—the culture of the mass of ex-Africans who found themselves in a new environment and who were successfully adapting to it.

Some understanding of the nature of this folk culture is important, not only in terms of the creole society to which it was to contribute within the time-limits of this study, but also because the changes in Jamaican society after 1865 involved the beginning of an assertion of this folk culture which was to have a profound effect upon the very constitution of Jamaican society. This assertion has become increasingly articulate since the gaining of political independence in 1962 and is now the subject of some study by scholars and intellectuals. This 'folk culture' is also being made use of by many Jamaican and West Indian artists and writers, though the nature of the creolization of this culture has made the effective validation of it more difficult than might be supposed. This is because, in M. G. Smith's phrase, 'the Creole culture which West Indians share is the basis of their division'.[2] White (European) and 'mulatto' (creole) values are still preferred to black folk values—even by black West Indians themselves.

---

[1] See M. J. Herskovits, *The Myth of the Negro Past* (New York, 1941); G. A. Beltrán, 'African Influences in the Development of Regional Cultures in the New World', in *Plantation Systems*, pp. 64–70, with comments by René Ribeiro, pp. 70–2; M. G. Smith, 'The African Heritage in the Caribbean', *Caribbean Studies: A Symposium*, ed. Vera Rubin (Seattle, 1960), pp. 34–46, with comments by G. E. Simpson and Peter B. Hammond, pp. 46–53; Roger Bastide, *Les Amériques Noires* (Paris, 1967).

[2] M. G. Smith, 'West Indian Culture' in *The Plural Society*, p. 9.

The African orientation of Jamaican folk culture

Folk culture, though usually autochthonous, may be said to be dependent upon a 'great tradition', in the sense defined by Redfield,[1] for its sanctions, its memories, its myths. In the case of Jamaica's slaves, the 'great tradition' was clearly in Africa, in the same way that white Jamaicans' was in Europe—both, in other words, external to the society.

Have you ever heard African Negroes speak of their own country?
—I have heard them speak very much in favour of their own country, and express much grief at leaving it. I never knew one but wished to go back again.[2]
Did you know any instances of African Negroes expressing themselves with affection of their native country, and desiring to return to it?
—I did, as I brought a Guinea woman to England who wished much to be sent back to her own country; and it is very common for Negroes when they are sick to say, they are going back to their own country.
Did they say it with apparent satisfaction?
—They certainly do, as they express always a great deal of pleasure when they think they are going to die, and say, that they are going to leave this Buccra country.[3]

Slave customs connected with the life cycle

(i) Birth

When a child was born, the placenta and navel string were carefully disposed of. 'The mother must guard it carefully and, after three days to a year from the time of birth, must bury it in the ground and plant a young tree over the spot, which henceforth becomes the property of the child and is called his "navel-string tree".'[4] The newborn was regarded as not being of this world until nine days had passed. 'Monk' Lewis was told by a slave midwife: 'Oh, massa, till

[1] 'In a civilization there is a great tradition of the reflective few, and there is a little tradition of the largely unreflective many. The great tradition is cultivated in schools or temples; the little tradition works itself out and keeps itself going in the lives of the unlettered in their village communities. The tradition of the philosopher, theologian, and literary man is a tradition consciously cultivated and handed down; that of the little people is for the most part taken for granted and not submitted to much scrutiny or considered refinement and improvement. . . . The two traditions are interdependent. . . . (Robert Redfield, *Peasant Society and Culture* (University of Chicago Press, 1956), 1965 imp., pp. 41–2.)
[2] *P.P.*, 1790–1, Vol. XCII (34), no. 746, p.196; Mark Cook's Evidence.
[3] ibid., p. 184; Davidson's Evidence. See also Montule, op. cit., p. 43. Kerr also describes (p. 31) present-day birth-customs and beliefs.
[4] Martha W. Beckwith, *Black Roadways* (Chapel Hill, 1929), p. 55. This custom persists. See Madeline Kerr, *Personality and Conflict in Jamaica* (London, 1952), 1963 ed., p. 29.

nine days over, we no hope of them'.[1] Dr. Dancer in his *Medical Assistant*,[2] said: 'The negro usage, of tying up the cut Navel-string with burnt rag, and never examining it for nine days, is attended sometimes with bad consequences.' After this period, the child was exposed 'to the inclemency of the weather, with a view to render [him] hardy'.[3] But was it as simple and crude as this? Dr. Patterson, in discussing the nine-day period of neglect, says it was due to the fear of tetanus in Jamaica.[4] On the other hand M. J. Field, describing the birth customs of the Ga people, has this account which corresponds, not insignificantly, with the Jamaican experience:

After the child is born it is 'kept like an egg' indoors for seven days. It is then held to have survived seven dangers, and is worthy to be called a person.

On the eighth day very early in the morning, about four o'clock, two women of the father's family are sent to bring the child from the mother's home, where it was born and where it will be suckled, to its father's house. The friends and relatives assemble in the yard outside the house for the *kpodziem*, or 'going-out' ceremony. . . .

. . . the child is laid naked on the ground under the eaves. . . . Then the 'godfather' takes water in a calabash and flings it three times on the roof, so that it trickles down on the child like rain. This is to introduce the child to the rain and to the earth. Then the child as it lies on the ground is blessed. . . . The child is now a member of the family and has assumed its own name. If it dies before the eighth day it is considered as having never been born and has no name, but it can die on the ninth day and its father and mother for the rest of their lives be called by its name—'*Dede* mother', '*Tete* father.'[5]

Martha Beckwith's *Black Roadways*, in fact, describes a Jamaican 'outdooring' observed in the 1920s:

The momentous time in an infant's life arrives on the ninth day after birth, when for the first time he is taken out of doors. During the first nine days the mother eats only soft food, like arrowroot, bread, and milk. On the ninth day, a bath is prepared for the child, a little rum thrown into it, and each member of the family must throw in a bit of silver[6] 'for the eyesight'.

[1] Lewis, op. cit. (1929 ed.), p. 87.
[2] Op. cit., p. 267.   [3] *Jamaica Magazine*, Vol. IV (Dec. 1813), no. 6, p. 893.
[4] Patterson, op. cit., p. 155.
[5] M. J. Field, *Religion and Medicine of the Ga People* (London, 1937; Accra/London, 1961), pp. 171 and 173. See also G. Parrinder, *West African Religion* . . . (London, 1949), pp. 110–11; Herskovits, *Myth*, pp. 188–9; *Dahomey: An Ancient West African Kingdom*, 2 vols. (New York, 1938), Vol. I, pp. 266–7.
[6] Yet another West African custom. See, for example, Field, *Religion and Medicine*, p. 166, who also stresses the importance of the initiatory bath.

... To ward off evil spirits, indigo blue is added to the bath, and the forehead marked with a blue cross ... the midwife offers a prayer before bringing the baby out into the air.[1]

(ii) *Sexual/Domestic unions*

It is a truth well known, that the practice of polygamy, which universally prevails in Africa, is also very generally adopted among the Negroes in the West Indies; and he who conceives that a remedy may be found for this, by introducing among them the laws of marriage as established in Europe, is utterly ignorant of their manners, propensities, and superstitions. It is reckoned in Jamaica, on a moderate computation, that not less than ten thousand of such as are called Head Negroes (artificers and others) possess from two to four wives.[2]

But

one only is the object of particular steady attachment; the rest, although called wives, are only a sort of occasional concubines, or drudges, whose assistance the husband claims in the culture of his land, sale of his produce, and so on; rendering to them reciprocal acts of friendship, when they are in want. They laugh at the idea of marriage, which ties two persons together indissolubly.[3]

(iii) *Children*

They exercise a kind of sovereignty over their children, which never ceases during life; chastizing them sometimes with much severity; and seeming to hold filial obedience in much higher estimation than conjugal fidelity.[4]

I can affirm, that the affections between the mothers and even spurious offspring are very powerful as well as permanent ... and with respect to black children, nothing is so sure to irritate and enrage them as cursing their mothers. ...[5]

negroes absolutely respect primogeniture; and the eldest son takes an indisputed possession of his father's property immediately after his decease. ...
they are in general [so] attached to their families, that the young will work with cheerfulness to maintain the sickly and the weak, and ... they are much disposed to pay to age respect and veneration.[6]

---

[1] Beckwith, *Black Roadways*, pp. 57–8.   [2] Edwards, op. cit., Vol. II, pp. 175–6.
[3] Long, *History*, Vol. II, pp. 414–15.   [4] ibid., p. 414.
[5] Bickell, op cit., pp. 17–18.   [6] Beckford, *Account*, Vol. II, pp. 323–4.

(iv) *Death, funerals and burial*

Before burial, a dead person was, if possible, laid out in state:

> an assemblage of slaves from the neighbourhood appears: the body is ornamented with linen and other apparel, which has been previously purchased, as is often the custom, for this solemn occasion; and all the trinkets of the defunct are exposed in the coffin. . . .[1]

A wake usually took place at this time, accompanied by what white observers called 'every kind of tumult and festivity'[2]—dirges, drumming, horn-blowing in the West African style,[3] praise-songs for the deceased, sacrifices of poultry and libations.[4] Interment took place in Negro burial grounds, if these were provided by the authorities, or 'promiscuously in the fields, and [near] their near and dear relations at the back of their huts, and sometimes under their beds'.[5] According to Lewis, they were

> always buried in their own gardens, and many strange and fantastical ceremonies are observed on the occasion. If the corpse be that of a grown person, they consult it as to which way it pleases to be carried; and they make attempts upon various roads without success, before they can hit upon the right one.[6]

Dr. Field's description of a Ga funeral procession is almost exactly similar:

> When the time comes for burial the body is put into a coffin—it used to be a basket—and is carried round the town. If any one is responsible for the death either by witchcraft, poison, or bad medicine, the coffin will lurch and plunge towards the house of the offender and refuse to pass it. Even when it has no accusation of this kind to make a coffin is always an unruly burden.[7]

At the graveside, libations were offered:

[1] Beckford, *Account*, Vol. II, p. 388.

[2] WMMS *Notices*, Vol. II, p. 151; Binning to John Purdom of Hull. Letter dated Montego Bay, 11 April 1819.

[3] See for instance, J. Goody, *Death, Property and the Ancestors* (London, 1962) pp. 97–104; Field, *Religion and Medicine*, pp. 198–201; David Brokensha, *Social Change at Larteh, Ghana* (Oxford University Press, 1966), pp. 191–3.

[4] See, among others, Long, *History*, Vol. II, pp. 421–2; Beckford, *Descriptive Account*, Vol. II, pp. 388–9; Stewart, *View*, pp. 274–6; Barclay, op. cit., pp. 134–7; WMMS, *Notices*, Vol. II, p. 312.

[5] Moreton, op. cit., p. 162. For a similar custom in West Africa, see Parrinder, op. cit., p. 118; G. J. Afolabi Ojo, *Yoruba Culture, A Geographical Analysis* (University of Ife, 1966), p. 192.   [6] Lewis, op. cit., p. 88. See also Leslie, op. cit., pp. 308–10.

[7] Field, *Religion and Medicine*, p. 200. For this custom among the Akan see R. S. Rattray, *Religion and Art in Ashanti* (Oxford University Press, 1927), 1954 ed., pp. 167–70. For West Africa generally, see Parrinder, op. cit., pp. 118, 166–7.

The manner of the Sacrifice is this: The nearest Relation kills [a hog], the Intrails are buried, the four Quarters are divided, and a kind of Soup made, which is brought in a Calabash or Gourd, and, after waving it Three times, it is set down; then the Body is put in the Ground; all the while they are covering it with Earth, the Attendants scream out in a terrible manner, which is not the Effect of Grief, but of Joy; they beat on their wooden Drums and the Women with their Rattles make a hideous Noise. . . .[1]

The dead body's spirit, however, would not yet be at rest. A period of forty days[2] had to elapse before this would be accomplished. As in parts of West Africa,[3] therefore, the first burial was considered temporary, and food was left by the graveside for the succour of the 'traveller':

After the Grave is filled up they place the Soup which they had prepared at the Head, and a Bottle of rum at the Feet. . . .[4]

There then followed the period of mourning—again West African in character (though Long[5] thought that he recognized in it the Scottish highland 'late-wake').

When the deceased is a married woman, the husband lets his beard remain unshaved, and appears rather negligent in his attire, for the space of a month;[6] at the expiration of which, a fowl is dressed at his house, with some messes of good broth, and he proceeds, accompanied by his friends, to the grave.[7]

Here now, about a month (or forty days) after the first interment,[8] the 'second', final (often symbolic only), burial took place.

Then begins a song, purporting, that the deceased is now in the enjoyment of compleat felicity; and that they are assembled to rejoice at her state of bliss, and perform the last offices of duty and friendship. They then lay a considerable heap of earth over the grave, which is called *covering it;* and the meeting concludes with eating . . . drinking, dancing and vociferation.[9]

Because of this 'two-burial' custom, some white Jamaican observers, lacking understanding, received the impression that the slaves

[1] Leslie, op. cit., p. 309.

[2] J. H. K. Nketia, *Funeral Dirges of the Akan People* (Achimota, 1955), p.15 mentions 'the 8th, 15th, 40th and 80th day of the funeral'.

[3] See, for instance, Parrinder, op. cit., pp. 118–19.

[4] Leslie, op. cit., p. 309. See also Hans Sloane, *A Voyage to the Islands, Madera, Barbados, Nieves, St. Christophers and Jamaica, with the Natural History . . . of the last of those islands*, 2 vols. (London, 1707, 1725), Vol. I, p. xlviii.

[5] *History*, Vol. II, p. 422.   [6] Cf., Field, *Religion and Medicine*, p. 201.

[7] Long, *History*, Vol. II, p. 421.   [8] Phillippo, op. cit., p. 246.

[9] Long, *History*, Vol. II, pp. 421–2.

did not care for their dead, but merely covered them lightly with a little earth.[1] The 'happy' songs and up-tempo rhythms used when returning from the graveside also contributed to this impression.[2]

Religious ideas

'The African negroes of the West Indies,' Stewart wrote,

whatever superstitious notions they may bring with them from their native country, agree in believing the existence of an omnipotent Being, who will reward or punish us in a future life for our good or evil actions in this....[3]

Another writer confirmed this, but went on to assume that this Being was not worshipped:

The Africans all acknowledge a Supreme Being; but they suppose him endowed with too much benevolence to do harm to mankind, and therefore think it unnecessary to offer him any homage....[4]

The slaves also believed that

after death, they shall first return to their native country, and enjoy again the society of kindred and friends, from whom they have been torn away in an evil hour....[5]

This led, as in Africa, to the recognition of the ancestors as active spirits or forces[6] and to the connected belief (or superstition) in duppies[7] and other forms of visible ghosts; 'Monk' Lewis in 1818 having to wonder if his slaves' general resistance to Christian doctrine did not betoken some religious beliefs of their own.[8]

[1] Long, *History*, Vol. II, p. 421; Phillippo, op. cit., p. 246; *Daily Advertiser*, 15 Sept. 1790.
[2] See Stewart, *View*, p. 275. A brilliant New Orleans re-creation of a Negro funeral is rendered by Louis Armstrong and his All Stars in 'Oh, didn't he ramble' on the LP *New Orleans Days* (Brunswick LA 8537), 1950.
[3] Stewart, *View*, p. 280.
[4] Dr. Winterbotham's 'Account of the Native Africans . . .', quoted in Watson, op. cit., pp. 15–16 (n.)   [5] Stewart, *View*, pp. 280–1.
[6] See Curtin, *Two Jamaicas*, p. 31; Beckwith, *Black Roadways*, p. 54.
[7] See Lewis, op. cit., p. 88, and J. G. Moore, 'Religion of Jamaican Negroes: A Study of Afro-Jamaican Acculturation', unpublished Ph.D. thesis, Northwestern University (1953), pp. 33–4: 'When a man is born, he has a personal spirit and a duppy spirit. The personal spirit is regarded as a man's personality, whereas the duppy spirit is [his] shadow. . . . The duppy spirit, or shadow, remains with the corpse in the grave. . . . When [he] feels that his body has not been buried properly, it is believed that he becomes restless and dissatisfied. . . ' For probable African derivation of the word, see F. G. Cassidy, *Jamaica Talk* (London, 1961), p. 247; Cassidy and Le Page, op. cit., p. 164 (Bube, *dupe*); M. J. Field, *Search for Security: An Ethno-psychiatric Study of Rural Ghana* (London, 1960), p. 44 (Ga-Adangme *adope*): and Patterson, op. cit., p. 204, n. 2.   [8] Lewis, op. cit. (1929 ed.), pp. 286–7.

Such a possibility, however, was not easy for white creoles to accept, though De la Beche found that

Some negroes entertain ideas of the transmigration of the soul; an old woman on my estate . . . stated her belief that people when they died turned into dust like brickdust; that those who behaved ill during their lives became mules, horses, flies, etc.; but that those who had led a good life were born again, and occupied similar situations to those they had previously filled; that blacks would be blacks again, and whites whites.[1]

Religious practice

As Lewis said,[2] it was difficult to know if the slaves had any real religious beliefs or practice, since the only external sign of a 'priest', was the obeah-man. Lewis was perhaps nearer than he knew to the truth about his slaves' religious beliefs and practices, but he did not understand the function of the obeah-man, since he was associated in the Jamaican/European mind with superstition, witchcraft, and poison.[3]

But in African and Caribbean folk practice, where religion had not been externalized and institutionalized as in Europe, the obeah-man was doctor, philosopher, and priest.[4] Healing was, in a sense, an act of faith, as it was in the early Christian church, and the fetish (*suman*) had come to mediate (in many instances to replace and obscure the connection) between man and god. More generally, however, the fetish was regarded as an attribute or token of the god. Each man was also, in a way not understood by Europeans, a priest, and through possession (induced by communal dancing to drums) could not only communicate with the gods, but become and assume the god.[5] In Jamaica, Black Baptist worshippers were often possessed, as were 'pagan' cultists, and not always under the prompting of drums:

---

[1] De la Beche, op. cit., p. 31. Dr. Field discusses the concept of reincarnation as it is expressed in the naming of Ga children in *Religion and Medicine*, pp. 174–5.

[2] Op. cit. (1929 ed.), p. 286.

[3] See also Marsden, op. cit., p. 40. Obeah (and myalism) are thoroughly discussed in Patterson, op. cit., pp. 185–95.

[4] See Field, *Search for Security*. In the Caribbean, the only African-derived functionary of this type to have received detailed study is the *houngan* of the Vodun 'cult' of Haiti. A useful summary is by H. Courlander and Rémy Bastien, *Religion and Politics in Haiti* (Washington D.C., 1966). For Jamaica see Moore, op. cit.; for Trinidad, G. E. Simpson, *The Shango Cult in Trinidad* (Rio Piedras, 1965).

[5] See Herskovits, *Myth*, pp. 215–17; J. H. Nketia, 'Possession Dances in African Societies' in *Journal of the International Folk Music Council*, Vol. IX (1957), pp. 4–8. Moore, op. cit., pp. 76–9, 136 and the discussion in *Caribbean Studies: A Symposium*, ed. Vera Rubin (University of Washington Press, 1957), 2nd ed. 1960, p. 36 (M. G. Smith), pp. 48–9 (Simpson and Hammond).

During the sermon, a heathen woman began to twist her body about, and make all manner of Grimaces. I bore it all for sometime till she disturbed the congregation, when I desired one of the assistants to lead her out, thinking she was in pain. When the service was over, I inquired what ailed her, and was told, that it was a usual thing with the negroes on M. estate, and called by them Conviction.[1]

Music and dance

Music and dance, though recreational, was functional as well. Slaves, as in Africa, danced and sang at work, at play, at worship, from fear, from sorrow, from joy. Here was the characteristic form of their social and artistic expression. It was secular and religious. There was no real distinction between these worlds in the way that a post-Renaissance European was likely to understand.[2] And because this music and dance was so misunderstood, and since the music was based on tonal scales and the dancing on choreographic traditions entirely outside the white observers' experience—not forgetting the necessary assumption that slaves, since they were brutes could produce no philosophy that 'reach[ed] above the navel'[3]—their music was dismissed as 'noise',[4] their dancing as a way of (or to) sexual misconduct and debauchery.[5] On the other hand, the 'political' function of the slaves' music was quickly recognized by their masters —hence the banning of drumming or gatherings where drumming took place[6]—often on the excuse that it disturbed the (white) neighbours, or was bad for the bondsmen's own health,[7] or both.

On the whole, therefore, the available descriptions of the slaves' music and dancing are picturesque only, though now and then a hint comes through of grace of form and discipline:

[1] John Lang's Diary in (Moravian) *Periodical Accounts*, Vol. VI (1816), p. 364. This cult, or something very similar was observed in eastern Jamaica in 1956 and described by Donald Hogg, in 'The Convince Cult in Jamaica', Yale University Publications in Anthropology, no. 58 in Sidney Mintz, comp., *Papers in Caribbean Anthropology* (New Haven, 1960).

[2] For a discussion of this, see J. B. Danquah, *The Akan Doctrine of God* (London and Redhill, 1944); Placide Tempels, *Bantu Philosophy* (Paris, 1959); Daryll Forde, 'Introduction' and P. Mercier (trans.) 'The Fon of Dahomey' in *African Worlds: Studies in the Cosmological Ideas and Social Values of African Peoples* (Oxford University Press, 1954); Janheinz Jahn, *Muntu: An Outline of Neo-African Culture* (trans. London, 1961), pp. 96–120; and *A History of Neo-African Literature: Writing in Two Continents* (trans. London, 1968), pp. 156–7; Marcel Griaule, *Dieu d'eau* (Paris, 1948).

[3] The phrase is from the St. Lucian poet, Derek Walcott, *In a Green Night* (London, 1962), p. 26.

[4] See, for instance, Edwards, op. cit., Vol. II, p. 106; Renny, op. cit., p. 168.

[5] See, among others, *The Diary of William Jones*, p. 12; Gardner, op. cit., pp. 99–100.

[6] See *Laws*, Vol. IV, p. 216; Stewart, *View*, p. 272.

[7] See, for instance, 32 Geo. III, 23, section 23 (1792).

nothing could be more light, and playful, and graceful, than the extempore movements of the dancing girl. Indeed, through the whole day, I had been struck with the precision of their march [Lewis is here describing a Christmas carnival], the ease and grace of their action, the elasticity of their step, and the lofty air with which they carried their heads. . . .[1]

The dances performed tonight seldom admitted more than three persons at a time: to me they appeared to be movements entirely dictated by the caprice of the moment; but I am told that there is a regular figure, and that the least mistake, or a single false step, is immediately noticed by the rest.[2]

Dancing usually took place, as in Africa, in the centre of a ring of spectator-participants, performers entering the ring singly or in twos and threes.[3] Sometimes male dancers expressed themselves acrobatically,[4] but more often, especially at private entertainments, the shuffle step was employed, the dancers stylistically confining themselves to a very restricted area indeed.[5] 'Sometimes there are two men dance with one woman; they follow, fan her with their handkerchiefs, court her and leave her alternately, and make you understand, as perfectly as any ballet-dancer in Europe, what they mean.'[6] As is still the custom in parts of West Africa, where coins are placed on the forehead of excellent performers, 'presents of ryals [were] thrust into [the] mouths or bosoms' of dancers who gave particular satisfaction to the audience, 'some officious negro going round the circle to keep back intruders'.[7]

Improvisation was also a feature of many of the slaves' songs. 'Guinea Corn' is an excellent example of this *genre*:

> Guinea Corn, I long to see you
> Guinea Corn, I long to plant you
> Guinea Corn, I long to mould you

[1] Lewis, op. cit., (1929 ed.), p. 57.   [2] ibid., p. 74.

[3] *A Short Journey*, Vol. I, p. 88; Stewart, *View*, pp. 269–70.

[4] 'performing the most extravagant and hyperbolical saltations'. Campbell, op. cit., p. 16.

[5] '. . . two of them generally dance together, and sometimes do not move six inches from the same place'. Marsden, op. cit., p. 34. This of course was 'apart' dancing, the couples not being in any physical contact. This style is perhaps the most common form of dancing, certainly among the Akan and related people of West Africa. See R. F. Thompson, 'An Aesthetic of the Cool: West African Dance', *Freedomways*, Vol. II (1966), no. 2, p. 97; and the descriptions in Geoffrey Gorer, *Africa Dances* (London, 1935); J. H. K. Nketia, *Folk Songs of Ghana* (University of Ghana, 1963), pp. 17–18. For comparative work on Negro dancing—mainly religious ritual—in Africa and the New World, see Pierre Verger, *Notes sur le culte des Orisa et Vodun à Bahia, la Baie de tous les Saints, au Brésil et à l'ancienne Côte des Esclaves en Afrique* (Dakar, 1957); Jahn, *Muntu*, pp. 62–95; Roger Bastide, op. cit., esp. pp. 175–96.

[6] *A Short Journey*, Vol. I, pp. 88–9.

[7] *Columbian Magazine*, Vol. II (May 1797), p. 768.

Guinea Corn, I long to weed you
Guinea Corn, I long to hoe you
Guinea Corn, I long to top you
Guinea Corn, I long to cut you
Guinea Corn, I long to dry you
Guinea Corn, I long to beat you
Guinea Corn, I long to trash you
Guinea Corn, I long to parch you
Guinea Corn, I long to grind you
Guinea Corn, I long to turn you
Guinea Corn, I long to eat you[1]

The climax of the song came with the word *eat*, when 'as though satiated with the food, or tired with the process for procuring it', the singers bestowed 'an hearty curse on the grain, asking where it came from'.[2]

Many of these 'impromptus' were, like 'Guinea Corn' (above) or like

Hipsaw! my deaa! you no do like a-me!
You no jig like a-me! you no twist like a-me!
Hipsaw! my deaa! you no shake like a-me!
You no wind like a-me! Go, yondaa![3]

and

Ying de ying de ying,
Ying de ying de ying,
Take care you go talk oh,
Min' you tattler tongue,
Ying de ying,
Min' you tattler tongue,
Ying de ying,
Min' you tattler tongue,
Ying de ying . . .[4]

songs of entertainment, used in ring games or while dancing. Some songs, on the other hand, had rebellious overtones or intentions,[5]

[1] See *Columbian Magazine*, vol. II (May 1797), p. 766.
[2] ibid., pp. 766–7.   [3] Moreton, op. cit., p. 156.
[4] Walter Jekyll, *Jamaican Song and Story* (London, 1907), reprint, New York, 1966, p. 38. This is a 'modern' song; there is no evidence of its having been sung during the period of this study, though it, or some version of it, may well have been. But as Jekyll himself points out, 'These songs however inaccurately recorded, are of the greatest value for the hint they give us of Jamaican music as it existed over two centuries ago (ibid., p. 283). 'Ying de ying' is in imitation of fiddle strings.
[5] See pp. 208, 211, above.

while many of them carried on the West African tradition of ridicule.[1] Some of these were merely concerned at laughing at Europeans, like the song Renny[2] reported hearing off Port Royal:

As soon as the vessel in which the author was passenger arrived near to Port Royal in Jamaica, a canoe, containing three or four black females, came to the side of the ship, for the purpose of selling oranges, and other fruits. When about to depart, they gazed at the passengers, whose number seemed to surprise them; and as soon as the canoe pushed off, one of them sung the following words, while the other joined in the chorus, clapping their hands regularly, while it lasted:

> New-come buckra,
>   He get sick,
> He tak fever,
>   He be die
>   He be die
>   New-come buckra, etc.

The song, as far as we could hear contained nothing else and they continued singing it, in the manner just mentioned, as long as they were within hearing.[3]

But very often the ridicule was turned as much against the masters as the singers themselves:

> If me want for go in a Ebo,
> Me can't go there!
> Since dem tief me from a Guinea,
> Me can't go there!
>
> If me want for go in a Congo,
> Me can't go there!
> Since dem tief me from my tatta,
> Me can't go there!
>
> If me want for go in a Kingston,
> Me can't go there!
> Since massa go in a England,
> Me can't go there![4]

Or

[1] See, for example, Theodore Van Dam, 'The influence of the West African Songs of Derision in the New World', in *African Music*, Vol. I, no. I (1954), pp. 53–6.
[2] Op. cit., p. 241.
[3] What is surprising here is that Renny did not notice and certainly did not comment on this song's derisive intent.
[4] Moreton, op. cit., p. 153.

Sarragree kill de captain,
O dear, he must die;
New rum kill de sailor,
O dear, he must die;
Hard work kill de neger,
O dear, he must die.

La, la, la, la
La, la, la, la . . .[1]

and

Bun-go Moo-lat-ta,
Bun-go Moo-lat-ta,
Who dé go married you?
You hand full a ring
An' you can't do a t'ing.[2]

A closer approximation to the African character of slave songs, however, may be observed in this phonetic transcription of a *cumina* invocation recorded by a field researcher[3] in the Morant Bay area of St. Thomas (in-the-East)[4] in the early 1950s. *Cumina* is a memorial ceremony for calling down ancestral spirits and African gods and is similar to, say, *vodun*, in Haiti.

Tangε langε Jeni di gal εva
Wang lang mama o
Di le kuwidi pangε le
　　So-so langε widi gal
So-so langε mama o
Owɔt kuqelaa zɔmbi di gal ɔlɔk
O widi pangε le
Gal ɔmɔt widi pangε le
Di le konakunda pangε langε e
Di lɔ wɔtɔ widingga le
Mɔnukɔ di lɔ kuwidi pangε le.[5]

Dance tall Jenny gal
Walk tall mama o
The dead come to greet you
Water long like the dead, gal
Water long, mama o
Look how the spirits look on the gal there

---

[1] Phillippo, op. cit., p. 189. Sarragree (sangaree) is a drink composed of lemon, water, and red wine.
[2] Jekyll, op. cit., p. 225.　　[3] Moore, *supra. cit.*, p. 218, n. 7.
[4] See Map I.　　[5] Moore, op. cit., p. 174.

O the dead greet her
The gal who greets the dead
They all come tall to greet her
The black ancestors from the water
Manuka of the spirits greets her.[1]

As in Africa, these songs were usually built on a statement and response pattern and except for work and digging songs, were customarily the province of women:[2]

The style of singing among the negroes, is uniform: and this is confined to the women; for the men very seldom, excepting upon extraordinary occasions, are ever heard to join in chorus. One person begins first, and continues to sing alone; but at particular periods the others join: there is not, indeed, much variety in their songs; but their intonation is not less perfect than their time.[3]

Musical instruments

These were almost entirely African. There were flutes: from the long bassoon-like 'Caramantee flute',[4] to the small 'Maroon'[5] nose-flute;[6] the *abenghorn*; a mouth violin or 'bender'[7] (Twi: *bentá*); the banjo (banja or bangil);[8] a box (tambourine) filled with pebbles, 'which they shake with their wrists';[9] the *rookaw*[10] and scraper (similar instruments),[11] corrugated sticks across which were (and are) rubbed a plain stick;[12] *jenkoving* (from the Ga *kofen*)[13] 'which is a way of clapping their Hands on the Mouth of two Jars';[14] and the 'jawbone':[15] the lower jaw of a horse, 'on the teeth of which, a piece of wood [was] passed quickly up and down, occassioning [*sic*] a

---

[1] My interpretation. Moore's translation (op. cit., p. 175) is as follows: 'Dancing erect, tall Jenny/Ever walking tall and erect,/Dead mama,/The person all the dead [*widi*] call [*ku*] to greet [*pange*]/Like clean water [*so-so*; Twi: *nso*] of the dead, this girl,/ Clean, clear water, dead mama,/ Oh what a day of the gods/When this girl is greeted by the dead/Who all greet her./ They who all come [*konakunda*], erect,/Greeting her,/Who would like to carry her away with them,/Even Manuka of the calling spirits/Comes to greet her.' The full text of the song, in Moore's translation, is reproduced in *Appendix IV*.

[2] See Nketia, *Folk Songs*, p. 16; *Funeral Dirges*, p. 8; Lewis, op. cit. (1929 ed.), p. 74.
[3] Beckford, *Account*, Vol. II, p. 121. See also *LNJ* (Cundall), pp. 65–6.
[4] Beckford, *Account*, p. 387.   [5] Cassidy, op. cit., p. 264.
[6] *LNJ*, Cundall, p. 101.   [7] Beckford, *Account*, Vol. II, p. 387.
[8] Leslie, op. cit., p. 310; Cassidy and Le Page, op. cit., p. 26.
[9] Beckford, *Account*, Vol. II, p. 387.   [10] Leslie, op. cit., p. 310.
[11] See Cassidy and Le Page, op. cit., p 385.   [12] ibid., p. 396.
[13] ibid., p. 245.   [14] Leslie, op. cit., p. 310.
[15] Beckford, *Account*, Vol. II, p. 387.

rattling noise'.[1] Above all, there were the various drums: the *cotter*[2] or *cotta*, the Eboe (Ibo) drum, the *bon* or *panya* (played with sticks), the gomba[3] (goombah,[4] gumbie or goombay[5] played with the hands.[6] One commentator claims that the gomba, goombah and goombay were different drums.[7] But this seems unlikely, though it is possible that the word 'gomba' (conga? congo?) might have been applied generically to a certain kind of dance drum. In any case, there are conflicting descriptions of the gomba. In *Marly* it appears played with 'a single stick'.[8] The confusion seems to have started with Long, (usually reliable in description). His is the first extant description of the gomba.[9] But what he appears to have described is the gomba ('tabor') and a kind of *etwie* drum 'which is played by rubbing the drum head with a stick':[10]

> The goombah . . . is a hollow block of wood, covered with sheep-skin stripped of its hair. The musician holds a little stick, of about six inches in length, sharpened at one end like the blade of a knife, in each hand. With one hand he rakes it over a notched piece of wood, fixed across the instrument, . . . whilst a second performer beats with all his might on the sheep-skin, or tabor.[11]

Belisario's description (in view of the modern equivalent) is probably more accurate:

Creolization

> [A] small square wooden frame, over which a goat's skin is tightly strained . . . , and being briskly struck several times in quick succession with one hand, and once only with the other, produces a . . . sound with but little vibration:—it is supported by a Bass-drum: *very unlike* that in the band at the 'Horse-Guards' in London . . . .[12]

There were also various rattles ('Shaky-shekies and Kitty-katties'),[13] made of gourds or cylindrical tin boxes, 'pierced with small holes,

---

[1] I. M. Belisario, *Sketches of Character in Illustration of the Habits, Occupations and Costume of the Negro Population in the Island of Jamaica*, 3 parts (Kingston, 1837–8), explanation to Plate 3.

[2] Beckford, *Account*, Vol. II, p. 387.   [3] ibid.

[4] Long, *History*, Vol. II, pp. 423–4.

[5] Michael Scott, *Tom Cringle's Log* (Paris, 1836), p. 112.

[6] ibid., Beckford, *Account*, Vol. II, p. 387.

[7] See R. Wright, op. cit., pp. 235–6.   [8] *Marly*, p. 46.

[9] Cassidy and Le Page, op. cit., p. 202.

[10] J. H. Nketia, *Drumming in Akan Communities of Ghana* (University of Ghana, 1963), p. 18.

[11] Long, *History*, Vol. II, p. 423.   [12] Belisario, op. cit., as at n. 1, above.

[13] Lewis, op. cit. (1929 ed.), p. 74.

and filled with beads, shots or gravel'[1] used, as in African music, as a kind of metronome.

It was in this area of most intense 'culture focus',[2] however, that, paradoxically (?), the greatest amount of creolization took place. As Stewart observed in 1823:

> In a few years it is probable that the rude music here described will be altogether exploded among the creole negroes, who shew a decided preference for European music. Its instruments, its tunes, its dances, are now pretty generally adopted by the young creoles, who indeed sedulously copy their masters and mistresses in every thing. A sort of subscription balls are set on foot, and parties of both sexes assemble and dance country dances to the music of a violin, tambarine, etc.[3]

But a distinction must be made here between public slave entertainment, like Christmas 'John Canoe' processions and the balls described by Stewart, and the more intransigent 'cult' observances of the slaves that were necessarily secret, or at any rate, private, and which centred around the drum. It was this drumming, which the authorities and the missionaries tried unsuccessfully to eradicate by legislation and persuasion, respectively, which retained and transmitted important and distinctive elements of African/folk culture into the period after Emancipation.[4]

Private entertainments

Dec 24, 1812
Being Christmas-eve, our evening-service was attended by most of our people from Elim, Two-mile-wood, Lancaster, and this place [Bogue]. The glad tidings of great joy . . . [were] heard with great attention. . . . [But] Scarcely was our worship closed, before the heathen negroes on the estate began to beat their drums, to dance, and to sing, in a most outrageous manner. The noise lasted all night, and prevented us from falling asleep.

Dec 25, 1812
After breakfast, I went down and begged the negroes to desist, but their answer was: 'What, Massa, are we not to dance and make merry at Christmas. We always did so.' I represented to them that this was not the

[1] Lewis, op. cit. (1929 ed), p. 74, footnote to 'French Set-Girls'.
[2] See Melville J. Herskovits, 'Problem, Method and Theory in Afroamerican Studies' (1945), reprinted in *The New World Negro* (Indiana University Press, 1966), pp. 43–61; M. J. and F. S. Herskovits, *Trinidad Village* (New York, 1947), p. 6.
[3] Stewart, *View*, p. 272.
[4] See, for instance, J. G. Moore and G. E. Simpson, 'A Comparative Study of Acculturation in Morant Bay and West Kingston', *Zaire* (1957, 1958), nos. 11, 12; G. E. Simpson, 'Jamaican Revivalist Cults, *Social and Economic Studies*, Vol. v (1956), no. 4; and *The Shango Cult in Trinidad*.

way to celebrate the birth of our Saviour, and expressed my surprise, that having heard the word of God for so many years, they still continued their heathenish customs. But all I could say was in vain. . . .[1]

Dec 26, 1813
These Christmas rejoicings among the negroes have certainly a very bad influence, even among Christian negroes, several of whom will find excuses for joining in what they call an innocent dance. . . .[2]

'Crop-over'[3] and the 'Habit of rambling to what are called Negro Plays, or nocturnal Assemblies',[4] the annual yam festival,[5] and wrestling,[6] were also among the entertainments of African origin in this category, as were games of chance like *warri* (Twi: *ware*; Fante: *əware*) which, like the musical instruments described above, survived the Middle Passage.[7]

Public entertainments

These took place during the legal seasonal holidays: Christmas, Easter, and Whitsun. They took the form, usually of street processions with music, dancing and costumes as in the Trinidad[8] and similar carnivals in the Catholic Caribbean today. As in Carnival, these entertainments were a brilliant fusion of African and European elements, deriving their energy and motifs, not from Catholicism in Protestant Jamaica, but from Africa, where many of their prototypes can still be observed, especially in the festivals of the coastal towns and villages.

In Jamaica, these Carnivals (Belisario uses the word)[9] rapidly became the cultural expression, *par excellence*, of the creole slaves and the free blacks and coloureds, rather than of the African or 'new' Negroes. The 'new' Negroes influenced by their African Great Tradition, tended to regard festivals as essentially religious in nature, and so kept them secret (or as secret as possible); thus forming the

[1] John Becker's Diary in (Moravian) *Personal Accounts*, Vol. V (1812), pp. 332–3.
[2] ibid., Vol. VI (1813), p. 82.   [3] *Marly*, p. 47.
[4] *P.P.*, Vol. LXXXIV (26), 1789, Jamaica A. no. 11, Fuller, Long, Chisholme Evidence.   [5] Bickell, op. cit., p. 232; Lewis, op. cit., p. 105.
[6] Leslie, op. cit., p. 310.
[7] Edwards, op. cit., Vol. II, p. 142. For *warri* in West Africa, see the article by G. T. Bennett in Rattray, *Religion and Art*, pp. 382–90. For 'Wari in the New World', see M. J. Herskovits, *Journal of the Royal Anthropological Institute* (1932), no. 62, pp. 23–37.
[8] For this, see Donald Wood, *Trinidad in Transition: The Years after Slavery* (Oxford University Press, 1968), pp. 243–7; and the special Carnival Issue of *Caribbean Quarterly*, Vol. IV (1956), nos. 3 and 4.
[9] Belisario, op. cit., note on 'Jaw-Bone, or House John-Canoe'.

basis of the various 'cults' that were to emerge after Emancipation. Many creole slaves and the bulk of the free people, on the other hand, tended to be grateful for the seasonal licence and encouragement[1] given them publicly by the white Establishment, and so responded enthusiastically to the occasion:

The Negroes enjoy the time from Christmas to new-Year's-day as holidays and the streets were now crowded with splendid processions, or choked up with crowds of dancers. . . . Their processions are really elegant, but as far as I could learn, they consisted principally of free Negroes. [The author is here writing of the North Coast, a dense plantation area.] They were well attired in muslins and silks, accompanied with bands of music. They walked arm in arm, males and females. Sometimes a female with a good voice sung a song, and the whole procession joined in the chorus. They carried, at certain intervals, large artificial trees, stuck full of burning tapers. They usually made a halt at the doors of the wealthier inhabitants, and after chanting some stanzas in praise of the occupant, received . . . gratuity in money.[2]

Perhaps because of these factors (participation by the free groups, Establishment encouragement), public entertainments in the island became increasingly orientated (externally, at least) towards European forms (silks, muslins, bands of music); at the same time reflecting the unquestionably *creole* colour/class divisions of the society. In the various costumed bands, for instance,

the *colours* were never blended in the same set—no blackie ever interloped with the browns, nor did the browns in any case mix with the sables—always keeping in mind—black *woman*—brown *lady*.[3]

This process of creolization from African motif to something local but (externally) European-influenced may be studied in the development of the masked (masque) bands like John Canoe.[4] Edward Long, writing just before the beginning of our period, described this manifestation as follows:

In the towns, during Christmas holidays, they have several tall robust fellows dressed up in grotesque habits, and a pair of ox-horns on their head, sprouting from the top of a horrid sort of vizor, or mask, which about the mouth is rendered very terrific with large boar-tusks. The masquerader, carrying a wooden sword in his hand, is followed with a

[1] Lewis, op. cit. (1929 ed.), p. 71.   [2] Campbell, op. cit., p. 16.
[3] Scott, op. cit., p. 266.
[4] Kerr, op. cit., pp. 143–4. A good summary account of John Canoe is in Cassidy, op. cit., pp. 256–62. Beckwith (*Black Roadways*, pp. 150–5), describes certain modern developments and syncretisms within the form.

numerous croud of drunken women [*sic*], who refresh him frequently with a sup of aniseed-water, whilst he dances at every door, bellowing out *John Connu!* with great vehemence. . . . This dance is probably an honourable memorial of John Conny, a celebrated cabocero at *Tres Puntas*, in Axim, on the Guiney[1] coast; who flourished about the year 1720.[2]

In 1769 'several new masks appeared; the Ebos, the Pawpaws, etc., having their respective Connús, male and female. . . .'[3] By 1815, however, when 'Monk' Lewis was writing his Jamaica *Journal*, this 'primitive' Connú had been creolized into

a Merry-Andrew dressed in a striped doublet, and bearing upon his head a kind of pasteboard house-boat, filled with puppets, representing, some sailors, others soldiers, others again slaves at work on a plantation . . . ,[4]

while De la Beche (1825) records an even further stage in the process:

I was much amused on Easter Monday by a party which came to my house from a neighbouring property, consisting of musicians, and a couple of personages fantastically dressed to represent kings and warriors; one of them wore a white mask on his face, and a part of the representation had evidently some reference to the play of Richard the Third; for the man in the white mask exclaimed, 'A horse, a horse, my kingdom for a horse!'[5]

In true Carnival spirit, however,

The piece . . . terminated by Richard killing his antagonist, and then figuring in a sword dance with him.[6]

The most beautiful moment in these seasonal festivities came, perhaps, with the procession of the Red and Blue 'Set Girls', originating, according to Lewis, in the Red and Blue divisions of the Royal Navy, and coming later to represent the English (Red) and Scots (Blue) in Kingston and elsewhere.[7] There were also French

[1] Gold.
[2] Long, *History*, Vol. II, p. 424. For John Conny, see John Atkins, *A Voyage to Guinea, Brazil, and the West Indies* (London, 1735), pp. 75–8. Dances similar in form to that described by Long may be seen during festivals in Nzima (Axim) and Fante coastal towns in Ghana today. For Nigeria, see Afolabi Ojo, op. cit., pp. 176–7.
[3] Long, *History*, Vol. II, p. 425.   [4] Lewis, op. cit. (1929 ed.), p. 53.
[5] De la Beche, op. cit., p. 42.   [6] ibid.
[7] 'It seems that, many years ago, an Admiral of the Red was superseded on the Jamaica station by an Admiral of the Blue; and both of them gave balls at Kingston to the "*Brown Girls*"; for the fair sex elsewhere are called the "Brown Girls" in Jamaica. In consequence of these balls, all Kingston was divided into parties: from thence the division spread into other districts: and ever since, the whole island at Christmas, is separated into the rival factions of the Blues and the Reds . . .' (Lewis, op. cit., 1929 ed., p. 54). Orlando Patterson (op. cit., p. 239) places this change-over from Blue to Red, and hence the beginning of Set Girls, to the 1780s, but does not cite his authority

Sets,[1] Golden Sets, Velvet Sets, Garnet Ladies, etc.;[2] and each set represented some variation of the society's complexity of colour:

They danced along the streets, in bands of from fifteen to thirty. There were brown sets, and black sets, and sets of all the intermediate gradations of colour. [The girls in each] set [were] dressed pin for pin alike, and carried umbrellas or parasols of the same colour and size, held over their nice showy, well-put-on *toques*, or Madras handkerchiefs, all of the same pattern, tied round their heads, fresh out of the fold.—They sang, as they swam along the streets, in the most luxurious attitudes . . . beautiful creatures . . . elegant carriages, splendid figures,—full, plump, and magnificent.[3]

Here, too, it was the brown girls who predominated, with their 'clear olive complexions, and fine faces'.[4] These, at least, were the ones most noticed, representing as they did, the Euro-tendency of this part of creole society.

First marched Britannia; then came a band of music; then the flag; then the Blue King and Queen—the Queen splendidly dressed in white and silver . . . his Majesty wore a full British Admiral's uniform, with a white satin sash, and a huge cocked hat with a gilt paper crown upon the top of it. . . .[5]

Jack-in-the-Green and the May-pole dance (using a 'spike of the yellow flowers of the American aloe' as pole),[6] were also popular forms of public amusement by the end of our period. These were post-1807 developments, reflecting the cutting off of demographic and cultural renewal from Africa, and the increasing influence of those browns and privileged blacks who could afford to spend time and money on costumed processions, and who wished, or tended, to imitate European models in these matters.

But the African influence remained, even if increasingly submerged, as an important element in the process of creolization. European adaptations or imitations could never be whole-hearted or complete. There might be apparent European forms, but the content would be different. There was developing a European-orientated creole form (Euro-creole) and an African-influenced creole form (Afro-creole);

for the date. In the 1780s, according to Clowes (*The Royal Navy: A History* . . . , London, 1898, 5 vols., Vol. III, pp. 537, 565–6) there was a change-over from White (Rodney) to Red (Pigot). For this and other issues connected with the provenance of Jamaican folk culture, see my review of *The Sociology of Slavery* in *Race*, Vol. ix (1968), no. 3, pp. 337–41.

[1] Belisario, op. cit.   [2] *Columbian Magazine*, Vol. iii (Oct. 1797), p. 288.
[3] Scott, op. cit., p. 265.   [4] ibid.
[5] Lewis, op. cit. (1929 ed.), p. 55.   [6] De la Beche, op. cit., p. 41.

and they existed together within, often, the same framework. It was a Negro fiddler who usually led the costumed bands; and it was the music of 'negroe drums, the sound of the pipe and tabor, negroe flutes, gombas and jawbones',[1] that moved them along. There were also large areas of public entertainment that remained intransigently African or Afro-creole. Those bands, for instance, who continued to dramatize or satirize aspects of the slave society—their and their masters' condition.[2] Outside the sets and masquerades, large groups of slaves 'from different districts in Guinea' wandered about, 'diverting themselves with their own peculiar singing, instruments and dances'.[3]

Dress

The general Clothing in Jamaica is what is called Osnaburgh Linen. On every well-regulated Estate, the annual Allowance is from Ten to Twenty yards to every Man; from Seven to Fifteen Yards to every Woman; and in proportion to the younger People. To every Negro, a Worsted Cap, Bonnet, or Hat, besides a Woollen Jacket, or Welch Blanket, to the Men; and a Petticoat and Blanket to the Women. The Petticoat is on many Estates of Perpetuana; a Quantity of common Check Linen is given on some Estates to the principal Negroes, such as Boilers, Drivers, Waggoners and Tradesmen; and several of our Planters furnish Handkerchiefs, Knives, Scissors, Thread, Needles, and short Tobacco Pipes. The Jamaica law enjoins sufficient Clothing to be given, and inflicts a Penalty on such Owners as disobey that Injunction. In general, the Negroes in Jamaica are well clothed; and there are very few Sugar Estates where the Negroes do not from their own private Earnings provide themselves with extra Clothes for Sunday and Holidays.[4]

In some houses, male domestics wore 'a coarse linen frock which buttons at the neck & hands, long trowsers of the same, a checked shirt, & no stockings'.[5] Servant maids appeared usually in' cotton or striped Holland gown[s]';[6] though of course there was often considerable variation between house and house, estate and estate, and town and country.[7]

Slave women, as in Africa, were 'fond of covering [their head] at

[1] As for n. 2, p. 231, above.
[2] See Scott, op. cit., p. 265. Paule Marshall in her novel, *The Chosen Place, The Timeless People* (New York, 1969) constructs, for a modern Barbados Carnival, a dramatizing procession (pp. 280–9).
[3] As for n. 2, 231, above.
[4] Fuller, Long, Chisholme, *P.P.*, Vol. LXXXIV (26), 1789, Part III, Jamaica, A. no. 6.
[5] *The Universal Magazine*, April 1773, p. 172.   [6] ibid.   [7] ibid.

all times, twisting one or two handkerchiefs round it, in the turban form . . .',[1] and at festivals, according to Lewis,[2] they tended to dress in white—an Akan colour of celebration;[3] though Christian missionary influence cannot be ruled out here. They also appeared during their holidays, according to Lewis, 'decked out with a profusion of beads and corals, and gold ornaments of all descriptions'.[4] Where the gold came from is not indicated or suggested. Is it possible that it could have been smuggled over on slave ships and accumulated over the years in the island? Writing of St. Vincent, Mrs. Carmichael noted that

The real value of their jewellery is considerable; it consists of many gold ear-rings, and rings upon their fingers. Coral necklaces, and handsome gold chains, lockets, and other ornaments of this description.[5]

Besides the usual ear-rings and necklaces, the slave belles produced African-influenced creole decorations of their own:

the women have at different times used as beads, the seeds of *Jobstears*, *liquorice*, and *lilac*; the vertebrae of the shark; and lately red sealing wax, which in appearance nearly resembles coral. Sometimes they sportively affix to the lip of the ear, a *pindal* or ground nut, open at one end; at other times they thrust through the hole bored for the ear-ring, the round yellow flower of the opopinax. . . .;[6]

while many slaves proudly displayed their tribal marks

with a mixture of ostentation and pleasure, either considering them as highly ornamental, or appealing to them as testimonies of distinction [from] Africa; where, in some cases, they are said to indicate free birth and honourable parentage.[7]

Under slavery, needless to say, these marks were supplemented with planters' initials on the shoulder or breast, stamped into the flesh 'by means of a small silver brand heated in the flame of spirits . . .'.[8]

Hair style was presumably 'Afro' or plaits, many females taking 'great pleasure in having their woolly curled Hair, cut into Lanes or

---

[1] Long, *History*, Vol. II, pp. 412–13.   [2] Op. cit. (1929 ed.), pp. 53, 69.
[3] See Field, *Religion and Medicine*, p. 172 n. 1; R. S. Rattray, *Ashanti* (Oxford, 1923), p. 158 and *passim*. It is not intended, by the use of these mainly Ga/Akan sources, to imply that Jamaican slaves came only or mainly from what is now Ghana. For a discussion on the origins of Jamaican slaves, see Patterson, op. cit., pp.113–44.
[4] Lewis, op. cit. (1929 ed.), pp. 69–70.
[5] Carmichael, op. cit., p. 146.
[6] *Columbian Magazine* Vol. III (July 1797), p. 109.
[7] Edwards, op. cit., Vol. II, p. 152.   [8] ibid, p. 154, note (d).

Walks as the *Parterre* of a Garden . . .';[1] as is still done in West Africa.[2]

Slave children, as children in West Africa still do, wore 'party-coloured beads tied round their loins'.[3] Sandals, 'cut from an ox-hide, which they bind on with thongs',[4] were also worn on occasion by adults. In general, however, slaves went barefoot and many of them, especially 'new' Africans and field slaves when working, were described as being naked or almost naked.[5] As in Africa, babies were often carried 'ty'd to their [mothers'] Backs, in a Cloth [used for that] purpose, one Leg on one side, and the other on the other of their Mother'.[6]

Houses and Furniture

The cottages of the Negroes usually compose a small village, the situation of which, for the sake of convenience and water, is commonly near the buildings in which the manufacture of sugar is conducted. They are seldom placed with much regard to order, but, being always intermingled with fruit-trees, particularly the banana, the avocado-pear, and the orange (the Negroes' own planting and property) they sometimes exhibit a pleasing and picturesque appearance.[7]

In general, a cottage for one Negro and his wife, is from fifteen to twenty feet in length, and divided into two apartments. It is composed of hard posts driven into the ground, and interlaced with wattles and plaister. The height from the ground to the plate being barely sufficient to admit the owner to walk in upright. The floor is of natural earth, which is commonly dry enough, and the roof thatched with palm . . . , or the leaves of the cocoa-nut-tree; an admirable covering, forming a lasting and impenetrable shelter both against the sun and the rain.[8]

By the end of our period, some of these huts were boarded, instead of wattle and daubed; and shingles ('wood split and dressed into the

[1] Sloane, op. cit., Vol. I, p. liv.
[2] See, for example, Boris de Rachewiltz, *Black Eros* (trans. London, 1964), photo. facing p. 240.
[3] Scott, op. cit., p. 124.
[4] Long, *History*, Vol. II, p. 412.
[5] See for instance, 'An accurate Account of whatever has appeared most remarkable [in Jamaica] . . .' in *The Universal Magazine*, April 1773, p. 172.
[6] Sloane, op. cit., Vol. I, p. lii. According to Sloane, the carrying of babies in this fashion accounted for the flatness of Negro noses and the broadness of Amerindian faces (ibid.). See also Lewis, op. cit. (1929 ed.), p. 273, where the cloth slipped. . . .
[7] Edwards, op. cit., Vol. II, p. 163.
[8] ibid., p. 164. Stewart (*View*, p. 266) adds that the branches of the mountain cabbage, a palm, durable for 30–40 years, were also used. Apart from this detail, however, Stewart's account of slave houses echoes Edwards's almost word for word.

shape of slates, and used as a substitute for them)[1] were in evidence on the roofs.

Of furniture they have no great matters to boast, nor, considering their habits of life, is much required. The bedstead is a platform of boards, and the bed a mat, covered with a blanket.[2]

Many slaves, in fact, slept on the floor or ground, causing a wit to remark that they don't go to *bed*, they simply go to sleep.[3] Other items inside the house included

a small table; two or three low stools; an earthen jar for holding water; a few smaller ones; a pail; an iron pot; *calabashes* of different sizes (serving very tolerably for plates, dishes, and bowls). . . .[4]

According to the slave laws,[5] certainly for the towns, slave huts, for control and security reasons, were not supposed to have more than one window and door. This, plus the very limited height of the structure, meant that little more than sleeping could be enjoyed inside the houses. 'Cookery', relaxing, story-telling, singing, etc., were all 'conducted in the open air'.[6]

This account of their accommodation, however, is confined to the lowest among the field-negroes: tradesmen and domesticks are in general vastly better lodged and provided. Many of these have larger houses with boarded floors, and are accommodated (*at their own expence it is true*) with very decent furniture:—a few have even good beds, linen sheets, and musquito nets, and display [such was the progress of their creolization] a shelf or two of plates and dishes of queen's or Staffordshire ware.[7]

The making of these houses was, as in a great deal of public Negro activity, communal.[8] Ingenuity and improvisation, as is so often the case in 'pre-industrial' situations, went into their construction—skills which were also applied to the building of plantation houses. The wood used in building, for instance, was often first burnt to prevent it from rotting. When nails could not be easily obtained, a notch was cut in the top of each post to receive the wall-plates, 'bestowing very little labour on any of their timber, except squaring one or two sides'.[9] The beams which crossed the wall-plates were held in their

---

[1] Stewart, *View*, p. 266.   [2] Edwards, op. cit., Vol. II, p. 164.
[3] Sloane, op. cit., Vol. I, p. xxxi.   [4] Edwards, op. cit., Vol. II, p. 164.
[5] See 35 Geo. III, c. 5 of 1795, for Montego Bay.
[6] Edwards, op. cit., Vol. II, p. 164.   [7] ibid., p. 165.
[8] See Bickell, op. cit., p. 201.
[9] *Columbian Magazine*, Vol. III (Sept. 1797), p. 250.

proper position by notches at the end where they overlapped. A ridge pole was placed in the forks of the uprights, at the ends and middle of the structure. The rafters, often of sweet-wood [1] were 'flatten'd at the upper ends and connected in pairs by wooden pins'.[2] The laths were bound to the rafters by strong withes, easily obtained from the surrounding woods.

The structure being thus far completed, the next concern is furnishing the sides with wattles. . . . Between every two posts in the wall, a small stick is placed perpendicularly & another nailed on each side of every post. The wattles are placed alternately; both ends of one bending inward, the next in a contrary direction. The interstices among the wattles are filled with clay and earth, into which some fibres of dried plantain leaves are rubbed to render the same more cohesive; and both the surfaces of the wall plaistered smoothly with the same composition: the whole is white washed when the mountain affords lime stone and the owner will be at trouble to burn it; otherwise the surface is left of its natural colour, a pale reddish yellow, red, or gray, as the loam employed in plaistering happens.[3]

Where hinges were unobtainable, un-dressed leather straps or wooden pivots were used. Locks, keys and bolts could also be made of wood. In the kitchen, which, as pointed out earlier, was out of doors, the trivet for supporting cooking-pots was replaced (as it still is in many rural areas) by three large stones. Ovens were made 'by scooping hollows in perpendicular sides of a bank; and covered with a shade of sticks & leaves to keep off rain. By frequent heating the cavity acquired sufficient hardness to answer its intention'.[4] Where the in-door householder used shelves, the 'kitchen-garden cook' had to improvise with forked sticks placed in the ground. An earthenware[5] water jar hung from the 'stem of a small tree with three prongs, fixed in one corner of [the] house'.[6] The water-cup (and one can still remember using these as a small boy) was a calabash, or small coco-nut shell, with a stick thrust through the sides. There were also calabashes, gourds, wooden plates, and bowls, *yabbas* (Twi: *ayawa*; earthenware vessels, crudely glazed, coming in all sizes), and the wooden mortar for pounding Indian corn,[7] plantain, etc., into *fufu* and *tumtum*.[8]

[1] Lewis, op. cit. (1929 ed.), p. 97.   [2] *Columbian Magazine*, Vol. III, p. 250.
[3] ibid.   [4] ibid.   [5] Edwards, op. cit., Vol. II, p. 164.
[6] *Columbian Magazine*, Vol. III, p. 252.   [7] Stewart, *View*, p. 267.
[8] For these, see Cassidy, op. cit., pp. 192–3.

Language

It was in language that the slave was perhaps most successfully imprisoned by his master, and it was in his (mis-)use of it that he perhaps most effectively rebelled.[1] Within the folk tradition, language was (and is) a creative act in itself; the word[2] was held to contain a secret power, as 'Monk' Lewis discovered one day on his estate:

The other day, . . . a woman, who had a child sick in the hospital, begged me to change its name for any other which might please me best: she cared not what; but she was sure that it would never do well so long as it should be called Lucia.[3]

'Perhaps', Lewis speculated,

this prejudice respecting the power of names produces in some measure their unwillingness to be christened.[4]

Lewis, like most Europeans in Jamaican slave society, was really unable to conceive of the possibility that the slaves did not wish to be christened because they had their own *alternative* to Christianity. The Bantu concept of *nommo* was unknown to him, though he did recognize that *some* principle of belief was at work.

They find no change produced in them [by Christianity], except the alteration of their name, and hence they conclude that this name contains in it some secret power; while, on the other hand, they conceive that the ghosts of their ancestors cannot fail to be offended at their abandoning an appellation, either hereditary in the family, or given by themselves.[5]

It is interesting to observe, though, how *nommo* was quickly creolized by Anancy into a secular device to avoid responsibility. This may be illustrated with the instance of the slave who, after having been baptized by a missionary, declared (the story is no doubt apocryphal, but it serves its turn):

'Me is new man now; befo me name Quashie, now me Thomas, derefo Thomas no pay Quashie debt.[6]

---

[1] This point is nicely made by Carlos Fuentes in a letter to the Editor of *The Times Literary Supplement* no. 3455 of 16 May 1969, p. 505, about Styron's *Confessions*. See also Jahn, *Neo-African Literature*, pp. 240–2. For specialist treatment of Jamaican creole, see Cassidy, op. cit.; Cassidy and Le Page, op. cit.; Beryl L. Bailey, *Jamaican Creole Syntax, A Transformational Approach* (Cambridge, 1966); R. B. Le Page and D. De Camp, *Creole Language Studies*, No. I: *Jamaican Creole* (London, 1960).

[2] Jahn, *Muntu*, pp. 121–55.   [3] Lewis, op. cit. (1929 ed.), p. 290.
[4] ibid.,   [5] ibid., pp. 290–1.
[6] Phillippo, op. cit., p. 203

Slave life

The Rev. G. W. Bridges recognized and analysed another aspect of *nommo* in discussing the power of Negro preachers over their congregations:

so susceptible are the Africans of the influence of that art which variously affects the mind by the mysterious power of sound, . . . they will scarcely give any attention to a religious instructor who possesses a harsh or discordant voice. Every good speaker, independently of the softness of his tones, raises and lowers them in strict musical intervals; so that, in fact, his discourse is as capable of being noted in musical characters as any melody whatever, becoming disagreeable only when those intervals ear uniformly the same, or when the same intonations are used to express sentiments of the most opposite import.[1]

'Of this qualification', the Negro congregations, with their African background of tonal speech (though Bridges did not know and certainly did not admit this) were 'naturally most extraordinary judges'.[2]

In their everyday lives, also, the slaves observed carefully the courtesies of language. Their greetings—'Good morning; how is family', followed by the asking after each member in turn,[3] their polite modes of address—'compliments of respect and friendship, when speaking of or to each other' (Uncle, Aunty, Granny, Tatta)[4]— all had their roots in West African forms of etiquette.

Then there was flattery (*Congo-saw*), as when an old slave woman, wanting to impress on 'Monk' Lewis her gratitude to him for a small favour, addressed him as '*my husband*' instead of Massa.[5] There were also proverbs and sayings such as 'Massa's eye makes the horse grow fat';[6] the response of the old man who, wakened from sleep by another with the question, '*You no hear Massa call you?*', replied, '*Sleep hab no Massa*' and returned to his dreams;[7] and the accurate description by the woman who, asked by a Baptist minister if she still felt sin, now that her heart was changed, admitted: 'It trouble me too much —it tick to me Massa, as close as de clothes to me back'.[8]

---

[1] Bridges, op. cit., Vol. II, p.442, and cf. David Lawton 'The Implications of Tone for Jamaican Creole,' in *Anthropological Linguistics*, Vol. X, no. 6 (1968), pp. 22–5.

[2] Bridges, op. cit., Vol. II, p. 442.   [3] *Marly*, p. 67.

[4] Moreton, op. cit., p. 159.

[5] Lewis, op. cit. (1929 ed.), p. 111.   [6] Gardner, op. cit., p. 157.

[7] Edwards, op. cit., Vol. II, p. 101.

[8] *Baptist Magazine* (1821), p. 226. For full treatment of this subject, see, among others, Violet Heaven, *Jamaica Proverbs and John Canoe Alphabet* (Kingston and Montego Bay, 1896); Jekyll, op. cit.,; Martha Beckwith, 'Jamaica Proverbs' in *Publications of the Folklore Foundation*, no. 6 (Poughkeepsie, 1925); I. Anderson and Frank Cundall, *Jamaica Negro Proverbs and Sayings* (London, 1927).

This language attained its freest expression in the folk tales, many, but not all, featuring the Akan spider-hero, Ananse, and known in the island as Anancy stories. Stories involving magic and rivers, and featuring spirit persons like the River Maid or Water Mama,[1] were (and are) also very common, since these elements ('magic' and rivers in flood) play such an important part in the life of the folk.

an, a so dem do. Dem kal de gyal, an she come. An im seh, Yu nyaam me peas today? Him seh, nuo ma, me no eat non. Him se, a'right, come, we go down a gully ya. We wi' find out. Him tek de gal an im go down a de gully. An when goin down to de gully, im go upan im laim tree, an im pick trii laim. Im guo in a im fowl nest, im tek trii eggs. Him guo in a geese nest, im tek trii. Das nine egg. An im tek trii dok eggs, mek wan dozen egg! An im staat, an haal im sword, an im go doun a de gully. An im go doun in a di gully. Him pu' down de gyal in a di lebl drai gully, an seh, See ya! tan op dey. Me de go tell you now, ef you eat me peas, you de go drownded, bot ef you nuo eat e, notn wuon do you. So swie, you bitch! swear! Seh you no eat e, while you know you eat e. An she lit [lick] doun wan a de laim a doti [dirty; earth. ground] so, *wham*! An de drai gully pomp op wata, cova de gyal instep. De gyal seh, Mai! puo me wan! A weh me de go to die? Him se, Swie! Swie! you bitch! An im lik doun wan nida laim so, *wham*! An de wata mount di gyal to im knee. De gyal seh,

laad ooi! Me Wilyam ooi!

(e im sweetheart im de kall)

me Wilyam ooi!
puo me wan ooi! Peas ooi!
oo, me dearis Wilyam oo!
ring doun peas oi ai A ring doun!
oo, ring doun.[2]

[1] See Peyraud, op. cit., pp. 370–1; Beckwith, *Black Roadways*, pp. 101–2.
[2] Adapted from Le Page and De Camp, op. cit., pp. 144–5. This corresponds in form and content to the Mammy Luna story in Lewis, op. cit. (1929 ed.), pp. 206–10 :

If da me eat Mammy Luna's pease-O,
Drowny me water, drowny, drowny!

But De Camp's version was chosen, though not contemporaneous with the period of this study, because of its advantage of verisimilitude over Lewis' version: ' "My neger, my neger," repeated Mammy Luna, "me no want punish you; my pot smell good, and you belly-woman. Come back, my neger, come back; me see now water above your knee"!' (Lewis, op. cit., 1929 ed., p. 207.)

PART FOUR

SOCIAL ACTIVITY AND SOCIAL CHANGE

16

THE HUMANITARIAN REVOLUTION

PETER DRUMMOND Overseer on Sunderland Estate Deposeth and saith that on Saturday the fifth day of July 1806 Deponent left the Estate and went to Montego Bay to attend Military Duty returned to the Estate in the Evening when the Driver said that most of the New Negroes had taken the day—On Monday the seventh Deponent went to the Field and began to call the list of Slaves the New Negroes being mostly in the first part of the List some of them did not answer and others improperly when about mid-way of the List a Negro named Pompey he answered in his Country Way and talked a great deal Deponent then ordered the Driver to bring said Pompey to him which he did on being questioned Spoke in his Country Tongue again again questioned he would not answer Deponent then ordered Driver to give him a Couple of Lashes on which order immediately said Pompey with Lyon Nelson, King, Cuthbert, Elliot, Pryce, Venture, Howe & Hope with other of the new Negroes threw down their Hoes and ran out of the Canes (they were hoing Ratoon Canes) The Driver ran after Pompey Deponent ordered said Driver to carry Pompey to the Hothouse and put him into the Stocks—The Driver seemed fearful on which Deponent went along with them all the new Negroes keeping near making great noise and very impertinent, near to the Works the said New Negroes took a short way when near the Place of Confinement They stripped off their Frocks and insisted said Pompey should not be put in the said Stocks, *the New Negroes very Riotous* Deponent stood on the Steps whilst the Driver took Pompey and put him into the Stocks the New Negroes very Riotous the Driver locked Pompey in the Stocks locked the Room and Door where the Stocks were and delivered the Keys to Deponent The said New Negroes then on the way to their Houses saying they would go and complain to their Master Deponent gave the Keys to the Hothouse Woman and went to the House when there about ten Minutes, heard the sound of a Shell or a Horn blowing in the Negro Houses Deponent went to the Back Door to take an Account of Rats caught (about 9 of the Clock A/M) The said New Negroes in presence of Deponent armed with Bills & Cutlasses (no Bill Work in the field) went to the Hothouse broke the Outer Door and liberated the said Pompey came out and again sounded the Shell or Horn singing in their Country Tongue Deponent says the said New Negroes were joined by two others named Green and Success previous to liberating

Pompey. Hothouse Woman came to Deponent saying Green had knocked her down cut her leg and threatened to Cut her Head off if she did not give the Key to Let Pompey out—Deponent from appearances judged the said Negroes intended to attack him in the House but Mr Tulloch and Mr Noelle who were alarmed by the Shell or Horn at that instant came galloping up to the House the said Negroes then dispersed.[1]

Jamaican slaves, like all the ex-African slaves in the New World, had a cultural life of their own that was as valid and meaningful as their masters'. In many respects, it was perhaps even more meaningful than theirs. But because of the fact of slavery and the arguments and attitudes that had been erected to justify it, this culture of the slaves was denied and finally (worst of all) forgotten—rendered invisible to the masters and to many of the slaves themselves. Within the slave section of Jamaican society, therefore, there was also (as within the Establishment), a dichotomy—a tension of values, an inhibiting choice of possibilities. One impulse tended towards an identification with and reinterpretation of their own folk and remembered African culture (such were the obeah-men and some of the more 'extreme' Black Baptists); the other tended towards coming to terms with their situation within their masters' image of them (such was Quashie-Sambo, and, though they were not technically slaves, many of the free coloureds). The creolization of the slaves, in other words, had a choice of forms, depending on the attitude, aptitude and opportunities of the particular slave or group of slaves, on the one hand; and on the degree of control and coercion (both physical and psychological) exerted by the master or, more effectively, by the white society as a whole, through its institutions. The development of the slave within creole society depended, to put it another way, as much on the efficiency of the white Establishment as on his own socio-cultural equipment and adaptability.

With regard to the (white) society as a whole, this study has so far dealt with its reaction to the break-up of the North Atlantic/American culture complex brought about by the American Revolution. The white élite was, to a large extent, thrown back upon its own resources and forced to think of the possibility of some measure of economic independence and internal self-government even though the logical goal of these considerations—constitutional independence—was never seriously examined. What happened, in fact, was that with the

[1] Montego Bay Resident Magistrate Court Kalendar Book, 1793–1841; Kalendar for July Slave Trials.

Economics

break-up of the American system, the island became more than ever dependent upon its other major cultural connection—that with Britain and the British mercantilist system. The Jamaican sugar economy became increasingly dependent upon the whims and requirements of the British economy; the Jamaican political constitution became increasingly under the surveillance of the British Crown after 1801 with the setting up in Britain of what was to become the Colonial Office.[1] The setting up of this new co-ordinating body for colonial administration reflected changes taking place in both British administration and British society, not least of which was concern with the facts of slavery in the West Indies. Linked with changing views in Britain with regard to administration and economic policy and needs,[2] this Humanitarian opinion was to have a profound effect on West Indian society, all the more so because of West Indian and Jamaican constitutional, economic and cultural *dependence* on Britain following the isolating effect of the American Revolution. The difference between the two 'events' with regard to Jamaica was this: The American Revolution made the need for social change implicit, if the island was to achieve political and economic viability. The Humanitarian Movement made the need for social revolution an explicit demand.

Haiti

In the nature of things, this Humanitarian Movement, since it emanated from outside Jamaica, and was directed only towards the conscience of the white élite (its only channel of communication) might, like the American Revolution, have affected only the superstructure of creole society. But coincident with this external Humanitarian Movement, there was in the Caribbean generally, a Humanitarian Revolt of an entirely different kind and emphasis, stemming from the French Revolution with its propositions, violently expressed, of liberty, fraternity, and equality for all men.[3] Under this impetus, slavery was abolished in Guadeloupe in 1794, confirmed by local

[1] See D. J. Murray, op. cit., p. 10.
[2] See Eric Williams, *Capitalism and Slavery* (University of North Carolina Press, 1944), New York ed., 1961, pp.126–77.
[3] See, J. Saintoyant, *La colonisation française sous l'ancien régime;* 2 vols. (Paris, 1929); *La colonisation française pendant la révolution 1789–1799*, 2 vols (Paris, 1930); *La colonisation française pendant la période napoléonienne, 1799–1815* (Paris, 1931); C. L. R. James, *The Black Jacobins; Toussaint L'Ouverture and the San Domingo Revolution* (London, 1938); Betty Russell, 'The Influence of the French Revolution upon Grenada, St. Vincent and Jamaica'.

Rebellion)

rebellion in 1797,[1] though it was re-established by Napoleon in 1802.[2] In St. Domingue, the slaves who had risen in revolt in 1791 were in effective control of the country by 1798 and (despite counter-attacks by British and Napoleonic forces) established the independent republic of Haiti on 31 December 1803. From its outbreak until as late as 1817, this 'dangerous example of the System of Equality at St. Domingo'[3]—the 'neighbouring colony of black barbarians'[4]—was to have a profound effect on Jamaica'.[5] In October 1791, the Governor of Jamaica was cautiously optimistic that the situation would soon be under control. He told the Assembly:

The last accounts from St. Domingo give room to hope for as favourable a termination of the insurrection there, as is possible after the destruction already committed. I have given them[6] all the assistance I thought compatible with your security, by supplying them with such arms and ammunition as could be spared from the magazines, without endangering a deficiency of what might be wanted for the militia.[7]

Replying, the Assembly used the occasion to declare their loyalty, their royalist sentiments and to confirm their slave-holding pictures of themselves as repositories of white civilization:

The dreadful example which the French islands present to us at this juncture, affords a melancholy proof of the fatal tendency of those wild enthusiastic notions, so widely reprobated by your excellency; and permit us, my lord, on this occasion, to observe, that, notwithstanding the calumnies to which we have been exposed in Great-Britain, from the misrepresentations of ignorance or malevolence, the just rights of mankind are no where more highly respected than in this part of his majesty's dominions; distinguishing, as propriety and necessity require, between civilized and uncivilized life.[8]

Still, the precaution was taken, on the Governor's suggestion, to have 'all the cannon which are lying about on the bays and shipping

[1] Saintoyant (1930), Vol. I, p.334; Henri Bangou, *La Guadeloupe, 1492–1848*, 2 vols (Paris, 1962), Vol. I, pp. 233–4.

[2] Bangou, op. cit., Vol. I, pp. 289–91.

[3] The Hon. Committee of Correspondence, Minute Book 1794–1833; Minute no. 1 of 11 Aug. 1797.

[4] Bridges, op. cit., Vol. II, p. 349.

[5] The connection between Haiti and the Humanitarian Movement in Britain and France should be noted. See E. L. Griggs and C. H. Prator, eds., *Henry Christophe and Thomas Clarkson. A Correspondence* (Berkeley and Los Angeles, 1952); James, op. cit., (New York ed. 1963), pp. 54, 134; H. Cole, *Christophe, King of Haiti* (London, 1967), *passim*; *The Columbian Magazine*, Vol. I (June 1796), pp. 8, 9.

[6] The French troops in Haiti.   [7] *JAJ*, IX, 2 of 25 Oct. 1791.

[8] ibid., 6 of 3 Nov. 1791.

places, . . . forthwith removed to places of safety, or be spiked up'[1] (Port-au-Prince had been burnt earlier that month);[2] and a request was sent off to London 'for a regiment of cavalry for the internal defence of [the] island'.[3] This was the first indication, from the Assembly, that a 'Haiti' was feared for Jamaica, because the cavalry was not asked for to repel an *invasion*, but to operate in the 'interior parts of the country',[4] where it was felt, quite wrongly, that they would be more effective than infantry. Soon after this, the first regulations prohibiting the entry of free negroes and people of colour from St. Domingue were introduced.[5] In March 1792, the Governor was asked that all forts at the free ports 'take an account of all negroes and mulattoes on board of any foreign vessels which may arrive at such ports, and not permit such vessels to depart . . . without carrying with them all such persons.'[6] Care was also to be taken that no Jamaican slaves travelled on vessels bound for or connected with St. Domingue.[7]

But as it turned out, it was not the Jamaican slaves, with or without Haitian and/or French Revolutionary inspiration or aid, but a section of the island's Maroons who challenged the System—though the authorities saw quite clearly a possible connection between all three sources of disquiet. 'If you destroy them [the Maroons] to five', General Walpole told the Governor, 'those five will be a rallying point for more runaways to resort to, and thus the war be perpetuated for years.'[8] Are you prepared 'to spin out the contest till foreign assistance may arrive? This may be followed up by another question. "If foreign assistance arrives, what will be the situation of the island"?'[9]

It was the Maroons, too, who prompted these remarks by Mrs. Brodbelt:[10] 'In my last letter', she wrote to her daughter in London,

I mentioned that an Insurrection had broken out among the Maroon Negroes in the Parish of St. James's, and I am sorry to add now, that peace is not yet restored among them, in consequence of which we have lost several Brave officers and men in the Militia, as well as in the regular troops. From the last accounts we have received I hope that the business is drawing nearer to a conclusion in *Favor* of the *Whites* than was expected a

---

[1] *JAJ*, IX, 20 of 16 Nov. 1791.   [2] James, op. cit. (1963 ed.), p. 101.
[3] *JAJ*, IX, 7 of 4 Nov. 1791.   [4] ibid.   [5] ibid., 50 of 6 Dec. 1791.
[6] ibid., 90 of 9 March 1792.   [7] ibid.   [8] ibid., 437 of 2 March 1796.
[9] ibid., 438.
[10] Mrs. Brodbelt was the wife of Dr. Francis Rigby Brodbelt (1746–95), a medical practitioner of Spanish Town. (See Wright, *LNJ*, p. 289; Mozley, op. cit., p. 141), Mrs. Brodbelt's *Letters to Jane* . . . is cited on p. 51, n. 2, above.

week ago; if so, everything will be right again, and it may be a very good lesson to others of the like description of people, to conduct themselves with that respect and proper attention which is due to those who are appointed to keep them in peace and quietness—for if that is not strictly observed they will shortly exert their power to throw the Island into confusion with a view of being assisted by our Neighbours the French, who from many things that have been lately discovered would most willingly lend their aid on such an occasion . . .[1]

What is significant here is the white reaction to these developments. For the first time, within this period, they are on the defensive; their society, as they had constructed it and as they understood it, seemed threatened:

Before this war was half over, what with desertions, *accidents* of one kind or another, sickness, real or *fictitious*, *retirements* from service under various pretences, it was disheartening to see the bulk of the militia companies with barely half their proper complement of officers and men—nay, some with less than one third, and a few left even without a commissioned officer! Nothing could shew more decisively than this circumstance the policy of concluding, on any admissable terms, as speedy a peace as possible, with an enemy so formidable by his activity, his cunning, the savage manner in which he carried on his hostilities, his inaccessibility against the ordinary modes of warlike attack, and by the probability of his becoming more daring by success, and at length carrying massacre and conflagration into every part of the island.[2]

The Maroons

The Maroon War was a result of white 'apartheid' policy. This small body of mountain-dwelling ex-slaves had won their independence in 1740, after a ten-year struggle against British/Jamaicans, but they had been relegated and confined to the area of their high and rather barren reservations. By the 1770s, with their population growing,[3] the Maroons began to show signs of restlessness. The land/man ratio was becoming a problem.[4] The Maroons could not (or were said to be too lazy to) grow all the food they needed on the territory allotted them. The Trelawny Town Maroons of St. James, for instance, where most of the trouble was coming from, had been apportioned 1,500 acres of land of which only a hundred acres were

[1] *Letters to Jane.* p. 119.   [2] *Montgomery*, Vol. II, pp. 438–9. Italics in text.
[3] See 33 Geo. III, c. 5. There were five Maroon towns. In 1770, the population of these was 885 (*JAJ*, VI, 311 of 8 Dec. 1770) and had grown to 1,400 by 1788. (Dallas, op. cit., Vol. I, p.120.)
[4] See 32 Geo. III, c. 4, section xxiv (1791); *Laws*, Vol. II, p. 562.

arable.[1] They began to encroach on white-settled plantations, both to plant and to steal. They also began complaining of a lack of social amenities. For instance, a petition of 1770 asked the Assembly that 'they . . . be allowed a doctor to visit them, once or twice a week, and oftener, should there be any emergency for it. . . .'[2] They also '[thought] it hard' that their government grants (as allowed under the 1742 treaty)[3] were not forthcoming.[4] When no redress was offered, the Maroons became restive, and there were incidents involving white surveyors, settlers, British soldiers, and merchantment.[5]

The Assembly reacted toughly. An Act of 1791[6] allowed the testimony of slaves to be accepted 'without reserve against the free Maroons';[7] restrictions against Maroon movement were renewed and reinforced, underlining the 'reservation' concept and designed to keep the Maroons from unnecessary social contact with the slave population:

And whereas several of the maroon negroes have frequently endeavoured to create factions and disputes among some of the slaves belonging to different plantations, and to persuade and entice others to run away from their owners, contrary to the articles upon which they surrendered. . . .[8]

The Maroons, in other words, were to confine themselves to their post-1740 role of slave catching. They were not to buy slaves, as it was 'apprehended that more slaves may be bought by them, which may be of ill consequence to [the] island, if not prevented'.[9] Whites were forbidden to employ Maroons unless a written agreement was entered into between the two parties, and, as a gesture of appeasement, any Maroon who felt unable to continue to live under these terms and conditions on the reservations, could, on public declaration before a justice, revoke his Maroon rights and enter the 'open' society with the rank and status of free coloured, as long as he enrolled in the militia within twenty days.[10]

But this was not only appeasement. It was also expediency. The Assembly, as it admitted, was offering these terms because it had no

[1] R. C. Dallas, op. cit., Vol. I, p. 84. See also *JAJ*, VI, 386 of 19 Dec. 1771.
[2] *JAJ*, VI, 311 of 8 Dec. 1770. [3] See *JAJ*, III, 594 of 1 May 1742.
[4] ibid., VI, 311.
[5] See, for instance, R. C. Dallas, op. cit., Vol. I, note to pp. 129–30, Add. MS. 12413: 'Extract of a Letter from the Hon. Bryan Edwards Esq. at Jamaica, to Mr. Mark Davis of Bristol, dated April 18, 1774'; *JAJ*, VI, 465–6 of 26 Nov. 1773; VII, 203 of 14 Dec. 1779; VIII, 204 of 2 Dec. 1786.
[6] 32 Geo. III, c. 4. [7] Southey, op. cit., Vol. III, p. 49.
[8] 32 Geo. III, c. 4 of 1791; *Laws*, Vol. II, p. 558. [9] ibid., p. 559.
[10] ibid., p. 562.

intention of granting more lands to the Maroons.[1] So although some Maroon families took advantage of the offer,[2] the basic grievance remained—land hunger—as the Trelawny Town Maroons pointed out a year after the 1791 Act.[3] Complaints, disputes and incidents therefore continued until the moment in 1795, at the Montego Bay workhouse, when two Maroons were (officially) whipped by a runaway slave, whom the Maroons themselves had captured.[4] This was an irreparable insult in a society where every free non-white had to guard his privilege and status as closely as the sweaty shirt sticking to his back. Maroon reprisal was followed by Government retaliation[5] and a resulting two-year war. Fighting took place between the 600-odd Maroons of Trelawny Town (in the parish of St. James), not more than 200 of whom would have been able-bodied fighting-men, and some 2,000 Government troops including 1,000 men of the British 83rd Regiment. The Maroons employed a highly developed guerrilla technique, suitable to the Cockpit country. The Government retaliated with a scorched-earth policy and finally sent in 100 Cuban bloodhounds, though the use and effectiveness of these is disputed. Government troops began reporting success when they, especially under Walpole,[6] started adapting their tactics to the terrain. The 764 Maroons of the other four towns did not take part in the war.[7] When the Maroons finally gave in, apparently on the understanding that their claims would be considered,[8] they were transported

[1] *JAJ*, IX, 175 of 6 Dec. 1792.

[2] ibid., 397 of 6 Nov. and 402 of 30 Nov. 1795; X, 523 of 24 Feb. 1801; Quarter Sessions Kalendar Book, 1793–1841, Resident Magistrate's Court, Montego Bay (in Jamaica Archives, Spanish Town); July Sessions, 1796: ten Maroon women, with ten mulatto children and four quadroon children, 'Each of [them] descendants from some of the Maroons of Trelawny Town Personally appeared in the present July Quarter-Sessions 1796 . . . and did then and there in open Court publickly and solemnly severally declare that they were severally desirous and willing to give up any right that they respectively might have to any part of the Lands which have been granted to the maroon Negroes, And that each of them was desirous and willing to reside in any other part of [the] Island except in any of the Maroon Towns.'

[3] See 'The humble petition of col. Montagu James, capt. John Jarrett, capt. Zachary Bayley, and capt. James Lawrence, officers of the Maroons in Trelawny-Town, on behalf of themselves and the rest of the maroons in the said town.' (*JAJ*, IX, 86 of 7 March 1792.)

[4] Cundall, *Historic Jamaica*, p. 327.

[5] *JAJ*, IX, 392–3 of 30 Sept. and 400 of 27 Nov. 1795.

[6] See pp. 106–7, above.

[7] See, for the war, R. C. Dallas, op. cit.; Edwards, op. cit., Vol. I, pp. 546–76; *JAJ*, IX, 368–76 of 22 Sept. 1795; 436–41, 457–68 of 2 and 23 March 1796. For estimate of Government troops, see *JAJ*, IX, 649; Edwards, op. cit., Vol. I, pp. 550, 551, 563, 566. For estimate of Maroons: *JAJ*, IX, 441, 452; X, 5, 89; Coke, *History*, Vol. I, p. 369. The C.O. 142/33 figure of 1,000 Trelawny Town Maroons in 1795 is far too high.

[8] *JAJ*, IX, 437 of 2 March 1796.

(man, woman and child) to Nova Scotia,[1] their town destroyed, their lands confiscated and sold.[2] With their departure, the threat of free black opposition to the regime was eliminated.

Slave rebellions, riots, and conspiracies

This is not to say, however, that opposition to white authority did not continue. There was, in fact, in Jamaica, considerable slave reaction against the regime—particularly noticeable *after* the Maroon War. Because of this war and its association with the Haitian and French Revolutions, these slave rebellions, riots, and conspiracies took on, for white Jamaicans, an added threat of danger. A slave leader, called Bowman, had played an active part in the Maroon War.[3] In 1797–8 there was a rebellion of runaway slaves in the parish of Trelawny.[4] This was so serious that again it was feared that it might lead to a second Haiti.[5] One of its leaders, Peter, had also led an independent insurrection during the Maroon War.[6] In 1798–9, it was reported that rebellious runaways in St. Elizabeth were retarding settlement in that parish.[7] The Government could not 'ascertain, with any precision', whether these rebel forces [were] 'exclusive or inclusive' of each other.[8] In 1799, there was the discovery and repression of a General Roume's attempt to instigate a rebellion in the island.[9] In 1802, 'a Town of Runaway Slaves' near Runaway Bay, in St. Ann,[10] had to be attacked; and in 1807 a rebellion broke out in St. George.[11] 'About the latter end of August 1808, fifty-four Chamba and Koromantyn negroes, who had been purchased to serve in the colonial corps, broke out into mutiny at Fort Augusta, while under drill, and massacred two of their officers, Major Darnley and Lt. Ellis, who had ridden up to them 'to enquire into the cause of the tumult'.[12] Bryan Edwards, reporting the incident in his *History*, claimed that it was a plot along Haitian lines.[13] The following year, the Kingston Common Council reported that they had unearthed a similar plot in the city.[14] During 1811, the *Royal Gazette* reported at

[1] The Assembly voted £25,000 for this. See Committee of Correspondence, 30 April 1796; Edwards, op. cit., Vol. I, pp. 572–3; 36 Geo. III, c. 34 of 1 May 1796.
[2] *JAJ*, IX, 509 of 23 April 1796.   [3] ibid., 437 of 2 March 1796.
[4] ibid., X, 106–14 of 13 June 1798.   [5] ibid., 111.
[6] ibid., 113–14.   [7] ibid., 253, of 20 Feb. 1799.   [8] ibid., 114.
[9] Frank Cundall, *Chronological Outlines of Jamaica History, 1492–1926* (Kingston, 1927), p. 26.
[10] See St. Ann Vestry Proceedings 1800–9, 28 Sept 1802, p. 77.
[11] *JAJ*, XI, 560–4 of 25 Sept. 1807.
[12] Edwards, op. cit. (1819 ed.), Vol. V, p. 97.   [13] ibid., p. 98.
[14] K.C.C. Proceedings, 1803–15, 15, 20, 27 March; 3, 10, 17, 24, 28 April; 1, 2 May; 9 June 1809.

least three cases of violent Negro activity.[1] In 1815 a Committee of the Assembly reported that

Affidavits are now in possession of your committee, stating the declarations of the young and violent, that if their freedom be not declared after Christmas, they must fight with the white men for it. . . .[2]

and that

They will not be long of accomplishing [their] object [Emancipation] by a way which they better understand; by fighting the white men, by attempting a general massacre, and ensuring a complete desolation and destruction of property.[3]

There was also trouble in Black River,[4] St. Ann,[5] and Bog Walk,[6] and there were runaway gangs in the Healthshire Hills of St. Catherine.[7]

But if this 'Black Power' action was the most dramatic manifestation of the operation of the spirit of the Humanitarian Revolution upon Jamaican society, there was a quieter, but no less significant social change taking place in the island, via the activity of the black preachers and the missionaries.

The missionaries

Moravian missionaries had arrived in Jamaica as early as 1754.[8] They set up a small station in the Bogue estate in St. Elizabeth,[9] but remained, throughout the period of this study, a small and (vis-à-vis the Establishment) rather co-operative group.[10] More dangerous, from the white creole point of view, were the 'real' Non-conformists (the Moravians did not regard themselves as Non-conformists in the strict sense).[11] The Methodists, established by

[1] R.G., XXXIII, 31, 17.   [2] JAJ, XII, 798 of 20 Dec. 1815.   [3] ibid.
[4] Lewis, op. cit. (1929 ed.), pp. 185–6 and p. 211, above.
[5] St. Ann Vestry Proceedings, 1817–23, 3 Oct. 1818, p. 89.
[6] R.G., XLI (1819), 14, 27.
[7] ibid., 38, 19; 39, 19; XLII, 14, 5; JAJ, XIII, 320 of 2 Nov. 1819 and 534 of 18 Dec. 1820; Stewart, View, pp. 322–3.   [8] J. H. Buchner, op. cit., p. 24.   [9] ibid.
[10] See Buchner, op. cit., pp. 27–8, 39; (Moravian) Periodical Accounts, Vol. I, p. 16; Vol. V, pp. 325–33, 485; the Moravian Missionary Diaries, MS. Malvern Archives, Jamaica; O. Furley, 'Protestant Missionaries in the West Indies: Pioneers of a Non-Racial Society' in Race, Vol. VI (Jan. 1965), no. 3, p. 233; 'Moravian Missionaries and Slaves in the West Indies', Caribbean Studies, Vol. V (July 1965), no. 2; Mary Reckord, Missions in Jamaica before Emancipation', Caribbean Studies, Vol. VIII (April 1968), no. 1, pp. 69–74. Anon., Succinct View of the Missions established among the Heathen by the Brethren . . . (printed pamphlet, London, 1771), p. 17; Minutes of the Society for the Furtherance of the Gospel, 28 Feb. 1803, p. 14; MS. in Moravian Archives, London.
[11] See JAJ, XII, 799 of 20 Dec. 1815; H. E. Stocker, Moravian Customs (Bethlehem, Penns., 1928).

Dr. Thomas Coke in 1789, during his first visit to Jamaica,[1] the Baptists and the Black Baptists under Liele, Moses Baker, and their followers and off-shoots, were the major contributors in this field.

George Liele (or Lisle, or Sharp)[2] arrived in Jamaica, according to his own account,[3] with his wife and four children[4] in 1783 from Savannah, Georgia.[5] He was by this time, it appears, a free man, having received his manumission on the death of his master, Sharp, who had been an officer in the British Army in North America[6] and a Deacon in the American Baptist Church.[7] Liele reckoned that he was 'about fifty years old' when he arrived in Jamaica, but he was not sure about this.[8] He established a chapel (completed 1793)[9] on the Windward Road, in East Kingston, which was to remain a centre of Baptist activity in Jamaica up to the eve of Emancipation and beyond.[10] He also began preaching on the Race Course in Kingston, where great numbers were attracted by the novelty of the spectacle,[11] and in Spanish Town; until he fell under the Establishment ban against unauthorized preachers in 1794, was charged with 'uttering dangerous and seditious words'[12] and was imprisoned, despite the failure of the charge, on a trumped-up accusation of debt.[13] His church began to fragment before his release from prison, however; ambitious followers forming their own independent sects.[14] Liele himself, like all the other black preachers, continued, in order to beat the ban, as an itinerant preacher until his death in 1822 or thereabouts.[15] Liele's activity, along with Moses Baker's,[16] was directly responsible for the decision of the British Baptist Mission to send missionaries to

[1] See p. 208, n. 6, above.

[2] See 'An Account of the Baptized Negro Churches' in *The Baptist Annual Register, 1798–1801*, p. 332.

[3] In the above-cited work, pp. 332–7, 343–4, in the form of letters. These are reprinted in *The Journal of Negro History*, Vol. I (1916), no. i, pp. 69–92.

[4] 'An Account', p. 335.   [5] ibid., p. 333.   [6] Cox, op. cit., Vol. II, p. 12.

[7] J. Clarke, op. cit., p. 11.   [8] 'An Account', p. 335.

[9] T. H. MacDermot, 'George Lisle and his work here', *Jamaica Times*, 1 May 1915, p. 12.

[10] ibid.; and J. H. Hinton, *Memoir of William Knibb, missionary in Jamaica* (London, 1847), *passim*.

[11] Gardner, op. cit., p. 343.   [12] *R.G.*, XVI, 14, 23 of 5 April 1794.

[13] Cox, op. cit., Vol. II, p. 14.   [14] ibid., pp. 14–16.

[15] J. Clarke, op. cit., p. 11. Liele paid a brief visit to England in 1822 at the invitation of the Baptist Mission. His son, for some years, assisted in and continued his work. (See K.C.C. Proceedings, 1803–15: 23 Aug. 1813.) One of his grandsons became a member of the Jamaica Assembly (Clarke, p. 11).

[16] See p. 162, above. In addition to Kingston and Spanish Town, Liele established chapels in Morant Bay and at Bethany in St. David. (MacDermot, op. cit., 1, 8 May 1915.)

Jamaica. The first of these arrived at Montego Bay in February 1814,[1] though a Baptist missionary had in fact been designated for work in Jamaica as early as 1803.[2]

There was, it must be pointed out, a fundamental difference in attitude and approach between the two sets of missionaries in Jamaica—the black and the white. The black preachers were essentially of the people and they appealed to the slaves because their ideas and their style of preaching[3] contained strong, syncretized African elements. 'The grand doctrine of these people', wrote the Rev. Hope Waddell, a Scottish missionary who had Jamaican as well as (West) African experience,

> was the Spirit's teaching. It gave life. The written word was a dead letter. If they could not read the Bible they could do without it, which was as good. The Spirit was sought in dreams and visions of the night, which thus became the source of their spiritual life. Without them inquirers could not be born again either by water or the Spirit. The leaders expounded these dreams to their kneeling followers in weekly class meetings; which, when judged to be of a right kind, were called 'the work', that is, of the Spirit, and supplied the place of knowledge, faith, and repentance. As Christ was led of the Spirit into the wilderness, his disciples must follow him into the wilderness to seek the Spirit. To the bush, the pastures, or the cane fields, these people resorted at night, when preparing for baptism, and were ordered to lie down, each apart, without speaking, but keeping eye and ear open to observe what way the Spirit would come to them....[4]

This, in other words, was not 'worship' or adoration of the Godhead in the European/Christian sense. It was a form of spirit-contact, or possession by the God, in the *vodun*, shango, pocomania, or West African religious sense.

> Doubtless they would see and hear strange things in their excited imaginations.... The result of such a system among such a people may be imagined....[5]

The point, though, is that worshipping in this way within a cultural 'style' that they understood and which made sense to them, gave the slaves a sense of freedom and dignity which they would not otherwise have had. It was no accident that Moses Baker could claim, in

[1] *Periodical Accounts relative to the Baptist Missionary Society*, 6 vols. (Clipstone, 1800–17); Vol. V, p. 502.
[2] *The Baptist Magazine* (1814), p. 41.   [3] See p. 238, above.
[4] Hope M. Waddell, *Twenty-nine years in the West Indies and Central Africa: a review of missionary work and adventure, 1829–1858* (London, 1867), p. 26.
[5] ibid.

1806, to have 3,000 followers.[1] But what was more dangerous, from the white Establishment's point of view, was that this religio-cultural freedom led the black missionary preachers, quite easily, into more terrestrial—and humanitarian—claims to freedom as well. The case of the Black River Baptists' song 'Take force by force! Take force by force!' has already been mentioned.[2] During the Maroon War, Moses Baker was arrested on a charge of sedition for quoting, in a sermon, the following verses from a Baptist hymn:

> Shall we go on in sin
>   Because thy grace abounds,
> Or crucify the Lord again
>   And open all his wounds?
>
> We will be slaves no more,
>   Since Christ has made us free,
> Has nailed our tyrants to the cross,
>   And bought our liberty.[3]

The white missionaries, by contrast, approached their slave congregations with all the prejudices of their white secular contemporaries. Their image of the Negro was as stereotyped as any creole planter's:

The dispositions of the slaves appear radically bad; both sexes are intemperate, laying no restraint upon their turbulent passions and appetites. . . . They are not diligent, their labour being wholly extorted by fear; they are greatly addicted to theft, and few believe it theft to purloin from their masters.

Many of them shorten their days by intemperance in drinking. The charges of laziness and want of fidelity are not without foundation.

Lying, theft, and sloth are habitual.[4]

To make good Christians of 'these people' it was necessary to convert lying and theft to probity, sloth to diligence and a sense of the morality of hard work. To achieve this, it was necessary for the missionaries to pluck out, root and branch, all vestiges of heathen (i.e.

---

[1] *The Baptist Annual Register, 1801–1802*, p. 1146.   [2] p. 211, above.
[3] John Clark, W. Dendy, and J. Phillippo, *The Voice of Jubilee: A Narrative of the Baptist Mission, Jamaica, from its commencement; with biographical notices of its fathers and founders* (London, 1865), p. 34.
[4] The statements quoted were excerpted from letters of various Methodist preachers to the Society in London, as collected in Watson, op. cit., p. 21.

African) practices from those over whom they had acquired influence.[1] The drum had to go. The dance had to go.[2] A plurality of wives or women had to be put out of mind.[3] Above all, obeah had to be confronted and defeated. 'Again and again', the Moravian Buchner told himself, 'we have to use all our authority and influence against [the] devices of the wicked one. . . . There is no sin against which a missionary, who knows the consequences, should be more watchful to guard his people.'[4] The missionaries were in despair when a little girl, 'being asked what she did pray', said: 'Lord, have mercy, Christ have mercy and spare me a little longer, make me live nam[5] a little more Christmas.'[6] Children, they remarked, imitate very much what 'those old people are telling them'.[7] On the other hand, they would become themselves childishly happy when faced with the 'many proofs of [the slaves'] sincerity of heart and their desire to be saved, and that they [the slaves!] caused such pains and sufferings to our Saviour by their sins'.[8]

A sister said, in her own dialect: Missir, me love our Saviour to [very] much; me crucified him, me slap him in he jaw, me pit [spit] in his face . . .[9]

But these hopes were often quickly cast down again as the slave or slaves in question back-slided. The evidence of the available missionary diaries[10] suggests, on the whole, a stubborn and remarkable

---

[1] See, for example, Minutes of Conference: Mesopotamia, Jan. 1798–Jan. 1818; 21 June 1798. Moravian Church Archives, Bethlehem, Malvern, Jamaica. Missionary activity in this respect increased after Emancipation. Drumming and shell-blowing became illegal (Curtin, *Two Jamaicas*, p. 169). There was, however, a determined, sometimes violent, resistance to this from the Jamaican peasantry and Baptist congregations (ibid.).

[2] See, for example, John Becker's Diary in (Moravian) *Periodical Accounts*, Vol. V (1815), pp. 332–3; Vol. VI, (1816), pp. 81–2, p. 421.

[3] See, for example, Minutes of Conference, as at n. 1, above; 27 Feb. 1798; *Instructions for Members of the Unitas Fratrum who minister in The Gospel among the Heathen* (London, 1784), pp. 36-7 and Appendix V which fictionally sums up white missionary ideas and concepts and incidentally illustrates the kind of price the African slave had to pay for his (Christian) creolization.

[4] Buchner, op. cit., p. 141.

[5] More usually *nyam* = eat or to eat (in this case, enjoy). A word of West African origin. See Cassidy and Le Page, op. cit., p. 325.

[6] Diary of Fairfield, 22 Aug. 1824; Moravian Church Archives, Bethlehem, Malvern, Jamaica.

[7] ibid.   [8] ibid., 8 Aug. 1824.   [9] ibid.

[10] For the West Indies, only Moravian Missionary diaries are available. The main depositories are at Bethlehem, Malvern, Jamaica and Sharon and Mt. Tabor Churches in Barbados—though the records at Sharon were not available at the time of visit. Of special interest for this study, were the following at Malvern: The Carmel Church Book 1813-37; Diaries for Fairfield 1824 and 1825, 1826, 1827, 1828, 1829; the Diary written by John Lang from Feb. 1805–Nov. 1819 (excerpts also available in the Moravian *Periodical Accounts*); Minutes of Conference, Mesopotamia, Jan. 1798–Jan. 1818.

resistance to Christian teaching—at least as far as the Moravians were concerned. This was so throughout the entire period of this study and beyond, and holds for Jamaica as well as, for example, Barbados:

This week we spoke with the new people and Candidates, but very few attended. We are often at a loss to know what to think of them and how to do to make them to come to speaking. When we see them numerously attending our evening meetings (at least some times) and listening attentively to the word of God, we cannot believe that anything else but desire after the word of God causes them to come, some even from distant places, *but when we endeavour to get personally acquainted with them* and invite them to come to speaking, they make fair promises but in vain we look for them.[1]

But the missionaries *knew* why this happened, even if they did not always admit it.

This may be owing to several reasons, but the chief among many is, we suppose, the mere system of works, depending upon the observance of an outward christianity to combine with Beliam [*sic*]. . . .[2]

'Beliam', for one thing, meant participating in the 'dance':

17th October (Saturday)
We saw many Negroes from Haynesfield passing on the road below our dwelling who went to a dancing, which was painful to us to see . . . as Mrs. Haynes wishes so much that her Negroes might attend the Church and go after such pleasure which is to be found in Christ Jesus.

18th October
Br. S. preached from James 4, 17. 'To them that knoweth to do good, and doeth it not, to him it is sin.' But not many had been to church because the Dance was not finished yesterday and carried on [to]day till late on the evening.

25th October (Sunday)
It was our painfull duty to exclude 6 person from the Congr. & 4 from the Candidates Class who went to the above mentioned dance.[3]

Estate List of Members of Fairfield Congregation, 12 Oct. 1824; List of Marriages at Fairfield, Manchester, 8 Feb. 1829 to 30 May 1840 (with note of Slave Marriages on cover); Register of Members 1824; Conveyance of lands from Alfred Henriquez to Mrs. Ruth Rock of Salem-Hope, the land being part of Fairfield in the parish of St. Thomas, 8 Dec. 1819.
[1] Mt. Tabor Diary, 14 Aug. 1830; Moravian Church Records, Mt. Tabor, Barbados, my italics.
[2] ibid.   [3] ibid. for 1829.

There was, in fact, a certain ambiguity[1] in the white missionaries'
attitude and position which the black preachers were not caught
balancing on. The white missionaries were, quite sincerely, as a
quotation above makes clear, endeavouring 'to get personally
acquainted with' the slaves, and their motives in trying to do this were
much 'purer' than a similar endeavour on the part of an average
secular creole would have been. The missionaries were also, on the
principle of their religious freedom alone, in opposition to the white
Establishment. Because of this they were, by implication, on the
'side' of the slaves. This appeared to be especially so of the Baptists in
Jamaica after 1820 and of individualists like John Smith in Guyana.[2]
But the slaves were still slaves, still seen as stereotypes, not people;
as souls to be saved, not selves to be respected. And this the slaves
must surely have realized and felt. There were, without doubt,
many sincere Christian slaves—really converted. But the evidence of
missionary diaries suggests that in general the slaves found the missionaries a convenience. They could offer them a certain prestige;
protection and privileges, sometimes. But above all, they could
supply, with their white man's religion, a new and another fetish.[3]

In a sense, both sides were using the faith as a fetish: the slaves, as
a charm against the System,[4] the missionaries as a charm against
political toothache. For the latter, Christianity was not to be the
revolutionary creed expounded by its founder; it was a way of separa-
ting the Spirit from the world, the Word from the flesh. Even the
Baptists, most distrusted (by the white élite) of Jamaican Non-
conformists, were instructed not to meddle with politics:

Remember that the object of your mission is not to teach the principles and
laws of an earthly Kingdom, however important a right understanding of
these may be, but the principles and laws of the Kingdom of Christ.
Maintain towards all in authority a respectful demeanour. Treat them with
the honour to which their office entitles them. Political and party discussion
avoid as beneath your office.[5]

[1] Goveia, *Slave Society*, p. 308.
[2] Smith was a representative of the London Missionary Society.
[3] 'Br. S. preached today from the Gospel Luke 16:10. During the preaching an old
Negro Woman came in thro' the door and straightway to Br. S behind the table,
stretching out her arm to shake with him, she was advised to sit down on the bench
with the rest. After the preaching was over, Br. Seiz asked her what she would. She
told him: "When I came in and saw your hand moving, it was to me, as you called,
come to me! . . ."' (Mt. Tabor Diary, 16 August 1829.) On the whole the German
Moravian diarists were more emotional (and more informative) than the English ones.
[4] See Appendix VI.
[5] Baptist Missionary Society, *Letter of Instructions* (London, n.d.), p. 13.

This, alas, was no new statement in the history of the Church; or, for that matter, in the history of recognized religions in Caesar's states. But it did very little to improve the quality of Jamaican society.

You are going to people in a state of slavery, and require to beware, lest your feelings for them should lead you to say or do anything inconsistent with Christian duty. Most of the servants whom the Apostle Paul addressed in his epistles to the Churches were slaves, and he exhorts them to be obedient to their own masters in singleness of heart, fearing God; and this, not only to the good and gentle, but also to the froward, etc. These exhortations must be your guide, and while you act upon them no man can justly be offended with you.[1]

Only one missionary (a Baptist), within the period of this study, ever dared to challenge his own Mission's decision of local political silence. He was dismissed.[2] As he wrote to his Committee in London (letter dated 5 August 1816):

Your counsel is always welcome, and if I were so near that I could obtain it at every turn when I need it, I would not move a step without it. But things in this island are sometimes so critical, that if I were always to wait for advice from home, before I made a movement, I might be falsely charged as an evil doer. . . .[3]

In general, however, the missionary societies were as 'colonial' as the political society in which they had been given permission to function. Their dilemmas were similar. As always, when actions and decisions were taken, they were taken by 'others', outside the society. Yet the missionaries' own ambiguous position, and the sharp, hanging *possibility* of their radicalism, kept them *personae non gratiae* with the white creole Establishment. In fact, the white creole Establishment saw these missionaries, the Haitian revolt, and the Humanitarian pressure in Britain for the abolition of (at least) the Slave Trade, as part of a general conspiracy against them. Early in 1800, the influential Simon Taylor[4] read to the Assembly a letter addressed to him from a friend in Edinburgh:

I have just learnt that a large body of missionaries embark for Jamaica in the ship Moreland, to sail in January; I do not know what doctrine they

---

[1] Quoted in Clarke, op. cit., p. 74.
[2] See the General Committee Minute Book of the Baptist Missionary Society, 1815–20, Oxford, Committee Meeting, 30 Sept. 1817, p. 7; in Baptist Mission Archives London.   [3] (Baptist) *Periodical Accounts*, Vol. VI, p. 74.
[4] See p. 40, above and Appendix I.

may pretend to preach, but I know that their strenuous advocates and supporters are for no less than a total abolition of slavery; and, whatever outward professions they may make, I am well assured their hidden sentiments are the same. I rather conceive, therefore, that their introduction will be pregnant with mischief to the colony, and thought it my duty to give you the earliest intelligence I could on this head.[1]

These missionaries, five Methodists, came out to join the four others of their sect already in Jamaica[2] who had established a small community in Kingston following Dr. Coke's visit in 1789. They established a station at Morant Bay.[3] With the Moravians at Bogue, Elim, Carmel and Mesopotamia in the St. Elizabeth highlands, they brought the number of mission stations in the island to six, in 1800, with a total following (excluding Black Baptists and other non-white-directed groups)[4] of about 1,000. Of these about 600 were Methodists,[5] 400 Moravians, though the number attending the four meeting houses of these latter does not appear to have averaged more than twenty per meeting at this time.[6]

Even with the relatively small numbers—the grain of mustard seed?—it was not a development that the Authorities welcomed. It brought about the prosecutions of Liele and Moses Baker, already mentioned[7], and the 1802 'Bill to prevent preaching by persons not duly qualified by law',[8] already mentioned in another context.[9]

Whereas there now exists, in this island, an evil which is daily increasing and threatens much danger to the peace and safety thereof, by reason of the preaching of ill-disposed, illiterate, or ignorant enthusiasts, to meetings of negroes and people of colour, chiefly slaves, unlawfully assembled, where-

[1] *JAJ*, X, 453 of 5 Feb. 1800. The letter was from David Dick, who himself became a member of the Assembly in a Kingston by-election in 1808. His letter is dated Edinburgh, 14 November 1799.
[2] See Coke, *History*, Vol. I, pp. 442–3.
[3] ibid., p. 443. For an account of this group's early (1802–3) difficulties with the Authorities, see the long letter from John Williams, one of the missionaries, dated Morant Bay, 13 May 1803 in Box Various: 3 (West Indies), Methodist Missionary Society Archives, London.
[4] Moses Baker, at this time (see p. 254, above) was claiming 3,000 followers. Thomas Swingle, another Black Baptist was reported as commanding a congregation of 700 in Kingston. (Clark, Dendy, Phillippo, op. cit., p. 33.)
[5] Coke, *History*, Vol. I, p. 442.
[6] These figures are derived from material in (Moravian) *Periodical Accounts*, Vol. I (1790), p. 16 and Vol. V (1812–13), pp. 325–33, 485. Compared with the Moravians in Antigua (see *Periodical Accounts*, Vol. I, p. 16), those in Jamaica appeared (at least to Buchner, op. cit., p. 35) to be rather too finicky about baptisms. But it was (and still is) general Moravian policy to confine themselves to small, select congregations.
[7] pp. 253 and 254, above.   [8] 43 Geo. III, c. 30.   [9] See p. 10, above,

Emancipatn

by not only the minds of the hearers are perverted with fanatical notions, but opportunity is afforded to them, of concerting schemes of much private and public mischief . . . [no person], not duly qualified and permitted, as is directed by the laws of this island and of Great Britain, shall, under pretence of being a minister of religion, presume to preach or teach, in any meeting or assembly of negroes or people of colour, within this island. . . .[1]

This legislation was rejected in Britain on the ground that (a) it did not define 'duly qualified' preacher and (b) it flew in the face of the principle of religious toleration as generally recognized and upheld by the British Parliament.[2] But the Jamaican Authorities got around this technical set-back by passing, as already discussed,[3] local annual bills on the subject and allowing local Vestries to put into operation prohibitive ordinances. Would-be preachers had to be licensed by the magistrates and preaching, even when allowed, was severely limited by certain 'curfew' hours, by the number granted licences and the places of meeting permitted.[4] This did not stop missionary activity, however. All Vestries were not hostile all the time;[5] there were a few friendly or sympathetic proprietors and officials,[6] and of course the whole business was watched, prodded and protested against by the missionaries' Societies in London— where it counted.

In November 1803, one of the Methodist ministers in Jamaica informed Dr. Coke that

The Kingston Society continues to increase, altho' not rapidly. Our congregations are large, especially at the Lectures at five in the morning,

[1] 43 Geo. III, c. 30 of 18 Dec. 1802; *Laws*, Vol. IV, p. 451.
[2] See A. L. Murray, op. cit., p. 25; WMMS *Report, 1807*, p. 20.
[3] p. 10, above.
[4] Meth. Miss. Soc. Archives (West Indies), Letters 1803–13, f. 245: William Ross, 'Statement', Spanish Town, 19 June 1807; Gardner, op. cit., pp. 348–9.
[5] In 1802/3, the local Methodist minister could not get a licence to preach in Morant Bay, but the Kingston minister could. (See John Williams' letter, referred to in n. 3, p. 260, above.) In 1811, Morant Bay had become the H.Q. of Methodist activity, with St. Mary, St. Thomas-in-the-Vale and St. Andrew furnishing the missionaries 'with a sufficiency of labour' (WMMS *Report, 1811*, pp. 11–12).
[6] See for instance, Coke, *History*, Vol. I, pp. 422, 432–3; Minutes of the Society for the Furtherance of the Gospel, Minute Books 1768–1817; Minutes for 5 Nov. 1804 in Moravian Church Archives, London; (Moravian) *Periodical Accounts*, Vol. III, pp. 159–60; *Baptist Magazine* (1814), p. 344; J. Wiggins to Miss. Ctte., 1817, WMMS Archives, WI Letter Box, 1814–15, f. 264; (Meth.) *Missionary Notices*, Vol. I (Nov. 1817), p. 188. Some of the missionaries also received support from some of the members of the Assembly. Coke in 1796, for instance, from Henry Shirley (Coke, *History*, Vol. I, p. 439); Shipman (Methodist) from James Stewart of Trelawny in 1815/16 (Duncan, op. cit., p. 110); the Methodists generally from J. C. Pownall in a letter to the Editor of *The Kingston Chronicle*, reprinted in *R.G.*, XXXVIII (1816), 46, 23.

which, for some time past, have been better attended than I ever knew them before.[1]

On April 12 1804:

The little flock, at Morant Bay, still continue steadfast . . .[2]

On April 26 1804:

You will not be surprised at the number of backsliders, when you consider how greatly the poor people are deprived of the means of grace; the Prayer-Meetings in particular, of which we used to have six in the week. The situation, also, of several of the slaves is such, that neither their Leaders nor myself can have access to them.[3]

Warren, a Kingston local preacher told Coke (19 May 1804):

The number of our People, who live at the Bay[4] amount to about 30. A few more live just nigh, who are those whom I generally see when I go up; and I can say for them, they are still endeavouring to please God, with the exception of four or five, who are not such as they should be. With regard to the other people, of whom the Morant-Bay Society consisted . . . I mean those belonging to the Estates,—I can say but very little of them. Some, I hear, are holding on; and others, I hear, have fallen . . . O what a difference will it make, when we shall have liberty to preach the Gospel without fear![5]

But with or without 'liberty', the missionaries were certainly preaching the Gospel. The figures of Methodist expansion between 1804 and 1820 may be taken as indicative of their progress:

	whites	coloured	black
1804			
Kingston	14	104	402[6]
1806			
Morant Bay	2	95	
Irish Town	—	38	
St. Mary's	—	34	
St. Andrew's	—	13	
Manchioneal	—	6	
Kingston	22	622	7
	24	808	

[1] Coke, *Account*, p. 27.   [2] ibid.   [3] ibid.
[4] Morant Bay.   [5] Coke, *Account*, pp .27–8.
[6] Fish to Benson, Kingston 26 April 1804; WMMS Archives; Letters, 1803–13, p. 230.   [7] In WMMS *Report*, Vol. I (1806), p. 4.

	whites	coloured	black
1817			
Spanish Town	1	76	
Morant Bay	2	1244	
Grateful Hill	—	144	
Kingston	22	2662	
	25	4126	1
1819			
Spanish Town	7	119	
Morant Bay	7	1959	
Grateful Hill	1	256	
Montego Bay & Falmouth	5	23	
Kingston	15	3095	
	35	5452	2
1820			
Spanish Town	3	160	
Morant Bay	8	2805	
Grateful Hill	1	424	
Montego Bay	6	84	
Kingston	14	3555	
	32	7028	3

The white Baptists, concentrating on the black population, (the free coloured favoured the Methodists),[4] made much slower progress during this period. In 1820, they had only three chapels (Kingston, Spanish Town, St. Ann's Bay)[5] and, together with the Moravians, had access to not more than ten or sixteen estates in the whole island.[6] But in the final analysis the white creole critics were right. Whatever the missionaries' 'official' policy, no matter how docile and dutiful some of them may have claimed Christianity would make the bondsmen—'more contented', as Dr. Coke argued, 'with their humble situation, than those who still adhere to the barbarous superstitions of pagan idolatry';[7] no matter what the missionaries' personal attitudes to and prejudices about black men might have been, no matter how much they might claim not to desire to interfere with the institution of slavery, the fact remains that they were not committed to its perpetuation either. It was this kind of non-commitment that the Establishment disliked and distrusted. But more than that, the

[1] In WMMS *Report*, Vol. I (1817), p. 28.
[2] ibid. (1819), p. xvii.   [3] ibid., Vol. II (1821), p. xiii.   [4] See pp. 209–11, above.
[5] See *A Tabular View of the Churches, Stations, Schools etc. in connection with the Baptist Mission in the Island of Jamaica* (London, 1836), p. 12.
[6] John Shipman, 'Thoughts on the Present State of Religion among the Negroes in Jamaica. A Plan for Their Moral and Religious Improvement', 2 MS. folios [London] 1820; f. I, p. 133 in WMMS Archives (London); Boxes, West Indies, B.1.
[7] Coke, *History*, Vol. I, p. 406.

Establishment disliked the missionaries' close personal contact with the slaves, bringing not whips, but a book, assuming that brutes, somehow, could be initiated into the secrets of the very spiritual core of Western civilization. Was a Christian Protestant slave any less a slave? There was just a chance that he might be. And if so, what then? It was this kind of subtle psychological intimation that the missionaries brought with them that upset the secular Establishment. And the presence of this disturbance was in itself a kind of change.

For the slaves, on the other hand, and for the non-whites generally, the missionary communities provided a new extra-plantation experience they had not known before. The new Christian communities, like their own ex-African religious beliefs and practices, provided them with embryonic organizations and ways and means of organizing. What is more, these Christian organizations were being encouraged, not discouraged like their African ones. The missionaries, in other words, whether they realized it or not, were giving to the slaves and non-whites, no matter how presented, new ideas to use, think about, reinterpret. They were providing a form of education and recharging the batteries of the slaves' imagination. But above all, the presence of the missionaries and their effect on the non-white population put the white élite, as did Haiti and the 'Intestine Jars',[1] on the defensive. It forced the need for change upon them, so that by 1812, through Establishment channels like Church of England curates[2] and the British and Foreign Bible Society[3] (five tons of Bibles were to be shipped from England in 1813),[4] the white Jamaican secular élite found itself attempting to institutionalize the conversion, baptism, and religious education of its slaves.[5] About this time, too, Church of England missionaries began to arrive in the island.[6]

[1] The phrase occurs in the anonymous poem, *The Politicks and Patriots of Jamaica* (London, 1718), p. 19.   [2] 57 Geo. III, c. 24, 25.

[3] Perhaps because this Society was supported by the Church of England and came in a more 'fashionable' way from the Mother Country than did the Non-conformist missionaries, it enjoyed considerable support in Jamaica during the period of this study. See John Owen, *The History of the First Ten Years of the British and Foreign Bible Society*, 2 vols. (London, 1816), Vol. II, pp. 289–94. White Jamaicans seemed only too happy to have their names in the papers as contributing to its funds. (See, for example, *R.G.*, XXXV, 17, 13.)   [4] *R.G.*, XXXV, 6, 17.

[5] See *JAJ*, IX, 444–5 of 5 March 1796; Minutes of the Society for the Furtherance of the Gospel, 14 June 1796; (Moravian) *Periodical Accounts*, Vol. VIII, p. 72; *R.G.*, XXXVIII, 26, 17; J. B. Ellis, op. cit., p. 59.

[6] ibid.; J. B. Ellis, op. cit., p. 59; Minutes of the Soc. for the Furtherance of the Gospel, 14 June 1796, pp. 88–9.

A position had been reached where, if the white Establishment did not change, the changes would be taking place without them. And here again there was a choice. Would these changes have to take place violently, through a rising crescendo of revolt, or peacefully through social recognition of 'the other's' personality? Would the effect of the Humanitarian Revolution destroy, divide or integrate the society?

17

(WHITE) SOCIAL ACTIVITY (1)

THE Humanitarian Revolution did not fatally destroy or divide Jamaican society because of other pressures or processes operating on and within it. For one thing, Jamaica remained a colony, still within the power-grasp, overall constitutional control, and cultural influence of the Mother Country. The influence of the increasingly powerful metropolis had a stabilizing effect on the colonial society. Perhaps even more important, however, was what was going on in Jamaica itself. There was the process of creolization; there was the white society's various means of controlling the slaves; and there was the creative activity of the white Establishment, especially the Assembly. Recognition of these points is important to an understanding of the nature and development of Jamaican society during and beyond the period of this study.

Because the island's was a slave society—a society, that is, of some brutality, callousness and inefficiency—it has been assumed by many writers that nothing—or nothing very much—'happened' during this period. It is not an attitude held, and this is perhaps significant, by those writers like Long,[1] Edwards,[2] or 'Monk' Lewis,[3] who came in their different ways to identify themselves with creole hopes and aspirations (even though they made their own telling strictures on the society). But it comes out in Moreton,[4] in Bridges' 'the inhabitants have imbibed the vices, without imitating the arts and institutions of European society',[5] in

> Necessity alone can bind
> His person to Jamaica's Isle

in Jack Jingle's 'Scrap Book',[6] and in increasing intensity in the works and tracts of anti-slavery writers and the diaries of some of the missionaries. This view of Caribbean society—another stereotype—was

[1] Op. cit.   [2] Op. cit.   [3] Op. cit.   [4] Op cit., *passim.*
[5] Bridges, op. cit., Vol. II, p. 11.
[6] The Omnibus or Jamaica Scrap Book: A thing of Shreds and Patches by Jack Jingle, MS. (*c.* 1824), f. 257, Institute of Jamaica.

continued by post-Emancipation visitors like James Anthony Froude,[1] and has been more recently expressed by some West Indians themselves, most impressively perhaps by the Trinidadian novelist V. S. Naipaul during the record of a Froude-like visit to his homeland in 1960:

How can the history of this West Indian futility be written? What tone shall the historian adopt? Shall he be as academic as Sir Alan Burns, protesting from time to time at some brutality, and setting West Indian brutality in the context of European brutality? . . . Shall he, like the West Indian historians, who can only now begin to face their history, be icily detached and tell the story of the slave trade as if it were just another aspect of mercantilism? The history of the islands can never be satisfactorily told. . . . *History is built around achievement and creation: and nothing was created in the West Indies.*[2]

Yet the slaves, as has been demonstrated by Elsa Goveia[3] and Orlando Patterson[4] (though with regard to the white society Patterson, too, falls into the stereotype)[5] had a real and living culture of their own, with its own sense of rewards, dignity and destiny. And so, it will now be submitted, did the whites.[6] The 'culture' of this group was not, however, as Bridges would have had it, the fashionable drawing-room efflorescence of the eighteenth- and early nineteenth-century English middle class and aristocracy. It was not, either, an urban, urbane society like that of the North American coastal cities. Here was a plantation, a 'frontier' society, with a practical, not an aesthetic focus. The function of the white Establishment was to 'run' the island—and keep it running—made up, as it was, of very disparate elements indeed. Had there been any lack of initiative on the part of this Establishment; had there been any prolonged loss of a sense of direction, the society might well have fallen apart. This did not happen because throughout the period of its power, the white Establishment continued to demonstrate a sense of social praxis; continued to adjust itself to flux and change and never lost control. Its activity, of course, was primarily directed towards, and was designed to be of benefit to, the white population in general and the white élite in particular. This, in the circumstances,

[1] See *The English in the West Indies* (London, 1887).
[2] V. S. Naipaul, *The Middle Passage. Impressions of Five Societies—British, French and Dutch —in the West Indies and South America* (London, 1962), pp. 28–9, my italics Naipaul has now written a history (Trinidad) of that 'futility': *The Loss of El Dorado* (London, 1969).   [3] *Slave Society.*   [4] Op. cit.
[5] See my review of *The Sociology of Slavery* in *Race*, Vol. IX (1968), no. 3, pp. 331–42.
[6] See Chapters 9 and 10, above.

was only to be expected. But the social activity of the Establishment was, willy nilly, of benefit to the society as a whole. After Emancipation, the results of this activity were to become available to an increasing number of the island's population.

For the purpose of illustration, three spheres of activity have been selected for examination in some detail here—the Establishment's work with regard to health, reform and education.

Education

In the eighteenth century and the years of the nineteenth covered by this study, the attitude to education, was, as in Europe, still predominantly the medieval and Renaissance one of initiative by clergy or lay patron. Jamaica was very much a part of this tradition, as the existence of Beckford's Free School in Spanish Town, Manning's Free School in Savanna-la-Mar, Wolmer's in Kingston and Rusea's in Lucea bear out; though unlike Europe, there were no clerical educational foundations except a few Sunday schools started, without much hope of real permanence, by Non-conformist missionaries.[1] Even with the established Free Schools, the quality and even frequency of opening was always in doubt,[2] and these were second-class schools for the children of poor second-class whites. Wealthier families sent their children to school in England and (before the Revolution) to North America,[3] 'like a bale of dry goods consigned to some factor'.[4] If not, tutors, like the Rev. William Jones,[5] were imported from England. *The Royal Gazette* carried this advertisement dated 9 April 1813:

Wanted, in a healthy part of the island, 18 miles from Kingston, a young MAN, capable of TEACHING three young Gentlemen the CLASSICS, ARITHMETIC and WRITING. His manners must be such as entitle him to a seat at the Table of a respectable Family.[5]

In 1828 Bridges, setting out to show that 'the inhabitants of Jamaica

[1] The Methodists had a schoolroom in Kingston in 1791 (Coke: *Extracts of the Journals of the late Rev. Thomas Coke L.L.D. comprising Several Visits to North America and the West Indies* . . . (Dublin, 1816), p. 158). In 1820 they were teaching, they claimed, 106 children in Jamaica. (WMMS *Reports*, Vol. II, p.ci.) In August 1816, the Baptist Missionaries reported that they had 'opened a school [in Kingston] without advertising, or any other parade . . .' (Baptist *Periodical Accounts*, Vol. VI, p. 238); and the Presbyterians announced that they had opened two schools in Kingston—one for free coloured children, the other for the 'higher classes'. (*JAJ*, XIII, 361 of 25 Nov. 1819.)

[2] See, for instance, *JAJ*, VI, 317–18 of 13 Dec. 1770; Bridges, op. cit., Vol. I, pp. 557–60.

[3] See pp. 65–6, above.   [4] Long, *History*, Vol. II, p. 246.   [5] *R.G.*, XXXV, 15, 9.

have not been illiberal' in their donations to charitable and educational institutions,[1] could not avoid recording that thirteen of the twenty-one parishes of the island were without any kind of school whatever;[2] though there appeared to be a large number of private schools.[3] 'Higher' education was, needless to say, hardly discussed at all.[4]

Faced with this situation, it is not surprising to find people in the 'poorer' parishes turning to the Assembly for help. There was, for instance, a petition from Portland Parish and Titchfield Town in 1784,[5] and petitions from St. James in 1790 and 1805.[6] But even before this, the Assembly was showing some concern for education. All private donations for the establishment of free schools had to be vested in trustees through an act of the legislature, and in 1770, a House committee was set up to investigate and report on the free school system.[7] There were, at that time, only five free schools in the island: St. Andrew's (established by an act of 1695), Wolmer's (1736), Mannings's (1738), Vere (1740) and Peter Beckford's school in St. Iago de la Vega (1744). Of these, the report disclosed, all but the St. Andrew's school were in operation. The St. Andrew's school, the report said, 'was established, and for some time kept up; but, for want of a proper fund, could not be supported. . . .'[8] Of the other

[1] Bridges, op. cit., Vol. I, p. 557.   [2] See ibid., pp. 557–60.
[3] Among these were Miss Snow's (*R.G.*, XVI, 41, 20), Miss Frogg's (ibid., 17, 17), William Jones' Grammar School (ibid., 23, 20), Miss Story's and Miss Walks's Boarding School (ibid., 27, 31), Francis Cuff's at St. Ann's Bay (St. Ann Vestry Minutes, 28 Sept. 1795), T. T. Sherlock's (*R.G.*, XXXV, 17, 24), the Port Maria Seminary (ibid., 23, 23); Mr. and Mrs. Collings' offering music, dancing, French, Writing and Arithmetic, Reading 'and every kind of fashionable and useful work' (ibid., XVI, 1, 20); Miss Smith, late from Queen Square, London (ibid., XVI, 25, 19); *LNJ* (Cundall), p. 80. The Kingston Common Council Minutes, no. 49 (1798), recorded that 'Mrs. O'Neal Tutoress of the parish house [was] at liberty to receive under her Tuition a certain number of Children of decent White parents. . . .'
[4] But see John Rippingham's plan in *JAJ*, XIII, 150 of 21 Nov. 1817, and his *Tract upon Education in General* . . . (Kingston, 1818). Rippingham, who 'appeared' in Jamaica around 1817, was a 'public lecturer' (from 'the Surrey Institution, London'), writer (*Jamaica Considered in its Present State* . . ., Kingston, 1817; *The Law and Usage of the British Parliament*, announced 1818), editor (*The Jamaica Journal*, Kingston, 1818, nos. 1 and 2), calligrapher, and adventurer (he seduced a parson's wife on board ship out to Jamaica.) In 1818 he had (announced) a School in the 'Great Room of the Old South Sea House, adjoining the Custom-House, in Port-Royal-street, Kingston'. He died in Kingston in 1819. The K.C.C. decided 'from the peculiar circumstances of the case, that [his estate] be relieved from the whole of the Parish Tax for the present year', and that 'A Piece of his Penmanship be placed in the Court House and framed.' (K.C.C. Minutes, 5 July, 20 Sept. 1819; *R.G.*, XXXIX, 32, 17; XL, 11, 9–10; 52, 13; XLI, 7, 23; 28, 18; Cundall, *Press and Printers*, pp. 61, 91; Rippingham, *Tract*); and pp. 273–7, below.
[5] *JAJ*, VIII, 26 of 24 Nov. 1784.
[6] ibid., 604 of 1 Dec. 1790 and XI, 329 of 8 Nov. 1805.
[7] ibid., VI, 317–18 of 13 Dec. 1770.   [8] ibid., 317 of 13 Dec. 1770.

schools, Wolmer's had four scholars, Manning's eight, Vere five and Beckford's eleven.[1] It was recommended that the regulations with regard to the Wolmer's Trustees should be revised,[2] and that a message should be sent to the Governor, suggesting that trustees be appointed for the St. Andrew's Free School. But the 7th Resolution of the committee perhaps most nearly reflects the hopes of some, at least, of the House at that time:

It is the opinion of this committee, that a free-school being established in each of the several parishes of this island, wherein no such school is now established, will not only tend early to improve the minds of the youth thereof, but also to render them better and more useful members of the community.[3]

In 1772, the Act[4] incorporating the Vere Free School was revised and made more effective.[5] The following year 'Mr. Haughton[6]. . . presented to the house, a bill for raising a tax on the parish of Hanover, for erecting and establishing a free-school in the said parish.[7] This became law as 14 Geo. III, c. 10 of 1773 but was repealed in 1777[8] because Martin Rusea's will had already (since 1764, in fact)[9] provided for the establishment of a free school in Hanover. The provisions of this will, plus a parochial grant, were therefore combined to set up Rusea's school. Meanwhile, in 1774, the reform of Wolmer's began with a complaint from the Kingston vestry that, because of the terms of Wolmer's will, only certain important office holders were allowed to be trustees of the school, and that since these gentlemen lived some distance from Kingston, the school was suffering from their neglected attendance. There had, in fact, been only two meetings of the school board in the previous five years. The House agreed to 'bring in a bill for rendering the said donation more useful'.[10] This bill, 15 Geo. III, c. 14, 'to repeal part of an act entitled "An Act to explain and enforce the last will and testament of John Wolmer . . . and to add to the number of trustees . . .",' became law on 3 December 1774. Two years later, the Assembly undertook to provide an annual grant of £2,000 to the Wolmer bequests,[11] though this was altered in 1799 to £1,500 p.a.[12]

[1] *JAJ*, VIII, 317–18.   [2] No action was taken, however, until 1774.
[3] *JAJ*, VI, 330–1 of 20 Dec. 1770.   [4] 13 Geo. II, c. 10 (1740).
[5] 13 Geo. III, c. 15.
[6] Member for Hanover from 1766 until his death in 1793. (Roby, op. cit.)
[7] *JAJ*, VI, 468 of 1 Dec. 1773.   [8] 18 Geo. III, c. 18.
[9] Bridges, op. cit., Vol. I, 559.   [10] *JAJ*, VI, 521 of 4 Nov. 1774.
[11] ibid., VI, 661 of 27 Nov. 1776.
[12] ibid., X, 410 of 20 Dec. 1799; 40 Geo. III, c. 33.

In 1780, Manning's Free School in Savanna-la-Mar was destroyed in the Westmoreland hurricane. On the 6 July 1781, the trustees of the school presented a petition to the Assembly for a grant of £405, on the ground that 'the school-house . . . was utterly demolished; the dwelling-house for the master, and the offices thereto belonging, very much damaged'.[1] The petition was referred to a small committee[2] but nothing further appears to have been said on the subject, though it must be assumed that repairs were carried out by means of one or other of the relief funds donated for the stricken area.[3]

In 1784, it was the turn of the people of the town of Titchfield, in Portland, to appeal to the House. When this specially-encouraged settlement was established in 1723,[4] one of the provisions was that there should be a free school there, and 350 acres had been set aside for this purpose.[5] No school, however, had been built. The petition to the House sets out the problem, as seen from Titchfield's point of view, quite clearly—a line of thought that would have gained support throughout much of Jamaica: '[If there is a school in Titchfield] it will be [the] means of having the succeeding generations properly educated, without putting parents to the enormous expence of sending their children off the island.'[6] There were a great number of people in this parish whose circumstances were such as to render them unable to bear the expense of sending their children to school at all, and who consequently 'must be brought up in ignorance, to the great detriment of the community in general'.[7] As a result of this petition, an act for 'vesting the common lands of the town of Titchfield, in the parish of Portland, in the trustees, for the purpose of raising a fund for making and maintaining a free-school in the said town' was introduced[8] and passed into law in December 1785.[9]

The Assembly then, when prodded by local authorities, was prepared to do something, though not very much, for at least existing schools or bequests for schools, in the island. But the running and maintenance of these schools remained a local responsibility, and though the Assembly tried to supervise the general administration of the schools, a great deal depended on the various *custodes rotulorum* and churchwardens, whose responsibility it was to seek out and relay information to the Assembly. In 1785 the Assembly requested the

[1] *JAJ*, VII, 371 of 6 July 1781.   [2] ibid., 372.   [3] See pp. 149-50, above.
[4] 10 Geo. I, c. 8 of 1723.   [5] See *JAJ*, VIII, 26 of 24 Nov. 1784.
[6] ibid.   [7] ibid.   [8] ibid., 152 of 19 Dec. 1785.
[9] Geo. III, c. 7 of 24 Dec. 1785.

'several custodes of the different parishes . . . to transmit . . . on or before the 1st day of July next, a state of the free-school funds in their respective parishes; also an account of all the landed and other real property belonging to such free-schools. . . .'[1] Similar requests in 1789[2] and 1806[3] suggest that not all local officials were at all times ready with the necessary information. In 1792 it was discovered that the trustees of the Manning's Free School had 'lent out the monies of the said free-school, without taking proper security for payment . . ., whereby the said monies [had] become lost to the . . . charity'.[4] The school was being run 'entirely on the rent of fifteen negroes', and a former headmaster of the school was owed 'upwards of £600', 'being for salary and other accounts'.[5] A bill (33 Geo. III, c. 13 of 1792) had to be introduced, giving permission to the school to sell part of its lands to discharge the debts.

In 1790, the House at last took what was perhaps the most sensible action in the circumstances. It appointed a committee 'to inquire into the state of the several free-schools in [the] island, the number of scholars maintained and educated in each, as also of the landed and other real property, funds, and securities for money, belonging to such free-schools. . . .'[6] The Governor also showed some concern, about this time, about the state of the schools when he asked the House, 'whether more advantage to the community may not be drawn from the present existing establishment for the education of youth'.[7] Later that year, a petition from the parish of St. James repeated the Titchfield Town argument that 'great inconveniences [arose] from the want of a proper seminary . . . for finishing the education of youth, so as to supersede the necessity of sending children to a distant country. . . .'[8]

---

[1] *JAJ*, VIII, 169 of 24 Dec. 1785.   [2] ibid., 543 of 16 Dec. 1789.
[3] ibid., XI, 479 of 19 Nov. 1806.   [4] ibid., IX, 160 of 23 Nov. 1792.
[5] ibid.   [6] ibid., VIII, 570 of 30 March 1790.   [7] ibid., 571.
[8] ibid., 604 of 1 Dec. 1790. Despite the obvious advantages of an education for their children abroad, parents were naturally, one supposes, not really happy about it—especially with regard to their daughters. As Jane Brodbelt's father wrote her in February 1793:

> I rejoice exceedingly that you considered how very right your good Governess acted in speaking to you about Mr. Raymond's kissing you when he called at Flint House, for it certainly was very wrong and indelicate, as such a liberty should only be taken by a Parent or a very near Relation, therefore never suffer Him or any Person to make use of such unbecoming familiarity. . . . I have placed great dependence in your returning to Me a thorough accomplished Girl, and which you may if you please, as I spare no expence, therefore you can easily judge what a Mortification it must be to a Parent for a Child to return not what he ought to expect, when an immense sum of money has been expended. . . . (*Letters to Jane*, p. 54).

The committee of the House set up in 1790 reported the following year, but only the parish of St. Ann was dealt with. Here it was found that £155,028 currency, accumulated from the will of Charles Drax, plus 'other charitable provisions made by sundry persons for the use of the poor of the said parish, . . . have never been carried into effect'[1] and it was therefore recommended that the St. Ann Vestry be empowered to impose a tax for the recovery of Drax's £155,000, 'as it meets . . . with the wishes of the major part of the inhabitants . . .'[2] This decision precipitated a long legal wrangle with William Beckford, the absentee inheritor of the Drax Estates, and the case was not settled until 1802, when it was agreed that Beckford would pay '£11,200 currency, in full discharge and satisfaction of all claims and demands'.[3] In 1805, £12,956 currency was vested in island securities to establish a school in St. Ann.[4]

In 1805, the parish of St. James again petitioned the House for 'an efficient school for the education of youth'.[5] Again the dilemma, as they saw it, was stated: either children were 'obliged to be sent to Europe' or 'from want of means, remain uneducated, from both which circumstances much evil and inconvenience have arisen to individuals and to the community.'[6] This time the petition was successful, and towards the end of the 1805 session, 'An act for the establishment of free-schools in the parish of St. James' was passed:[7]

Whereas there is no efficient school for the education of youth in the parish of St. James . . . and the inhabitants thereof are desirous that they may be enabled, by law, to tax themselves for the purpose of raising a sufficient fund to establish, support, and maintain seminaries of learning within the said parish: For the effecting so good and desirable a purpose . . . ,[8]

the justices and vestry were authorized to collect, on the parish tax, an extra education tax of not more than £1,400 per annum.[9] The trustees were empowered to appoint masters, mistresses (Church of England only), and also such 'treasurer, officer or officers, servant or servants,'[10] as necessary. They (the trustees) were to 'have power to import from the united kingdom of Great Britain and Ireland, or to purchase within [this] island, a sufficient quantity of decent and good clothing for the poor children, also desks, benches, tables, and other

[1] *JAJ*, IX, 13 of 11 Nov. 1791.   [2] ibid.
[3] ibid., XI, 34 of 24 Nov. 1802.
[4] ibid., 313, 314 of 5 July 1805; Bridges, op. cit., Vol. I, 557.
[5] *JAJ*, XI, 329 of 8 Nov. 1805.   [6] ibid.   [7] 46 Geo. III, c. 27 of 23 Dec. 1805.
[8] *Laws*, Vol. V, pp. 148–9.   [9] ibid., p. 149.   [10] ibid., p. 151.

furniture, school-books, and other stationary',[1] as should seem necessary, and

upon the said poor childen attaining a sufficient age, or having received a sufficient education, to be determined by the said trustees and their successors, [the trustees were] to remove or discharge them, or any of them, and to receive others in their place and stead: [the discharged children to be apprenticed] to such professions, occupations, or manual trades, as the said trustees . . . shall, in their discretion, [deem] fit.[2]

The next committee report (of November 1806) shows, in fact, that the House, or at any rate its Committee on Education, was becoming more fully aware than hitherto, of the need for a planned educational system in the colony. As always, information from the parishes was unreliable. As the committee put it:

a full and comprehensive detail cannot be expected unless the secretary of the island be directed to make out a list of dockets of the charitable devises and donations, which may appear in his office, similar to that presented to the house in the year 1737.[3]

This was the first hint of possible co-ordination in this field during this period. Catching some of the parochial enthusiasm, the committee went on to make out a plea for the establishment of 'a public seminary, for the instruction of youth, on a liberal and extensive scale, as a measure highly essential to the future welfare and prosperity of the island'.[4] Without an institution of this kind, the committee argued, 'children are of necessity sent to Great-Britain . . . , the expence of which is intolerable to all but the most affluent inhabitants: That the consequences are estrangement from their parents, and the impoverishment and depopulation of the colony.'[5]

Then comes at last a sign of real initiative from this Committee. Because of the poor handling of donations and funds by local bodies,[6] 'the donors' intentions must prove ineffectual without the interposition of the house'.[7] They were of opinion 'that permanency and general utility are only to be expected from a public seminary founded and supported by legislative authority and protection'.[8]

---

[1] *Laws*, Vol. V, p. 151.   [2] ibid.   [3] *JAJ*, XI, 479 of 19 Nov. 1806.
[4] ibid.   [5] ibid.
[6] The Titchfield Trustees, for example, waited ten years before they reported to the Assembly in 1815 that their trust lands had been occupied by battalions of soldiers since the martial law of 1805, thus making it impossible for them to maintain 'more than four scholars on the trust, in addition to the salary of the master and other contingent charges.' (*JAJ*, XII, 727 of 23 Nov. 1815.)
[7] *JAJ*, XI, 479 of 19 Nov. 1806.   [8] ibid.

Recognizing the hopelessness and inefficiency of the existing educational structure, the committee proposed a plan that, had it been taken up, would have introduced the idea of 'centralized', as opposed to local/parochially-based, education into Jamaica even before it was considered in England.[1] Why not, the committee asked, amalgamate 'former donations for parochial free-schools, as are incapable of effect on the original plans'?[2] Such a seminary would allow a parish 'to maintain and educate more children at an easier rate than they can now possibly do', especially since 'the expence of the erection and repair of buildings would be saved'.[3] There was precedent for this, the committee argued, in the action taken by the House with respect to alterations in the constitutions of the Wolmer and St. Catherine Free schools, and in the Vere and other charities, 'and, although the effect has not been answerable to the end proposed, they owe their present existence, such as it is, to the interference of [the] house'.[4]

The committee proposed to begin this new centralizing experiment using Drax Hall school:

The advantage that charity possesses at present over other similar donations consists in the command of a very considerable fund. . . .

Besides:

The trustees of Drax's charity are in treaty with eminent masters; the committee have observed with great pleasure that those masters are to be clergymen; that not only literary but moral and religious instruction will be afforded, and that tried and well known characters may, at stated periods, be selected for the incumbencies of this island.[5]

A '*General Outline of a plan for rendering Drax's free school, for the education of white children, extensively beneficial, and for the foundation and endowment of a college in the island of Jamaica*',[6] appended to the Report, sets out the ideas and thinking of the Assembly in this matter. What is particularly interesting is the way the Committee, perhaps influenced by Long,[7] saw the proposed seminary as an integral part of (white) creole society and as a means, not only of education, but of improving the quality of settlement in

---

[1] See Mary M. Carley, *Education in Jamaica*, Social Survey Series no. 1 (Kingston, 1942). A similar plan had apparently been proposed as early as 1787. See the clipping from *The Essayist* in Add. MS. 12414.
[2] *JAJ*, XI. 479 of 19 Nov. 1806.   [3] ibid.   [4] ibid.
[5] ibid.   [6] ibid., 480.   [7] See his *History*, Vol. II, pp. 251–60.

the island, though the model for the establishment would continue
very much to be the Mother Country.

The first consideration, they felt, was health. The proposed site for
the new school, 300 acres at Walton pen, near Moneague, possessed
'general and easy communication, and the salubrity of its air is
attested' by 'the concurrent testimony of men of professional
eminence'.[1]

2nd: Regarding moral and religious instruction of greater importance to
the rising generation than literary acquirements, it is designed . . . to
promote the welfare of the youth of this colony by rendering them equally
virtuous and wise. With that in view it is proposed that the head-master of
the college shall be a clergyman of known probity, learning, and abilities,
who has had a regular academical education, and can produce the requisite testimonials: The under-masters also to be clergymen of the established church. . . .[2]

The headmaster was to receive £560 per annum, two assistants
£420 and £280 respectively, a teacher of modern languages £280,
and a writing master £200 per annum.

3rd: Having in contemplation the increase of population and the improvement of agriculture, it is proposed . . . that six skilful white gardeners . . .
be indented from Great-Britain for a fixed term; that a regular succession
of the number should be kept up; that a preference be avowed for those
that are married, and that the women be employed in the higher domestic
offices.[3]

Twelve white servants, rather than slaves, at a wage of £70 per
annum were also to be employed at the school. Horticulture was to
be encouraged

to its greatest extent, not only as a means of amply supplying the foundation with culinary herbs, vegetables, and roots of every description, but
for the purpose of making useful experiments in husbandry, of gratu-
itously dispensing rare and valuable plants, and of promoting the knowledge of botany.[4]

Fifty boys were to be clothed, fed and instructed at this school, at
a total cost of £7,780. Of this, £6,500 would be met from the Drax
fund, the rest from the consolidation of various charities.[5]

The bill for setting up this idea—the Jamaica Free School Bill—

[1] *JAJ*, XI. 480.   [2] ibid.   [3] ibid.   [4] ibid.   [5] ibid.

passed through the House, after some opposition,[1] in December 1806, but was rejected by the Council on the ground that it was a private Bill (education still being a 'private' not a 'state' affair), and that there were no fees available with which to enregister it.[2] A move in the House to declare the bill a public one, was defeated 11 to 18.[3] It was, however, reintroduced in the next session as a public bill and passed into law as 48 Geo. III, c. 25 of 1807. Proposals to establish free schools for all three counties were also introduced in December 1806 and November 1807, but these failed to pass the House.[4]

In 1815 the Jamaica Free School, along with Wolmer's (£1,500 p.a.), Manning's (£128) and Vere (£540) was receiving an annual grant of assistance of £1,120 from the House.[5] In 1828, it had an enrolment of sixteen boys and two masters[6]—a fall of twenty-four boys and three masters from the original plan, but, Bridges claims, the establishment had risen to be 'the first in the island' and that 'public examinations took place [there] twice a year'.[7] It was moved to St. Andrew in 1789 renamed Jamaica College in 1902,[8] and is today, along with Wolmer's, Manning's and Vere, among the leading secondary schools in the island.

[1] The voting on the third reading was 21 to 16.
[2] *JAJ*, XI, 537 of 16 Dec. 1806.   [3] ibid., 537–8.
[4] ibid., 540–1 of 17 Dec. 1806; 603, 607 of 3 and 5 Nov. 1807.
[5] ibid., XII, 828 of 21 Dec. 1815.   [6] Bridges, op. cit., Vol. I, p. 557.   [7] ibid.
[8] See Anon., *The regulations for the management of the Jamaica College. With some account of the history of the College* . . . (Kingston, 1916), p. 2; Frank Cundall, *Some notes on the history of secondary education in Jamaica* (Kingston, 1911), p. 8.

18

(WHITE) SOCIAL ACTIVITY (2)

Health

In social affairs, individuals (in most of Western Europe, the Church as well), rather than secular governments, were expected to provide 'welfare' (certainly hope and charity) for the needy. In Jamaica, a colony without well articulated and established religious foundations[1] and without very obvious and outstanding individuals, bodies, or organizations willing to carry out this kind of work, a great deal more social work devolved upon the local secular government as outlined in the previous chapter, than was the case in England (or North America). Or to put it more accurately: in Jamaica, the secular government enjoyed a greater measure of monopoly over social work and welfare than was normally the case in England and North America at that time, though of course the plantations provided their own kind of built-in 'benefits'.[2] In any case, in an island like Jamaica, endemic with dysentery, yellow fever, and malaria; with these fevers regularly, in the towns and especially among the unseasoned soldiery, reaching epidemic proportions; with small pox, yaws and related disorders pervasive among the mass of the population,[3] the government could hardly be expected to sit idly by while sickness took its toll. John Hunter, an Army physician who served as superintendent of military hospitals in Jamaica from 1781 to 1783,[4] gives the following mortality figures for some of the regiments in the island for the period 1779–83: of the 630 men of the 1st Battalion 60th Regiment, 200 died on the expedition to Fort Juan in Nicaragua.[5] In 1782 and 1783, about 80 of this battalion died at their

[1] See pp. 23–5, above.
[2] See, for example, *The Worthy Park Plantation Register*, *1787–91*, Phillips, 'A Jamaica Slave Plantation', pp. 543–58.
[3] See Dancer, *Medical Assistant, passim*; WMMS *Notices*, Vol. II (1819), p. 169, n.1.
[4] Ragatz, *Guide*, p. 374.
[5] For details of this expedition, see Thomas Dancer, *A Brief History of the late Expedition against Fort San Juan, so far as it relates to the Diseases of the troops* (Kingston, 1781).

quarters in Spanish Town. Of 1,008 men of the 74th Regiment
stationed in Kingston in 1779, 910 were dead by 1783; some of these
deaths occurred on the Nicaragua expedition, but roughly a quarter
died in Kingston in 1782–3. In the entire Army in Jamaica during
1780–3, large numbers fell sick and the average annual death rate
was one in four. 'In less than four years', Hunter concluded, 'there
died in the island of Jamaica 3,500 men. . . . In April 1782, when
Jamaica was expected to be attacked, though upwards of 7,000 men
had been sent there in the three preceding years, there were not above
2,000 men fit for duty.'[1]

On Hunter's analysis, the major contributory factor for this
prodigal wastage of human life was the kind and location of quarters
in which the soldiers were placed.[2] These quarters were hot, damp and
overcrowded. In 1806, the Deputy Inspector of Hospitals and the
Surgeon to the Forces reported to the Lt.-Governor that:

the present mode of lying on the floor or on platforms appears to us not
only to be totally devoid of every kind of comfort, but also evidently
pernicious to health.[3]

It was recommended that

each soldier should be provided with a canvas hammock, a blanket or rug,
and a pillow; that the platforms should be removed, and bars or stan-
chions placed in the barracks for the purpose of slinging the hammocks
at the hour of going to rest. This accommodation for sleeping has been
furnished . . . in all the Windward Islands for many years past, and is
found considerably to improve their situation and preserve their health.
This mode secures to the soldier a clean and dry birth [sic] to retire to
after his day's fatigue, an advantage seldom to be derived from the present
plan, particularly during the rainy seasons, the floors and platforms being
so walked on through the day.[4]

Not only the soldiers; the missionaries also suffered, especially
before they had a chance to become acclimatized. Of the 193 Moravian ministers who went out to Jamaica in the 100-year period
1754–1854, sixty–four died in the island; six within less than a year,
ten after only one year, and seven after only two years.[5] John Rowe
(see below), the first white Baptist preacher, landed at Montego
Bay on 23 February 1814. Just over two years later (7 June 1816),

[1] Hunter, *Observations*, p. 60. The main body of this paragraph is based on detailed
figures supplied by Hunter, pp. 34–9.
[2] ibid., p. 57.   [3] *JAJ*, XI, 455 of 11 Nov. 1806.   [4] ibid.
[5] See Buchner, op. cit., p.14.

he was dead. Of his four successors, Coultart, who arrived on 9 May 1817, lost his wife within a few weeks and himself went back to England for his health (though he returned in 1820). Kitchin, who arrived in 1818, died after two years, and Godden, who arrived in April 1819, was dead by 19 December.[1] William Knibb, in a letter to his mother dated 9 September 1828, said: 'Since I have been here fourteen Missionaries have died—and almost as many of their Children. . . .'[2]

James Pinnock's *Diary*,[3] provides a picture of Jamaican mortality on the domestic front. The following all took place in 1780:

July 24
My mother Mrs. Mary Pinnock died exactly at Midnight at the Great House at Halfwaytree in the 63rd year of her Age, after a short sickness of 4 days being fits of Epileptick Nature. . . .

August 18
The only Child of my Brother George, named Thomas, died of a Putrid Sore Throat in Kingston. . . .

August 23
The only child of Augustin and Sarah Gwyn, named Sarah, died of the like disorder at my House in Kingston, whither she had been carried to be nearer the Doctor.

Sept. 17
Emma Pinnock, my 3rd Daughter, died at 3/4 after 8 o'clock in the Morning at which time, exactly on Friday morning, she had been seised with a fit, though at 8 of the Clock she was playing at my Knee at the Breakfast Table. [It] was thought at first to be occasioned by Worms, but . . . the Body being opened after her Death, neither Worm nor the Egg of a Worm [was] found. . . .[4]

A sadder, even more harrowing picture of conditions for the sick and dying in Jamaica is provided in an account by Moses Baker of the death of John Rowe, the Baptist Missionary Society preacher, on June 1816. Rowe and his wife had both taken ill with fever in a Montego Bay boarding house. The landlady told them she wanted the room as 'it was court week' (when, in a sense, the social life of Montego Bay would begin). Rowe promised to quit as soon as possible. But the couple grew worse.

[1] See (Baptist) *Magazine for 1814–1821* (London, 1821); (Baptist) *Annual Register for 1819* (London, 1819), p. 37.
[2] Baptist Missionary Society Archives, London: West Indies, Box 3.
[3] Add. MS. 33316.   [4] ibid.

The sister [a Baptist convert who was trying to look after the couple] told me that the doctors had ordered him to be kept out of the room where Mrs. Rowe was. . . . But he was anxious to see her, and went to the door, and when he found it fastened he seemed very unhappy. He clapped his hands together and said, 'Oh me! what shall I do!?' He then began to bleed at the nose, and fell on his knees, putting his hands together for prayer. The blood then began to clod together, and choked him, and so he departed. The good woman said, she was persuaded that he was desirous of taking leave of his wife. . . .[1]

It might be said in extenuation of this persistent death-rate, that the eighteenth-century miasmatic theory of infection had not been challenged by the knowledge of the mosquito vector in malaria or yellow fever.[2] It was believed that the swampy exhalations and vapours at sunrise and sunset were the main cause of these illnesses.[3] There was also a notion that in the tropics the body's temperature should be kept constant at all times, and, to effect this, some doctors[4] and others[5] recommended the wearing of flannel next to the skin—a not really suitable arrangement for the tropics. But sanitation generally—the filth of the towns in particular—was something which required not science but a sense of social responsibility (though here, as in so many things, Jamaica was no better or worse than its metropolitan model).

In Kingston some [houses] were tolerably stately, but sanitary arrangements were unknown, dunghills abounded, and from these the ruts in the streets and lanes were filled up after every heavy rain. In the early morning negro slaves might be seen bearing open tubs from the various dwellings, and emptying their indescribable contents into the sea. The churches were for a long time used as places of sepulture; the marshes around the city were undrained . . . and the inhabitants generally set at defiance every law of health, and paid the penalty.[6]

On this subject, the Rev. William Jones noted in his *Diary*:

I have known many persons who have complained of a noisome stench from the carcases which have been interr'd within the walls, & inveighed

---

[1] (Baptist) *Periodical Accounts*, Vol. VI (London, 1816), p. 72.
[2] The *Aedes aegypti* mosquito, carrier of yellow fever, was not identified as such until after 1900.
[3] Wood, op. cit., p. 26.
[4] See, for example, Mosley, *A Treatise on Tropical Diseases* . . . p. 132.
[5] See Robert Hibbert, Jnr., *Hints to the Young Jamaica Sugar Planter* (London, 1825), pp. 2–3.
[6] Gardner, op. cit., p. 165.

against the continuance amongst Xtian [*sic*] Protestants of a custom which originated in Popery. . . .[1]

Here then was a massive and serious problem. The Assembly did what it could. In 1789, it legislated against burials in churches 'especially within the several towns . . . found dangerous to the health of the inhabitants . . .', introducing special dispensations only in the case of Governor Lord Effingham and his wife, who were buried in Spanish Town Cathedral within a month of each other.[2] Other public health measures included the control of inoculation 'for the small-pox, measles, or any other contagious or infectious disease or distem-per'[3] (no 'physician, surgeon, apothecary, or other person whatso-ever'[4] was to provide inoculations without a licence), the attempt to control the spread of 'canine madness',[5] the quarantine act of 1801[6] the introduction of a sewerage system from the Spanish Town barracks to the Rio Cobre,[7] the anti-dysentery action at Savanna-la-Mar in 1812,[8] and throughout the period, inspection, improve-ment and extension of the various hospitals.[9]

Most satisfactory progress was perhaps made with respect to vaccination against the small pox. In 1803, Lady Nugent was still importing 'the vaccine virus' from England and praying that it would succeed;[10] but by 1813[11] there was a Vaccine Establishment in Jamaica. Operating from Kingston Hospital, it was open to the public for vaccination '*gratis* every Tuesday and Friday'.[12] The Director of the project, Dr. Alex. MacLarty, reported to the Assem-bly on 31 October 1815 as follows:

The principal object of the Jamaica vaccine establishment is the pre-servation of the succession of vaccine matter for the public at large, as well as for medical practitioners. This the institution has effected, and charges of vaccine lymph have been distributed to most of the parishes in this island. . . . The number of persons vaccinated at the public hospita

[1] *William Jones*, p. 40.
[2] The dispensing bills were introduced on 23 November 1791 and passed the House on the 26th. (*JAJ*, IX, 24, 25 32, 33.) The Countess was buried on 28 October; Effing-ham on 22 November. (*JAJ*, IX, 4, 22.)
[3] *Laws*, Vol. II, p. 254.   [4] ibid.   [5] 33 Geo. III, c. 10 of 1792.
[6] 41 Geo. III, c. 16.   [7] See 47 Geo. III, c. 23 of 1806.
[8] See *Laws*, Vol. VI, p. 165.   [9] See pp. 285–90, below.
[10] *LNJ* (Cundall), p. 236. The year before, in fact, Maria Nugent had been using the older method of small-pox inoculation. The cowpox vaccine, introduced by Jenner in Paris in 1798, did not come into general use in Jamaica until after 1809. See Dancer *Medical Assistant* (1809 ed.), footnote on pp. 155–6.
[11] *JAJ*, XII, 552, 553 of 30 Nov. 1813.
[12] ibid., footnote to 695 of 31 Oct. 1815.

amounts only to [122]; but, as the popular prejudices against vaccination seem to be rapidly losing ground, the number, in all probability, will soon be much increased.[1]

Two years later, in November 1817, the 'director and surgeons of the Jamaica vaccine establishment' were reporting that

although prejudices still exist here (in common with most other parts of the world) against the practice of vaccination, yet a greater number have been vaccinated throughout this island since the last report[2] than at any former period.

So universally has it been resorted to in Kingston, that as far as your reporters have been able to ascertain, no case of small-pox has occurred there or in the vicinity during the last six months.[3]

In November 1818, Dr. MacLarty told the House (prematurely) that 'small-pox seem [sic] now extinct, for, according to the best information . . . not a case has occurred in any part of [the] island for nearly two years. . . .'[4] The next year, however, brought an admission of public resistance to the vaccine. Although the demand had 'been greater than in any preceding [year]',[5] fifty-one packets of vaccine matter had been distributed to medical practitioners in eighteen parishes and 'Our island happily continues still exempt from small-pox. . . .'[6] We lament to state that there are many persons in this island, who are still adverse to its adoption. Some from prejudice, others from apathy, having had no recent cause of alarm. . . .'[7]

The following year there *was* cause for alarm:

Since our last report . . . a case of small-pox, in its most loathsome and horrible form, has been brought to Kingston from St. Jago de Cuba, in the schooner *Aimable Theresa*. This person, Juan Bello, was sent to the public hospital on the 10th of July last, being two days after the arrival of the vessel in this harbour.

From the aggravated nature of this case . . . there was no reason to expect a favourable termination, but the risk of propagating a dreadful contagion in this island, which had been exempt from this disease for several years, was truly alarming, and called for every exertion to avert.[8]

[1] *JAJ*, XII, 695.
[2] In November 1816. See *JAJ*, XIII, 32 of 12 Nov. 1816.
[3] *JAJ*, XIII, 146 of 19 Nov. 1817.
[4] ibid., 241, of 17 Nov. 1818.
[5] ibid., 351 of 23 Nov. 1819.
[6] ibid.   [7] ibid.
[8] ibid., 469 of 21 Nov. 1820.

The Kingston Public Hospital, from which this work originated,[1] was established by 17 Geo. III, c. 31 of 1776.[2] Until about 1782, however, the Assembly did not appear fully to appreciate the connection between health and a well-trained medical establishment, or at any rate, it was prepared to allow its quarrel with the British Government over who was responsible for the 'supply' to troops in Jamaica to affect its chance of recruiting first-class people. In December 1779, for instance, the Physician-General of Troops (in London) submitted a plan to the House, through the Governor, for setting up, in view of the continuing poor health of the troops, a Military Hospital in or near Kingston. The Assembly was to subsidize this and provide some of the equipment (100–50 cradles, cooking and bath utensils, two mates, a nurse, a washerwoman for every ten men, etc.).[3] The Assembly replied that they

hope his excellency will not think it presuming in the house, to say, that they are of opinion, if the troops were sent into *country quarters*, it would greatly alleviate, if not entirely relieve, their present distress.[4]

In March 1782, the Governor informed the House of 'the arrival of a physician for the use of his majesty's troops in Jamaica, and a regular medical staff under his direction'.[5] Although this staff was a military one, it would almost certainly have been of benefit to the island as a whole. But the Assembly's reaction was a selfish one. The arrival of a medical staff, it was felt, could only mean a reduction in the number of locals employed as surgeon's mates. In other words, 'jobs for the boys' was more important than any consideration of efficiency. (A settlement was reached when the Governor pointed out that a reduction in the number of local surgeon's mates would help to reduce island expenditure, but that in any case, most of the local mates would be allowed to retain their rank of ensign in the military hierarchy.)[6]

By 1791, however, (on the evidence of the report of a committee

[1] Dr. MacLarty, the Director of the Vaccine Establishment, was a physician at the Kingston Public Hospital, and it seems that the Vaccine Establishment was financed out of the Assembly's annual vote to the Hospital. There is no record, at any rate, of a separate vote for the Vaccine Establishment; but three of its officers—the clerk, the registrar and the surgeon (Director) were paid direct by the Assembly.

[2] Before this period of study, the St. Andrew Hospital for Sailors had been established by 13 Geo. II, c. 11 of 20 Dec. 1740; and the Port Royal Hospital for Seamen by Geo. II, c. 18 of 22 Dec. 1756.

[3] *JAJ*, VII, 188 of 3 Dec. 1779.   [4] ibid., 199 of 10 Dec. 1779, my italics.
[5] ibid., 458 of 1 March 1782.   [6] ibid., VII, 459 of 1 March 1782.

of the House appointed 'to inspect the several gaols, hospitals, and workhouses, in the county of Surrey'),[1] the situation had changed. Considerable attention was now being given to the question of health and to the condition of the hospital, even though the report, one feels, was not as critical or objective as it might have been. The report provides, first, a picture of the Kingston Hospital's establishment:

The committee found the establishment . . . to consist, first, of a physician, who, at that time, was the late doctor Langley, one of the most eminent of the profession in Kingston, with a salary of 100(£) *per annum*; he attends daily for an hour or less, as occasion may require; secondly, of two surgeons and apothecaries . . . with a salary of 200(£) *per annum*, for which they perform amputations and other surgical operations, and make up and prepare medicines, which are all of the best quality, being annually imported from Apothecaries Hall, agreeably to a list made out by the physician; thirdly, of an assistant, with a salary of 50(£) *per annum*, who is maintained by, and constantly resides in, the hospital; fourthly, of a white matron, with a salary of 80(£) *per annum*; she also lives in the hospital, her duty being to attend to the diet of the patients, to see that the medicines are duly administered, and that the bedding and cradles are aired, and the wards kept clean; she is assisted by five women slaves, who are hired at the rate of 5s each *per* week, and 1s 10½d each for their allowance. The supervisor of the workhouse, which joins the hospital, purchases provisions for the hospital, and is allowed a salary of 50(£) *per annum*; he accounts to the treasurer, who is always the acting churchwarden of Kingston. The expences of the hospital amount, upon the average, to 180(£) *per* month, which is provided for partly by a tax on shipping, which produces about 950(£) *per annum*, partly from the profits of the workhouse, and partly by grants from this house. . .[2]

They found

the wards for the accommodation of sick persons and invalids, and convalescents, to be clean and roomy, and that individuals of all descriptions and countries, and from all parts of the island, are admitted therein. . . .

On inspecting the books, they found that the number of patients admitted from the first of November, 1788, to the 1st of November, 1789, amounted to 399, of whom 61 had died; and that, from the 1st of November, 1789, to the 1st of November, 1790, 413 had been admitted, of whom 41 had died; the remainder had been discharged cured, unless in some few

[1] *JAJ*, VIII, 634 of 19 Feb. 1791.   [2] ibid., 634–5 of 19 Feb. 1791.

instances, where the disorders [were] of such a nature as to render the prospect of cure in a warm climate very dubious.[1]

These few had been sent back to Great Britain at the hospital's expense.[2] It is the Committee's conclusion, however, which seems rather sanguine:

The committee consider that (making due allowances for the inconveniences to which patients in a public hospital, in so warm a climate, must unavoidably be subject) the proportion of deaths is small, and a manifest proof that due care and attention is paid to them.[3]

But to obtain a clearer picture of conditions at the Hospital, it will be necessary to look at actual Hospital Returns and at complaints about conditions from some of its aggrieved inmates. The Kingston Hospital Returns for the period 1 January 1793 to 31 December 1793, according to the *Royal Gazette*[4] were as follows:

Trade/Occupation of those Admitted	
Seamen	358
Mercantile line	6
Shopkeepers	3
Planting line	14
Carpenters	5
Surgeons	4
Bakers	3
Pedlar	1
Silversmith	1
Royal Artillery	1
Tanner	1
Farrier	1
Gardener	1
Fisherman	1
Disabled soldiers	2
Shoemakers	3
Slater	1
Town-guard	4
	410

[1] *JAJ*, VIII, 634. [2] ibid.
[3] ibid. [4] *R.G.*, XVI, 6, 20.

Diseases/Complaints	Number	Died
Asthma	1	1
Abscess	3	1
Bruises and sprains	10	1
Consumptions	17	6
Dysentery	39	25
Dropsy	7	3
Dislocated shoulder	1	—
Epilepsy	1	1
Fevers	108	68
Fractured arm	1	—
Fractured collar bone	1	—
Gunshot wound	1	—
Insane	9	1
Jaundice	1	—
Obstructed viscera	1	—
Ophthalmia	2	—
Palsy	2	—
Rheumatism	13	1
Scurvy	10	—
Small Pox	1	—
Ulcers	147	14
Venereal	10	—
Wounds	4	—
[Other]	20	—
Total admitted/Dead	410	122

'18 of whom were dead or dying before they reached the wards.'[1]

What is interesting here is that although the total number of deaths is only 29·7 per cent of the total admitted, the deaths from the really virulent diseases—dysentery and 'fevers'—amount to 63·2 per cent of those admitted under these two heads. Looked at another way, of course, this could mean that apart from the virulent diseases, the Kingston Hospital's record for the year 1793 was very satisfactory. The majority of deaths seemed to take place, at the Hospital, in the second half of the year—during that is, the hot months of July and August and the rainy season, September to November.

No. admitted during each month		Dead in each month
January	41	4
February	34	3
March	27	6
April	17	1
May	24	4
June	36	9
July	47	10
August	30	10
September	32	19
October	25	17
November	58	16
December	39	21[2]

[1] R.G., XVI, 6, 20.   [2] ibid.

From 1 November 1814 to 31 October 1815 (to take the latter part of our period) the incidence of death from 'fevers' and dysentery was again higher than other ills, though the proportions this time were more favourable: a total of 403 admitted for 'fever', 44 dead; 22 admitted with dysentery, 8 dead. Total admissions for the year 1814–15 were recorded as 883, with a total of 94 deaths—fractionally over 10 per cent.[1]

Complaints about the working of the Hospital, though denied and refuted by the Kingston Common Council (the body directly responsible for the Hospital) are interesting because of their ring of familiarity, and because they provide, too, a useful corrective to the official reports. On 23 September 1816, the Hospital Committee of the Kingston Common Council, laid before the Council 'the memorial of Williams and others[2] containing matters of complaint. . . .'[3]

Gentlemen, the improper conduct carried on in this Institution is really a disgrace to human nature. In the first case, the unfortunate patients although ordered by the doctor to get a sufficient quantity of nourishment . . . never get any, and the consequence of which there are a great many died through the want of it, especially in No. 6 Ward.

Secondly, not long ago there was a man died with the fever. His bed was thrown out and in the course of two hours hafter [sic] it was given to a man that was brought in with another complaint. Thirdly, there is only three pounds of sugar allowed to five pail of coffee—if such it can be called—and the tea which is more than three-quarters of an ounce to each man. The soup is [so] shocking bad for the want of ingredients that one-half of the people throws it away. The allowance of beef is shameful. The best half i bones and what remains is put in the store and by the next day it is tainted And this is likewise given to the poor unfortunate sick.

Fourthly, the abusive language made use of by the nurses to the patient is too bad to be made mention of and should you complain to the matron she gives you no kind of satisfaction. The wards are not kept in a prope manner clean. But gentlemen, the nurses are not to be blamed. Altogethe the matron gets drunk mostly every evening. She associates with then [i.e. the nurses; blacks], in consequence of which all is neglect . . . for i cannot be expected that negroes will care anything about a white person who makes a companion of them. Several other improprieties is carrie on which you will hear of should an investigation take place.[4]

A Mr. Oliver, a dispenser, wrote a letter to Assemblyman Stewar

[1] K.C.C. Minutes, December 1819.
[2] Clearly patients or ex-patients of the Hospital.
[3] K.C.C. Minutes, 23 Sept. 1816.   [4] ibid.

of Trelawny, which came before the Investigating Committee of the Kingston Common Council that same month.[1] 'A number of patients', Oliver wrote,

are admitted in a dying state . . . to save funeral expenses.[2] The only thing many of them get is a Coffin—and an instance occurred lately of a person being brought to the Hospital after he was dead—the body, however, was not admitted.

Patients are admitted by an order of the Magistrate and such an order is obtainable by any person and in any state: the magistrate in fact seldom sees them.

There are several persons in the Hospital whose connexions are in affluence and ought to prevent them being a burden to the public. [Because of this, a lot of deserving people cannot get into the hospital.]

In an examination of the Purveyor's Books lately they were found in such a state of confusion that the number of patients in the Hospital could not be ascertained in order to regulate the quantity of Beef taken from the Butcher or loaves of bread supplied by the Baker. It was then reported that the Cash Book was kept in a slop-work way. [More money, for instance, was spent on patients' food in 1817 than in 1816—£50 more, in fact—although there were 300 patients less.] It would seem from that mode of expenditure that the fewer the patients the greater the expense.[3]

A lot of money, Oliver went on, was spent in sending people off the island, 'several of whom have never been in the Hospital.'[4]

There is a negro man for whom an allowance is made of 13/4 for attending a person who has not been in the Hospital since the beginning of 1817—nearly two years which money is charged as voted by the Common Council for attending one Mr. P. Edwards.—The negro's name is William Jordan—and it is said that this has been going on so far back as 1816.

It is alleged that the contracts entered into for supplying the Establishment are given to the particular friends of the Corporate body to the prejudice of others—. The accounts should be carefully examined before they are paid by disinterested individuals of that body—and not by the Purveyors who, it is said, have been robbing the public of considerable sums of money for a very long time past.[5]

In these two instances, the Kingston Common Council instituted 'investigations', and in both cases the allegations were refuted point by point, some of the witnesses backing down when faced by the Councillors. When the Assembly's Hospital Committee reported

[1] K.C.C. Minutes, 23 Nov. 1818.
[2] This point was also made in the *Royal Gazette* (1793–4) Vol. XVI, 6, 20.
[3] K.C.C. Minutes, 23 Nov. 1818.   [4] ibid.   [5] ibid.

on the institution in 1810,[1] 1813,[2] 1814,[3] and 1818[4], no complaints of the nature quoted above showed through. The 1818 Committee, like that of 1791, seemed very satisfied with the institution. They found the condition of the wards satisfactory (except for the bedding).[5] The number of (local white) patients was steadily increasing[6] and the Hospital was slowly expanding to meet the pressure of numbers although there was still gross overcrowding. 'In some wards' the 1819 report pointed out, 'fourteen patients are contained, which ought to receive only seven or eight'.[7] £5,000 was voted as a result of this report, for expansion and improvements.[8] Special large grants for expansion and improvement were also made in 1802, 1803, 1809, 1810, 1814 and 1816,[9] and on the whole, for the period 1797 to 1820, the Assembly spent over £50,000 on the Kingston Hospital alone.[10] When it is realized that there were, in addition to the Kingston Hospital, four other hospitals,[11] three Spas—the Jamaica Spa,[12] the Bath of St. Thomas the Apostle,[13] and the Milk River Bath,[14]—a lunatic asylum,[15] the expanding Vaccine Establishment, a Negro Hospital and Asylum in Kingston,[16] plus the parochial workhouses also used as hospitals and asylums, it may be posited that the Assembly's contribution to 'Health' in Jamaica was financially[17] and legislatively[18] not inconsiderable.

[1] *JAJ*, XII, 311 of 4 Dec. 1810.   [2] ibid., 527 of 23 Nov. 1813.
[3] ibid., 602 of 6 Dec. 1814.   [4] ibid., XIII, 281 of 9 Dec. 1818.
[5] ibid., XIII, 281 of 9 Dec. 1818.
[6] 63 in 1810; 87 in 1813 (XII, 527); and 117 in 1814 (XII, 602). All references *JAJ*.
[7] *JAJ*, XIII, 281.   [8] ibid., 413, of 13 Dec. 1819.
[9] ibid., XI, 58 (1802): £3,500; 142 (1803): £4,500; XII, 232 (1809): £1,471. 16s. 7d. 321 (1810): £2,286. 10s. 3d.; 608 (1814): £4,423. 9s. 7¾d.; XIII, 69 (1816): £3,000.
[10] To the above add: *JAJ*, X, 45 (1797): £1,000; XI, 266 (1804): £600; XI, 405 (1805): £500; XII, 91 (1808–9): £600; XII, 477 (1812): £320. 15s. 10d.; XII, 477 (1812): £704. 13s. 4d.; XIII, 82 (1816): £3,525. 19s. 5¼d.; XIII, 177 (1817): £2,458. 12s. 1d.; XIII, 295 (1818): £3,088. 19s. 3½d.; XIII, 379 (1819): £3,116. 6s. 5½d.; XIII, 413 (1819): £5,000; XIII, 505 (1820): £4,320. 7s. 2d.
[11] The St. Andrew Hospital for Sailors (13 Geo. II, c. 11 of 20 Dec. 1740), the Port Royal Marine Hospital (29 Geo. II, c. 18 of 22 Dec. 1756), the Montego Bay Hospital 'for the reception of sick seamen' (see 35 Geo. III, c. 35 (1795), clause 46), the Savanna-la-Mar Marine Hospital (53 Geo. III, c. 22 of 11 Dec. 1812). The hospitals, however, were run and maintained on parochial funds.
[12] In St. Andrew. See Cundall, *Historic Jamaica*, p.233.
[13] In St. Thomas-in-the-East. Opened in 1699. See Cundall, *Historic Jamaica*, p. 247.
[14] This spa was established by the Vere Vestry in October 1791 as a public bath. (See *JAJ*, IX, 168–9 of 4 Dec. 1792.)
[15] '[The] only hospital for lunatics in the whole island'. Lewis, op. cit. (1929 ed.), p. 281.
[16] Kingston Vestry Minutes, 7 April 1788, no. 96; nos. 146, 149, 158 of May–June 1788.
[17] Expenditure on Health for 1816, not including medicines, etc. to the various gaols and workhouses, was as shown at foot of p. 291.
[18] See foot of p. 291.

Reforms

But the activity of the white Establishment was not confined to social work and welfare. Responding directly to the Humanitarian Revolution, it was able, through the Assembly, to initiate reforms in all sectors of the society.

The free coloureds

One of the first reactions to the Maroon War, for instance, with its attendant fear of a St. Domingue in Jamaica, was a lowering of some of the barriers against the free coloured—though only after they had 'proved' themselves loyal. In 1795, an 'Act to make provision for the females of such free people of colour, and of free negroes, enrolled in the militia, as shall be killed or disabled in the public service',[1] was introduced and passed in the Assembly. The following year, a more direct acknowledgement of the loyalty of the free coloured and the part they had played in the recent discontents was made:

Whereas, during the present rebellion of the Trelawny Town maroons, essential services have been rendered to this island by the zeal and prompt obedience of the free persons of colour and free negroes serving in the

[1] 36 Geo. III, c. 15 of 22 Dec. 1795.

---

[18] The Assembly's main legislative acts during this period, under this head, were as shown below.

Bath, Milk River: an add. grant	£500	(XIII, 85)
Bath, St. Thos the Apostle	£700	(XIII, 44)
Bath: physician's salary for 1816–17	£400	(ibid.)
Bath: buildings and roads	£500	(XIII, 65)
Hospital: in aid of funds	£3,000	(XIII, 69)
treasurer's balance	£3,525. 19s. 5¼d.	(XIII, 82)
Vaccine Est.: clerk's salary	£50	(XIII, 69)
registrar's	£150	(ibid.)
surgeon's	£150	(ibid.)

17 Geo. III, c. 31 of 1776: establishing a public hospital.
33 Geo. III, c. 10 of 1792: to prevent the spread of canine madness.
35 Geo. III, c. 35 of 1795: The Montego Bay Police laws which made provision, among other things, for the erecting of a marine hospital there.
39 Geo. III, c. 10 of 1798: purchasing lands and buildings in Port Royal for the use of H.M.'s naval hospital. (Repeated: 59 Geo. III, c. 14 of 1818.)
40 Geo. III, c. 16 of 1801: general quarantine Act. In 1793 a quarantine Act affecting ships from 'different parts of America and other foreign places' had been passed.
47 Geo. III, c. 23 of 1806: sewerage system from the Spanish Town barracks to the Rio Cobre.
53 Geo. III, c. 22 of 1812: making provision for the establishment of a marine hospital at Savanna-la-Mar.

militia, who thereby manifested their faithful attachment to His Majesty's government: And whereas it is just and necessary that they should be . . . protected by law against all violences that may be committed against them . . .[1]

By 1813, with pressure from the free coloureds and the Colonial Office increasing,[2] they (the coloureds) were allowed 'to give evidence in all cases, civil and criminal';[3] 'to navigate all droggers, vessels, or boats, plying round [the] island for hire',[4] and 'to save deficiencies for their own slaves and for the slaves of each other'.[5] Conciliation, in other words, was being used to keep this group within the System.

The slaves

Similarly with regard to the slave population, there was a 'humanitarian' response. As early as 1781, mutilation and dismemberment as a form of punishment had been legislatively forbidden,[6] and in 1787 a more generous form of slave court was set up whereby, instead of two justices and three freeholders, three justices and nine freeholders would sit in judgement over slave crime and delinquency.[7] This Act (29 Geo. III, c. 2) of 1787 was, in fact, the second[8] in a series of ameliorative Consolidated Slave Acts which, among other things, decreed that slaves should not be confined or 'kept to hard labour' in public workhouses for more than three months without trial; that slave families, when sold, should be preserved as far as possible in their familial units;[9] that the killing of a slave by a white man should be considered and treated as a case of murder or manslaughter and not as felonious assault as formerly;[10] and that all persons, including slaves, suffering sudden death, should be examined as soon as possible by a coroner.[11] The wholesale selling of slaves in discharge of debts was to be controlled.[12]

[1] 36 Geo. III, c. 23 of 25 March 1796; *Laws*, Vol. III, pp. 233–4.
[2] M. C. Campbell, op. cit., pp. 76–86.   [3] 54 Geo. III, c. 19 (1813).
[4] ibid. This act, first introduced in 1805 (46 Geo. III, c. 29), allowed Negroes, mulattoes and free people of colour to be master pilots.
[5] 54 Geo. III, c. 20 (1813).
[6] 22 Geo. III, c. 17.
[7] 29 Geo. III, c. 2.
[8] See *JAJ*, VIII, 427 of 12 Nov. 1788.
[9] 32 Geo. III, c. 33 (1791).
[10] See 8 Gulielmi III, c. 2 (1696). It should be noted, however, that under this Act, anyone found guilty of a *second* offence 'of willingly wantonly or "bloodymindedly" ' killing a Negro or slave, could be convicted of murder. See *Acts of Jamaica, 1681–1737* (London, 1738), p. 8. Before this, punishment was three months' imprisonment and a £50 fine payable to the owner of the murdered slave.
[11] 58 Geo. III, c. 23 (1817).
[12] 50 Geo. III, c. 21 (1809); J. H. Howard, op. cit., Vol. I, pp. 79–80.

The Establishment also decided to 'join' the Non-conformist missionaries in working socially among the slaves. Curates were appointed to introduce religion to such as could, in the eyes of the Authorities, be made 'sensible of a duty to God, and the Christian faith',[1] and baptism was to be allowed and encouraged.[2] Two days a month, exclusive of Sundays and holidays, were to be set aside for these things.[3]

With the cutting off of manpower supplies from Africa, it became necessary to look more carefully after the health and fertility of the resident black work-force. One day per fortnight (Mondays),[4] except during crop time and in addition to the Christmas, Easter and Whitsun holidays, was to be given to the slaves so that they could attend their provision grounds. They were not to be worked on Sundays, except, of course, when the canes were being brought in. Bounties were to be paid to overseers to encourage 'breeding women', and females (queen bees) with six living children, whether their own or adopted, were to be exempted from hard labour. Old, infirm, and superannuated slaves were to be looked after by their estates and not turned out into the wilds or on to the public, and a fund was set up to help disabled Negroes (and the free poor) in the workhouses. Public slave whippings were cut down to ten lashes if the owner or overseer was not or could not be present to witness, and to not more than the Mosaic thirty-nine otherwise. Iron collars, investment in heavy chains, etc., were forbidden; and Parochial Councils of Protection were set up to listen to slave complaints of ill treatment.[5] In this way, the white Establishment hoped to justify its ways to God, the Humanitarians, perhaps the slaves themselves, and certainly to the men in the Colonial Office.

Administration

But more importantly, the Establishment, responding to post-1795 changes in the society, was also concerned to reform itself. The militia, for instance, as discussed earlier,[6] was put on a more military

---

[1] 57 Geo. III, c. 24 (1816); 57 Geo. III, c. 25, section ii of 19 Dec. 1816.
[2] See *JAJ*, XIII, 41 of 20 Nov. 1816.
[3] 57 Geo. III, c. 24, section iv.
[4] *JAJ*, XIII, 35 of 15 Nov. 1816. The original resolution proposed the Monday of each week.
[5] 41 Geo. III, c. 26 (1801); 57 Geo. III, c. 25 (1816). A list of laws relating to slaves is included in Appendix VII.
[6] See p. 30, above.

footing. The staffing of forts was tightened up[1] and plantations were, by law, to be in a reasonable state of self-defence.[2] A streamlining of public offices was initiated. Fees for most posts were revised,[3] the Chief Justice[4] and Receiver General[5] were put on salary; Collecting Constables, as public officers, were excluded from sitting in the Assembly,[6] following criticism of them.[7] Reforms were introduced into the entire administration of justice,[8] for the 'more speedy and effectual collection of the public taxes and the arrears thereof';[9] the whole Church of England ecclesiastical establishment was brought under local control;[10] and Kingston was given corporate status.[11]

There were also small but significant reforms of detail, such as the revision of the 1750 Act dealing with weights and measures. This was now (1804) revised and made applicable 'to the circumstances of the present time'.[12] Similarly, the new Highway Regulations of 1801,[13] though they did not alter the statutory dimensions of public roads in the island,[14] consolidated and systematized the business of repair, upkeep, and responsibility for these. In 1801, also, it was found that punishment of burning in the hand 'in clergyable offences' was not only 'often ineffectual, and disregarded by hardened offenders', but was sometimes 'too severe and ignominious'.[15] This, plus the provision that coroners were in duty bound to hold inquests as soon as possible,[16] indicates that, even within the plantocracy, the Humanitarian Revolution was producing significant alterations in the

[1] *Laws*, Vol. V, pp. 176–7.

[2] ibid., p. 508. 'And whereas many proprietors suffer great inconvenience by being unable to procure arms and accoutrements, directed by law to be provided and kept for the white persons in their service and resident on their plantations. . . . Every proprietor . . . liable to pay deficiency, who shall be desirous of obtaining such arms . . . shall be entitled to receive from the island storekeeper a musket and bayonet, cartouch box and cross belts, for every white man which this or any other law shall oblige the said proprietor to keep on their, his or her estate. . . .'

[3] 40 Geo. III, c. 15 of 13 Dec. 1799; *Laws*, Vol. IV, pp. 39–43.

[4] 45 Geo. III, c. 17 of 18 Dec. 1804.

[5] 41 Geo. III, c. 10 of 11 March 1801.

[6] 43 Geo. III, c. 1 of 29 Oct. 1802.

[7] See *JAJ*, X, 566 of 11 March 1801.

[8] ibid., XII, 234–5 of 8 Dec. 1809; 51 Geo. III, c. 27 of 15 Dec. 1810; *Laws*, Vol. VI, pp. 76–8.

[9] 42 Geo. III, c. 16 of 10 Dec. 1801.

[10] 38 Geo. III, c. 24 (1797) and pp. 23–5, above.

[11] 41 Geo. III, c. 29 of 15 March 1801.

[12] 45 Geo. III, c. 18 of 18 Dec. 1804.

[13] See 41 Geo. III, c. 14 of 11 March 1801; *Laws*, Vol. IV, pp. 119–38.

[14] The statutory dimensions were as follows: width in standing wood, 60 feet; width, wood on one side only, 40 feet; width, open ground, 24 feet (Long, *History*, Vol. I, p. 467).

[15] 42 Geo. III, c. 18 of 10 Dec. 1801; *Laws*, Vol. IV, p. 302.

[16] 41 Geo. III, c. 13 of 11 March 1801; and pp. 292–3, above.

stereotype. Even so critical a person as Coke, writing of the period 1800 to 1808, thought he noticed a wind of change.[1]

But these changes, especially in the most crucial area of slavery, were to be gradual. As a Committee of the House declared in 1817:

Every view, which [we] can take of the present and future condition of the slave population, confirms [us] in [the] opinion, that the improvement of their religious, moral, and civil state can only be effected by *gradual* and progressive measures, and that any experiments, which have a tendency to produce a sudden change in their present state, by the introduction of principles which are unknown to, and inconsistent with, the policy of colonial institutions, and the habits of the slaves themselves, would be as fatal to them as dangerous to the security of the island. . . .[2]

In terms of the colonial/creole complex as described in this study, no more could have been expected. Action to alter the basis of the society and the disposition of its two main cultural groups in relation to each other could have come only from some new positive move (probably revolution by the slaves) by one or other of them. The action by the British Government in 1833–4 in emancipating the slaves, in a sense removed that possibility, so that the slaves entered free society with their cultural relationship to white society practically unaltered. Creolization, in this sense, was an aspect of white control and the Assembly's function was, in the final analysis, to express this, ensure this, and perpetuate it. Its record, within this context, was most impressive. When, in 1865, it felt it could no longer function as an effective expression of the society, when, in other words, creole society as established during slavery at last began to crack and transform itself into new patterns and alignments—the white Establishment destroyed itself. But even this was a political and colonial event, not a creole and cultural one. The initiative remained with the whites, not with the ex-slaves. Why this should have been so, and why the society did not disintegrate after Emancipation and after 1865, is a question that still remains to be considered. It is being suggested here that an 'answer' lies in the nature of the black/white acculturative process that this study has tried to explore.

[1] Coke, *History*, pp. 294, 340.   [2] *JAJ*, XIII, 181 of 9 Dec. 1817, my italics.

19

CREOLIZATION

THE single most important factor in the development of Jamaican society was not the imported influence of the Mother Country or the local administrative activity of the white élite, but a cultural action—material, psychological and spiritual—based upon the stimulus/response of individuals within the society to their environment and—as white/black, culturally discrete groups—to each other. The scope and quality of this response and interaction were dictated by the circumstances of the society's foundation and composition—a 'new' construct, made up of newcomers to the landscape and cultural strangers each to the other; one group dominant, the other legally and subordinately slaves. This cultural action or social process has been defined within the context of this work as creolization. Mrs. Duncker has described it, in general terms in so far as it affected white settlers and visitors:

Although there were some people who came to the West Indies and refused to conform, the power of the society to mould new-comers was strong. However oddly constructed West India society might appear in England, for the English people coming to the West Indies it was only a short time before they were caught up in the system. J. B. Moreton observed of men from other countries when they became inured to the West Indies, 'how imperceptibly like wax softened by heat, they melt into their manners and customs'. Perhaps it was because the standards were laxer than in the society from which the newcomers came that they were so easy to acquire. Even a strong willed person faced with . . . loneliness, heat and probable fever would find it hard to resist the consolations of the island. A man like William Knibb forearmed against the life of the island by a positive creed, recognized the compelling force of constant use. When he arrived he said 'I have now reached the land of sin disease and death, where Satan reigns with awful power and carries multitudes captive at his will'. Four years later he said of slavery: 'I am fearful of becoming habituated to its horror; sincerely do I hope I never may.'[1]

[1] Duncker, op. cit., pp. 231–2.

Maria Nugent must have said the same thing to herself when, after watching her dance with an (elderly) black slave, her hostesses broke down and cried from horror and outrage.[1] We are faced here with an obscure force, working upon an entire section of society, which makes them all conform to a certain concept of themselves; makes them perform in certain roles which, in fact, they quickly come to believe in. Those who could or would not perform were simply censored out of the situation.[2]

'. . . And as a stranger, allow me to advise you to adopt the opinion generally entertained by the white inhabitants of this country, which, though somewhat illiberal, is pretty true in fact; "that whenever you see a black face, you see a thief." '[3]

Marly now imperceptibly began to lose his former favourable opinion of the Negroes being a much calumniated race, and to resort to the one formed by persons daily conversant in their management, and which he had been advised to adopt, that when he saw a black face, he saw a thief.[4]

This alteration of perception, conformity to the stereotype, was an essential stage in Marly's creolization. Was it the influence of slavery that was responsible for this? Was it some factor in eighteenth-century Britain and Europe, creating this disposition in those who went or were sent overseas; to the overseas tropics?[5] Or was it the action of an as yet undiscovered 'law' which operates when groups or cultures come into contact with each other, the one in a 'superior', the other in an 'inferior' position? 'How', Boris Gussman has asked, speaking of modern Rhodesia,

can these primarily British settlers so readily align themselves with the forces of racial prejudice? How can they accept the pass law system, the segregation of residential areas, the many and varied restrictive practices that characterize the scene in Central Africa today? Why is their behaviour so different to our own?[6] Does the situation create the man or does man create the situation?[7]

A similar kind of pressure towards conformity (Anancy/De Bundo

---

[1] See p. 191, above.   [2] See pp. 106–7, above.
[3] Overseer to Marly in *Marly*, p. 36.   [4] *Marly*, p. 41.
[5] For some light on this, see Wylie Sypher, 'The West Indian as a "character" in the Eighteenth century'; *Guinea's Captive Kings*; Eldred Jones, *Othello's Countrymen* . . . (Oxford University Press, 1965); Curtin, *The Image of Africa*; Mannoni, op. cit.; Goveia, *Historiography*.
[6] Written before Britain's 'Immigration Problem'.   [7] Gussman, op. cit., p. vii.

were exceptions) operated also on the generality of slaves. The nature of their capture in West Africa, their transport, sale and 'seasoning' in the West Indies is crucial to an understanding of this.[1] Slaves in Jamaica came from a wide area of West Africa, within the period of this study, mainly from the Gold Coast and the Niger and Cross deltas.[2] They were an agricultural non-literate people, with a political and social background based on the tribe, the clan, and the village. They were uprooted from this context on capture, and further disorientated at the trading forts on the West African coast, on the ships of the 'middle passage', and when sold and distributed on their arrival in Jamaica. Creolization began with 'seasoning'—a period of one to three years, when the slaves were branded, given a new name and put under apprenticeship to creolized slaves.[3] During this period the slave would learn the rudiments of his new language and be initiated into the work routines that awaited him.

These work routines, especially for plantation slaves, were the next important step in creolization. Plantation work was so designed that a slave could become (had to become) identified with his work. Discontent and sense of loss were usually sublimated in this way, and with success at job-accomplishment, a certain pride in the work would most likely be developed. Acceptance of the conditions would also grow if conditions of work were comfortable—the acquisition of a house, a woman, a home, a plot of land. From this followed 'socialization'[4]—participation with others through the gang system, and through communal recreational activities such as drumming and dancing and festivals. From this would follow identification with the group (necessary for a man whose social culture was based on the clan), and with local symbols of authority—the proprietor, the overseer, the driver, the obeah-man—according to temperament or circumstance. Slaves, like most people wholly involved in agricultural or industrial routine, were also conservative, disliking, even fearing, change; becoming attached to places and/or persons with whom they had identified themselves.[5] For the docile there was also the persuasion of the whip and the fear of punishment; for the venal, there was the bribe of gift or compliment or the offer of a

[1] See, for example, *Equiano*, ed. Paul Edwards, pp. 15–32.
[2] Patterson, op. cit., p.143.
[3] Beckford, *Remarks*, p. 27; Edwards, op. cit., Vol. II (1819 ed.), pp. 155–6.
[4] Patterson, op. cit., 145–259, discusses this in detail.
[5] Long, *History*, Vol. II, p. 410; Beckford, *Account*, Vol. II, p. 323; *P.P.*, Vol. XCII (34), 1790–1, no. 745, p. 206 (Fitzmaurice); *A Short Journey*, Vol. I, pp. 67–8, 82–3; Lewis, op. cit. (1929 ed.), p. 196.

better position, and for the curious and self-seeking, the imitation of the master.

This imitation went on, naturally, most easily among those in closest and most intimate contact with Europeans, among, that is, domestic slaves, female slaves with white lovers, slaves in contact with missionaries or traders or sailors, skilled slaves anxious to deploy their skills, and above all, among urban slaves in contact with the 'wider' life. Any man, John Shipman, the Methodist missionary said, 'will soon see how the Negroes have acquired [the] knowledge [of civil affairs] by going into some companies' [sic].[1]

Their table is surrounded by domestic servants, especially in the country; where perhaps for want of other subjects, they introduce the favourite topic, the conduct of negroes, and their particular management of them. On these occasions every thing relative to them is freely discussed: the colonial laws, the observations made upon them at home, and in the public prints in this island, together with those instances that have occurred of trials before Magistrates, etc., respecting any violation of the laws. This being the real state of the case, can it be wondered at, that the negroes are increasing their knowledge of civil affairs? Don't we know that servants have got *eyes* and *ears* as well as ourselves? And that it is natural enough for them when they are chatting together, to rehearse the observations of their masters, when those have a particular reference to themselves?[2]

But knowledge of white society is one thing. Imitation of its mere externals is another. Certain aspects of this have already been discussed. But the examples given in Chapter 15, taking place within a still strong Afro-creole context, retained a certain vitality. The kind of charade described by Maria Nugent in 1801 is of a different order:

Then there was a party of actors— . . . a little child was introduced, supposed to be a king, who stabbed all the rest. They told me that some of the children who appeared were to represent Tippoo Saib's [sic] children, and the man was Henry the 4th of France— . . .[3]

'Monk' Lewis saw the same thing happening in 1816:

A play was now proposed to us, and, of course, accepted. Three men and a girl . . . made their appearance; the men dressed like the tumblers at Astley's, the lady very tastefully in white and silver, and all with their faces

[1] Shipman, 'Thoughts', MS. Second volume, p. 90, WMMS Archives, Box. B. 1. West Indies.
[2] ibid., pp. 90–1.   [3] *LNJ* (Cundall), p. 66.

concealed by masks of thin blue silk; and they proceeded to perform the quarrel between Douglas and Glenalvon, and the fourth act of 'The Fair Penitent'. They were all quite perfect, and had no need of a prompter. ... The first song was the old Scotch air of 'Logie of Buchan', of which the girl sang one single stanza forty times over. But the second was in praise of the Hero of Heroes. ... [1] It was not easy to make out what she said, but as well as I could understand them, the words ran as follows—

> Come, rise up, our gentry,
> And hear about Waterloo;
> Ladies, take your spy-glass,
> And attend to what we do;
> For one and one makes two,
> But one alone must be.
> Then singee, singee Waterloo,
> None so brave as he!

—and then there came something about green and white flowers, and a Duchess, and a lily-white Pig, and going on board of a dashing man of war; but what they all had to do with the Duke, or with each other, I could not make even a guess. ... [2]

It was one of the tragedies of slavery and of the conditions under which creolization had to take place, that it should have produced this kind of mimicry; should have produced such 'mimic-men'. But in the circumstances this was the only kind of 'white' imitation that would have been accepted, given the terms in which the slaves were seen; and it was this kind of mimicry that was largely smiled upon and cultivated by 'middle class' Jamaican (and West Indian) society after Emancipation. *The snow was falling in the canefields* became typical of the 'educated' West Indian imagination.

But it was a two-way process, and it worked both ways, as the anonymous author of *A Short Journey in the West Indies*[3] admitted in 1790.[4] The markets and the Army camps were the places of inter-racial concourse, despite efforts by the authorities to uphold the principle of 'apartheid'.[5] The Army favoured black recruitment, and accepted it under the egalitarian conditions of military discipline.[6] White civilian Jamaicans in Kingston were often shocked to see a

---

[1] Wellington.   [2] Lewis, op. cit. (1929 ed.), pp. 56–8.
[3] Loc. cit., p. 118, n. 1.
[4] 'The negroes that are already in the West Indies form a part of our society.' (*A Short Journey*, Vol. I, p. 87.)
[5] See p. 106, above.
[6] A. B. Ellis, op. cit., *passim*. There were, however, differences in pay (see n. 2, p. 161) and in chances of promotion.

black sergeant commanding a troop of white soldiers.[1] 'Sailors and Negroes', one observer asserted,[2]

are ever on the most amicable terms.[3] This is evidenced in their dealings, and in the mutual confidence and familiarity that never subsist between the slaves and the resident whites. There is a feeling of independence in their intercourse with the sailor, that is otherwise bound up in the consciousness of a bitter restraint, that no kindness can overcome; and, instead of sympathy, the white inhabitants very generally affect a supercilious personal superiority over them and the free people of colour. In the presence of the sailor, [however], the Negro feels as a man. . . .

In white households the Negro influence was pervasive, especially in the country areas:

Those, who have been bred up entirely in the sequestered country parts, and had no opportunity of forming themselves either by example or tuition, are truly to be pitied. We may see, in some of these places, a very fine young woman aukwardly dangling her arms with the air of a Negroe-servant, lolling almost the whole day upon beds or settees, her head muffled up with two or three handkerchiefs, her dress loose, and without stays. At noon, we find her employed in gobbling pepper-pot, seated on the floor, with her sable hand-maids around her. In the afternoon, she takes her *siesto* as usual; while two of these damsels refresh her face with the gentle breathings of the fan; and a third provokes the drowsy powers of Morpheus by delicious scratchings on the sole of either foot. When she rouzes from slumber, her speech is whining, languid, and childish. . . . Her ideas are narrowed to the ordinary subjects that pass before her, the business of the plantation, the tittle-tattle of the parish; the tricks, superstitions, diversions, and profligate discourses, of black servants, equally illiterate and unpolished.[4]

'They disdain', Long wrote in exasperation—almost in desperation —of young white mothers,

to suckle their own . . . offspring! they give them up to a Negroe or Mulatto wet nurse, without reflecting that her blood may be corrupted, or considering

[1] The Hon. Cttee. of Correspondence, 10 June 1809. See also Stewart, *View*, p. 157.
[2] James Kelly, *Voyage to Jamaica, and Seventeen Years' Residence in that island: chiefly written with a view to exhibit Negro Life and Habits* . . . 2nd. ed. (Belfast, 1838), pp. 29–30.
[3] This is confirmed by books like *Tom Cringle's Log* (loc. cit., p. 226, n. 5, above). Bryan Edwards (Add. MS. 12413) relates an incident at Old Harbour where a ship's captain was killed in a 'fray' involving Maroons hunting a runaway. The slave challenged by the Maroons was defended by a party of sailors headed by the captain.
[4] Long, *History*, Vol. II, p. 279.

the influence which the milk may have with respect to the disposition, as well as health, of their little ones. . . .[1]

'Another misfortune', he continued,

is, the constant intercourse from their birth with Negroe domestics, whose drawling, dissonant gibberish they insensibly adopt, and with it no small tincture of their aukward carriage and vulgar manners; all which they do not easily get rid of, even after an English education, unless sent away extremely young.[2]

Maria Nugent made the same point

The Creole language is not confined to the negroes. Many of the ladies, who have not been educated in England, speak a sort of broken English, with an indolent drawling out of their words, that is very tiresome if not disgusting. I stood next to a lady one night, near a window, and, by way of saying something, remarked that the air was much cooler than usual; to which she answered, 'Yes, ma-am, *him rail-ly too fra-ish*'.[3]

To preserve the pure dialect of the tribe (at least of the females) planters had to send to England for governesses and practically locked their daughters away from Negro influence.[4] 'I have heard it observ'd as a fault of the white Inhabitants,' William Jones wrote in his *Diary*, 'that, instead of correcting the rude speech of the Negroes & better informing them, they descend so low as to join them in their Gibberish, & by insensible degrees almost acquire the same habit of thinking & speaking.'[5]

Many white creole ladies affected the kind of head-ties worn be their African slave women[6] and cleaned their teeth with 'chaw-stick[s]'.[7] As to food, Bryan Edwards, as he did in so many ways, showed himself the perfect creole:

To my own taste . . . several of the native growths, especially the chocho, ochra, Lima-bean, and Indian-kale, are more agreeable than any of the esculent vegetables of Europe. The other indigenous productions of this class are plantains, bananas, yams of several varieties, calalue (a species of spinnage), eddoes, cassavi, and sweet potatoes. A mixture of these, stewed with salted fish or salted meat of any kind, and highly seasoned with Cayenne-pepper, is a favourite olio among the negroes. For bread, an

[1] Long, *History*, Vol. II, p. 276.
[2] ibid., p. 278.   [3] *LNJ* (Cundall), p. 132. Italics in text.
[4] Long, *History*, Vol. II, p. 278.   [5] *Dairy of William Jones*, p. 16.
[6] Long, *History*, Vol. II, pp. 412–13.   [7] ibid., p. 271.

unripe roasted plantain is an excellent substitute, and universally preferred
to it by the negroes, and most of the native whites.[1]

At (white) dances, Stewart said,

Even if the music of the violins were better than it is, it would be spoiled
by the uncouth and deafening noise of the drums, which the negro
musicians think indispensable, *and which the dancers strangely continue
to tolerate.*[2]

And (this from Moreton)[3]

though a Creole was languishing on his death bed, I believe the sound of
the gumbay or violin would induce him to get up and dance till he killed
himself.

So necessary, in fact, had the Negro become, not only to the European's wealth, but to his vision of himself, that it was possible for the
Royal Gazette to print the following 'Satire';

> A West-Indian dandy (not Bond-Street alone
> Can claim the dear exquisite thing as its own)
> Stood fix'd by the Glass while the new suit displays,
> And all of its charms of stiff collars, short waists, and tight stays—
> 'Don't I look very well?' (here the mirror was eyed),
> 'Massa look like a lion,' a Negro replied.
> 'Where have you seen a lion?'—'Oh! me see it each day—
> Ah! there's its long ears—it is coming this way.'
> One moment the beau turn'd away from the glass,
> Look'd back, and beheld his resemblance—an Ass.[4]

But it was in the intimate area of sexual relationships that the
greatest damage was done to white creole apartheid policy and where
the most significant—and lasting—inter-cultural creolization took
place.[5] Black mistresses made convenient spies and/or managers[6] of
Negro affairs, and white men in petty authority were frequently
influenced in their decisions by black women with whom they were
amorously, or at any rate sensually, connected.

Saturday morning between five and six o'clock, the negro girl named
Prancer, came to Golden Spring hot house, with four others; after making
the strictest examination, they were dismissed, conceiving their complaints
frivolous, and that they were by no means eligible objects of admission.

[1] Edwards, op. cit., Vol. I, p. 255.   [2] Stewart, *View*, p. 207, my italics.
[3] Op. cit., p. 105.   [4] *R.G.*, XLII. 45, 18.   [5] Curtin, *Two Jamaicas*, p. 18.
[6] Marsden, op. cit., p. 8.

The next morning the mother of Prancer, named Fanny, brought her daughter, as related by Mr. Kelly . . . and with the most insolent and unbecoming gestures and language, did publicly accuse me of dismissing her daughter from the hot house (knowing her to be sick), *from revenge and disappointment*. After waiting some little time in hopes that Mr. Kelly as Overseer, would conceive notice of Fanny's improper conduct, but being myself disappointed, I applied to him demanding redress, when Mr. Kelly said he would punish her till I was satisfied. On Monday evening . . . I did ask if he had forgot or had intentionally omitted, punishing Fanny as to his promise. . . .[1]

Dr. Cumming, the complainant here, had underestimated Fanny's influence. In 1817, an irate slave owner complained to the Kingston Common Council in the following terms:

Sir—

I feel it necessary to complain to you of the conduct of the Overseer or Supervisor of the Kingston Workhouse. A Negro woman belonging to me named Diana was sent into the Workhouse by Mr. B. Williams as a punishment for frequent running away—but instead of being worked she was taken into the Overseer's House and when I sent my Overseer and Bookkeeper at different times to take her out, she refused to return, and she further told many of my negroes that she was very comfortable, and that they need not be afraid of the Workhouse. . . .[2]

But it was at the book-keeper or 'walking buckra'[3] level that black/white contact was most revealing and most mutually accepted:

On Wednesday an indictment, against Robert Edmeston, late bookkeeper on Cardiff-Hall estate, in the parish of St. Thomas in the East, was tried, for an assault committed by him, under circumstances, as the Attorney General stated, of the most unusual ferocity. . . . There were four counts in the indictment, the first and third accusing the prisoner with having assaulted and wounded two female slaves, Jane Murphy and Susannah Baxter . . . with a razor fastened to a stick, with intent to kill. The other two counts charged him with committing the assault and inflicting the wounds. . . .

Mr. Ward:— Knows the prisoner; he was a bookkeeper on Cardiff Hall estate with him; knows Jane Murphy and Susannah Baxter; recollects Edmeston coming to the estate on the 9th February in the forenoon, between twelve and one o'clock; witness went up to the overseer's house, where he saw prisoner, and took a little weak rum and water with him,

---

[1] *Daily Advertiser*, 21 June 1790.   [2] K.C.C. Minutes, 1815–1820: 6 June 1817.
[3] *Marly*, p. 45.

when he returned to the still-house, where his particular duty was; in a few minutes he heard a great noise, and saw a negro running out, when he hastened to the house, and found prisoner and Jane Murphy engaged with each other in a scuffle, the former having a knife or razor, and a musket with fixed bayonet. On witness entering, prisoner made an attempt at him, or one of the negroes who accompanied him, with the musket, but Jane Murphy seizing hold of the butt, thrust the point to the ground.... Murphy had been in habits of intimacy with prisoner.—Recollects that he was disturbed one night by her noise, and when he inquired what was the matter, she replied that Edmeston would not let her get her clothes.[1]

But it was common for all ranks of white society to have black mistresses. As Moreton, who tended, though, to exaggerate in these matters, said:[2]

It is quite common for an attorney to keep a favourite black or mulatta girl on every estate, which the managers are obliged to pamper and in-indulge like goddesses. Tom Coldweather, a gentleman in Spanish-Town, was attorney for about forty plantations, and had thirty or forty doxys of this kind in keeping: I suppose each flattered the debauchee that they waited chaste for his coming....

The visible and undeniable result of these liaisons was the large and growing coloured population of the island, which, in its turn, acted as a bridge, a kind of social cement,[3] between the two main colours of the island's structure, thus further helping (despite the resulting class/colour divisions) to integrate the society. Even the whippings and the more subtle reported cruelties of some of the clearly neurotic white women[4] were, in a sense, admissions of this interaction which, as the 'mulatto culturalists' hold,[5] must have had not only physical, but metaphysical effects as well. The development of creole society in Jamaica must be seen within this context and dimension.

[1] *R.G.* (1816), XXXVIII, 34, 11.   [2] Op. cit., p. 77.
[3] See Long, *History*, Vol. II, p. 333, and M. C. Campbell, op. cit., *passim.*
[4] 'the clergyman's wife at Port Royal was a remarkable cruel woman; she used to drop scalding hot sealing wax on her Negroes, after having punished them by flogging. ...' (*P.P.*, Vol. XCII, *Accounts and Papers*, 1790–1 (34), no. 746, p. 152.)
'I have seen several Negro girls at work with ... needles in the presence of their mistresses, with a thumb screw upon their left thumb, and I have seen the blood gush out from the end of them.' (ibid., p. 180.)
[5] Especially J. A. Crow, 'An Interpretation of Caribbean Society through Literature', in *The Caribbean at Mid-Century*, ed. A. C. Wilgus (University of Florida Press, 1951), p. 243. See also Gilberto Freyre, *The Masters and the Slaves*; and *The Race Factor in Contemporary Politics* (University of Sussex, 1966); Wilson Harris, *Palace of the Peacock* (London, 1960), esp. p. 40. 'Mulatto culturalists' are essentially concerned with the integration of the society.

20

CONCLUSION

CREOLIZATION, then, was a cultural process that took place within a creole society—that is, within a tropical colonial plantation polity based on slavery. As a colonial polity, the island was attached to and dependent on the British raj for its economic well-being, its protection and (from the point of view of the whites), its cultural models. The American Revolution, which took place at the beginning of the period under discussion, isolated the island from any chance of a wider or alternative British American development, possibly leading to constitutional independence, and placed the island firmly within the mercantilist spider-web operating from the Mother Country. This isolation and these restrictions, along with what, in this study, has been nominated the 'Humanitarian' Revolution, gave an impetus to the creolization of the society—though even here, except socially, development continued to be limited by the colonial relationship.

These social 'creole' developments within the society, however, were more substantial, and from the point of view of the future of the island, more important, than they have generally been given credit for by writers of the island's history who, in the main, have been concerned with the mercantilist and colonial aspects of its economy and constitution. If the assumption is that Jamaica was a mere declining appendage of Great Britain from the seventh decade of the eighteenth century, and, what is more, if it is assumed that its own internal structure and body was, at best, a parody of the metropolitan, at worst, a disorganized, debased and uncreative polity, then of course the picture of Jamaica as drawn, say, by Moreton,[1] Ragatz,[2] Pitman[3] and Patterson[4] emerges.

It has been the burden of this investigation, on the other hand, to demonstrate that this assumption is based on a partial appreciation of the achievements of the island. This study has attempted to show

---

[1] Op. cit., pp. 104–6, 108, 129–32, 160, 161.
[2] *Fall*, Chapter I, esp. pp. 5, 27, 28, 33, 34.   [3] *The Development*, p. 41.
[4] Op. cit., pp. 9, 10, 34, 41, 42, 51.

that despite the imitation, despite the inefficiency, despite debasements caused by slavery, Jamaica was a viable, creative entity during the period of this study; that rather than being a loose 'collection of autonomous plantations'[1] it had developed, from the beginning of its history, an Establishment of governmental and social institutions capable not only of organizing and controlling life within its territory, but comparable, in many ways (at least up to the American Revolution), to similar institutions on the mainland of British North America. The success and failure of white Jamaica should be seen as much from within the context of these local creole institutions as from the more familiar and traditional colonial point of view.

Even more important for an understanding of Jamaican development during this period was the process of creolization, which is a way of seeing the society, not in terms of white and black, master and slave, in separate nuclear units, but as contributory parts of a whole. To see Jamaica (or the West Indies generally) as a 'slave' society is as much a falsification of reality, as the seeing of the island as a naval station or an enormous sugar factory. Here, in Jamaica, fixed within the dehumanizing institution of slavery, were two cultures of people, having to adapt themselves to a new environment and to each other. The friction created by this confrontation was cruel, but it was also creative. The white plantations and social institutions described in this study reflect one aspect of this. The slaves' adaptation of their African culture to a new world reflects another. The failure of Jamaican society was that it did not recognize these elements of its own creativity. Blinded by the need to justify slavery, white Jamaicans refused to recognize their black labourers as human beings, thus cutting themselves off from the one demographic alliance that might have contributed to the island's economic and (possibly) political independence. What the white Jamaican élite did not, could not, would not, dare accept, was that true autonomy for them could only mean true autonomy for all; that the more unrestricted the creolization, the greater would have been the freedom. They preferred a bastard metropolitanism—handed down to the society in general after Emancipation—with its consequence of dependence on Europe, to a complete exposure to creolization and liberation of their slaves.

Blinded by the wretchedness of their situation, many of Jamaica's

[1] Patterson, op. cit., p. 70.

slaves, especially the black élite (those most exposed to the influence of their masters), failed, or refused, to make conscious use of their own rich folk culture (their one indisputable possession), and so failed to command the chance of becoming self-conscious and cohesive as a group and consequently, perhaps, winning their independence from bondage, as their cousins in Haiti had done. 'Invisible', anxious to be 'seen' by their masters, the élite blacks and the mass of the free coloureds (apart from the significant exceptions already discussed within the body of this work, and those who, after Emancipation, were to establish, against almost impossible odds, the free villages and small peasantries of rural Jamaica),[1] conceived of visibility through the lenses of their masters' already uncertain vision as a form of 'greyness'—an imitation of an imitation. Whenever the opportunity made it possible, they and their descendants rejected or disowned their own culture, becoming, like their masters, 'mimic-men'.[2]

The crucial test for the society came with the American Revolution. Had there not been the physical and psychological barriers between master and bondsman as had developed as a result of the nature of slavery in the New World, it might have been possible for the Jamaican politicians to present a more united and positive front to British mercantilism than was in fact possible or was felt to be necessary. Had the white creole élite not demeaned itself by debasing its labour-force it might have been possible for British European culture to have made a more radical contribution than it did to the process of creolization, and a Jamaican 'identity' with deeper white Anglo-Saxon Protestant foundations might have been the result. As it was, the white contribution to Jamaica remained structural only, and resulted, because of its prestige position in relation to the mass, in the formation of a cultural dichotomy.

A second opportunity for social and cultural integration presented itself at Emancipation. But here again the physical and psychological barriers proved to be insurmountable. When, by 1865, the white élite admitted failure and, still refusing to co-operate with the black masses, accepted (and were made to accept) the knock of the British

---

[1] For this, see Douglas Hall, *Free Jamaica*; G. E. Cumper, op. cit., pp. 37–86.
[2] This condition has been observed by several West Indian novelists. See, among others, George Lamming, *Of Age and Innocence* (1958); Andrew Salkey, *The Late Emancipation of Jerry Stover* (1968); Neville Dawes, *The Last Enchantment* (1960); Orlando Patterson, *An Absence of Ruins* (1967); V. S. Naipaul, *The Mimic Men* (1967); Garth St. Omer, *Shades of Grey* (1968). (All publications London.)

imperial hammer,[1] colonial forms, in the descendant since 1728, rushed back in to fill the void created by the failure of the creole élite, and the society became even more estranged from itself and from its several parts. The result was a further widening of the gap between colonial and metropolitan, colonial and creole, between élite and the mass of the population; and post-Emancipation industrial and political development in Europe and America have further retarded the possibility of creole autonomy.[2]

Whether it can or will continue to survive in these terms is another matter. Jamaican society has in common with all other societies, one assumes, a natural built-in drive or gravitational tendency towards cultural autonomy. Cultural autonomy demands a norm and a residential correspondence between the 'great' and 'little' traditions within the society. Under slavery there were two 'great' traditions, one in Europe, the other in Africa, and so neither was residential. Normative value-references were made outside the society. Creolization (despite its attendant imitations and conformities) provided the conditions for and possibility of local residence. It certainly mediated the development of authentically local institutions, and an Afro-creole 'little' tradition among the slave 'folk'. But it did not, during the period of this study, provide a norm. For this to have been provided, the Euro-creole élite (the one group able, to some extent, to influence the pace and quality of creolization) would have had to have been much stronger, culturally, than it was. Unable or unwilling to absorb in any central sense the 'little' tradition of the majority, its efforts and its continuing colonial dependence merely created the pervasive dichotomy which has been indicated in this study.

The presence of this dichotomy has led to the agnostic pessimism of writers like Derek Walcott, Orlando Patterson, and Vidia Naipaul. It has also led to the intellectual pessimism of the sociologists' formulation of the concept of 'the plural society' with its prognosis (Despres) of tension and violent conflict,[3] or negation (Smith):

[1] See F. R. Augier, 'The Passing of Representative Government in Jamaica in 1865', Dept. of History, Staff/Graduate Seminar Paper, [1965]; and 'Before and After 1865' in *New World Quarterly*, Vol. II, no. 2 (Croptime, 1966), pp. 21–40.

[2] For this, in their different ways, see J. J. Thomas, *Froudacity: West Indian Fables by James Anthony Froude, Explained* . . . (London, 1889); *Philosophy and Opinions of Marcus Garvey*, 2 vols., ed. Amy Jacques-Garvey (New York, 1923, 1926); Fanon, op. cit.; George Lamming, *The Pleasures of Exile* (London, 1960), esp. pp. 9–50.

[3] Leo A. Despres, *Cultural Pluralism and Nationalist Politics in British Guiana* (Chicago, 1967), esp. pp. 268–85.

It follows that interpretations of events by reference to one or another of these competing moral systems [white, brown, black] is the principal mode of thought that characterizes Jamaican society, and also that such sectional moralizations normally seek to define a negative, extrasectional and disvalued pole in contrast to a positive, intrasectional and esteemed one. Thus Jamaicans moralize incessantly about one another's actions in order to assert their cultural and social identity by expressing the appropriate sectional morality. For such self-identification, negation is far more essential and effective than is its opposite; hence the characteristic appeal of negativism within this society, and its prevalence.[1]

If 'negativism' is in fact a prevalent feature of contemporary Jamaican life, it can certainly not be predicted from the kind of socio-historical record set out in this study. My own reading of contemporary Jamaica, likewise, returns a much more positive signal than Smith's. The difference, perhaps, lies in the conceptual models being used. The classic plural society paradigm is based on an apprehension of cultural polarity, on an 'either/or' principle, on the idea of people sharing common divisions instead of increasingly common values. My own idea of creolization is based on the notion of an historically affected socio-cultural continuum, within which (in the case of Jamaica), there are four inter-related and sometimes overlapping orientations. From their several cultural bases people in the West Indies tend towards certain directions, positions, assumptions, and ideals. But nothing is really fixed and monolithic. Although there is white/brown/black, there are infinite possibilities within these distinctions and many ways of asserting identity. A common colonial and creole experience is shared among the various divisions, even if that experience is variously interpreted. These four orientations may be designated as follows: European, Euro-creole, Afro-creole (or folk), and 'West Indian'. (The 'East Indian' problem, since it introduces new complexities, and does not (yet) significantly relate to Jamaica, will not be unrolled here.)

The acceptance and continuation of the idea of a 'plural' society, with the consequences and assumptions already outlined, has been taken from Smith and absorbed into the bloodstream of West Indian

[1] M. G. Smith, *The Plural Society*, p. 175. For other contributions to the plural society debete, see, among others, H. Hoetink, 'The Concept of Pluralism as Envisaged by M. G. Smith', *Caribbean Studies*, Vol. VII (April 1967), no. 1, pp. 36–43; Malcolm Cross, 'Cultural Pluralism and Sociological Theory: A Critique and Re-evaluation', *SES*, XVII (Dec. 1968), no. 4, pp. 381–97; H. I. McKenzie, 'The Plural Society Debate . . .', *SES*, XV (March 1966), no. 1, pp. 53–60; and the papers and discussions in *Social and Cultural Pluralism in the Caribbean*, ed. Vera Rubin (New York, 1960).

thought by the last of the 'orientations' listed above—the educated middle class, most finished product of unfinished creolization; influential, possessed of shadow power; rootless (eschewing the folk) or Euro-orientated with a local gloss: Creo- or Afro-Saxons. For them the society is 'plural' in so far as it appears to remain divided into its old colonial alignments. They are 'West Indian' in that they are (or can be) critical of the colonizing power. But they are also dependent upon it. Unlike the Euro-creole élite, or the plantocracy of our period, they lack confidence, economic power, and the ability to create structures. In this sense, then, the concept of a 'plural society' would appear to be a colonial rather than a creole contribution. The creole society of the period of slavery did not conceive of itself as 'plural', but as made up of two *separate* (superior and inferior) cultures.

With political power now in the hands of the black majority of the population, it remains to be seen whether the society will remain conceived of as 'plural'—the historical dichotomy becoming the norm[1]—or whether the process of creolization will be resumed in such a way that the 'little' tradition of the (ex-)slaves will be able to achieve the kind of articulation, centrality, prestige and influence— assuming, that is, that it is not by now too debased—that will provide a basis for creative reconstruction. Such a base, evolving its own residential 'great' tradition, could well support the development of a new parochial wholeness, a difficult but possible creole authenticity.[2]

[1] See R. Dahrendorf, *Class and Conflict in Industrial Society* (1957; trans. London, 1959), esp. p. 289; John Beattie, *Other Cultures: Aims, Methods and Achievements in Social Anthropology* (London, 1964), 2nd ed. 1966, pp. 241–50.
[2] See Roger Bastide's chapter, 'Les Chemins de la Négritude' in *Les Amériques Noires*, pp. 217–31. For a light-hearted but penetrating account of the operation of the Afro-creole norm in Cuba, see Tony Harrison, 'Shango the Shaky Fairy', *London Magazine*, Vol. X (April 1970), no. 1, pp. 5–25.

PART FIVE

DOCUMENTATION

APPENDIX I

(*Ref. pp. 27, 28, above*)

OFFICES HELD BY MEMBERS OF THE JAMAICA ASSEMBLY IN
1787[1]

Hon. Samuel W. Haughton (*Hanover*)
    Speaker
    Lt.-Col. of Militia
    Magistrate, Clarendon Precinct
Wm. Mitchell (*St. Catherine*)
    Dep. Receiver-General
    Clerk of the Supreme Court
    Attorney at Law
    President of the St. Catherine Workhouse
    Magistrate, St. Catherine Precinct
    Captain of Militia
John Rodon (*St. Catherine*)
    Attorney at Law
    J.P., St. Catherine Precinct
    Magistrate, Clarendon Precinct
    Member of Vestry, St. Catherine
Phillip Redwood (*St. Catherine*)
    Barrister admitted to plead in Supreme Court
    Magistrate, St. Mary Precinct
    Captain of Militia
Robert Hibbert (*Kingston*)
    Magistrate, St. Mary Precinct
    Magistrate, Kingston
    Magistrate, St. George
    Captain (Artillery), Militia
John M'Lean (*Kingston*)
    J.P., Kingston
Archibald Galbraith (*Kingston*)
    J.P., Kingston
    Magistrate, St. Andrew
    Contractor for supplying H.M. ships with fresh beef

[1] Information for this Appendix compiled mainly from *Jamaica Almanack for 1788*.

Matthew Wallen (Port Royal)
    Colonel of Militia
William Gray (Port Royal)
    Magistrate, Port Royal
    Magistrate, St. George
Archibald Thomson (Port Royal)
    Magistrate, Port Royal
    Magistrate, St. Andrew
Hon. Wm. Jackson (St. Dorothy)
    Asst. Judge, Supreme Court
    Custos, Port Royal
    J.P., St. Catherine Precinct
    Major of Militia
Hon. John Grant (St. Dorothy)
    Chief Justice
    Magistrate, St. Catherine Precinct
    Ex-officio Trustee, Wolmer's Free School
Thomas Brooks (St. John)
    Magistrate, St. Catherine Precinct
    Magistrate, Port Royal
    Lt.-Col. of Militia
Joseph Woodhouse (St. John)
    Asst. Judge, Supreme Court
    Magistrate, St. Catherine Precinct
    Magistrate, Port Royal
    Major of Militia
Sir Charles Price (St. Thomas-in-the-Vale)
    Magistrate, St. Catherine Precinct
    Maj.-General of Militia
Henry Rennalls (St. Thomas-in-the-Vale)
    J.P., St. Catherine Precinct
    Lt.-Col. of Militia
Thomas Goldwin (Clarendon)
    Magistrate, Clarendon Precinct
William Thompson (Clarendon)
    J.P., St. Catherine Precinct
    Captain, Militia
Robert Richards (St. David)
    Barrister admitted to plead at the Supreme Court
    Magistrate, St. Thos.-in-the-East and St. David
    Magistrate, St. Mary Precinct
Benjamin Allen (St. David)
    J.P., Port Royal
    Magistrate for St. Thos.-in-the-East and St. David

Thos. Cockburn (St. Andrew)
  Attorney at Law
  Magistrate, St. Andrew
  Governor, St. Andrew's Free School
  Member of Vestry, St. Andrew
  Lt.-Col. of Militia
Hinton East (St. Andrew)
  Attorney at Law
  Judge-Advocate-General of Militia
George Murray (St. Elizabeth)
  Master in Ordinary
  Asst. Judge of Supreme Court
  Dep. Island Secretary (Sav. la Mar)
  Dep. Receiver-General (Sav. la Mar)
  Dep. Naval Officer (Sav. la Mar)
  Comptroller of Customs (Sav. la Mar)
  Quarter-Master-General of Militia
John Vanheelen (St. Elizabeth)
  J.P. for St. Elizabeth
  Captain of Militia
William Blake (Westmoreland)
  Asst. Judge, Supreme Court
  Magistrate, Westmoreland
John Lewis (Westmoreland)
  Asst. Judge, Cornwall Assizes
  Magistrate, Westmoreland
George Scott (Hanover)
  Asst. Judge, Cornwall Assizes
  Magistrate, Westmoreland
  Magistrate, Hanover
  J.P. for St. Elizabeth
Hon. Simon Taylor (St. Thos. in the East)
  Custos, St. Thos.-in-the-East and St. David
  Magistrate, St. Andrew
  Maj.-General of Militia
Sir Thomas Champneys (St. Thos. in the East)
  Magistrate, St. Thos.-in-the-East and St. David
  Major-Commandant (Artillery), Militia
  Superintendent of Forts (Windward)
Donald Campbell (St. George)
  Magistrate, St. Mary Precinct
  Magistrate, St. James
  Magistrate, St. George

Maj-General of Militia

Captain, Fort Frederick, St. James

Henry Shirley (St. George)

Magistrate, St. George

J.P. for St. Thos.-in-the-East and St. David

Charles Bernard, Jnr. (St. James)

Asst. Judge, Cornwall Assizes

Magistrate, St. James

George C. Barrett (St. James)

J.P. for St. James

J.P. for Trelawny

Second Cornet, Trelawny Horse Militia

James Irving (Trelawny)

Magistrate, Trelawny

Dep. Receiver-General (Montego Bay)

Major-Commandant and Superintendent for Cornwall Militia Artillery

Bryan Edwards (Trelawny)

J.P. for St. Mary Precinct

Hon. A. Fullerton (St. Ann)

Asst. Judge, Supreme Court

Commissioner for Affidavits, St. Ann

Custos, St. Ann

John Blagrove (St. Ann)

J.P. for Trelawny

Dr. Archibald Sympson (Vere)

Magistrate, Vere Precinct

Physician General of Militia

Hon. Richard Batty (Vere)

Master in Ordinary

Asst. Judge, Supreme Court

Member of Vestry, St. Catherine

Magistrate, St. Catherine Precinct

Custos, Vere

Lt.-Col. of Militia

Wm. Innes (Portland)

Magistrate, St. Thos.-in-the-East and St. David

Thos. Prince (Portland)

J.P. for Portland

Thos. Murphy (St. Mary)

Magistrate, St. Mary Precinct

Hon. Francis Dennis (St. Mary)

Asst. Judge, Supreme Court

Custos, St. Mary

APPENDIX II

(*Ref. p. 44, above*)
Jamaica Assembly: numbers voting 1774–1816, obtained from 'division' figures for the period. (Not all years cited.) All refs. *JAJ.*

Year								Reference	
1774	25	25	25					(VI.	506, 560, 570)
1775	23							(VI.	603)
1776	31							(VI.	662)
1777	29							(VII.	18)
1778	25	35	31	26	32			(VII.	70, 83, 88, 125, 129)
1779	25	34	30					(VII.	162, 171, 213)
1780	28	35	34	35	31			(VII.	249, 264, 269, 325, 336)
1781	24	25	29	23	21	28	27	(VII.	349, 385, 396, 403, 412,
	28								431, 433, 442)
1782	nil								
1783	22	24	33	28				(VII.	555, 606, 621, 646)
1784	23	37	26	23	27			(VIII.	23, 56, 88, 91)
1785	27	30	30	29	29	29	28	(VIII.	130, 149, 149, 151, 153,
	30	23	31						153, 156, 159, 167)
1786	37	35	31	34	26	24	24	(VIII.	189, 191, 211, 215, 241,
	23	22	28	24					245, 246, 252, 253, 258,
									259)
1787	38	38	28	34	39	39	39	(VIII.	272, 272, 273, 288, 292,
	39	38	32	33	28	33	35		292, 293, 293, 293, 301,
									301, 303, 319, 341)
1788	34	33	32	29	29	29	24	(VIII.	364/5, 365, 367, 373, 373,
	26	29	27	26	33	22	31		376, 376, 395, 407, 410,
	33	34	27	30	30	31	33		411, 415, 420, 421, 425,
	24	30	28	29	26				436, 452, 454, 461, 462,
									463, 476, 479, 480, 482,
									485)
1791	28	31	28	31	25	29	28	(IX.	10, 13, 17, 19, 43, 61, 62,
	28	28	23	27					62, 63, 64, 64)
1792	25	23	28	24	26	27	22	(IX.	81, 93, 101, 102, 109, 109,
	20	29	29	25	27	32	32		115, 121, 142, 142, 178,
	31	31	31						179, 186, 186, 186, 194,
									194)

1795 26 28 23 29 31 31 31 (IX. 385, 393, 405, 422, 423,
       29 31   423, 424, 428, 433)

1796 24 29 29 25 29 29 28 (IX. 445, 449, 450, 473, 473,
       34 30 26 29 30 31 34   474, 489, 513, 525, 525,
       33 35 28 29 32 30   533, 536, 541, 566, 580,
                                    580, 580, 598, 625, 628)

1798 21 26 27 27 28 26 33 (X. 155, 159, 165, 170, 215,
       33 33 33 30 30 30 30   220, 227, 229, 229, 229,
       29   249, 249, 249, 249, 249)

1800 24 24 25 27 26 22 22 (X. 446, 446, 452, 466, 467,
                                 470, 472)

1801 23 27 26 30 28 31 32 (X. 540, 567, 575, 611, 616,
                                 623, 641)

1802 27 27 33 32 32 33 32 (XI. 4, 20, 38, 38, 39, 41, 58)

1804 28 27 27 19 32 32 28 (XI. 180, 189, 252, 266, 271,
       29 27   273, 281, 282, 291)

1805 32 34 34 27 28 25 27 (XI. 353, 377, 377, 394, 407,
       25   408, 430, 430)

1807 20 22 29 23 22   (XI. 555, 558, 606, 608, 609)

1808 24 27 34 36 36   (XII. 9, 17, 26, 28, 29)

1810 26 30 27 31 32 31 31 (XII. 249, 251, 253, 255, 278,
       31 30 22 29   310, 315, 315, 320, 320,
                                 347)

1812 35 36 28 31 29 36   (XII. 449, 461, 468, 475, 477,
                                 485)

1814 31 32 30 33 29 29   (XII. 597, 599, 600, 605, 679,
                                 679)

1815 24 25 30 32 30 33 30 (XII. 694, 700, 721, 727, 735,
       29 31   745, 772, 781, 826)

1816 29 28 32 31 31 32 32 (XIII. 23, 27, 30, 32, 33, 34, 35,
       34 25 28 35 37 36 37   40, 41, 41, 41, 55, 55, 60,
       37 37 35 36 36 29 33   61, 61, 62, 62, 62, 65, 66,
       36 34 35 35   66, 78, 82, 82)

1819 29 31 32 22 30 29 35 (XIII. 331, 347, 347, 347, 376,
       30 32 32 32 32 31 32   380, 384, 389, 414, 414,
       30 30 27 27   414, 422, 423, 423, 423,
                                 424, 426, 426/7)

1820 35 31 26 26 32 31 35 (XIII. 430, 436, 440, 442, 458,
       33 37 34 33 33 31 31   469, 472, 479, 479, 498,
       37 36 36 35 33 35 35   498, 498, 498, 498, 503,
       21   505, 505, 506, 508, 525,
                                 526, 559)

APPENDIX III

(*Ref. p. 153*)

A GENERAL LIST OF THE NEGROES ON AND BELONGING TO THE
WORTHY PARK PLANTATION TAKEN THE 1ST JANUARY, 1789

MALES

	Names	*Qualifications*	*Condition*
	Quashie	Head Carpenter	Old & Infirm
	Mo Aleck	Carpenter	Infirm
	Hamlet	do.	Able
	London	do.	Old & Infirm
5	Anthony	do. & Cabinet Maker	Able
	Mo George	Carpenter	Subject to Sores and bone ach [*sic*]
	Cambridge	do., a Man Boy	Able
	Minute	do., but now old, infirm & a watchman	
	Adam	do., a Stout boy	Able
10	Mo Gardener	do. do.	do.
	Mo John	Blacksmith	Subject to bone ach [*sic*]
	Hampshire	do., a Man Boy	Able
	Mo Billy	Mason do.	do.
	Joe	do., learning	do.
15	Joan's Cudjoe	Head Sawyer & Plowman	Rhumatic
	Will	Sawyer, learning	Able
	Darby	Head Driver	Ruptured
	Guy Quashie ⎫ Creole Scotland ⎭	Under do.	Elderly
20	Pembroke	Head Muleman	Able
	Pool ⎫ Waller ⎪ Rippin ⎪ Sam ⎭	Head Boilers & in the Field occasionally	Elderly & Infirm
25	Nero	a Driver occasionally and in the Field	Elephantisas [*sic*]
	McGregor	Field & Boiler	Able
	McDonald	do. & Sugar Potter	do.

Names	Qualifications	Condition
McKein	Field & Sugar Potter	Able
Dryden	Carrys [sic] Grass	Elderly
30 Prussia	Field	Able
McKay	do. & Boiler	do.
Cumberland	do.	do.
McPherson ⎫		Weakly
McAllister ⎭	do. & distiller	Able
35 McLeod	do.	indifferent
McLean	do. & distiller	asthmatic
Toney	do.	Able
Tim: Cobina	do. & boiler	do.
Juba's Quashie	Head Wainman	do.
40 Dontcare	Wainman	Infirm
Maurice	Wainman	Able
W^m· Tom	do.	Old & Infirm
Ben^a: Cuffee	do.	Able
Cicily's Quamina	Field & Boiler	do.
45 Douglas Cuffee	do. & do.	do.
Worcester	Watchman	Infirm
Quaco Thombo	Field	Able, but a skulker
Venus Quaw	do.	Able
Ned	do.	do.
50 Coot	do.	do.
Robert	do. & boiler	do.
Philip	do.	Infirm
Pope	do.	Able & ill dispos'd
Italy	do.	do.
55 L. Anthony	do. & Wainman	Able
Adam	do. & do.	do.
Greenwich	do. & do.	do.
Fergus	do.	do.
Counsellor	do.	do.
60 May	do. & Wainboy	do.
Bossue	do.	do.
Spain	In the Garden	Subject to Sores
Punch	Field & distiller	Weakly
Germany	Watchman	do.
65 Portugal	Field	do.
Ishmael	good for nothing	[no entry]
Samson	Field	Weakly
L. Tom	Carrys [sic] water & Grass	Weakly
Jasper	Cattle Man	Able

Names	Qualifications	Condition
70 Eugene	[no entry]	full of Ulcers
Arthol	[no entry]	good for nothing
Penzance	Cook Great house	Infirm
Teckfords	Head Cattle Man	Old & Infirm
Mo Willmeck	Second do.	Able
75 Timothy	with do.	Old & Infirm
Cre: C: Cuffee	Field	a sad Runaway
Falmouth	Watchman	Infirm
Quas: Prapra	makes Pads	Old & Infirm
Will Morris	Doctor's Assistant	Able
80 Boot Cudjoe	Head Watchman	Elderly
Robin	do.	do.
Mingo	do.	do.
Peter	[no entry]	very Old & Infirm
Cor. Scotland	Watchman	Elderly
85 Withy· Tom	do.	do.
Mercury	do.	do.
Yaw	do.	do.
Wakefield	do.	do.
Hopkins	do.	do.
90 Frank	do.	do.
Hannibal	do.	do.
Boston	do.	do.
Titus	do.	do.
Stephen	do.	Lame on one Leg
95 Somerset	do.	distempered
Bristol	do.	do.
Julius	do.	Elderly
Dickie	do.	distempered
York	Field	Elderly
100 Fletcher	Watchman	do.
Johnstone	Watchman	Subject to Fits
Bute	do.	Elderly
Windsor	do.	distempered
Homer	do.	Lame
105 Tim	do.	very Old
Villain	Field	Subject to Fits
Solomon	[no entry]	Subject to bone ach [*sic*]
October	[no entry]	Able
Harry	[no entry]	do.
110 McBean	Greathouse	do.

Names	Qualifications	Condition
M° Davy	with Cattle	do.
Duncan	Field	do.
Ralph	do.	do.
Mutton	do.	do.
115 Fondling	with Cook at Greathouse	do.
Emanuel	Field	do.
M° Dick	looks after Stock	do.
Andrew	Field	do.
Boy	[no entry]	bad feet good for nothing
120 Green	Field	Able
Donald	a Sad Runaway	do.
Bob	with Cattle	Subject to bone ach [*sic*]
Strap	do.	[no entry]
Martin	[no entry]	[no entry]
125 Dennis	Field	Able
Qua^n. Charles	Yaws	[no entry]
Cupid	do.	[no entry]
Sambo John	Overseers	Able
Ireland	Field	do.
130 Richmond	Carrys [*sic*] hogmeat	do.
L. Sam	Yaws	
Mars	Field	Able & ill disposed
Oxford		
Wapping		
135 Winter		
Ketto		
Isaac		
Joseph		
Beckford		
140 York		
Robert		
Scipio	Young & healthy	[no entry]
Warwick		
Frank		
145 L. Kent		
Duke		
Guy		
Prince		
John Maurice		
150 Little Peter		

Names	Qualifications	Condition
Cyrus		
Trash		
Rodney	Young & healthy	[no entry]
William		
155 Polydore	[no entry]	[no entry]
Lambert	[no entry]	[no entry]
Newell	[no entry]	[no entry]
Abraham	[no entry]	[no entry]
Strafford	Field	Able
160 Stepney	fowlhouse	Infirm
Hob	watches	Lame in one hand
Vulcan	Cooper	Able

FEMALES

Grace	Driver to the small gang	Elderly
Badday	Field	Able
Emma	do.	do.
Cre. Betty	do.	Old & weakly
5 Rachel	do.	Able
Delia	do.	Elderly
Betty Madge	having many young children	do's no work
Empress	Field	Able
Lilly	do.	Sickly
10 Bessie	do.	Able
Bella	do.	do.
Sickie	do.	Sickly
Big Mirtilla	do.	Elderly
Little Mirtilla	do.	Able
15 Flora	do.	do.
Sarah	do.	do.
Ellen	do.	do.
Little Bess	do.	do.
Becky	do.	do.
20 Suckie	do.	do.
Cre. Cuba	Yaws house	Old & weakly
Agnes	Stockhouse	Sickly
Venus	[no entry]	Old & weakly
Diligence	[no entry]	do.
25 Dido	[no entry]	do.
Juba Lilly	Field	Weakly
Ann	do.	Able

Names	Qualifications	Condition
Amaryllis	do.	do.
Phibba	do.	do.
30 Pomelia	do.	do.
Yellow Cuba	do.	Old & weakly
Lady	do.	Able but a Runaway
Dorothy	do.	Elderly
Clair	do.	Able
35 Phillis	do.	do.
Present	do.	do.
Jean	do.	unhealthy
Judy	do.	Able
Chloe	do.	of little use
40 Con° Betty	do.	Elderly Runaway
Christⁿ Grace	Field	Able
Succuba	do.	do.
Juliett	do.	do.
Love	do.	Weakly
45 Pheba Girl	do.	Able, but a sad skulker
Pallas	do.	Weakly
Charlotte	do.	do.
Esther	do.	Able
Strumpet	do.	do., but a Skulker
50 Gipsey	do.	do.
Little Yabba	do.	Lame
Little Benneba	do., but a worthless Runaway	
Whore	do.	do.
Cicily	do.	Able
55 Abba	Field Cook	lost one hand
Dolly	Field	Infirm
Clementina	do.	Able
Abba Moll	[no entry]	full of Sores
Lucretia	Superintends Great h°.	Old
60 Franky	at do.	Sickly
Joany	do.	Able
Mary	do.	Elderly
Harodine	Overseers h°.	Able
Fogo	do.	do.
65 Counsellor Cuba	do.	Old & weak
Juba	Washer	do.
Jenny	do.	Able
Pruc	do.	do.

Names	Qualifications	Condition
Susannah	Washer Great house	Elderly
70 Cimbrey	Nurse at the Hott hᵒ	do.
Henrietta	Assist. to do.	Able
Molly		good for nothing
Little Kelly	Field	Able
Prudence	do.	do.
75 Princess	do.	do.
Eve	do.	Sickly
Queen	do.	Able
Woman	do.	do.
Penny	do.	do.
80 Lucinda	Field	Able
Daphne	do.	do.
Sally	do.	do.
Eddie	do.	do.
Countess	do.	do.
85 Margaretta	do.	do.
Behaviour	do.	do.
Sambo Sally	do.	do.
Emmy	do.	do.
Hannah	do.	do.
90 Lucy	do.	do.
Parthenia	do.	do.
Little Agnis	do.	do.
Mᵒ Peggy	Overseers house	Healthy
Belinda	Field	[no entry]
95 Sucky		
Juno		
Cre. Sue		
Clair's Joan		
Rose		
100 Little Rachel		
Elsie		
Melia		
Judy	Young and healthy	
Friendship		
105 Phoeba		
Calistra		
Tency		
Kitty		
Mᵒ Patty		
110 Joan's Molly		

Names	Qualifications	Condition
Lewey		
Violet		
Nellie		
Cynthia	Young and healthy	
115 Helena		
Diana		
Ann		
Little Abba		
Amelia		
120 Maxie		
Spr^g. Gard^n: Juliet		
Quad^n Nancy	Young children	
do. Nellie		
Lizette		
125 Mary's Molly		
Constantia		
Douglas		
Benney		
Baddu		
130 Luida's Nancy		
Jugg		
Fushabah		
Silvia		
Marowttah		
135 Cre. Bennebah		
Cor: Cuba		
Hersey	Old & infirm	
Old Cicily		
Withy^{wd}. Abba		
140 Maria		
Old Venus		
Dido		
Kelly		
Quashebah		
145 Peggy Nanny		
Olive		
Old Lucy		

APPENDIX IV

(Ref. p. 224)
TANGE LANGE JENNY
(Translation)

Dancing, erect, tall Jenny,
The girl ever of the calling spirits
Who greet her;
The girl he is waiting to greet,
Dead mama,
All the dead call to greet her.

Dancing, erect, tall Jenny,
Ever walking tall and erect,
Dead mama,
The person all the dead call to greet
Like clean water of the dead, this girl,
Clean, clear water, dead mama,
Oh what a day of the gods
When this girl is greeted by the dead
Who love her,
This girl loved by the dead
Who all greet her.
They who all come, erect,
Greeting her,
Who would like to carry her away with them,
Even Manuka of the calling spirits
Comes to greet her.

Dancing, erect, tall Jenny,
Ever dancing so erect and tall,
Dead mama,
Jenny, mama, the erect tall girl.
Ah, the clean, erect tall girl,
Dead mama.

The girl of the Gaws
Whom all the calling dead spirits come to greet.
The girl like clean clear water,
Dead mama.
Hailed by the watching dead.
The girl who ever dances.
So erect and tall,
Dead mama,
This wonderful, all-spirits-attracting girl,
Whom they greet.
All watching this girl of the spirits,
This erect, tall girl,
Dead mama,
Jenny, erect, tall Jenny,
The girl who always dances so erect and tall,
Dead mama,

So clean and clear.
The ancestral spirits who come
From the Mondungo, Gaw, Madinga nations,
Dancing erect and tall,
Dead mama,
Greet big Jenny, the great, erect, tall dancer,
Dead mama.

Dancing, erect, tall Jenny,
The girl who is ever greeted
By all the calling spirits,
This Madonga girl, so big and clean,
Who dances so sweetly, erect and tall,
Dead mama,
Greetings to my Jenny are coming
From all the calling dead spirits,
Even you now, dead mama,
Are calling my Jenny,
Joining with all the great calling spirits,
This girl who dances so erect and tall,
Dead mama,
The dancing, great, tall, calling
Ancestral spirit, Manuka Vola,
Is dancing erect and tall,
Dead mama,

With this clean, beloved girl,
Big Jenny, the beloved,
Of even the greatest calling spirits
Who greet her as she dances, erect and tall,
With the greatest of ancestral calling spirits, Manuka,
Receiving greetings from all the calling dead
Who greet her.

(Moore, op. cit., pp. 175–6.)

APPENDIX V

(*Ref. p. 256, above*)
A CONVERSATION ON MARRIAGE

I

Missionary: Well Quacco it is now three weeks since you and I had a serious and I hope profitable conversation on your marrying Quasheba. I trust that you have been following the advice I then gave you and that you now see more clearly the path of duty and are fully disposed to walk in it.

Quacco: I do as you tell me, Massa. I think about it. I pray about it.

Missionary: Stop Quacco! What hurry! I have wished to have a little serious Conversation with you for some time, but you always get out of the way as soon as you see me, as if you suspected that I wanted to talk with you about some subject of which you are ashamed. You are now at liberty and I hope you will listen to me a few minutes.

Quacco: O no Massa! Me no ashamed to talk with you. Why me ashamed to do so, Massa? You say nothing to aw-we but for our good.

M.: True, Quacco. This is what we aim at always; but then when people are living in bad practices they do not like to hear that which is good.

Q.: I hope, Sir, you do not think I am guilty of bad practices. My owner knows that I am an honest, industrious and faithful slave; and if you ax the negroes on the Estate they will all of them tell you, Sir, that I would not hurt the feather of a fowl.

M.: All that you say, Quacco, may be very true and I dare say it is so. Your Master speaks well of you and the people on the property give you a good character: but then you know we have a Master Who is in heaven! and although we may be living so as to give satisfaction to our fellow creatures and to ourselves, yet it is quite possible at the same time to be living in the neglect of those duties which we owe to God. . . .

Q.: But I do not neglect my God, sir. I have been Christened; and I say my prayers; and when I can get time I go to Church or Chapel.

M.: This also may be true but God looks for more than this. . . . You have sinful connexions with different women and the one that you profess to live with as your wife is not so for you have never been married to her. All this is wrong and will be the ruin of your soul if you die in your sins. . . . No fornicator shall enter into the Kingdom of heaven Gal. V. 19th and [the Lord] hath most solemnly assured us that they who do such things shall have their portion in the lake which burneth with fire and brimstone. . . .

Q.: If all this be true, Massa, God help poor negroe & plenty beside he.

M.: It is true, Quacco, I assure you. It cannot be otherwise for it is the Word of God and he cannot lye. . . .

Q.: Massa! I know & feel that it is wrong to go from home and I will not do it again. But I cannot marry Quasheba.

M.: Why not? She is a very respectable, well behaved, clean and industrious woman. I believe she loves you and she appears to have been very faithful to you. You have several children by her and I am sure their tidy and healthy appearance Especially on a Sunday, do her credit, and show her to be a good mother. . . .

Q.: But Massa! Why negroe for to marry? Negroe not fit. White people marry and that is good: but it no right for Negroe to marry! What he do with a married wife? Massa, me no hear of such a thing until Missionary come . . . Besides, Buccra have woman plenty without marry and he can read Book. . . . [Besides], Sir, you know we are both slaves and perhaps after marriage we may be separated and then you know, Massa, that would be a very painful thing. Perhaps in that case we might not see each other again and we could not take up with any body else after we had been married. Could we, Sir?

M.: No! certainly not. Nothing but death and adultery can separate married people. . . .

Q.: I wish to do right, Massa. I do wrong, I begin to see, long enough; but me Massa, negroe on the Estate very wicked and they make mock of we if we get married; and if I was to marry Quasheba, he would think too much of himself and not give me much satisfaction.

M.: You mean that *she* would think too much of *herself.* You should never say *he* for a woman nor *she* for a man. You frequently confuse strangers when they are talking to you by doing so. I understand your objection and particularly the latter part of it very well. You mean to say that if you were married your wife would not have the fear of your leaving her and taking up with another woman to keep her in subjection! But let me tell you that this is a most unmanly and unchristian mode of Reasoning and it is a reproach to any man to adopt it. I have always observed, Quacco, a disposition among negroe men who are not good Christians, to keep those with whom they live in a kind of brutal subjection and to view them more in the light of slaves than companions. All this however is contrary to the word of God and to the habits of christian men and Countries.

Woman it is true was made for man, but not that he might act towards her the part of a brute; nor that he might keep her in subjection by fear and violence. No, she was made for mans happiness, made as his equal—'a help meet for him' Gen. II. 20—and man is required not to rule over her with *fear* of any kind, much less with the base fear of leaving her in the way you mean, but in *love*. . . .

Q.: Massa give me a little time to think about it? Me begin to feel different about it since you talk with me so much.

M.: Certainly! I do not wish you hastily to decide upon so important a step. Think about it seriously; pray over it fervently; and talk to Quasheba about it affectionately; and may the blessing of God go with you! . . .

II

Quasheba: Good Morning, Massa. How dee? How Missis . . . & chilens?

M.: Thank you Quasheba, we are all *so so.* I have required you to be called in that I might have some conversation with you about . . . Quacco . . . I have had two or three serious conversations with him about his manner of living and the necessity of amendment, and as one of the first steps to this I have urged him to marry you directly. He, I am glad to say, has consented and has promised by the grace of God, to do better, but says that you wont listen to him. . . .

Quash: Massa, dont you believe him. He no mean to mend, Massa. He often say so and never become better but worser. You no no him Massa. He got woman every where. Massa, he run about too much too much. Ax Negroe on the Estate and them tell you . . . plenty about he, Massa. . . . He give all he got to dem women on the Estates, and he no care for me nor for he pickanees, not so much as so [*showing the end of her finger*]. Massa, me work hard for he! Me wash he clothes! Me mend 'em! Me get him victuals! Me bring up [him] pickanee well. Me raise plenty of stock & me take 'em to market and sell 'em! Me work in he negroe ground! Me make cassava bread! Massa, me do everything to please he and to give he satisfaction. Me work sometimes till second cock crow for he and he only abuse me, curse me, and sometimes lick me. . . .

Q. (*very angrily*)*:* Massa, she tell lye. Dont you—

M.: O Quacco, I am ashamed to hear you Express yourself in such a way and to see you yielding so much to passion. Quasheba's feelings are wrought up at the recollection of what she has often been called to suffer, and although perhaps every thing that she has said may not be true in the way that she has described it; yet you know that she has had just cause for the complaints which she has made. You ought to know that such a spirit as that which has just made its appearance in you, is quite contrary to the religion of Christ which I trusted that you was earnestly engaged in seeking. . . .

Q.: Massa! I ask you pardon. It was one bit of the devil that come into me heart & me no watch. I wont do it again, Massa. . .

M.: You do not I hope, Quasheba, object to marriage itself, but only to Quacco, in consequence of his past unkind conduct to you.

Quash.: O no Massa, me no object to marriage. Me think that is good, but me cannot marry Quacco. . . .

M.: There is no other man I hope that you like better, Quasheba? Do you feel love for him? and do you think that you could live happy with him if he was to change for the better and become a good Christian?

Quash.: Me no like any body like he. Me true with him since me a girl so [*lifting her hand to her chin*] and me have all me pickanees for him; and if he was to live a Christian life, I would wish to do the same and then, Massa, me should be happy.

M.: I am glad to hear thus much from you, Quasheba. Pray, how has he been going on for the last month? Have you had any of those causes for complaint of which you have been speaking . . . ?

Quash.: No Massa. He has been as if he was sick and cast down & this has made him steady. But Massa, me no think any ting about that! He do so before & turn back again.

M.: Allow me to say, Quasheba, that I do not think he was ever in that state of mind he is [in] now. He may have made attempts to mend, but then as he did not feel [the] need of God's help when he made them, they came to nothing. Now however I believe the Spirit of God is at work in his heart and he is going to make an effort by the strength & blessing of God to turn & find grace . . . Quacco? I hope that I am not saying more for you than I ought to say. You are I believe truly penitent for your sins to God: heartily sorry for your unkind treatment of Quasheba, and being 'strengthened with might by the Holy Spirit in your inner man', you are resolved to deny yourself of all ungodliness & worldly lusts & to live soberly and righteously in this present world.

Q. (*weeping*): I am, Massa, by the help of God.

M.: Quasheba? What do you say? I am glad to see you so much affected.

Quash. (*weeping*): Massa, I make friends with he now. I do as you tell me, and (*dropping a curtsey*) Massa I thank you and may God Almighty help you.

M.: Thanks be to God who is the author of peace & lover of concord. Now let me see you shake hands with one another, according [to] your plan of making friends. I could wish however to see you under such circumstances . . . *kiss* each other. This is a scriptural civilized & christian custom, practised as you know by the Whites. . . .

Q. & Quash.: Massa, we thank you. We will do as you tell us and may
   God reward you (*falling on their knees*) for your pains with all we.
M.: Oh! do not kneel to me but to God. It is an act of homage due to none
   but him. 'Come let us together worship, and fall down; and kneel
   before the Lord our Maker' . . .

Methodist Missionary Society Archives (London); Boxes, West Indies BI
(MS.): Series of Tracts for Slaves in the West Indies. 'A Conversation on
Marriage, Between Quacco the Head Driver and Quasheba his Companion
and the Missionary who visits the Estate.'
'By a Wesleyan Methodist Missionary.'

APPENDIX VI

(Ref. p. 258, above)

NEGRO SPIRITUAL

A good example of (the Christian) religion being seen and used as a fetish, may be seen in the American Negro spiritual, 'I got religion':

> Well, I know I got religion now
> So glad
> I know I got religion now
> So glad
> I know I got religion now
> So glad
> *The world can't do me no harm*

African concepts of the deity are present, also, in the second stanza of this spiritual:

> Meet me, Jesus, meet me
> Meet me in the middle of the air
> Meet me, Jesus meet me
> Meet me in the middle of the air
> If my wings should fail me, Lord
> I want to meet me with another pair
>
> 'Cause I know I got religion now
> So glad. . . .

APPENDIX VII

(*Ref. page 293*)

JAMAICAN SLAVE LAWS, 1770–1817

11 Geo. III, c. 3 (1770)
An act for remedying the inconveniences which may arise from the number of negro huts and houses, built in and about the town of St. Iago de la Vega, Port Royal and Kingston.

11 Geo. III, c. 6 (1770)
An act for raising and setting out parties for suppressing any rebellion in this island . . .
(Annual to 1784, renewed 1787, 1790, 1802.)

12 Geo. III, c. 14 (1771)
An act for the better order and government of the negroes, belonging to the negro-towns, and for preventing them from purchasing slaves; and for encouraging the said negroes to go in pursuit of runaway slaves . . .
(Also 17 Geo. III, c. 10 (1776), 21 Geo. III, c. 6 (1780) 28 Geo. III, c. 16 (1787).)

12 Geo. III, c. 15 (1771)
An act to repeal an act entitled 'An act for the more effectual preventing negroes and other slaves from deserting from their owners, and departing from this island in a clandestine manner; and to punish such persons as shall be aiding, assisting or abetting, such slaves in their escape'; and for the more effectual preventing negroes and other slaves from deserting from their owners . . .

14 Geo. III, c. 15 (1773)
An act to repeal an act entitled 'An act to prevent the enticing or inveigling of slaves from their possessors; and for the preventing the transportation of slaves by mortgagers and tenants for life and years . . .'; and to prevent the hiding, concealing, inveigling, detaining. knowingly harbouring, or employing, the slaves of others . . .
(Also 15 Geo. III, c. 23 (1774), 28 Geo. III, c. 23 (1787), 29 Geo. III, c. 2 (1788).)

14 Geo. III, c. 19 (1773)
An act to prevent negro and other runaway slaves from being harboured and entertained, by establishing a constant patrolling party in

each parish throughout the island; and to prevent slaves from being carried from this island by masters of ships and other vessels.
(Also 15 Geo. III, c. 23 (1774), 17 Geo. III, c. 29 (1776).)

15 Geo. III, c. 18 (1774)
An act for regulating the manumission of negro, mulatto or other slaves; and to oblige the owners to make provision for them during their lives.

16 Geo. III, c. 14 (1775)
An act to regulate the devises of negro, mulatto and other slaves, in wills.

17 Geo. III, c. 7 (1776)
An act to prevent improper levies being made on the negroes or other slaves of minors; and to regulate the sale of slaves taken on writs against persons who have only an estate for a term of years, or for their own lives, or for the lives of any other persons, in negro or other slaves.

18 Geo. III, c. 20 (1777)
An act to prevent masters of ships, and other vessels, from clandestinely carrying off this island negro and other slaves.

19 Geo. III, c. 5 (1778)
An act to repeal an act entitled 'An act for vesting runaway slaves, not claimed by proprietors within a certain time, in his majesty, to be employed in the service of the public'; and to direct how those slaves, now vested in his majesty by virtue of the said act, shall be disposed of.

19 Geo. III, c. 12 (1778)
An act to explain, alter and amend, an act, passed in [1696] entitled 'An act for the better order and government of slaves.'

19 Geo. III, c. 18 (1778)
An act to prevent negro and other slaves from keeping horses, mares, mules, geldings or asses.

22 Geo. III, c. 17 (1781)
[First Amelioration Act]
An act to repeal several acts, and clauses of acts, respecting slaves, and for the better order and government of slaves . . .

25 Geo. III, c. 8 (1784)
An act to prevent slaves, standing charged with any crime or offence, from availing themselves, on their trials, of manumissions granted them after the commission of the crime or offence . . .

25 Geo. III, c. 17 (1784)
An act to prevent captains, commanders and masters of ships, and all other vessels whatsoever, from clandestinely carrying off this island negro or other slaves.
(See also 18 Geo. III, c. 20, above, and 54 Geo. III, c. 19 of 1813.)

28 Geo. III, c. 6 (1787)
    An act to repeal several acts and clauses of acts respecting slaves, and
    for the better order and government of slaves.

29 Geo. III, c. 2 (1788)
    [First Consolidated Slave Act]
    An act to repeal an act entitled 'An act to repeal several acts, and
    clauses of acts, respecting slaves; and for the better order and govern-
    ment of slaves; and for other purposes'; and also to repeal the several
    acts, and clauses of acts, which were repealed by the act entitled afore-
    said; and for consolidating, and bringing into one act, the several laws
    relating to slaves; and for giving them further protection and security;
    for altering the mode of trial of slaves charged with capital offences;
    and for other purposes.
    (Also 32 Geo. III, c. 22 and 23 of 1791.)

32 Geo. III, c. 4 (1791)
    An act to repeal 'An act for the better order and government of the
    negroes belonging to the several negro towns, and for preventing them
    from purchasing of slaves . . .'; and for giving the maroon negroes
    further protection and security; for altering the mode of trial; and for
    other purposes.

32 Geo. III, c. 11 (1791)
    An act for establishing Public Workhouses in the several Parishes in
    this Island.

32 Geo. III, c. 13 (1791)
    An act to repeal an act entitled 'An act for licensing hawkers and
    pedlers . . .'; and for prohibiting the practice of hawking and pedling
    within the parishes of this island.
    (Designed, in part, to stop slaves selling stolen plantation silverware, etc.)

32 Geo. III, c. 33 (1791)
    An act to repeal an act entitled 'An act to regulate the sales of newly-
    imported negroes; and to prevent, as far as possible, the separation of
    different branches of the same family'; and to regulate the sales of
    newly-imported negroes; and to prevent, as far as possible, the separa-
    tion of different branches of the same family.

32 Geo. III, c. 34 (1791)
    An act to prohibit the purchasing, hiring or employing, certain foreign
    slaves, except as therein mentioned.

35 Geo. III, c. 10 (1792)
    An act to prevent the spreading the infection of canine madness, by
    restraining slaves from keeping unnecessary dogs.

35 Geo. III, c. 22 (1794)
    An act to provide further regulations for such slaves as have been

admitted into this island; and to regulate the admission of slaves of a certain description [from St. Domingue].

35 Geo. III, c. 35 (1795)
An act for the better regulating the police within the town of Montego Bay . . .
(Sections deal with control of slaves; housing, etc.)

36 Geo. III, c. 10 (1796)
An act to repeal certain acts, and clauses and parts of acts . . . to prevent the hiding, concealing, inveigling, detaining, knowingly harbouring or employing, the slaves of others . . .

36 Geo. III, c. 11 (1796)
[An act to repeal an act of 1744 dealing with possession of gunpowder and firearms.]

36 Geo. III, c. 21 (1796)
An act to prevent gunpowder and firearms from falling into the hands of maroons, slaves and other improper persons . . .
(Also 38 Geo. III, c. 11 of 1797.)

38 Geo. III, c. 18 (1797)
An act for laying a duty on all negro slaves that shall be imported into this island, from the coast of Africa, who shall be above a certain age; and for regulating the manner of ascertaining such age.
(Also 39 Geo. III, c. 31 of 1799 and 42 Geo. III, c. 15 of 1801.)

38 Geo III, c. 22 (1797)
An act in aid of the party law now in force, . . . empowering the commander-in-chief . . . to raise and fit out parties.
(The act allowed for a number of slaves to be raised for carrying arms or baggage.)

39 Geo. III, c. 21 (1798)
An act to repeal an act, passed in the year [1744] entitled, 'An act to regulate the selling of gunpowder, and to prevent the selling of fire-arms to slaves'; and to prevent the improper use of gunpowder and fire-arms.
(See also 36 Geo. III, c. 11 of 1796, above, and 40 Geo. III, c. 9 of 1799.)

39 Geo. III, c. 29 (1798)
An act to prevent any intercourse and communication between the slaves of this island, and foreign slaves of a certain description . . .

41 Geo. III, c. 26 (1801)
An act to repeal the several acts, and clauses of acts, respecting slaves . . .; and for the better order and government of slaves . . .

42 Geo. III, c. 18 (1802)
An act for explaining and amending the laws relating to manslaughter.
(This act made the wilful killing of a slave by a white man a capital offence.)

48 Geo. III, c. 20 (1808)

An act to repeal several acts therein mentioned respecting slaves, to declare slaves assets for payment of debts and legacies, and in what manner they shall descend and be held as property, and be sold and conveyed in certain cases.

(Also 50 Geo. III, c. 21 of 1810.)

49 Geo. III, c. 30 (1809)

An act to permit a slave named Affleck [Sir Eyre Coote's slave] . . . to remove to England, and to emancipate the said slave.

50 Geo. III, c. 16 (1810)

An act for the protection, subsisting, clothing, and for the better order, regulation and government of slaves . . .

57 Geo. III, c. 15 (1816)

An act for a more particular return of slaves in this island, and the enrolment thereof.

57 Geo. III, c. 16 (1816)

An act for manumizing a slave, named Prince William, belonging to the public.

57 Geo. III, c. 18 (1816)

An act in furthrance of the provisions of the abolition laws within this island.

57 Geo. III, c. 24 (1816)

An act for providing curates for the several parishes in this island, and for promoting religious instruction amongst the slaves.

57 Geo. III, c. 25 (1816)

An act for the subsistence, clothing and the better regulation and government of slaves; for enlarging the powers of the council of protection; for preventing the improper transfer of slaves; and for other purposes.

58 Geo. III, c. 23 (1817)

An act for further regulating the duties of the office of coroner.

(Under this act, cases of sudden death of all persons, including slaves, were to be reported; and slave testimony to be acceptable at inquest.)

58 Geo. III, c. 24 (1817)

An act to declare in force the slave act passed in the year 1809 [50 Geo. III, c. 16], so far as concerns the punishment of crimes committed during the continuance thereof.

BIBLIOGRAPHY

This consists only of works cited in this study. Short titles, especially of printed works, are used whenever possible, since full titles are provided in the footnotes.

MANUSCRIPT SOURCES

Government—Central

British Museum

Add. MS. 11410: 'The Relation of Collonell Doyley . . .'

Add. MS. 12411: 'General Dalling's Plan for the Security and Defense of Jamaica'(1781).

King's Manuscripts, 214: 'A Memoir Relative to the Island of Jamaica, 1782 . . . by Major General Archibald Campbell.'

Jamaica: Government Archives, Spanish Town

Commissioners for Forts, Fortifications and Public Buildings, Minute Book, 1773–83.

Governors—Head of Correspondence, 1789–91.

House of Assembly Poll Book, 1803–43.

Jamaica: Institute of

The Hon. Committee of Correspondence Minute Book, 1794–1833.

Public Record Office, London

C.O. 137/28	C.O. 137/131	C.O. 139/35
C.O. 137/71	C.O. 137/140	C.O. 139/37A
C.O. 137/81	C.O. 137/142	C.O. 139/47
C.O. 137/91	C.O.137/154	C.O. 139/51
C.O. 137/100	C.O.137/175	C.O. 142/33
C.O. 137/110	C.O. 138/1	C.O. 325/12
C.O. 137/114	C.O. 138/44	C.O. 325/17
C.O. 137/118	C.O. 139/5	C.O. 325/19
C.O. 137/125		

Government—Local

Jamaica: Government Archives, Spanish Town

Clarendon Register of Baptisms (1804–19), Marriages (1805–34), Burials (1805–30).

Hanover: Slave Court, Lucea, 1819, 1820, 1821.

Kingston Common Council Minutes, 1795–1805.

Kingston Common Council Minutes, 1803–15.

Kingston Common Council Minutes, 1815–20.

Kingston Common Council Register of Freeholders, 1803–32.

Kingston Register of Marriages, 1713–1814.

Kingston Vestry Accounts, 1760–92.

Kingston Vestry Minutes, 1744–9.

Kingston Vestry Minutes, 1769–70.

Kingston Vestry Proceedings, 1781–8.

Kingston Vestry Register of Slaves, 1761–95.

Montego Bay: Resident Magistrate's Court, Quarter Sessions Kalendar Book, 1793–1841.

St. Ann Register of Baptisms, Marriages, Burials, 1790–1813.

St. Ann Vestry Minutes, 1785–93.

St. Ann Vestry Orders, 1767–90.

St. Ann Vestry Orders, 1791–1800.

St. Ann Vestry Proceedings, 1800–9.

St. Ann Vestry Proceedings, 1817–23.

St. Catherine Register of Baptisms, Marriages and Burials, 1693–1836.

St. Catherine Register of Marriages (St. Thos.-in-the-Vale), 1816–37.

St. Catherine Vestry Minutes, 1799–1807.

St. David Vestry Minutes, 1785–93.

St. David Vestry Minutes, 1793–1800.

St. David Vestry Minutes, 1806–13.

St. Elizabeth Parish Register of Baptisms, Marriages, Burials, 1707–1820.

St. James Parish Register of Marriages and Baptisms, 1774–1809.

Church and Mission Records

Baptist Missionary Society London

General Committee Minute Book of the Baptist Missionary Society, 1815–20.

Church of England, Fulham Palace

General Correspondence, West Indies, Vol. XVIII, Jamaica, 1740— undated: ff. 53–4; 65–70 (1788); 100–1 (1798); 102–5 (1798); 171–2.

Moravian Church, Barbados
Mt. Tabor Diary, 1829, 1830.

Moravian Church Archives, Malvern, Jamaica
The Carmel Church Book, 1813–37.
Conveyance of Lands (Fairfield), 1819.
Diary of Fairfield, 1824, 1825, 1826, 1827, 1828, 1829.
Estate List of Members of Fairfield Congregation, 1824.
John Lang's Diary, 1805–19.
List of Marriages at Fairfield, 1829–40.
Minutes of Conference, Mesopotamia, 1798–1818.
Register of Members of Fairfield Congregation, 1824.

Moravian Church Archives, London
Minutes of the Society for the Furtherance of the Gospel, vols. III–V (1768–1831).

Wesleyan Methodist Missionary Society, London
Letters from Missionaries in Jamaica to the Committee in London, 1803–13, 1815–34, West Indies.
  Anon., A series of tracts for Slaves in the West Indies:
    'A conversation on marriage.'
  Shipman, John: *Thoughts on the Present State of Religion among the Negroes in Jamaica. A Plan for Their Moral and Religious Improvement*, 2 vols., 1820.

British Museum
  Long, Add. MS. 12, 404; 12, 407; 12, 408; 12, 412–14; 12, 419; 12, 431.
  Add. MS. 12, 436, 'List of Landholders in Jamaica, 1750'.
  Add. MS. 18, 273.
  Add. MS. 33, 316: James Pinnock Diary, 1758–94.

Institute of Jamaica
  Nugent Papers (1806): 'Sketch of the Characters of certain Individuals . . .'
  The Omnibus or Jamaica Scrap Book: A thing of Shreds and Patches by Jack Jingle (*c.* 1824).
  Wolmer's Old Minute Book, 1736–1826, 2 vols.

West India Committee Library
  West India Committee Minutes, West India Merchants, Vol. I, 1769–79.

Worthy Park, Jamaica
The Worthy Park Plantation Register, 1787–91.

OFFICIAL DOCUMENTS

Acts of Assembly, Passed in the Island of Jamaica; From the year 1681, to the year 1754, inclusive (St. Iago de la Vega, 1769).
Acts of Assembly Passed in the Island of Jamaica, From 1770 to 1783, inclusive (Kingston, 1786).
Acts of Jamaica, 1681–1737 (London, 1738).
Acts of Parliament: Great Britain: Public General Acts (London, 1825).
American Archives, 1774–1776, 6 vols. (Washington, 1837–46), ed. P. Force.
Calendar of State Papers (Colonial), America and West Indies, 1574–1660, 1661–8, 1669–74, 1675–6, 1677–80, 1685–8.
Journals of the Assembly of Jamaica, 1663–1826, 14 vols. (Jamaica, 1803–26).
Laws of Jamaica, 1681–1816, 6 vols. (St. Iago de la Vega, 1792, 1802, 1793–1817).
Laws of Jamaica, 2 vols. (London, 1684–98).
Laws of Jamaica, 1817 (St. Iago de la Vega, 1818).
Laws of Jamaica, 1818 (St. Iago de la Vega, 1819).
Laws of Jamaica, 1819 (St. Iago de la Vega, 1820).
Laws of Jamaica, 1820–1 (St. Iago de la Vega, 1821).
The Laws of Jamaica, Passed in the Assembly and Confirmed by His Majesty in Council, April 17, 1684 (London, 1684).

Parliamentary Papers:
Accounts and Papers, Vol. LXVII (9), 1785; Vol. LXXXIV (26), 1789; Vol. LXXXVII (29), 1790; Vol. LXXXVIII (30), 1790; Vol. XCII (34), 1790–1; Vol. XXXVI (2), 1833.
Commission of Inquiry into the Administration of Justice and Criminal Justice in the West Indies. First Report. 2nd Series, Jamaica, 1826–7.
Reports from Committees, Vol. XX (16), 1831–2.
Thurloe, John. *A collection of State Papers . . . 7 vols.* (London, 1742).

REGISTERS AND ALMANACS

Alumni Cantabrigienses.
Alumni Oxonienses.
Chambers' Biographical Dictionary.
Dictionary of American Biography.
Dictionary of National Biography.
Eton College Register, 1753–1790 (Eton, 1921).

The Eton School Lists, from 1791 to 1850 (London and Eton College, 1864).
Handbook of Jamaica (Kingston, 1882, 1883).
Jamaica Almanacs, 1787–1828 (Kingston, 1779–1829). Titles vary.
The Harrow School Register, 1571–1800 (London, 1934).
The Harrow School Register, 1801–1823 (London, 1894).
Men at the Bar, comp. J. Foster (London, 1885).
Middle Temple Register, 1501–1902, 2 vols. (London, 1949).
Records of the Hon. Society of Lincoln's Inn, 1420–1893, 2 vols. (London, 1896).
Register of Admissions to Gray's Inn, 1521–1889, comp. J. Foster (London, 1889).

NEWSPAPERS

The Cornwall Gazette (Falmouth).
The Daily Advertiser (Kingston).
The Daily Gleaner (Kingston).
The Jamaica Courant (Kingston).
The Jamaica Gazette (Kingston).
The Jamaica Mercury and Kingston Weekly Advertiser (Kingston).
The Kingston Journal (Kingston).
The Royal Gazette (Kingston).
The St. Iago de la Vega Gazette (Spanish Town).
The Sunday Gleaner (Kingston).

MAGAZINES AND PERIODICALS

Used as primary source material

The Baptist Annual Register, 1790–1820 (London, n.d.–1820).
The Baptist Magazine, 1814–21 (London, 1821).
The Baptist Missionary Society *Annual Report*, 1819, 1820 (London, 1819/20).
Caribbean Quarterly, Vol. IV, nos. 3 and 4 (Port-of-Spain, 1956).
The Columbian Magazine (Kingston, 1796–1800).
The Jamaica Journal (Kingston, 1818).
The Jamaica Magazine, 1812–15 (Kingston, 1812–15).
Journal of Negro History (Washington, 1916).
Moravian *Periodical Accounts*, 1816–20 (London, 1816–20).
Moravian *Personal Accounts* (London, 1812).
Periodical Accounts relative to the Baptist Missionary Society, 6 vols. (Clipstone, 1800–17).
Periodical Accounts relative to the Baptist Missionary Society (Bristol, 1816).
The Universal Magazine (London, April 1773).

The Wesleyan Methodist Missionary Society *Annual Report* 1818–20
(London, 1818–20).

The Wesleyan Methodist Missionary Society *Missionary Notices*, 1818–20
(London, 1818–20).

The West India Committee Circular (1906, 1933).

PRINTED WORKS

Contemporary

ANON., *Colonization of the Island of Jamaica* (no imprint, 1792).

ANON., *The Election, A Poem* (Kingston, 1788).

ANON., *Hamel, the obeah man*, 2 vols. (London, 1827).

ANON., *The Importance of Jamaica to Great Britain considered* (London,
n.d.).

ANON., *Instructions for Members of the Unitas Fratrum* . . . (London, 1784).

ANON., *Jamaica, a poem in three parts* . . . (London, 1777).

ANON., *Marly* (Glasgow, 1828).

ANON., *Montgomery: or the West Indian Adventurer*, 3 vols. (Kingston,
1812–13).

ANON., *A narrative of recent events connected with the Baptist Mission* . . .
(Kingston, 1833).

ANON., *Negro Slavery* . . . (London, 1823).

ANON., *The politicks and patriots of Jamaica* (London, 1718).

ANON., *The Present State of the West Indies* . . . (London, 1778).

ANON., *The Privileges of the Island of Jamaica vindicated* (Jamaica, 1766).

ANON., *A Short Journey in the West Indies*, 2 vols. (London, 1790).

ANON., *Succinct View of the Missions established among the Heathen by
the Brethren* . . . (London 1771).

ATKINS, JOHN, *A voyage to Guinea, Brasil and the West Indies* (London,
1735).

BAPTIST MISSIONARY SOCIETY, *Letter of Instructions* (London, n.d.).

BAPTIST MISSIONARY SOCIETY, *A Tabular View of the Churches, Stations,
Schools, etc. in the Island of Jamaica* (London, 1836).

BARCLAY, ALEXANDER, *A Practical view of the present state of slavery in the
West Indies* (London, 1826).

BAYLEY, F. W. N., *Four Years' Residence in the West Indies, during the
years 1820–1829* (London, 1833).

BECKFORD WILLIAM, *A Descriptive Account of the Island of Jamaica*, 2 vols.
(London, 1790).

—— *Remarks upon the situation of the negroes in Jamaica* . . . (London,
1788).

BELISARIO, I. M., *Sketches of Character in Illustration of the Habits
Occupations and Costume of the Negro Population in the Island of
Jamaica*, 3 parts (Kingston, 1837–8).

BICKELL, R., *The West Indies as they are* . . . (London, 1825).

BRIDGES, G. W., *The Annals of Jamaica*, 2 vols. (London, 1827).

[BRODBELT, MRS.], *Letters to Jane from Jamaica, 1788–1796*, ed. Geraldine Mozley (London, n. d.).

BROUGHTON, ARTHUR, *Hortus Eastensis* . . . (Kingston, 1792).

CAINES, CLEMENT, *Letters on the cultivation of the otaheite cane* . . . (London, 1801).

CAMPBELL, CHARLES, *Memoirs of Charles Campbell* . . . (Glasgow, 1828).

CARMICHAEL, A. C., *Domestic manners and social condition of the white, coloured, and negro population of the West Indies*, 2 vols. (London, 1833).

COKE, THOMAS, *An account of the rise, progress, and present state of the Methodist missions* (London, 1804).

—— *Extracts of the journals of five visits to America* (London, 1793).

—— *Extracts of the Journals of the late Rev. Thomas Coke. LL.D.* . . . (Dublin, 1816).

—— *A History of the West Indies* . . . , 3 vols. (Vol. I, Liverpool, 1808; Vols. II and III, London, 1810, 1811).

—— *A Journal of the Rev. Dr. Coke's Visit to Jamaica and his Third Tour on the Continent of America* (London, 1789).

—— *Statement of the receipts and disbursements for the support of the missions established by the Methodist Society for the instruction and conversion of the negroes in the West Indies* (London, 1794).

COOPER, THOMAS, *Facts illustrative of the condition of the negro slaves in Jamaica* (London, 1824).

DALLAS, R. C., *The History of the Maroons*, 2 vols. (London, 1803).

DANCER, THOMAS, *A Brief History of the late Expedition against San Juan, so far as it relates to the Diseases of the troops* . . . (Kingston, 1781).

—— *The Medical Assistant* (Kingston, 1801).

—— *Some Observations respecting the Botanical Garden* (Kingston, 1804).

DE LA BECHE, H. T., *Notes on the present condition of the negroes in Jamaica* (London, 1825).

DICKSON, WILLIAM, *Mitigation of Slavery* (London, 1814).

DIROM, ALEXANDER, *Thoughts on the State of the Militia of Jamaica, November, 1783* (Jamaica, 1783).

EDWARDS, BRYAN, *The History, Civil and Commercial, of the British Colonies in the West Indies*, 2 vols. (London, 1793); 3 vols, 1801 ed.

EQUIANO, OLAUDAH, *The Interesting Narrative* . . . 2 vols. (London, 1789).

—— *Equiano's travels* . . . edited by Paul Edwards (London, 1967).

GOSSE, PHILLIP, H., *A Naturalist's Sojourn in Jamaica* (London, 1851).

GRANT, JOHN, *Notes of Cases adjudged in Jamaica, from May 1774 to December 1787* (Edinburgh, 1794).

HIBBERT, ROBERT JNR., *Hints to the Young Jamaica Sugar Planter* (London, 1825).

HIGGINS, BRYAN, *Observations and advices for the improvement of the manufacture of muscovado sugar and rum*, 4 parts (St. Iago de la Vega, 1797, 1800, 1801, 1802).

HOWARD, R. M., *Records and Letters of the Family of the Longs of Long-ville, Jamaica, and Hampton Lodge, Surrey*, 2 vols. (London, 1925).

HUNTER, JOHN, *Observations on the diseases of the army in Jamaica . . .* (London, 1788).

JONES, WILLIAM, *The Diary of the Rev. William Jones, 1777–1821*, ed. O. F. Christie (London, 1929).

KELLY, JAMES, *Voyage to Jamaica . . .* (Belfast, 1838).

LESLIE, CHARLES, *A new history of Jamaica* (London, 1740).

LEWIS, M. G., *Journal of a West India Proprietor, kept during a residence in the island of Jamaica* (London, 1834).

LONG, EDWARD, *The History of Jamaica*, 3 vols. (London, 1774).

M'MAHON, BENJAMIN, *Jamaica Plantership* (London, 1839).

MARSDEN, PETER, *An Account of the Island of Jamaica . . .* (Newcastle, 1788).

MATHIESON, GILBERT, *Notes respecting Jamaica* (London, 1811).

MONTULE, E., *A voyage to North America, and the West Indies, in 1817* (London, 1821).

MORETON, J. B., *Manners and Customs of the West India Islands* (London, 1790).

MOSELEY, BENJAMIN, *A Treatise concerning the Properties and Effects of Coffee* (London, 1785).

—— *A treatise on Sugar* (London, 1799).

—— *A Treatise on Tropical Diseases . . .* (London, 1787).

NUGENT, MARIA, *A journal of a voyage to, and residence in, the island of Jamaica . . .* (London, 1839).

—— *Lady Nugent's journal . . .* edited by Frank Cundall (London, 1907).

—— *Lady Nugent's journal . . .* edited by Philip Wright (Kingston, 1966)

OWEN, JOHN, *The History of the First Ten Years of the British and Foreign Bible Society*, 2 vols. (London, 1816).

PHILLIPPO, J. M., *Jamaica: its past and present state* (London, 1843).

PINCKARD, GEORGE, *Notes on the West Indies . . .* 3 vols. (London, 1806).

RAYNAL, ABBÉ, *Histoire philosophique et politique . . .* 4 vols. (Amsterdam, 1770).

RENNY, R., *A History of Jamaica* (London, 1807).

RIPPINGHAM, JOHN, *Jamaica considered . . .* (Kingston, 1817).

—— *Tract upon education* (Kingston, 1818).

ROBERTSON, JAMES, *Map of the County of Cornwall . . . Jamaica* (London, 1804).

—— *Map of the County of Middlesex . . . Jamaica* (London, 1804).

—— *Map of the County of Surrey . . . Jamaica* (London, 1804).

ROBY, JOHN, *Members of the Assembly of Jamaica* . . . (Montego Bay, 1831).

—— *Members of the Assembly of Jamaica for the parish of St. James* (Montego Bay, 1837).

ROUGHLEY, THOMAS, *The Jamaica Planters' Guide* . . . (London, 1823).

SCOTT, MICHAEL, *Tom Cringle's Log* (Paris, 1836).

SENIOR, B. M., *Jamaica as it was, as it is, and as it may be* . . . (London, 1835).

SLOANE, HANS, *A voyage to the islands* . . . 2 vols. (London, 1707, 1725).

SOUTHEY, THOMAS, *Chronological history of the West Indies*, 3 vols. (London, 1827).

STEPHEN, JAMES, *The slavery of the British West India colonies delineated*, 2 vols. (London, 1824, 1830).

[STEWART, J.], *An account of Jamaica and its inhabitants* (London, 1808).

STEWART, J., *A brief account of the present state of the negroes in Jamaica* (Bath, 1792).

—— *A view of the past and present state of the Island of Jamaica* . . . (Edinburgh, 1823).

THOME, J. A., and KIMBALL, J. H., *Emancipation in the West Indies* . . . (New York, 1838).

VERNON, J. B., *Early recollections of Jamaica* . . . (London, 1848).

WATSON, RICHARD, *A defense of the Wesleyan Methodist Missions in the West Indies* (London, 1817).

WILLIAMSON, JOHN, *Medical and miscellaneous observations* . . . 2 vols. (Edinburgh, 1817).

YOUNG, WILLIAM, *The West-India Common-place Book* . . . (London, 1807).

Modern

ACWORTH, A. W., *Buildings of architectural or historic interest in the British West Indies* (London, 1951).

—— *Treasure in the Caribbean: A First Study of Georgian Buildings in the British West Indies* (London, 1949).

ANDERSON, I., and CUNDALL, F., *Jamaica Negro proverbs and sayings* (London, 1927).

ANDRADE, JACOB, *A Record of the Jews in Jamaica* . . . (Kingston, 1941).

ANON., *The Political Constitution of Jamaica* (London, 1844).

ANON., *The regulations for the management of the Jamaica College* . . . (Kingston, 1916).

BAILEY, BERYL L., *Jamaican Creole Syntax* (Cambridge University Press, 1966).

BECKWITH, MARTHA, W., *Black Roadways* (Chapel Hill, 1929).

BLACK, CLINTON, V., *The Story of Jamaica* (London, 1965).

BUCHNER, J. H., *The Moravians in Jamaica* (London, 1854).

BURNS, ALAN, *History of the British West Indies* (London, 1954).

CALDECOTT, A., *The Church in the West Indies* (London, 1898).

CARLEY, MARY, M., *Education in Jamaica* (Kingston, 1942).

CASSIDY, F. G., *Jamaica Talk* (London, 1961).

CASSIDY, F. G. and LE PAGE, R. B., *Dictionary of Jamaican English* (Cambridge University Press, 1967).

CAULFEILD, JAMES, E., *One Hundred Years' History of the Second Battalion West India Regiment, from the date of raising, 1795 to 1898* (London, 1899).

CLARK, J., DENDY, W. and PHILLIPPO, J., *The Voice of Jubilee. A Narrative of the Baptist Mission, Jamaica* (London, 1865).

CLARKE, JOHN, *Memorials of Baptist Missionaries in Jamaica* (London, 1869).

COX, F. A., *History of the Baptist Missionary Society from 1792 to 1842*, 2 vols. (London, 1842).

CRATON, M., and WALVIN, J., *A Jamaican plantation: the history of Worthy Park, 1670–1970* (London, 1970).

CUNDALL, FRANK, *A brief history of the parish church of St. Andrew in Jamaica* (Kingston, 1931).

—— *Chronological Outlines of Jamaican History, 1492–1926* (Kingston, 1927).

—— *Historic Jamaica* (London, 1915).

—— *The Press and Printers of Jamaica Prior to 1820* (Worcester, Mass., 1916).

—— *Some notes on the history of secondary education in Jamaica* (Kingston, 1911).

CURTIN, PHILIP D., *The Atlantic slave trade: a census* (University of Wisconsin Press, 1969).

—— *The image of Africa* (University of Wisconsin Press, 1964).

—— *Two Jamaicas* (Harvard University Press, 1955).

DALLAS, JAMES, *The history of the family of Dallas . . .* (Edinburgh, 1921).

DEERR, NOEL, *The history of sugar*, 2 vols. (London, 1949–50).

DELANY, FRANCIS X., *A History of the Catholic Church in Jamaica . . .* (New York, 1930).

DUNCAN, PETER, *A Narrative of the Wesleyan Mission to Jamaica* (London, 1849).

ELLIS, A. B., *The History of the First West India Regiment* (London, 1885).

ELLIS, JOHN B., *The Diocese of Jamaica* (London, 1913).

Essays in colonial history; presented to C. M. Andrews (New Haven, 1931).

EYRE, ALAN, *The Botanic Gardens of Jamaica* (London, 1966).

FEURTADO, W. A., *Official and other personages of Jamaica, from 1655 to 1790* (Kingston, 1896).

FORTESCUE, J. W., *A History of the British Army*, vol. IV (London, 1915).

GARDNER, W. J., *A History of Jamaica* (London, 1873).

GOVEIA, ELSA V., *A Study on the Historiography of the British West Indies to the End of the Nineteenth Century* (Mexico, 1956).

HALL, MAXWELL, *The Meteorology of Jamaica* (Kingston, 1904).

—— *Notes of Hurricanes, Earthquakes, and other Physical Occurrences in Jamaica up to . . . 1880* (Kingston, 1916).

HEAVEN, VIOLET, *Jamaica Proverbs and John Canoe Alphabet* (Kingston and Montego Bay, 1896).

HENDRICK, S. P., *Sketch of the History of the Cathedral Church of St. Iago de la Vega* (Spanish Town, 1911).

HENRIQUES, F., *Family and Colour in Jamaica* (London, 1953).

HINTON, J. H., *Memoir of William Knibb* (London, 1847).

HOWARD, JOHN H. (ed.), *The Laws of the British Colonies in the West Indies . . .* 2 vols. (London, 1827).

[JACOBS, H. P., and CONCANNON, T. A. L.], *Falmouth 1791–1970* (The Georgian Society of Jamaica, Kingston, 1970).

JEKYLL, WALTER, *Jamaican Song and Story* (London, 1907)

KERR, MADELINE, *Personality and conflict in Jamaica* (London, 1952).

LE PAGE, R. B. and DE CAMP, D., *Jamaican Creole*, Creole Language Studies I (London, 1960).

LINDSAY, A. W., *Lives of the Lindsays: or a memoir of the houses of Crawford and Balcarres*, 4 vols. (Wigan, 1840), 3 vols. (London, 1849, 1858).

LIVINGSTON, E. B., *The Livingstones of Livingston Manor* (New York, 1910).

METCALF, GEORGE, *Royal Government and Political Conflict in Jamaica 1729–1783* (London, 1965).

MURRAY, D. J., *The West Indies and the Development of Colonial Government, 1801–1834* (Oxford, 1965).

OLIVIER, SYDNEY H., *Jamaica, the blessed island* (London, 1936).

PARES, RICHARD, *Merchants and Planters* (Cambridge, 1960).

—— *Yankees and Creoles* (London, 1956).

PARRY, J. H. and SHERLOCK, P. M., *A Short History of the West Indies* (London, 1956).

PATTERSON, ORLANDO, *The Sociology of Slavery* (London, 1967).

PENSON, LILLIAN, *The Colonial Agents of the British West Indies* (London, 1924).

PEYTRAUD, LUCIEN, *L'esclavage aux Antilles françaises . . .* (Paris, 1897).

PHILLIPS, U. B., *American Negro Slavery* (New York, 1918).

PHILO SCOTUS (pseud.), *Reminiscences of a Scottish gentleman* (Edinburgh, 1861).

PITMAN, F. W., *The Development of the British West Indies, 1700–1763* (New Haven, 1917).

—— *Plantation Systems of the New World* (Washington, D.C., 1959).

RAGATZ, L. J., *Absentee Landlordism in the British Caribbean, 1750–1833* (London, 1931).

—— *The Fall of the Planter Class in the British Caribbean, 1763–1833* (New York, 1928).

—— *A Guide for the Study of British Caribbean History, 1763–1834* . . . (Washington, 1932).

ROBERTS, G. W., *The Population of Jamaica* (Cambridge, 1957).

RUBIN, VERA (ed.), *Plantation systems of the New World* (Washington, D.C., 1959).

SAINTOYANT, J., *La colonisation française pendant la période napoléonienne, 1799–1815* (Paris, 1931).

—— *La colonisation française pendant la révolution 1789-1799*, 2 vols. (Paris, 1930).

SAINTOYANT, J., *La colonisation française sous l'ancien régime*, 2 vols. (Paris, 1932).

SCHUCHERT, CHARLES, *Historical geology of the Antillean-Caribbean region* (New York, 1935).

SIBLEY, INEZ K., *The Baptists in Jamaica* (Kingston, 1965).

SIEBERT, W. H., *The Legacy of the American Revolution to the British West Indies and Bahamas* (Columbus, Ohio, 1913).

SMITH, M. G., *The Plural Society in the British West Indies* (University of California Press, 1965.)

SPURDLE, F. G., *Early West Indian Government* (Palmerston North, New Zealand [1962]).

STOCKER, H. E., *Moravian Customs* (Bethlehem, Penns., 1928).

SYPHER, F. W., *Guinea's Captive Kings* (Chapel Hill, 1942).

THORNTON, A. P., *West-India Policy under the Restoration*, (Oxford, 1956).

WADDELL, HOPE M., *Twenty-nine years in the West Indies and Central Africa* . . . (London, 1867).

WEST, R. C. and AUGELLI, J. P., *Middle America: Its Lands and Peoples* (New Jersey, 1966).

WHITSON, A. M., *The Constitutional Development of Jamaica, 1660–1729* (Manchester University Press, 1929).

WRIGHT, P. and WHITE, P. F., *Exploring Jamaica* . . . (London, 1969).

WRIGHT, RICHARDSON, *Revels in Jamaica, 1682–1838* (New York, 1937).

Supporting Material

ADAMS, JOHN, *The Works of John Adams*, ed. C. F. Adams, 10 vols. (Boston, 1856).

ADAMS, R. G., *Political Ideas of the American Revolution* (Durham, North Carolina, 1922).

ARMSTRONG, LOUIS, *New Orleans Days* (long playing record, Brunswick LA 8537, 1950).

BAILYN, BERNARD, *The New England Merchants of the Seventeenth Century* (Cambridge, Mass., 1955).

BANGOU HENRI, *La Guadeloupe, 1492–1848*, 2 vols. (Paris, 1962).

BASTIDE, ROGER, *Les Amériques Noires* (Paris, 1967).

BEATTIE, JOHN, *Other Cultures* (London, 1964).

BOORSTIN, D. J., *The Americans*, vol. I, *The Colonial Experience* (New York, 1958).

BROKENSHA, DAVID, *Social Change at Larteh, Ghana* (Oxford University Press, 1966).

CLOWES, WILLIAM LAIRD, *The royal navy: a history*, 5 vols. (London, 1898).

COLE, H., *Christophe, King of Haiti* (London, 1967).

COULBORN, R. (ed.), *Feudalism in History* (Princeton University Press, 1956).

COURLANDER, H. and BASTIEN, RÉMY, *Religion and Politics in Haiti* (Washington, D.C., 1966).

CRUMP, HELEN J., *Colonial Admiralty Jurisdiction in the Seventeenth Century* (London, 1931).

DAHRENDORF, R., *Class and Class Conflict in Industrial Society* (trans. London, 1959).

DANEY, M. S., *Histoire de la Martinique*, 3 vols. (Fort Royal, 1846).

DANQUAH, J. B., *The Akan Doctrine of God* (London and Redhill, 1944).

DAVIS, D. B., *The Problem of Slavery in Western Culture* (Cornell University Press, 1966).

DAWES, NEVILLE, *The last enchantment* (London, 1960).

DE RACHEWILTZ, BORIS, *Black Eros* (trans. London, 1964).

DESPRES, LEO A., *Cultural pluralism and nationalist politics in British Guiana* (Chicago, 1967).

EATON, C., *The Growth of Southern Civilization 1760–1860* (New York, 1961).

ELKINS, M., *Slavery* (University of Chicago Press, 1959).

FANON, FRANTZ, *Peau Noire, Masques Blancs* (Paris, 1952).

FIELD, M. J., *Religion and Medicine of the Ga People* (London, 1937).

FIELD, M. J., *Search for Security* (London, 1960).

FORDE, DARYLL (ed.), *African Worlds . . .* (Oxford University Press, 1954).

FREYRE, GILBERTO, *The masters and the slaves* (trans. New York, 1946).

—— *The race factor in contemporary politics* (University of Sussex, 1966).

FROUDE, J. A., *The English in the West Indies* (London, 1887).

GARVEY, AMY JACQUES (ed.), *Philosophy and opinions of Marcus Garvey*, 2 vols. (New York 1923, 1926).

GENOVESE, EUGENE D., *The Political Economy of Slavery* (New York, 1961).

GLUCKMAN, MAX, *Custom and conflict in Africa* (Oxford, 1956).

GOODY, J., *Death, Property and the Ancestors* (London, 1962).

GORER, GEOFFREY, *Africa Dances* (London, 1935).

GOVEIA, ELSA, *Slave Society in the British Leeward Islands at the End of the Eighteenth Century* (Yale University Press, 1965).

GREAVES, H. R. G., *The civil service in the changing state* (London, 1947).

GRIAULE, MARCEL, *Dieu d'eau* (Paris, 1948).

GRIGGS, E. L. and PRATOR, C. H., *Henry Christophe and Thomas Clarkson. A Correspondence* (Berkeley and Los Angeles, 1952).

GUSSMAN, BORIS, *Out in the Mid-day Sun* (London, 1962).

HALL, DOUGLAS, *Free Jamaica* (Yale University Press, 1959).

HALL, HENRY L., *The Colonial office; a history* (London, 1937).

HALL, ROBERT, *Pidgin and Creole Languages* (New York, 1966).

HANDLIN, OSCAR, *The Americans* (New York, 1963).

HANSEN, M. L., *The Atlantic Migration, 1607–1860* (Cambridge, Mass., 1940).

HARLOW, V. T., *A History of Barbados, 1625–1685* (London, 1926).

HARRIS, MARVIN, *Patterns of Race in the Americas* (New York, 1964).

HARRIS, WILSON, *Palace of the peacock* (London, 1960).

HEARNE, JOHN, *Stranger at the gate* (London, 1956).

HERNTON, CALVIN, *Sex and Racism in America* (New York, 1965).

HERSKOVITS, M. J., *Dahomey*, 2 vols. (New York, 1938).

—— *The Myth of the Negro Past*, (New York, 1941).

—— *The New World Negro* (Indiana University Press, 1966).

—— *Trinidad Village* (New York, 1947) with F. S. Herskovits.

JAHN, JANHEINZ, *A History of Neo-African Literature* (trans. London, 1968).

—— *Muntu* (trans. London, 1961).

JAMES, C. L. R., *The Black Jacobins* (London, 1938).

JEFFRIES, CHARLES, *The colonial empire and its civil service* (Cambridge University Press, 1938).

JONES, ELDRED, *Othello's countrymen* (Oxford University Press, 1965).

JONES, LEROI, *Blues people* (New York, 1963).

KERR, W., *Bermuda and the American Revolution, 1760–1783* (Oxford University Press, 1936).

KLEIN, HERBERT S., *Slavery in the Americas* (Oxford University Press, 1967).

LAMMING, GEORGE, *Of age and innocence* (London, 1958).

—— *The Pleasures of Exile* (London, 1960).

LE PAGE, R. B. (ed.), *Proceedings of the Conference on Creole Language Studies* (London, 1961).

LOVEJOY, ARTHUR, *The Great Chain of Being* (London, 1936).

LOWIE, R. H., *Social Organization* (London, 1949).

MAKINSON, DAVID H., *Barbados, A Study of North American–West Indian Relations, 1739–1789* (The Hague, 1964).

MANNONI, O., *Psychologie de la Colonisation* (Paris, 1950); trans. New York, 1956, as *Prospero and Caliban.*

MAQUET, J. J., *The Premise of inequality in Ruanda* (trans., Oxford University Press, 1961).

MARSHALL, PAULE, *The chosen place, the timeless people* (New York, 1969)

MORSE, JOHN T., *The Life of Alexander Hamilton* (Boston, 1876).

NAIPAUL, V. S., *The loss of El Dorado: a history* (London, 1969).

—— *The Middle Passage* (London, 1962).

—— *The mimic men* (London, 1967).

NETTELS, C. P., *The Roots of American Civilization* (New York, 1938).

NKETIA, J. H., *Drumming in Akan Communities of Ghana* (University of Ghana, 1963).

—— *Folk Songs of Ghana* (University of Ghana, 1963).

—— *Funeral Dirges of the Akan People* (Achimota, 1955).

NYE, R. B., *The Cultural Life of the New Nation, 1776–1830* (New York, 1960).

OJO, G. J. AFOLABI, *Yoruba Culture* (University of Ife, 1966).

PARES, RICHARD, *War and Trade in the West Indies, 1738–1763* (Oxford, 1936).

—— *A West India Fortune* (London, 1950).

PARRINDER, G., *West African Religion* (London, 1949).

PATTERSON, H. Orlando, *An absence of ruins* (London, 1967).

PORTER, A. T., *Creoledom* (London, 1963).

RAGATZ, L. J., *The West Indian Approach to the Study of American Colonial History* (London, 1935).

RATTRAY, R. S., *Ashanti* (Oxford, 1923).

—— *Religion and art in Ashanti* (Oxford University Press, 1927).

REDFIELD, ROBERT, *Peasant Society and Culture* (University of Chicago Press, 1956).

RODNEY, WALTER, *A History of the upper Guinea coast, 1545–1800* (Oxford University Press, 1970).

ROGERS, C. A. and FRANTZ, C., *Racial Themes in Southern Rhodesia* (Yale University Press, 1962).

RORIG, V. F., *The Medieval Town* (trans. London, 1967).

RUBIN, VERA (ed.), *Caribbean studies: a symposium* (University of Washington Press, 1957, 1960).

—— *Social and cultural pluralism in the Caribbean* (New York, 1960).

ST. OMER, GARTH, *Shades of grey* (London, 1968).

SALKEY, ANDREW, *The late emancipation of Jerry Stover* (London, 1968).

SIMPSON, G. E., *The Shango Cult in Trinidad* (Puerto Rico, 1965).

SMITH, R. T., *The Negro Family in British Guiana* (London, 1956).

STYRON, WILLIAM, *The Confessions of Nat Turner* (New York, 1967).

TANNENBAUM, FRANK, *Slave and Citizen* (New York, 1947).

TEMPELS, PLACIED, *Bantoe-filosofia* (English trans. Paris, 1959).

THOMAS, J. J., *Froudacity* . . . (London, 1889).

TONER, J. M. (ed.), *The Daily Journal of Major George Washington in 1751–1752* (Albany, New York, 1892).

TURNER, F. J., *The Frontier in American History* (New York, 1920).

VERGER, PIERRE, *Notes sur le culte des Orisa et Vodun* . . . (Dakar, 1957).

WADDELL, D. A. G., *British Honduras* (London, 1961).

WAGLEY, CHARLES and HARRIS, MARVIN, *Minorities in the New World* (New York, 1958).

WALCOTT, DEREK, *In a Green Night* (London, 1962).

WILLIAMS, ERIC, *Capitalism and Slavery* (University of North Carolina Press, 1944).

WOOD, DONALD, *Trinidad in Transition* (Oxford University Press, 1968).

WRIGHT, L. B., *The Cultural Life of the American Colonies, 1603–1763* (New York, 1957).

ZAVALA, S., *The colonial period in the history of the New World* (trans. and abridged, Mexico, 1962).

ARTICLES

ACWORTH, A. W., 'Georgian Architecture in the British West Indies', in *The Connoisseur Yearbook* (London, 1953).

ADAMS, R. N., 'On the Relation Between Plantation and "Creole Cultures",' in *Plantation Systems of the New World*.

ANON., 'An account of the baptized Negro churches', in *The Baptist Annual Register* (1798–1801).

—— 'Characteristic traits of the Creolian and African Negroes in the island . . .', in *The Columbian Magazine* (1797).

—— 'Letters showing the rise and progress of the early negro churches in Georgia and the West Indies', in *Journal of Negro History* (1916).

—— 'View of Certain Regulations of Customs, subsisting at Charleston, South Carolina, and in Kingston, Jamaica', *Columbia Magazine* (1797).

—— 'The West Indian Merchants and the American Revolution', in *West India Committee Circular* (1906).

AUGIER, F. R., 'Before and After 1865', in *New World Quarterly* (1966).

BARNES, V. F., 'Land Tenure in the English Colonial Charters of the Seventeenth Century', in *Essays in Colonial History* (New Haven, 1931).

BASTIEN, R., Comments on 'The relation between plantation and "creole cultures" ', in *Plantation Systems*.

BECKWITH, MARTHA, 'Jamaica Proverbs', in *Publications of the Folklore Foundation* (1925).

BELL, H. C., 'The West India trade before the American Revolution', in *American Historical Review* (1916–17).

BELTRAN, G. A., 'African Influences in the Development of Regional cultures in the New World', in *Plantation Systems*.

BELTRAN, G. A., 'Races in 17th Century Mexico', in *Phylon* (1945).

BENNETT, N. R., 'Christian and Negro Slavery in Eighteenth Century North Africa', in *Journal of African History* (1960).

BRAITHWAITE, LLOYD, Comment on 'Skin color and social class', in *Plantation systems*.

—— 'Social Stratification in Trinidad', in *Social and Economic Studies* (1953).

BRATHWAITE, EDWARD, 'Creative literature of the British West Indies during the period of slavery', in *Savacou* (1970).

—— 'Jamaican Slave Society', in *Race* (1968).

CLARKE, MARY P., 'Parliamentary Privilege in the American Colonies'— *Essays in Colonial History* (New Haven, 1931).

CONCANNON, T. A. L., 'Houses of Jamaica', in *Jamaica Journal* (1967).

COOPER, J. I., 'The West Indies, Bermuda and the American Mainland Colleges', in the *Jamaican Historical Review* (1949).

CROSS, MALCOLM, 'Cultural pluralism and sociological theory', in *Social and Economic Studies* (December 1968).

CROW, J. A., 'An interpretation of Caribbean society through literature', in *The Caribbean at mid-century*, ed. A. C. Wilgus (University of Florida Press, 1951).

CUMPER, G. E., 'Labour Demand and Supply in the Jamaican Sugar Industry 1830–1950', in *Social and Economic Studies* (1954).

DEGLER, CARL, 'Slavery and the Genesis of American Race Prejudice', in *Comparative Studies in Society and History* (1959).

DIGGS, IRENE, 'Color in Colonial Spanish America', in *Journal of Negro History* (1953).

FORDE, DARYLL, Introduction to *African worlds* (Oxford University Press, 1954).

FREMMER, RAY, 'Fort Balcarres', in the *Daily Gleaner* (May 1970).

—— 'The Stirlings of St. James', in the *Daily Gleaner* (May 1970).

FUENTES, CARLOS, Letter to the Editor, *Times Literary Supplement* (May 1968).

FURLEY, O., 'Moravian missionaries and slaves in the West Indies', *Caribbean Studies* (1965).

—— 'Protestant Missionaries in the West Indies', in *Race* (1965).

FURNESS, A. E., 'The Maroon war of 1795', in the *Jamaican Historical Review* (1965).

GOVEIA, ELSA V., 'The Caribbean: Socio-Cultural Framework', in *Caribbean Artists Movement Newsletter* (1967).

—— 'The West Indian Slave Laws of the Eighteenth Century', in *Revista de ciencias sociales* (1960).

GREENE, J. C., 'The American Debate on the Negro's Place in Nature', in *Journal of the History of Ideas* (1954).

HALL, DOUGLAS, 'Absentee-Proprietorship in the British West Indies, to about 1850', in *Jamaica Historical Review* (1964).

—— 'Incalculability as a Feature of Sugar Production during the Eighteenth Century', in *Social and Economic Studies* (1961).

—— 'Slaves and Slavery in the British West Indies,' in *Social and Economic Studies* (1962).

HALL, MAXWELL, 'The Jamaica Hurricane of October, 3, 1780', in *Quarterly Journal of the Royal Meteorological Society* (1917).

HARRISON, TONY, 'Shango the shaky fairy', in the *London Magazine* (April 1970).

HEARNE, JOHN, 'Landscape with faces' in *Ian Fleming introduces Jamaica*, ed. Morris Cargill (London, 1965).

HERSKOVITS, M. J., 'Problem, method and theory in Afro-american studies', in *The New World Negro*.

—— 'Wari in the New World', in *Journal of the Royal Anthropological Institute* (1932).

HOETINK, H., 'The concept of pluralism as envisaged by M. G. Smith', *Caribbean Studies* (April 1967).

HOGG, DONALD, 'The Convince Cult in Jamaica', in *Papers in Caribbean Anthropology*, compiled S. Mintz (New Haven, 1960).

JACOBS, H. P., 'The Earl of Effingham', in the *Sunday Gleaner* (May 1970).

—— 'Roger Hope Elletson's letter book' in the *Jamaican Historical Review* (1949).

JAMAICA INFORMATION SERVICE, 'List of Public Monuments in Jamaica', *Sunday Gleaner* (June 1966).

JAMESON, J. F., 'St. Eustatius in the American Revolution', in *American Historical Review* (1903).

LAWTON, DAVID L., 'The Implications of Tone for Jamaican Creole', in *Anthropological Linguistics* (1968).

LEYBURN, JAMES G., Comment on 'Skin color and social class', in *Plantation Systems*.

MACDERMOT, T. H., 'George Lisle . . .', in *The Jamaica Times* (April, May 1915).

McKENZIE, HERMAN I., 'The plural society debate', in *Social and Economic Studies* (1966).

MAY, ARTHUR J., 'The Architecture of the West Indies', in *West India Committee Circular* (1933).

MERCIER, P. (trans.) 'The Fon of Dahomey', in *African worlds*.

MILLER, ERROL, 'Body image, physical beauty and colour among Jamaican adolescents', in *Social and Economic Studies* (1969).

Moore, J. G. and Simpson, G. E., 'A Comparative Study of Acculturation in Morant Bay and West Kingston', in *Zaire* (1957, 1958).

Nketia, J. H., 'Possession Dances in African Societies', in *Journal of the International Folk Music Council* (1957).

Nogueira, Oracy, 'Skin Color and Social Class', in *Plantation Systems . . .*

Phillips, U. B., 'A Jamaica Slave Plantation', in *American Historical Review* (1914).

Penson, Lillian, 'The London West India Interest in the Eighteenth Century', in *English Historical Review* (1921).

Pitman, F. W., 'The Settlement and Financing of British West India Plantations in the Eighteenth Century', in *Essays in Colonial History*.

—— 'Slavery on the British West India Plantations in the Eighteen Century', in *Journal of Negro History* (1926).

Ragatz, L. J., 'The West Indian Approach to the Study of American Colonial History' (American Historical Association Pamphlet, 1934) (London, 1935).

Reckord, Mary, 'Missions in Jamaica before emancipation', in *Caribbean Studies* (1968).

Ribeiro, René, Comment on 'African influences . . .', in *Plantation Systems*.

Rodney, Walter, 'African slavery . . .', in *Journal of African History* (1966).

Seal Coon, F., 'How healthy is "Hell"?', in the *Daily Gleaner*, October 1969).

Sheridan, R. B., 'Planter and Historian: The Career of William Beckford', in *Jamaican Historical Review* (1964).

Simpson, G. E., 'Jamaican Revivalist Cults', in *Social and Economic Studies* (1965).

Simpson, G. E. and Hammond, P. B., 'The African Heritage in the Caribbean', in *Caribbean Studies: A Symposium*, ed. Vera Rubin (University of Washington Press, 1957, 1960).

Sio, Arnold, 'Society, Slavery and the Slaves', in *Social and Economic Studies* (1967).

Smith, M. G., 'Slavery and Emancipation in Two Societies' in *The Plural Society in the British West Indies*.

—— 'The African Heritage in the Caribbean', in *Caribbean Studies: A Symposium*, ed. Vera Rubin (University of Washington Press, 1957, 1960).

Sypher, F. W., 'The West Indian as a "Character" in the Eighteenth Century', in *Studies in Philology* (1939).

Thompson, R. F., 'An Aesthetic of the Cool: West African Dance', in *Freedomways* (1966).

Tylden, G., 'The West India Regiments, 1795–1927', in *Journal of the Society for Army Historical Research*, Vol. XL.

VAN DAM, THEODORE, 'The influence of West African Songs of Derision in the New World', in *African Music* (1954).

VENDRYES, H. E., 'Bryan Edwards, 1743–1800', in the *Jamaican Historical Review* (1943).

WESLEY, C. H., 'The emancipation of the free coloured population in the British Empire', in the *Journal of Negro History* (1934).

WHITSON, A. M., 'The Outlook of the Continental American Colonies on the British West Indies, 1760–1775', in *Political Science Quarterly* (1930).

THESES AND UNPUBLISHED PAPERS

ALLEYNE, M. C., 'The Cultural Matrix of Caribbean Dialects'. Unpublished paper, University of the West Indies, Mona, Jamaica [n.d.].

AUGIER, F. R., 'The Passing of Representative Government in Jamaica in 1865', Dept. of History, Staff/Graduate Seminar Paper, University of the West Indies, Mona, Jamaica [1965].

CAMPBELL, M. C., 'Edward Jordan and the free coloureds: Jamaica, 1800–1865'; unpublished Ph.D. thesis, University of London [1968].

CUNDALL, FRANK, 'Architecture in Jamaica', stencilled paper, Institute of Jamaica, Kingston, n.d.

DUNCKER, SHEILA, 'The Free Coloured and the Fight for Civil Rights in Jamaica, 1800–1830'. Unpublished M.A. Thesis, University of London, 1960.

HIGMAN, BARRY, 'Some Demographic Characteristics of Slavery in Jamaica, *c.* 1832', Dept. of History, Post-graduate Seminar Paper, University of the West Indies, Mona, Jamaica, 1969.

MOORE, J. C., 'The Religion of Jamaican Negroes . . .' Unpublished Ph.D. Thesis, Northwestern University, 1953.

MURRAY, A. L., 'Constitutional Developments in Jamaica, 1774–1815'. Unpublished M.A. Thesis, University of London, 1956.

RECKORD, MARY, 'Missionary Activity in Jamaica before Emancipation'. Unpublished Ph.D. Thesis, University of London, 1964.

RUSSELL, BETTY, 'The Influence of the French Revolution upon Grenada, St. Vincent and Jamaica', Dept. of History, Postgraduate Seminar Paper, University of the West Indies, Mona, Jamaica, 1967.

SCHULER, MONICA, 'Slave Resistance and Rebellion in the Caribbean during the Eighteenth Century', Dept. of History; Postgraduate Seminar Paper, University of the West Indies, Mona, Jamaica [1966].

[TIKASINGH, GERAD], 'A method for estimating the free coloured population of Jamaica', Dept. of History, Staff/Graduate Seminar Paper, University of the West Indies, Mona, Jamaica, [1967].

INDEX